CODES FOR NORTH

Foundations of the Canadian Avant-Garde Film

STEPHEN BROOMER

Codes for North

Foundations of the Canadian
Avant-Garde Film

CANADIAN FILMMAKERS DISTRIBUTION CENTRE
Toronto, Canada

ISBN 978-0-9696721-2-8

Library and Archives Canada Cataloguing in Publication

Broomer, Stephen, author
Codes for north : foundations of the Canadian avant-garde film / Stephen Broomer.

Includes bibliographical references and index.
ISBN 978-0-9696721-2-8 (softcover)

1. Experimental films--Canada--History and criticism. 2. Painting, Canadian--20th century--Themes, motives. 3. Chambers, Jack, 1931-1978--Criticism and interpretation. 4. Snow, Michael, 1928- --Criticism and interpretation. 5. Wieland, Joyce, 1930-1998--Criticism and interpretation. I. Canadian Film-Makers Distribution Centre, issuing body II. Title.

PN1995.9.E96B76 2017   791.43'611   C2017-906868-7

The Canadian Filmmakers Distribution Centre gratefully acknowledges the financial assistance of the Canada Council for the Arts, the Ontario Arts Council and the Toronto Art Council.

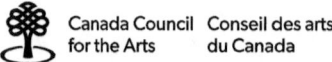 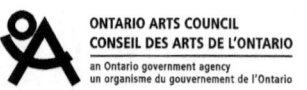

Cover: film strips from Jack Chambers' *The Hart of London*, Michael Snow's *La Région Centrale* and Joyce Wieland's *Reason Over Passion*, courtesy of the CFMDC. Scan by Jesse Brossoit. Design by Stephen Broomer and Emmalyne Laurin, in tribute to Richard Kerr's film weavings.

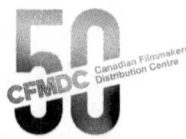

CONTENTS

ACKNOWLEDGEMENTS

The works discussed in this book have been a part of my life since childhood. I dedicate this study to my parents, Cherie and Stuart Broomer, who first introduced me to the paintings and films of Jack Chambers, Michael Snow and Joyce Wieland. My thanks to them, my brother Geoffrey and my partner Emmalyne for their love and support.

Few have dedicated themselves to writing the history of the Canadian avant-garde film as passionately as R. Bruce Elder. No comprehensive text has appeared on this subject since Elder's *Image and Identity: Reflections on Canadian Film and Culture* (1989), a volume that covered the much larger territory of Canadian philosophy and vision. *Codes for North* gathers a view of this field that is guided by the role of difficult aesthetics in the origins of the Canadian avant-garde film. None of this would be possible without the insight of Elder, who has spent his career to date advancing the cause of a poetic cinema.

The masterful bibliographies and collections of Kathryn Elder have been among the central resources in my education on this subject. Her anthologies on Jack Chambers and Joyce Wieland, and her bibliographic chronicling of Michael Snow, testify to her diligence and devotion to this cinema and are among the most rigorous accounts of these filmmakers. In her role as the librarian at York University's Sound and Moving Image Library, she has also been one of the most generous supporters of this work, facilitating my access to prints of these films.

This text began as my doctoral dissertation in the joint programme in Communication & Culture at York University and Ryerson University. It was supported through the years by a number of fellowships and awards, including the Ted Rogers Doctoral Fellowship, the Ontario Graduate Scholarship, the Liss Jeffrey Award for Research in New Media and a Scholar-in-Residence position at the Modern Literature and Culture

Research Centre at Ryerson University. I am grateful to Irene Gammel, the Jeffrey family and Jo Ann Mackie for their support.

My writing on this topic developed through many animated conversations. For this I thank Seth Feldman, Bart Testa, Izabella Pruska-Oldenhof, Don Snyder, Clint Enns, Dan Browne, Michael Zryd, Siobhan McMenemy, Christine Lucy Latimer and Mark Loeser. Sebastian di Trolio and Brett Kashmere were a tremendous help in gathering research materials, as were the staff of the Art Gallery of Ontario archives and the Library & Archives Canada.

Eva Kolcze, formerly of the Canadian Filmmakers Distribution Centre, facilitated my access to films and other research materials. Our ongoing discussions have helped me to better understand the place of this work in the world. Jim Shedden was one of the manuscript's first readers and has been a generous champion of the book through its many stages. Our discussions have helped me in clarifying my relationship to the Canadian nationalist project and he has been a guide in understanding this movement and its social history and meaning. Daniel Barnett, filmmaker and theorist, was another early reader who furnished me with generous insights to the improvement of the text.

The Canadian Filmmakers Distribution Centre (CFMDC) published this book on the occasion of their 50th Anniversary. I am grateful for the enthusiasm and support of Lauren Howes and Genne Speers. This book was completed while I was serving as the CFMDC's inaugural Scholar-in-Residence (2016). CFMDC staff, past and present, provided further support for my research, including Larissa Fan, Aimée Mitchell, Edward Fawcett Sharpe and Jesse Brossoit. Thanks to the generosity of John Chambers, Michael Snow, and Raven Amiro of the National Gallery of Canada, a number of paintings have been reproduced throughout to contextualize the full scale of these artists' achievements. Reproductions have been provided by Jill Offenbeck and Tracy Mallon-Jensen of the Art Gallery of Ontario's Rights and Reproductions division.

I owe a great debt to Cameron Moneo, who has spent countless hours working through these films and many others with me. Our common vision through the years has done much to shape my understanding of cinema and whatever contribution this work makes to this movement is his as well as mine. Likewise, Emmalyne Laurin has spent many hours working through and discussing these films with me and her insights did much to illuminate my own thinking about the relation of this cinema to the other arts.

Stephen Broomer, 2017

FOREWORD

Seth Feldman

It has been forty to fifty years since the events presented in this, Stephen Broomer's insightful, erudite book. At this distance from the fact we find ourselves in a time of transition. Living memory (and an assumption of shared living memory with an audience) is giving way to historical analysis and its reception based solely on archival material. Complicating matters is an in-between stage of the transitory period. It is peopled by those historians who relate to their studied period as post-memory, a state in which they are so immersed in the time frame they study that it affects them as if it were personally experienced.

Stephen Broomer falls into this category and he comes by it honestly. [Full disclosure: I have known Stephen since he was a student in one of my undergraduate classes and was involved with his graduate studies up to the point of being both a reader and examiner of the dissertation that served as the basis for this work.] His first book, *Hamilton Babylon* examined this same mid-1960s to the mid-1970s period through the work and tribulations of the remarkable university students who styled themselves as the McMaster Film Board. Choosing that particular name can be read as an exercise in unfettered hubris. The student filmmakers appropriated the role of Canada's only distinguished cinematic institution, the National Film Board, while at the same time daring to undertake what so many luminaries only talked about: make independent films in Canada. Broomer's research on their exploits was all but obsessive, taking him to dimly lit corridors of Canadian film history to document forgotten and often lost works as well as the individuals who made them.

The students of the McMaster Film Board began by working in

a mode that was, at the time, familiar to almost no one in Canada. New American Cinema had its roots in a small number of films made in the 1940s and its ancestry in the avant-garde movements of the 1920s. Its numbers–of filmmakers, screenings, critics and audiences–grew in the 1950s. The New York-based artistic and organizational genius, Jonas Mekas, began showing, writing about and fighting for the work of a cadre of exceptionally talented individuals. By the early 1960s, their films had audiences in museums, galleries and university campuses. The movement, no longer new and by then not entirely American, began to be known as "experimental" or "avant-garde cinema."

Avant-garde cinema's Canadian debut came with the work of Michael Snow, Joyce Wieland and Jack Chambers, the filmmakers Broomer addresses here. Broomer's visceral connection to the three pioneers is more than a matter of his scrupulous research into them. In his own creative life, Broomer is a Canadian avant-garde filmmaker of some stature. He is likely the first of his generation to inspire a book about his films. That book's title, *The Transformable Moment*, refers to Broomer's understanding of his creations. As he defines the phrase:

> The transformable moment is the moment turning into both its opposite and its other, and meaning arises in the gap between opposition and otherness. By this transformation, the moment departs from the assurances of memory and becomes a breathing passage.[1]

On one hand this "transformational moment" describes Broomer's role as historian, departing from "assurances of memory." On another, the transformable moment as artistic catharsis echoes Henri Cartier-Bresson's "decisive moment" and Roland Barthes' definition of the photographic "punctum." There also seems to be, as we learn in this volume, a resonance with Jack Chambers' "wow" moments. Broomer's films, like Cartier-Bresson's photographs and Chambers' paintings, are extrapolations. In these instances, we are made to see not only the subject of the work, but its transformation from captured image to icon.

As Broomer demonstrates in *Hamilton Babylon* as well as in this book, "transformation" works equally well as historiography. We know that anything photographed or filmed is necessarily an image of the past, history begging for reconciliation with our point of view. The mechanically reproduced image "departs from the assurances of memory and becomes

---

[1] Stephen Broomer, "The Transformable Moment," in *The Transformable Moment: The Films of Stephen Broomer* (Ottawa: Canadian Film Institute, 2014), 5.

a breathing passage" while being pulled away from its context and toward its discovery. In this sense, as Broomer proves in both his writing and his films, all media are time-based.

The notion of transformational moments–art as history, history as art–is especially pertinent as Broomer examines the emergence of his three film artists as it takes place during a time of intense visual transformation. It is easy to point to the psychedelic colours and patterns of the 1960s and 1970s or indeed the prevalence of hallucination itself as strikingly new images, unexpected and uncalled for. New icons abounded: the ubiquitous peace symbol, the marijuana leaf, the art of the album cover. Costume and grooming (or lack thereof) were redefined. Accompanying this was the tectonic shift of the artist's subject matter brought on by Pop Art.

The look of the period also included more prosaic yet equally fundamental changes. In architecture, the long-standing uses of glass and metal in the International Style were challenged by the Brutalists' poured concrete. Postwar triumphalism in the design of bigger and ever less practical automobiles began giving way to its opposite in the form of small, more rational European and Japanese designs. Between 1965 and 1975 both commercial cinema and broadcast television changed from primarily black and white imagery to almost exclusively colour. Black and white cinema became an affectation in feature filmmaking and took on the connotation of authenticity in documentary. Fuzzy black and white images familiar from early television lived on only in the small gauge video art and documentary that questioned the dominant commercial use of the medium.

Canada too witnessed the arrival of these visual innovations and to them added its own transformational moments. This was the era when Frye's "garrison mentality" was giving way to Atwood's "survival" via McLuhan's "global village." It was the technological environment we created for ourselves rather than the enormity of the landscape in which we lived that now drove the national purpose.

This intellectual transformation can be seen in the two most significant Canadian visuals of the time. The first is the new national flag that was adopted in 1965. Abandoning the Red Ensign was a trauma for some and for others, the sharing of a post-colonial liberation being celebrated globally with a hundred other new national flags. The flag's design was touted as an interactive process with the nation as a whole being asked to give some thought to images that would link heritage to the future. In the end, the thousands of designs submitted, including the Prime Minister's choice, lost to simplicity. Complex heraldry gave way to a minimalist logo. Seemingly overnight, the new flag was flying everywhere in Canada and traveling the world sown onto an army of backpacks.

A second Canadian visual revolution took place on the grounds of Expo '67. The fair's architecture – including Buckminster Fuller's American Pavilion, and Moshe Safdie's Habitat 67 – challenged the limitations of inhabitable space. Other pavilions were designed to complement the visual experiments they contained. Among them were: the multiscreen theatres of the National Film Board's *Labyrinth*; *Kaleidoscope* in which a multiscreen work was projected on the interior of a two-story cylinder; and the Man the Explorer Pavilion, designed around *Polar Life*, a large screen immersive production that proved to be the prototype for IMAX.

It was within this cacophony of new visuals that Snow, Wieland and Chambers emerged. Each made a distinct contribution to and reflection upon the period in the form of what Broomer describes as "difficult pleasures." Indeed, their films could clear an auditorium – save for those few who were committed to understanding them. The films required the same sorts of skills the archaeologist uses to find cultural patterns in obscure objects. Conversely, the artists took on the task of building these Rosetta Stones.

Michael Snow worked as the trickster of time and space. His "walking woman" sculptures functioned as minimalist logos unattached to any entity outside themselves. Larger manifestations of the woman mounted as public art looked (at least to my over-heated imagination) like a hurried urbanite rushing past a piece of public art. Commissioned to provide a sculpture for the elephantine Eaton's Centre shopping mall, Snow sculpted a flock of Canada geese. They flew through the mall's pretensions of being bigger than all outdoors. Toronto's new baseball stadium got an oversized, cartoonish manifestation of what its builders were trying to sell: the sports event as transcendental experience for the true and unthinking fan.

In a similar manner, Snow's films gave devoted cineastes what they thought they wanted. If one measure of an auteur was his or her reference to off-screen space, here is *Wavelength*, a film whose entire narrative consists of the production of that feature. *One Second in Montreal* celebrated the moving image's use of stasis. His *Side Seat Paintings Slides Sound Film* is a discourse on audience perspective, reception theory without the theory. And Snow's greatest work of the period, *La Région Centrale*, is a deliberately exhausting demonstration of framing and camera movement. That its images are made by a machine is also a bit of meditation on the "apparatus," an understanding of film as technology.

Labeled as a "structuralist," (a term derived from its original manifestation as a Soviet revolutionary aesthetic), Snow might also be seen

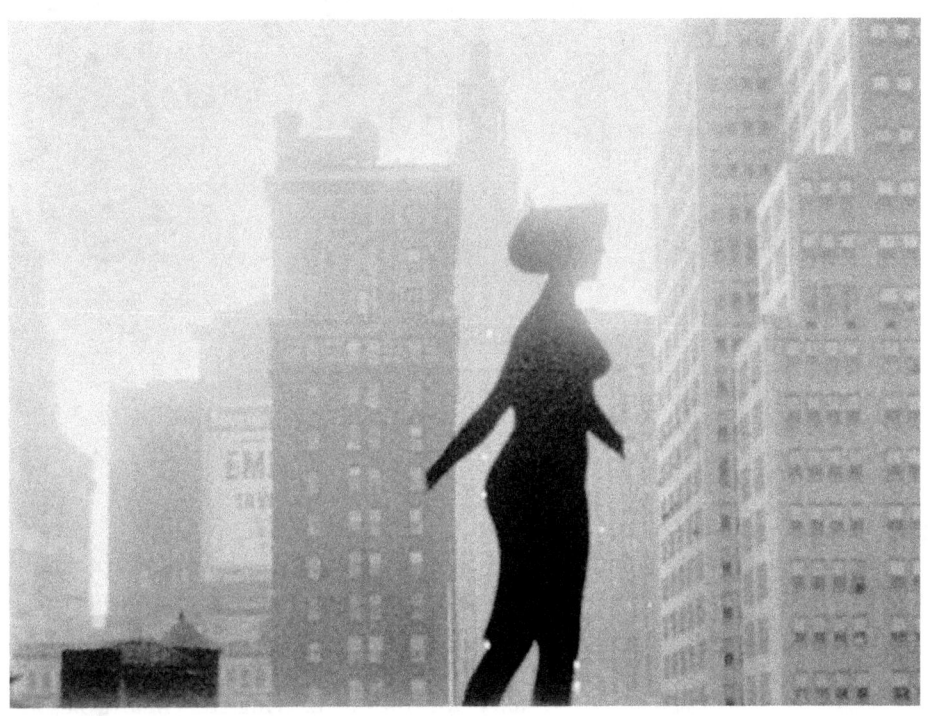

New York Eye and Ear Control *[Film Still]*, 1964
16mm film, 34 minutes, black and white, sound
Courtesy of Michael Snow

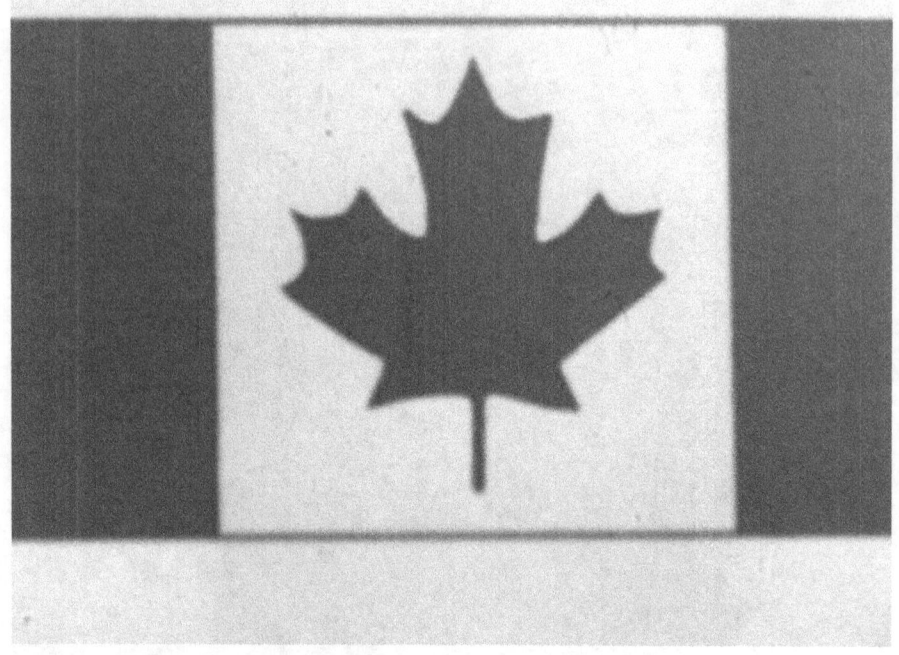

Reason Over Passion *[Film Still]*, 1969
16mm film, 84 minutes, colour and black and white, sound
Courtesy of CFMDC

as a pre-eminent commentator on the era's visual values. His partner at the time, Joyce Wieland, functioned as a curator of its sensibilities. Her hand-sewn fabric art with its innocent Canadian iconography was a collection of proposals for another more humble and more distinctly female, Canadian banner. The vast number of drawings she made for her feature film, *The Far Shore*, could be taken together as a living storyboard, i.e. a Canadian theatrical release that had nothing to do with the Canadian Film Development Corporation's limited definition of CanCon.

Wieland's most remembered experimental film of the period is *Reason Over Passion*, a deconstruction of the phrase that Pierre Trudeau claimed as his guiding principle. The film's visuals consist of long takes of Canadian landscape filmed from a moving car. These are subtitled with an ever changing hodgepodge of the letters that compose Trudeau's phrase. Here the curator of Canadian sensibilities exams the irony of Canada's most cerebral Prime Minister taking power on a wave of Trudeau-mania. She also cites the primal fact of Canada's history, its vast and largely empty landmass. Her work, as a would-be detractor labeled it, had reached the pitch of "passion over reason."

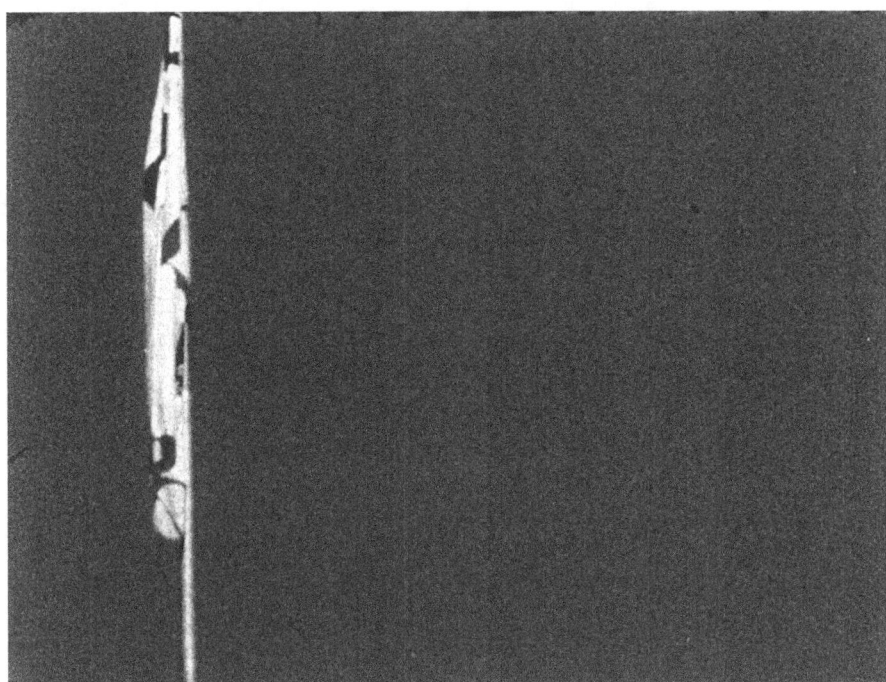

The Hart of London *[Film Still]*, 1968-70
16mm film, 79 minutes, colour and black and white, sound
Courtesy of CFMDC

On his part, Jack Chambers chronicled his moment in history in one unchanging location. Chambers lived almost all of his life in London, Ontario, a city that, with its Thames River, Covent Garden Market and Oxford Street, is the "other and opposite" of its namesake. And just as Chambers lived in London, London lived in Chambers. That dour and grim town in a dour and grim period found a place for its artistic son. London trained him as a draftsman and commercial illustrator. Later, Chambers upgraded his skills at the Franco-era San Fernando Academia de Bellas Artes in Madrid, a repository of Renaissance discipline. The result was paintings that convey the dialectic between the precocious child artist and the precision-tooled vocation that shaped his expression. Chambers theorized his approach as "Perceptual Realism," a theory of alternative visions escaping from strictly crafted reality.

Chambers came to work in any number of artistic media, including film. His cinematic masterpiece, *The Hart of London*, is certainly the most emotionally charged Canadian film ever made about the idea of place. Created almost entirely from the throwaway images of London's local television news, *The Hart of London* is, among its many other accolades, one of the greatest achievements of archival filmmaking. It is to the quotidian historical documentary what Walter Benjamin's *Arcades Project* is to a standard history of nineteenth century merchandising. And yet, typical Chambers, it is nothing more or less than the geography as he found it.

If Snow worked with his satirical wit and Wieland with her passion, Jack Chambers' palette was the unbearable precision of his own experience. In all three cases we are looking at work that is, at least in a metaphorical sense, submitted to the new flag committee. These are our banners, just as they are our alternative Expo, small and simple, single screen productions just as subversive as the Expo films in pushing the limits of the cinematic frame.

Together, the three artists presented in this book converge as chroniclers of a moment of rapid visual change and all that those visions might represent. Stephen Broomer's commendable achievement as historian-artist-theorist is to study their contributions in tandem and, I believe, to find the sum that is greater than the historical parts they played. He is to be commended for his intellectual achievement as he and we are welcomed into the era he depicts.

CODES FOR NORTH

Foundations of the Canadian Avant-Garde Film

INTRODUCTION

The Invention of Difficulty

The Canadian avant-garde film emerged through the work of three artists. Each bore separate stylistic and thematic debts and each shaped those
styles and themes to their distinct visions. Jack Chambers pursued painting
and later filmmaking from his hometown of London, Ontario. He had
returned to London in 1961 after seven years in Spain, where he gathered his voice through the Spanish legacy of figurative painting and the
mysteries of the Castilian landscape. Michael Snow and Joyce Wieland,
married artists, both born in Toronto, had met in the mid-1950s while
working together at the animation firm Graphic Associates. In 1962, they
left Toronto to live and work in New York City, and there experienced
the aftermath of Abstract Expressionism, a vacuum of colliding modern
and postmodern movements, before their ultimate return to Toronto in
1971. This book considers the aesthetic debts of these filmmakers, the
metamorphosis of those influences into their individual styles, their major works and the ways in which their art is fortified against ready comprehension, presenting perceptual challenges, resisting interpretation and
bearing complex meanings. Such difficult modern aesthetics manifested in
the Canadian avant-garde film and became central to its character. These
bodies of work became unified around an aesthetic of purposeful difficulty,
even as the strategies, intentions and perceptual character of the works
remained distinct. Later, as the school of Canadian experimental film was
formalized, a narrow set of themes and subjects—landscape, autobiography, material self-consciousness—would supplant the subtler unity of difficulty that had been sown through the foundational works: Joyce Wieland's
Reason Over Passion (1969), Jack Chambers' *The Hart of London* (1970) and
Michael Snow's *La Région Centrale* (1971).

The Invention of Difficulty

Difficult aesthetics cannot be said to have a fixed point of origin, an hour
of invention, much less to have entered the world as a symptom of the

modern era. A long-advancing impulse toward difficult forms in art con-
spired with the epistemological transformations of the post-Victorian era
to bring us into the modern, to create a difficult modern art, an art that
is a contest of complex pleasures. Difficulty evolved in tandem with modernism, a radical break from the past that simultaneously bound itself to
that past. To map the evolution of difficult art is to map the precursors of
modernism.

Difficult aesthetics have their origins in medieval and renaissance
literature, from the pantheistic allegories, self-reflexivity and vernacular of
Dante Aligheri's *Divine Comedy* (1321), to the intertextual and metatheatrical strategies of Miguel De Cervantes's *Don Quixote* (1605).[1] In the visual
arts, a primitive difficulty begins in the telltale emblems of painted saints,
for example, in the cross, skull, Bible and lion that indicate St. Jerome
even as other aspects of his appearance change to reflect the era of that
representation. This encyclopedia of symbols signalled the world as the
text of God. Slowly we would come to engage the perceptual difficulties of
dynamism and perspective, but difficult aesthetics began from an understanding of the work of art as a container into which one could collapse
the world into symbol and allegory. When the Moderns arrived, they were
not only responding to political and social transformations and to the new
and different experiences, sensations and visions that came with the industrial age, but also to a rare urge that runs through the history of cultural
production, to "bring light to bear upon a dark age."[2] Their work emerged
out of a heritage of paintings and texts that employ self-conscious devices,
texts that are steeped in obscurities, ontological barriers, slang, complex
programmes, iconography and ambiguities. These texts necessitate inter-
preters whose task is seemingly infinite, toiling in the total library of a
deep history. This concept for literature finds its apotheosis in James Joyce's
Ulysses (1922), its world constricted and magnified, detailed to minutiae, the

---

[1] A book of particular value to the study of difficulty in literature, specific to Dante, is
James Wilhelm's *Il Miglior Fabbro: The Cult of the Difficult in Daniel, Dante, and Pound* (Orono:
National Poetry Foundation, 1982). Wilhelm explores the deeper motivations that guide
difficult periods in literature and his argument pivots on the notion that difficulty "does
not necessarily arise in every period of literary history," but emerges primarily in the
medieval and the modern. It is a great challenge to locate difficult forms in Romantic
and Victorian art and literature to bridge the medieval and the modern, but my position
diverges from Wilhelm's in that I believe Dante tested the boundaries of medieval thought
even as he shaped it, and so is among the earliest emissaries of the modern.

[2] Frederick R. Karl, *Modern and Modernism: The Sovereignty of the Artist 1885–1925* (New
York: Atheneum, 1985), 9. Karl characterizes this notion, of modern thought as light
and traditional thought as darkness, as "an unjust frame of reference which (...) enabled
Modernists to justify their work." It simultaneously denigrates the past (the dark age) and
establishes that past as the base material of cultural production (light as illumination of a
dark age).

tiniest detail rich with ambiguous meaning, yet still by its roots in Homer a cosmic odyssey; and in Ezra Pound's *The Cantos* (1915–1962), a text that integrated many languages and Chinese logograms, a text of sudden allusion without transition, holding to its own mysterious logic and its oracular rhetorical strategies, a text under endless construction terminating only with the life of the author. In 1891, the poet Stephane Mallarmé observed that, "everything in the world exists to end up in a book."[3] Such books-to-end-all-books, books to contain all knowledge, all insight, all experience, became the mission of twentieth-century modernist literature. Those who set themselves to the task of this writing—Joyce and Pound foremost—were following in a tradition older than Mallarmé, a tradition passed across disciplines in rare, visionary works that had heralded the modern. The makers of this art-to-end-all-art would produce works that were conscious of their own mediation of reality, that would contain not only a vastness of experience and information, but which would also have inbuilt obstacles. These works would be fortified against ready understanding, posing challenges that would involve the reader in the construction of meaning.

All schools of painting have codes. Diego Velázquez's *Las Meninas* (1656), a painting of perspectival enigmas, contains at once a self-portrait of the artist at work, a royal portrait seen in a reflection, a high-ceilinged room decorated with paintings and mirrors, and the titular subject of the painting, the maids of honour and other members of the royal entourage as they attend to the young Margaret Theresa of Spain.[4] Michel Foucault wrote that *Las Meninas* was the midpoint between the classical and the

---

[3] Mallarmé's original remark, "Le monde est fait pour aboutir dans à un beau Livre," given in an interview with Jules Huret (*Revue Blanche*, 1891), is translated as the common expression given here. A fuller account of Mallarmé's intended meaning, and his later modulations of this statement, is offered by Roger Pearson in his *Mallarmé and Circumstance: The Translation of Silence* (New York: Oxford University Press, 2004): that the book is a "human accessory [waiting] to serve its purpose as an 'instrument spirituel'", a book an assemblage of the component parts of a global totality, and that Mallarmé's remark is not the "Wildean claim that the purpose of life is to be turned into (literary) art," but rather a neutral expression of the relationship between words and things (Pearson, 255). The most comprehensive discussion of Mallarmé's difficult aesthetic strategies is in Malcolm Bowie's *Mallarmé and the Art of Being Difficult* (Cambridge: Cambridge University Press, 1978), which, as with other studies of difficulty, focuses on the audience as decoder of complex texts.

[4] When he first encountered *Las Meninas*, the painter Luca Giordano is said to have declared it the "theology of painting." Antonio Palomino, who recorded this remark, explained it as an expression of praise: that this work is to painting what theology is to 'lesser' branches of knowledge. This is a reductive interpretation of this statement. The work contains, as did Giordano's own work that followed it, a totality of vision, a representation of every possible hierarchy, aligning its governing perspective with the eyes of the royal subject, a confluence of social and aesthetic hierarchies. This work was the theology of painting for it was an enclosed visual system, a realization of the potential of art to vanish into itself.

modern, that within it "representation, freed finally from the relation that was impeding it, can offer itself as representation in its pure form," and yet even freed, that pure representation had a history embedded in it.[5] The painting is simultaneously an erasure and a container of its world and its predecessors, recalling Frederick Karl's thesis that modernism sought "to capture the present while denying the past, and yet to use every aspect of the past to develop ideas of presentness."[6] The paintings that hang on the walls are scenes from Ovid's *Metamorphoses*, first painted by Peter Paul Rubens, copied by Velázquez's son-in-law and assistant Juan del Mazo. *Las Meninas* therefore contains Velázquez's representation of Mazo's copies of Rubens' paintings. By this mimetic echo, by its inventory of perspectives, by its metatheatrical staging, *Las Meninas* foretells the impulse in modern art to subsume the world.[7] The veil between representation and the perceptual experience of reality was under duress in the Baroque paintings of Velázquez and his contemporaries, for example, in Luca Giordano's *Rubens painting the Allegory of Peace* (1660). Giordano, with coexisting planes and perspectives, depicts Rubens sitting in the world of his own paintings, selecting a detail from the limitless universe of his fantasy, a fantasy of luminous and divine erotomania. These painters knew the traps of vision. Their labours would cause painting to break from the restrictions of realist representation.

In the twentieth century, crises of perspective and of the subject would become the governing theme in art. But in the decades leading up to the twentieth century, a crisis of vision would already begin to play out, in the shift away from naturalism and toward abstraction. Photography displaced the value of realism in painting. From the photograph's evolution beginning in the 1840s, through to its assumption as the essential medium of realist representation, painters gradually turned their attention to the expression of interior experience. The photograph, as a tool for precise documentation, gave form to a scientific record of reality. This not only freed painters to develop representations of inner life, but also gave rise to art that engaged with a scientific understanding of optics.[8] The divisionism

---

[5] Michel Foucault, *The Order of Things: An Archeology of Human Sciences* (New York: Vintage Books, 1970), 16.

[6] Frederick R. Karl, *Modern and Modernism: The Sovereignty of the Artist 1885–1925* (New York: Atheneum, 1985), 13.

[7] The composition of *Las Meninas* has also become an iconic tableau, repeated through the history of art. It inspired works by Francisco Goya, Salvador Dalí, Richard Hamilton and perhaps most famously a Pablo Picasso series of 58 interpretations (1957).

[8] The junction of the science of vision and Post-Impressionist painting is explored in José A. Argüelles's study of Charles Henry, a French librarian who conceived of the doctrine of the psychophysical in the age of Post-Impressionism. His was a pursuit of a harmony beyond symbolism, a harmony between scientific knowledge and the expression of interior

and pointillism of Paul Signac and Georges Seurat is a sea change in the formal representation of vision in painting, not as concerns perspective or symbol, but in its relation to the physics of vision. By choosing as his subject *A Sunday Afternoon on the Island of La Grand Jatte* (1884), Seurat remained connected to the tradition of conventional representation, a tradition dominated by the ready pleasures of naturalism and realist figuration. The method of the painting held to realism, but the divisionist form suggests the composition of photographic vision, understood as the granular makeup of the photograph, a complex mimesis arising from a scientific knowledge of perception; this form extends even to the frame, now realized as simply a margin of the whole, as the divisionist pattern continues outwards, extending the composition to the limits of the art object.[9] The divisionist painter breaks down his scene into granular fragments that reassemble into representation. Even this Post-Impressionism, with its ostensible ties to the tradition of realist depiction, was embracing a coming fragmentation and recombination of vision, a departure from classical ideas of time, space and sight. The modern movements of the early twentieth century would see a further dispensation with realism, a detachment of form from representation, toward freer, improvisatory, gestural, content- and form-dense work. The perceptual possibilities of such work would further foster resistance to realist conventions.[10]

Visual art pressed forward through the fragmentation of Italian Futurism, the prismatic imagination of analytic and synthetic Cubism, and the anti-art of Dada. This series of movements showed a pronounced resistance to realism. Futurism had prefigured the fragmented vision that, in Cubism, pushed toward a fuller abstraction. Cubism in turn partly prefigured Dada, in its plastic aspects: the affixing of paper fragments directly to the canvas foreshadowed Dada collage, but to a vastly different end. Dada was, by Hans Richter's account, "anti-art," anti-aesthetic, anti-tradition, a

experience through art. For further information, see *Charles Henry and the Formation of a Psychophysical Aesthetic* (Chicago: University of Chicago Press, 1972).

[9] With *Evening, Honfleur* (1886), Seurat again painted the frame, again penetrating the very boundaries of painting that separate representation from reality. This act forces the eye to seek continuity between Seurat's divisionist pattern on the frame and the ends of his exposed canvas, as if the scene that he depicts will pass out of art and into reality. In *A Sunday Afternoon on the Island of La Grand Jatte*, there was such continuity. But two years later, with *Evening, Honfleur*, the pattern of the frame is fully abstract. It resists continuing the scene from the canvas and does not extend that scene to the limits of its objecthood. By doing so it sets an impasse between reality and its representation.

[10] This is not to say that photography would remain a slave to scientific observation; on the contrary, the desire amongst visual artists to explore interior experience would soon be extended to photography, and as photography developed as an art form, it too would engage a resistance to realism.

rage against the demoralization of man in the shadow of progress. Dada was ushered in with the Great War and lasted from roughly 1915 to 1924, beginning in Zürich and spreading out to other European territories and to America. It was an ideology arising out of the disgust that its artists and poets felt in the course of the War, an outraged response to the fatal logic of bourgeois capitalist society. It was a rejection of the cold reason and strategy that had choked men with chlorine on the front. Against the scale and horror of the War, it was an embrace of the irrational, the intuitive, and, despite the weight of its protest, the comic. These themes took form in the performances and poetry of Tristan Tzara, the collages of Hannah Höch and the sound poetry of Kurt Schwitters. Form, even photorealist form, took on an abstract dimension in the associative collage of Dada. The art object, increasingly abstracted since the 1880s, had steadily divorced from realist representation. Through Dada, art would reconnect with a perceptual reality, in the tremors of hearing, in the disfigurative collage. The world of art was no longer slave to the uncanny pleasures of realist rendering; real things, drawn out of the everyday, could now be declared art, and in that declaration the purity of their forms would take on manifold meanings. Dada's subversion of the everyday is most prevalent in Marcel Duchamp's readymades, for instance, *Fountain* (1917), an ordinary object, a urinal, signed and declared as art. Against this reality, an embattled realism could not stand.

Dada was a prelude to the postmodern, to the Neo-Dada, Pop Art and Situationist movements, but its immediate descendent and the recipient of its anti-realist tendencies was Surrealism.[11] Surrealism emerged with the decline of Dada, formalized in André Breton's 1924 manifesto, which stated its intention "to resolve the previously contradictory conditions of dream and reality."[12] The nonsense of Dada extended here into an embrace of the sublime, the surprise, by logic of dreaming; it was an embrace of the processes of the unconscious, of automatism as a process to bring the maker and the viewer closer to the realities of perception, and to assemble new unities out of the discontinuities of perceptual experience. Automatism joined creative action to the crude structures of the subconscious, of the unguided hand. In Surrealist painting, familiar forms and figuration would be compromised by dream and fantasy, for example in the automatic drawings of André Masson, whose spontaneous webs of pen strokes suggest the reordering of a conventional subject; in

---

[11] Surrealists, on an individual basis, employed sources such as Symbolist literature and painting, itself an important rejection of naturalism and realism in painting.

[12] André Breton, "Manifesto of Surrealism," (1924) republished in Breton, *Manifestoes of Surrealism*, translated by Richard Seaver and Helen R. Lane (Ann Arbor: University of Michigan Press, 1969).

the paintings of René Magritte, where hats rest on phantom heads; those of Salvador Dalí, where temporal and spatial distortions of his subjects bely a bridge between dream and reality; or in the boxed assemblages of the American Surrealist Joseph Cornell, in which commonplace objects gathered from thrift stores form lyrical and nostalgic juxtapositions. This movement would last until the Second World War and the rise of Nazism displaced a great number of European artists.[13]

With the end of the Second World War, the American Abstract Expressionist movement took up the modern impulse against realism. A movement primarily based in New York City, Abstract Expressionism signalled the end of common figuration, as individual expression became dominant in the act of painting. Paint would be applied for expressive purpose, for its raw colours and textures, and artists would master new forms of craftsmanship based in a comprehensive knowledge of their materials and the application of that knowledge to spontaneous forms. Such craftsmanship might appear ingenuous to those entrenched in more traditional schools. Theme and symbol remained in the programme of works such as Robert Motherwell's *Elegies to the Spanish Republic* (1948–1991) and Barnett Newman's *Abraham* (1949), but form, having long abandoned the representational aspects of earlier modern movements, was becoming increasingly radicalized. The great envoy of Abstract Expressionism was the critic Clement Greenberg. For Greenberg, modernism had established the autonomous expression, which in turn created a pure art, freed from the traps of representation to pursue its own agenda. Raw material engagement was the path of bare expression. External influence was eliminated, privileging the elements of picture plane, frame, depth, consistency and the application of paint and other materials to the canvas. Abstract Expressionism aspired toward a confrontation with pure form. Vision would have to surrender its search for reality in art, to give itself over to form, mechanism and pluralism.

Difficulty had reached a new height in Abstract Expressionism, for the paintings placed a direct demand on the viewer's perceptual faculties, suspending their search for referent and symbol.[14] Abstract Expressionism was soon followed with post-painterly abstraction. The dense surfaces

---

[13] Surrealist Antonin Artaud, conceptual architect of the Theatre of Cruelty, once called rational discourse a field of "falsehood and illusion." His work extends the resistance to realist representation and its basis in the rational. For Surrealists, the rational discourse of politics, like the rational discourse of pre-modern movements, was a disconnection from reality.

[14] This is not true of all Abstract Expressionist paintings; while the search may have been suspended, there was still symbolic and referential intention. Consider Motherwell's *Elegies to the Spanish Republic*; the artist has described the oval black forms that dominate the canvas as an invocation of bull testicles.

of Abstract Expressionist paintings were a site of obscurity; by contrast, post-painterly abstractionist paintings achieved a greater clarity in precision of paint application, and that clarity was simply an evolution and refinement of that obscurity. Post-painterly abstraction went further than abstract expressionism in abandoning the link between art and reality, minimizing the marks of its own construction. Coming in close step with post-painterly abstraction, and to a vastly different end, was Neo-Dada, which drew from the methods and spirit of the Dada movement, for example, in the tool sculptures of Jim Dine and the collage and sculptural works of Robert Rauschenberg. In Neo-Dada, the execution and labour of the work itself was more important than its concept, its objecthood suspended beyond the contemplation and emotion of process. In the branch of Neo-Dada that became Pop Art, painters and sculptors reclaimed the realist project, with a newly pliable line between conceptualism and formalism. For Andy Warhol, contemporary iconography, in the form of mass media images, was elevated to the order of the empty signifier, against interpretation. In his photorealist canvases, of repeating images of Elvis Presley, Marilyn Monroe and Elizabeth Taylor, the repetition itself became iconic, the granules of halftone newsprint and Polaroid colour palettes casting these icons as an echo of an echo, the tireless gesture of post-modernity.[15] The absurdist soft sculptures of Claes Oldenburg, such as *Floor Cone* (1962), undermined the familiar, a continuity of Marcel Duchamp's readymades. For artists such as Warhol, Oldenburg and Jasper Johns (who had come through the American Neo-Dada), Pop Art was as much a reaction to realism as it was to abstraction, and its confrontation repurposed the modes of Dada, and the power of its subjects, into a realm of apathy and indifference.[16] Its surfaces were impenetrable, and in it, mimetic realism was replaced by the reality of the mass media cliché.

Conceptual and perceptual challenges pervaded modern art movements, from the fragmentation of Cubism and Futurism, to the ineffable power of Abstract Expressionism, to the allegorical indirection of Pop Art.[17] All were engaged in a resistance of realism. This project was

---

[15] Warhol did not confine this strategy to his iconographic paintings; he did the same in *Birmingham Race Riot* (1964), a work that, like his celebrity paintings, and despite the apparent social meanings conferred on its subject, held no inherent social ideology.

[16] In Donald Kuspit's "Pop Art: A Reactionary Realism," (*Art Journal* 36:1, Fall 1976, 31-38), Kuspit argues that Pop Art—specifically the art of James Rosenquist, Roy Lichtenstein and Andy Warhol—endorsed the mass media clichés that dominated their work, that they became "part of that organization of optimism so essential to consumer capitalist society, and had nothing to do with the derision of that society socialists imagined they saw in it."

[17] Other modern and post-modern movements excluded from this cursory introduction to difficulty, such as Fauvism, Suprematism, Fluxus, Minimalism, the particularities of Orphic Cubism, and so on, are not irrelevant to this discussion. I have elected to focus on only one

not restricted to the visual arts, but was also at the core of modern and post-modern literature and music, from the opaque poetry of John Ashbery to the dissonance and spatial fragmentation of Ornette Coleman's *Free Jazz* (1961). The modern, in response to the age of enlightenment, introduced into culture forms of knowledge and art that are full of restrictions and barriers. "In modernity," Maurice Merleau-Ponty wrote, "we have a representation of the world which excludes neither fissures nor lacunae, a form of action which is unsure of itself, or, at any rate, no longer blithely assumes it can obtain universal assent."[18] In modern art, the art object itself critiques and departs from representation. It is less assured of the definitive and singular meaning, less assured of the value of meaning, less concerned with speaking directly. By the 1960s, modern difficulties had reached a point of such diversity that the boundaries of art were in continuous development. Even the densest of difficult forms could lie ahead, in a radical domain of the arts that was ever opening to new expressions. To others, aesthetic difficulties would remain a point of contention, the product of a cloistered elite, to be defeated with the insurgence of an all-accessible realism.

A Typology of Difficulty

William Wordsworth, in his preface to *Lyrical Ballads*, speculated on the sources of delight in poetry. He determined that delight formed through "the music of harmonious metrical language, the sense of difficulty overcome, and the blind association of pleasure which has been previously received from works of rhyme or metre of the same or similar construction, an indistinct perception perpetually renewed of language closely resembling that of real life, and yet, in the circumstance of metre, differing from it so widely."[19] For Wordsworth, the pleasure of poetry came in part from conquering difficulties of comprehension, and yet also recognizing in poetic language and rhythm a description of experience distinct from 'real life', a subtlety of perception that encompasses another world of perception. In this statement, delight begins in the ready pleasures of harmony, and is then enriched by the labour of learning dissonances and by perceptual reveries that are innately mysterious.

Modern poetry brought with it new mysteries. Where the audiences for ancient Alexandrian and medieval poetry could resolve the difficulties of their texts to agreed-upon meanings, decided by a common

strata of this evolution, and even then, there are admitted limitations to this line.

[18] Maurice Merleau-Ponty, *The World of Perception* (New York: Routledge, 2004), 106.

[19] William Wordsworth, preface to Wordsworth and Samuel Taylor Coleridge, *Lyrical Ballads, with a Few Other Poems* (London: J. & A. Arch, 1798).

readership, modern audiences were now faced with texts that resisted such agreement. In modernism, the common reader vanished. Modern poetry was bewilderingly new, in continuity with the difficulties that had preceded it but new in its ambiguity and indirection, new in its capacity to pass beyond mere puzzles of comprehension. Wordsworth's statement on the delight of poetry could not account for the possibility of complex difficult pleasures. Decodification evolved, from the ready pleasure of solution, to the complex pleasures of polysemic immersion. The reader began to participate in the creation of meaning, to confront and celebrate the subjective and the improvisatory, and to meet the absolute boundaries of their comprehension. Literary criticism and philosophy wrestled with these qualities in modern poetry, and as they turned to the relationship between artist and receiver, a modest discourse would form within that field to describe the challenges posed to the reader, and the ways in which a text gives delight and pleasure, beyond Wordsworth's ideal of difficulty overcome.

In 1978, the literary critic and philosopher George Steiner published "On Difficulty," an essay through which he attempted to classify the difficulties posed by modern poetry to its audience. Steiner divides these difficulties into categories of contingent, modal, tactical and ontological, each representing a different form of reader engagement and, arguably, a different experience of pleasure.[20] His four difficulties all, in different ways, reinforce the obscurity of modernism, and that obscurantism is most readily understood as referential, in relating the modern text to greater bodies of knowledge. But these four difficulties also suggest forms of strategic fortification and the role of taste and engagement that distance modern aesthetics from encyclopedism.

In contingent difficulty, the poem is guarded by allusions to particular knowledge, to past works of art, or to doctrines, ideas, words and expressions that have faded from common knowledge. The pleasure of the text depends upon knowledge that exists beyond the text, in history, or science, or other works of art and literature. The text introduces the

---

[20] George Steiner's text is not the final word in difficulty. The scholar to most fully commit himself to this subject, in its broadest application to art, is Leonard Diepeveen, who has written a number of substantial texts on difficulty in literature and in visual art, in particular, his rigorous monograph *The Difficulties of Modernism* (New York: Routledge, 2002) and *Art with a Difference: Looking at Difficult and Unfamiliar Art* (co-authored with Timothy van Laar, Mayfield, 2001). Other authors who have written book-length studies of difficulty, in the relation between artist and audience, are Vernon Shetley and Bob Perelman. Shetley's *After the Death of Poetry: Poet and Audience in Contemporary America* (Durham: Duke University Press, 1993), is a call to restore the difficult experience of poetry; Perelman's *The Trouble with Genius: Reading Pound, Joyce, Stein and Zukofsky* (Berkeley: University of California Press, 1994), is an indictment of academic discourse surrounding the major works of late modern literature, with attention to the dysfunctional exchange between society and radical texts.

reader to particularities of knowledge by drawing from them in explicit or subtle ways. This is a form of difficulty that meets with a ready resolution, in that the obstruction—here, absent knowledge—can be remedied if necessary with encyclopedias and readings of past literary and philosophical works, rendering primary texts secondary in the pursuit of the difficult text's decodification. This form is primary in the writings of Eliot, Joyce and Pound. For Eliot's debts to James George Frazer, *The Golden Bough* (1890) could be regarded as a primer for *The Waste Land* (1922). The call of the Frog Chorus from Aristophanes's *The Frogs* (405 B.C.) that commences James Joyce's *Finnegans Wake* (1939) is one of many gestures that implicate the classical tradition in literature and drama among Joyce's sources. Steiner describes contingent difficulty as "the homework of elucidation."[21] They are obstacles that can be solved, in part, through labour. As this difficulty passes from poetry and prose into music and the visual arts, the perceptions required likewise shift, toward the recognition of patterns, sequences, symbols, and other contents unique to each media.

In modal difficulty, Steiner writes, "the centre holds against us." Put simply, the text does not engage the reader. This beholder, despite their understanding "of the rough and ready sort represented by paraphrase," cannot engage the work, for the work is fortified by displeasure of form or by a disagreement of form to content. This difficulty occurs when we cannot find justification for form, when "the root-occasion of the poem's composition eludes or repels our internalized sense of what poetry should or should not be about."[22] And it resists solution, for despite gaining an awareness of the standards by which the poem was composed, of the greater movement that encompasses it, and coming to a fuller understanding of its aesthetics, it may still be met with resistance or dismissal, for its sheer otherness. Here, Steiner's typology shifts toward the subjective, as the burden of classifying a work by modal difficulty now involves personal subjectivity on the part of the beholder. Gertrude Stein's *Tender Buttons: Objects, Food, Rooms* (1914) represents one height of modal difficulty in twentieth century modern poetry, for how Stein uses language to alienate the reader from even the most mundane and familiar subject, for instance, her umbrella: "Coloring high means that the strange reason is in front not more in front behind. Not more in front in peace of the dot."[23] John Ashbery is an example of one of George Steiner's contemporaries, a late modern poet whose work is defiantly difficult, and whose collection *The Tennis Court Oath* (1962) represents a radical and impenetrable vanguard in

[21] George Steiner, "On Difficulty," *The Journal of Aesthetics and Art Criticism*, 36:3 (Spring 1978), 267.

[22] Ibid.

[23] Gertrude Stein, *Tender Buttons: Objects, Food, Rooms* (New York: Claire Marie, 1914), 22.

American poetry, our comprehension strained by its modal incongruity.

Modal difficulty is evident in the advance of modernism through the early-to-mid twentieth century across several art forms. For example, in music, this difficulty is evident from the radical piano compositions of Henry Cowell, e.g., *The Banshee* (1925) and the piano roll compositions of Conlon Nancarrow, to the violent extensions of a free jazz vanguard evident in Peter Brötzmann's *Machine Gun* (1968). Modal difficulty challenges our preconceptions of form, but it does so in an elusive way. There is no guarantee to a rich aesthetic engagement at the end of the trial of this difficulty, and the pleasure varies from beholder to beholder. Modal difficulty is subject to individual taste, but given more objective consideration, it is a matter of distance between 'ordinary discourse', the ordinary discourse of realism and convention—or simply discourse made ordinary by the logic of our expectations—and the dislocated discourse of the new.

Tactical difficulties manifest as the poet shapes language as a vehicle for their individual voice, through the use of neologism, archaism, elision, distortion and displacement that "shape the common idiom into an instrument of individual expression."[24] Like contingent and modal difficulties, tactical difficulty weighs on the condition of intelligibility between text and reader, but unlike the contingent and the modal, the tactical lies in an intention of the poet to achieve a personal and distinctive style out of the impersonal and uniform system of language. It is therefore less a result of confrontation with the audience, than it is a confrontation with language itself. More than the allusions of contingent difficulty and the otherness of modal difficulty, tactical difficulty is an act of encoding text. The material is shaped into individual expression by allegorical indirection, by challenging the impersonal and resistant medium, of language, of paint, of scale and key. Tactical difficulty conceals the work; in poetry it might do so through fragmentary syntax, through slang and word creation, and in the visual arts there is the tactic of décollage and the disfiguration present across Dada and Surrealism. If the tactical seems to be joined to fragmentation and recombination, as the contingent is to allusion, this is only one of its manifestations. The tactical difficulties of the visual arts lie in all manner of perspectival subversion. The enigmas and distortions of the modern image are strategies that resist realism, just as those same tactical difficulties bend and distort language in modern literature. The individuation of tactical difficulty haunts twentieth century art, with artists approaching the conventions and idioms of their media with a need to individuate, to sculpt and mark those traits into new standards of the

---

[24] Vernon Shetley, *After the Death of Poetry: Poet and Audience in Contemporary America* (Durham: Duke University Press, 1993), 8.

distinct and authentic expression, authentic in the strangeness of the art-ist's invention.

These difficulties challenge directness of meaning and by exten-sion the value of realism, its ideological codification, its simplicity of alle-gory, its guided meaning. The final form of difficulty identified by Steiner, ontological difficulty, departs from this inquiry. It is instead a subversion of the contract of intelligibility that exists within a medium between art-ist and audience, and its presence disconnects the two, revealing the gulf between their expectations of communication. In Steiner's words, onto-logical difficulties are those that "confront us with blank questions about the nature of human speech, the status of significance, the necessity and purpose of the construct which we have (...) come to perceive as a poem."[25] An ontological difficulty is a confrontation with a terrifying sublime, one that overturns the material reality of a work and its base perception (as speech is to poetry, as hearing is to music, as vision is to painting). Meaning and purpose are eclipsed. To recognize the ontologically difficult is to real-ize that unanswerable questions lay at the roots of our search for meaning. Such art challenges its receiver into confronting this uneasy search, and to confront the experience and perception of art in a general sense. It admits that there are qualities beyond description and beyond knowledge, in the outermost regions of aesthetic inquiry. The ontological difficulty is a crisis of idiom, of culture itself, identified with the urge to revolt against the authority of the past, through esotericism, and the urge to return to a past state when form, freed from the conventions of the common beholder, was "open to the truth of being, to the hidden sources of all meaning."[26]

This typology was offered for application to modernist poetry, and there are many instances in the poems of Zukofsky, Ashbery, Celan, Olson and others in which one or several of these difficult strategies are present. Steiner's conclusion is decidedly enigmatic, reminding that difficulty is es-sentially a mysterious trait, and that its presence within a text opens the reader to profound spiritual questions of meaning. He writes, in reflection on Celan, "the poet is not a persona, a subjectivity 'ruling over language,' but an 'openness to,' a supreme listener to, the genius of speech."[27] The mystery of difficulty, and the mystery of form, reminds us that there re-mains a fundamental problem of perception beyond resolution. Resolution may not be the aim of such mysteries. Steiner's typologies are not prescrip-tive. The strategies of modern aesthetics resist typologies and definitions. I have referred to the myriad forms of modern art, but a more accurate

---

[25] Steiner, 273.

[26] Ibid., 274.

[27] Ibid., 275.

description would be to say that modern forms undergo endless improvisation and modulation, that they are utterly inexhaustible for their response to all of history and all manner of perception. It is tempting, in following Steiner's typology, to still regard modern art by the laws of a puzzle, in continuity with Wordsworth, its difficulty merely a thing to overcome. It is likewise tempting to consider it as fortified against interpretation, those semantic enclosures the boundaries of its meaning. But to see modernism as merely enigmatic, or as obscure to the point of meaninglessness, is shortsighted. The modern is a clearing out of the past, a break from history. It is the birth of a new age through complex meanings, presences and systems. Modern art is no longer slave to the illusion of realism. In its break from realism and from the common beholder, art opens to boundless possibilities of experience and perception.

In the discourse of difficult art, critics have been polarized by the question of whether difficulty lies in the eye of the beholder or is a property of the work itself. Leonard Diepeveen and Timothy van Laar have argued that "a work's difficulty is subjectively determined; it is a mix between a work's implied instructions for use and a viewer's personal abilities."[28] This notion arises from the belief that difficulty is a behaviour, a contract between artist and receiver, and therefore, that difficulty is a variable, existing only for the receiver. The puzzle holds no mystery to the puzzle-maker. By this argument, the perceived difficulty of a work changes as society becomes more or less comfortable with it, an argument that has causation on its side, in the growing comfort with which audiences endorse, for instance, Post-Impressionism, but which cannot account for deviations, such as the enduring perceptual difficulties of Ezra Pound or John Cage.[29] Diepeveen and van Laar's argument is in continuity with the role of taste and subjectivity in Steiner's notion of modal difficulty, but also, it extends Wordsworth's notion of difficulty to be overcome. Mid-century modernism achieved forms in which such comfort became increasingly impossible, as the common reader vanished. The difficult aesthetic strategies of modernism can be identified and isolated in relatively objective terms, existing as both a property and a behaviour. While a dedicated audience

---

[28] Leonard Diepeveen and Timothy van Laar, *Art with a Difference: Looking at Difficult and Unfamiliar Art* (Mayfield, 2001), 101. This is also a central idea in the essays in James Purves's anthology *The Idea of Difficulty in Literature* (Buffalo: SUNY Press, 1991).

[29] Leo Steinberg makes this argument in *Other Criteria: Confrontations with Twentieth-Century Art* (London: Oxford University Press, 1972). He writes, "no art seems to remain uncomfortable for very long. At any rate, no style of these last hundred years has long retained its early look of unacceptability." (5) I believe that counter to this, the codification of works, the position that much radical late modernism takes against familiarity, and the taxing perceptual encounters of those works place rigorous demands that have continued to agitate and confound the audience.

can acclimate to the difficulties of early modernism, the difficulties of late modernism fortify the text against assent. The enduring difficulty of such works enriches the experience of them for both initiate and novice.[30]

When we speak of difficulty, it is inevitable that we do so in the subjective, perceptual terms by which we relate experience. Such difficulty develops between artist and audience, and to approach difficulty by more abstract terms implies a particular mode of engagement with a text. It announces the trial of a text as something inseparable from the experience of it; the perceptual challenge and the individual struggle become entangled. Art's difficulty does not, in this sense, exist solely as an isolated variable inherent within a work, fashioned in the artist's process, but rather lies dormant until it is beheld. As difficult aesthetic strategies evolved in tandem with an encroaching modernism, so too was the audience evolving. That audience had been tuned through their readings, their comprehensive knowledge of history, literature and art, their maturing knowledge of science, and their distinctly modern skepticism toward the text itself, to meet the perceptual demands of those difficult strategies. The audience would now participate in the creation of meaning, and would join the artist in contesting extant systems of meaning.[31]

The audience was the variable, flawed and uneven, and artists would create their work for an ideal beholder, inevitably a mirror of themselves.[32] In a catalogue text accompanying an exhibit of the Prinzhorn Collection of outsider art, Constance Perin wrote that encounters with such works of art "invite us to enter into their doubts, and we can accept

---

[30] One might argue in turn that the works of James Joyce, Ezra Pound and Gertrude Stein have gained universal assent as the essential works of twentieth-century modern literature, but the act of reading their texts remains a confrontation. If the initial shock of Marcel Duchamp's *Fountain* (1917), John Cage's *4'33"* (1952), or Albert Ayler's *Bells* (1965) has softened, their perceptual challenge and essential ontological difficulty remains; the same is true of difficult texts that emerged out of later twentieth-century literature, such as the works of John Ashbery and Thomas Pynchon, in which style and codification remain obstacles, and the pleasures of the texts are still derived by studied confrontation. The same can no longer be said for late-nineteenth-century modernism, which is now popularly embraced and misunderstood as a stylized realism (as in the case of Post-Impressionism).

[31] An essential study of this modern audience is Lawrence Lipton's *The Holy Barbarians* (New York: Julian Massner, 1959), which understood the world of the Beats as one enmeshed in history, its artists struggling with an inheritance of myth.

[32] What I am calling the ideal beholder is rooted in Anthony Burgess's statement on his ideal reader: "The ideal reader of my novels is a lapsed Catholic and failed musician, short-sighted, colour-blind, auditorily biased, who has read the books that I have read ... every author wants to make his audience. But it's in his own image, and his primary audience is a mirror." (John Cullinan, "Anthony Burgess, The Art of Fiction No. 48," *The Paris Review* 56, Spring 1973, 118-163) The ideal beholder is the artist and is as much an antithesis to the common reader as is the individual to the masses.

only insofar as our own capacities for deciphering them permit."[33] Perin's romantic treatment of the challenge of outsider art might be readily applied to the experience of difficulty in modernism, be it the elusive depths of contingent knowledge, the boundaries of modal engagement, the strategies of tactical obstruction, or the sublime and contemplative ends of existence, thought and objecthood itself. Perin argues that this invitation leads to a direct communion between artist and beholder, but in the realm of purposeful difficulty, the artwork itself forms an experience beyond artist or beholder. By taxing the limits of comprehension through purposeful difficulty, the modern artist builds an edifying experience, and by their engagement, the beholder approaches the ideal.

A Poetic Vanguard in Cinema

In the nineteenth-century, photography displaced the realist impulse in painting, challenging the painter's role as witness and the canvas as a descriptive medium. Photography led to the invention of motion pictures, each medium bridging art, commerce and science. But from cinema emerged a separate aesthetic lexicon, primarily one that extended the project of realism, however, at the fringes of that realist project, new and radical possibilities for vision emerged. As in the modern impulses in the visual arts, literature and music, newly machined visions would develop to counter folk cultures, romanticism and classical perspective. In Europe, an artists' cinema emerged out of the early modern movements of Futurism, Dada and Surrealism, as in the work of Anton Giulio Bragaglia, Fernand Léger and Man Ray. The restlessness of these movements, their aesthetic philosophies and the urgency of their politics were reflected in their cinema, be they pushing toward abstraction of the visual plane, or taming film form to the will of more mystic, psychoanalytic, or dreamlike values, which became possible in the associative tensions of editing and through illusory photography. Luis Buñuel and Salvador Dalí took up the movie camera to make a film against reason, and therefore, against the pretenses of Paris's intellectual bourgeoisie, deposing what Dalí would later call the "little maniacal lozenges of Monsieur Mondrian."[34] The resulting film, *Un Chien Andalou* (1929), treated cinema as a psychic analogue, one that could, to paraphrase Buñuel, cast qualities of dreaming without the form of a dream. This idea that cinema could be used to mirror the psychological interior was taken further in America's postwar avant-garde, in the

---

[33] Constance Perin, "The Reception of New, Unusual and Difficult Art," in *The Artist Outsider: Creativity and the Boundaries of Culture* (Washington and London: Smithsonian Institution Press, 1994), 197.

[34] Salvador Dalí, *The Secret Life of Salvador Dalí* (New York City: Dial Press, 1942), 212.

psychodramas of Maya Deren, Gregory Markopoulos, Curtis Harrington, Sidney Peterson and James Broughton.[35]

Stan Brakhage, who would become the key figure of the American avant-garde film, emerged as a son of this movement, making his first films in this psychodrama style before taking the medium in the direction of personal vision.[36] By the time a third wave of avant-garde film had taken hold in America, it had adopted a variety of radical stances. There was the notion of a third-eye cinema, where plastic abstraction became a metaphor for a 'closed eye' vision of the psychic interior, but there was also, in keeping with the political dissidence of early twentieth-century modernism, a regard for cinema as a vehicle for the political and social concerns of its makers. This ranged from the obscure programme of the Beats to the rage of the anti-nuclear, civil rights and youth movements. Many concurrent movements within avant-garde cinema formed, defined by region, aesthetic philosophy, or the work's subversive relation to the dominant conventions of mainstream cinema. Avant-garde cinema had assumed these manifold forms and intentions, but as the 1960s wore on, formalism began to dominate. Like their counterparts in late modern painting, avant-garde filmmakers vanished increasingly into their work.

Jonas Mekas, an artist, poet, musician and journalist who emigrated from Lithuania during the Second World War, would become a leading critic and organizer of this movement, which he called the New American Cinema. Mekas would describe it as something profoundly mystical, for he saw its artists as monastic vessels whose orders were to sing in a new age, "through their intuition that the eternity communicates with us, bringing a new knowledge, new feelings."[37] Mekas's spoke of this cinema as an "art of light," light most mystical and serene, into which the artist might vanish. By the late 1960s, ideological divides would develop between styles that would, through discourse, be termed 'lyric' and 'structural' filmmaking. Even as this revealed a hazardous competition, it affirmed an overarching

---

[35] This concept for the history of avant-garde film–that it has three successive waves that bring it into the 1960s–has its roots in the writings of Sheldon Renan (*An Introduction to the American Underground Film*, 1966), Parker Tyler (*Experimental Film*, 1969) and P. Adams Sitney (*Visionary Film*, 1974). This is a useful typology that, like Steiner's typology of difficulty, should be used only as a loose guide. Terms such as 'generations' and 'waves' falsely imply knowledge of predecessors, a fixed causality, or at least a conscious break, and gloss over the more complex interpenetrations of avant-garde movements.

[36] Some of these early psychodramas include *Unglassed Windows Cast a Terrible Reflection* (1953), *Interim* (1953) and *The Extraordinary Child* (1954). Later, through his lyric works and beyond, Brakhage would conceive of perspective as, among other things, the betrayer of the fatal competition of earthly things.

[37] Jonas Mekas, "Where are We–the Underground?" in *New American Cinema*, ed. Gregory Battcock (New York: Dutton, 1967), 21.

harmony between the constructive systems of cinema and of poetry. This critical discourse was an acknowledgement, however subtle, that the forms that cinema had assumed, outside of the dominant ideologies of fiction and documentary form, evolved toward the similar expressions of modern poetry.

Avant-garde film found correlatives in modern poetry, fraught with difficulties and discontinuities, sudden turns in perception, resisting the boundaries of experience that a classical realism could lend it. Although links between cinema and poetry had been evident in earlier movements and the films and writings of earlier makers, it was in the work of Stan Brakhage that this bridge between literary and visual systems was stated most clearly and passionately, advanced in his first book, *Metaphors on Vision* (1963). Brakhage's films shared in the perceptual character of Charles Olson's projective verse, a text as an assembly of perceptions built in the wake of other perceptions, or other breaths. This perceptual character is also shared in the improvisatory processes of late modern painting and musical free improvisation.[38] Brakhage's films, and the works of many of his peers in the New American Cinema movement, are essentially rhythmic in their transcription of experience, wherein visual experience takes on characteristics we might explain best as language, as speech, but which were intended as innately visual. This was especially true of the films of Jonas Mekas, in which experience is given in episodic sequences, his elliptical photography taking on the lacunae of remembered speech and of fragmented syntax. [39]

Visual syntax–the ordering of visual experience to achieve a particular effect–takes hold in this movement, for instance in the films of Brakhage, such as *Anticipation of the Night* (1958) and *Cat's Cradle* (1959). In addition to this cinema's relation to sound and music, its rhythmic sensibilities could find analogues in poetic meter. Rhythms were built through

---

[38] The relation between Brakhage's films and modern poetry, and in particular his relation to the projectivists, is discussed extensively in R. Bruce Elder, *The Films of Stan Brakhage in the American Tradition of Ezra Pound, Gertrude Stein, and Charles Olson* (Waterloo: Wilfred Laurier Press, 1999).

[39] Although his earliest films reflected narrative ambitions in the underground film movement (*Guns of the Trees*, 1962; *The Brig*, 1964), by the time he made *Award Presentation to Andy Warhol* (1964), Mekas had begun to work more exclusively in a mode of episodic diarism, which he would continue through several long films (*Walden [Diaries, Notes, and Sketches]*, 1969; *Reminiscences of a Journey to Lithuania*, 1971–72; *Lost, Lost, Lost*, 1976). That this form was marked by an overarching theme of loss becomes most apparent in his epic *He Stands in a Desert Counting the Seconds of His Life* (1969–1985), in which the rapid start-stop style of his photography takes the viewer on a trajectory spanning 16 years of parties, births, deaths, vacations, encounters and scenes of ordinary experience magnified to their poetic potential.

cutting and shot juxtapositions. In metric film editing, by contrast, measurement was divorced from the rhythms of visual composition, the film cut into strips of particular lengths and joined metrically, as in the syllabic structures of poetry, as in the regular rhythms of music. The most dramatic examples of metric film editing come in flicker films such as Peter Kubelka's *Arnulf Rainer* (1960) and Tony Conrad's *The Flicker* (1965); but such aspiration toward the even measure had been apparent in avant-garde cinema through the evolution of visual music with its careful rhythmic structures. Likewise, juxtapositions and agreements between images might be taken to mirror the relation created by rhyme and dissonance in poetry, just as those systems in poetry likewise mirror states of perception. Forms of cinema that dealt with a direct engagement with the picture plane, unmediated by the camera, such as the photogram films of Man Ray or the painted films of Stan Brakhage, were largely divorced from the apparatus and grew further from realism, developing a direct relation between the artist and vision itself. However, through rhythmic structures and titular allusions, these works remained a product of poetic thought, should we take 'poetic thought' to be an adequate description of the artist's interface between thought and expression.

P. Adams Sitney's *Visionary Film* (1974) would offer the first considered view of a poetic vanguard in cinema. Sitney's analysis was not so narrow–his primary ambition was to chart the relation of individual works to the overarching careers of their makers, to discuss the works within the discourse of modern aesthetics, and to relate those makers to one another as a means of gathering movements and themes. He gave the field of avant-garde film a comprehensive sense of definition while declaring and championing a body of major works, from the psychodrama collaborations of Maya Deren and Alexander Hammid, and Sidney Peterson and James Broughton, to the book's contemporary avant-garde, of filmmakers such as Michael Snow, Hollis Frampton and Owen Land, whose work emphasized predetermined structures and in doing so achieved a heightened self-consciousness. Sitney argued that the relation of avant-garde film to commercial cinema was like that of poetry to prose; and while his arguments tied film's history to a greater history of aesthetics, it was specifically the relation between cinema and poetry that guided his terminology. The terms used by Sitney—lyrical, structural and mythopoeic—have roots in poetic forms. The most difficult of these is, arguably, the structural film, a style marked by predetermination and an insistence on its shape; and the 'mythic' absolute film, not to be confused with the 'absolute' abstract films of Hans Richter and others that were made in the 1910s and 1920s, rather films that embody a totality of experience to the final enclosure of the object and its field, following in the tradition described by Stephane Mallarmé as the "books to end all books."[40] The structural and the absolute impulses are entangled in a number of films. Sitney offers Ken Jacobs' structuralist epic *Star Spangled to Death* (1959–2004) as an example of the absolute film, but other examples of American avant-garde films that align with this ambition, though not necessarily with one another, include Andy Warhol's *Empire* (1964), Stan Brakhage's *The Art of Vision* (1965), Hollis Frampton's cycles *Hapax Legomena* (1971–72) and *Magellan* (1974–84, unfinished), and Bruce Baillie's *Quick Billy* (1971), each work approaching enclosure, finality and totality in distinct and even oppositional ways and yet unified by their ambition to be the films to end all films. By their levelling reflection on the medium, such works embody ontologically difficult art.

If we accept the premise that avant-garde film shares common ground with poetry, in terms of its construction, the character of its authorship and its perceptual effect, it then becomes possible to explore Steiner's typology in relation to this cinema. The common reader of literature becomes the common beholder of the visual arts, already in decline through the nineteenth century, fully splintered in the twentieth. The common beholder would remain, in cinema, as a patron of the fiction and documentary traditions, but there was no common beholder for avant-garde cinema. Contingent difficulties within the avant-garde film are signalled by image, text, or symbol, suggested elusively through setting or through a mimetic relation to, or an integration of, other films and works from other media. Tactical difficulties have much the same manifestation in the visual aspect of cinema as they do in painting, in a shaping of the material into a particularity of voice, in an act of individuation, and in forming obstructions to vision, in an uneasy confrontation with material form. In cinema this is enhanced further through the techniques of editing, which can allow vision to bear repetition, motifs, or sudden turns; in addition, editing and composition both impact on the communication of space, which can be obstructed, invented through composite photography, or given false dimensions. In film sound, these values are carried over, in effecting auditory fragmentation, feedback and signal distortion, and in the construction of

---

[40] That Sitney repeatedly refers to this as the "myth of the absolute film" (241, 281-2, 338) emphasizes his recognition that such projects seek to perform an impossible task. My use of this particular term from *Visionary Film* is informed in part by Fred Camper's use of the same term in his essay "*The Hart of London*: Jack Chambers' Absolute Film." Despite the confusion that arises from the other historical movement for which this term has been used (the abstract animated films of the 1920s made by Hans Richter, Walter Ruttmann, Oskar Fischinger and Viking Eggeling), I choose to use it here as a statement of totality in intention, the absolute film's simultaneous assumption of and independence from all things that lie beyond its borders, its lack of relation to the other works of its kind, the sui generis quality of the rare absolute films and cycles of the avant-garde cinema.

aural space.

Modal difficulties are perhaps most readily discernible in the American modernist avant-garde film, where work is typically offered up with a knowledge of the surrounding field, of the artist's other work, of the artist's sources and contemporaries. The audience's acclimation to that mode impacts their comprehension. As with poetry, painting and music, many modalities can come to bear on a film, and these can manifest in cinema in confounding ways. For example, in endurance, be that endurance a matter of flicker or the long take, which so readily resist the expectations of a viewer accustomed to the conceits of dominant cinema. Finally, while ontological difficulty exists across many of these films, it is of central importance to the absolute films, in their capacity to challenge the nature of cinema and of art itself. Artists working in avant-garde film face an overarching ontological difficulty inherent in the material itself; in the particular manifestation of their work as a creative act of many meanings; and in the challenge that artists put to the receiver in the predetermined shape of their work. By this last value, the filmmaker subverts the expectations of the frame and composition plane, as well as length, elongating or stunting the dimensions of works out of the bounds of what is common. The presence of the object itself also challenges, in its relation to temporality, its experience as not a representation of time but as time itself. Through this line of inquiry, other aesthetic strategies begin to emerge, in photographic and editorial processes that are the marks of individual artists, and which are then taken up and absorbed into the processes of those that follow. In the American avant-garde film, such processes would become essential to the continuity of the field, and would serve as the primary anchor of this tradition, even as they became a sign of the detritus and derivation that would lead to a call to bury or redeem the avant-garde cinema.

In Canada, underground film culture would not form until the mid–1960s. It arrived first in the form of audiences, not filmmakers, through campus screening societies and later dedicated repertory cinemas. It was a film culture that drew heavily from American resources, for at its start, those were virtually the only resources it had.[41] Its evolution mirrored the dispersed progress toward poetic forms in the American avant-garde. Student screening societies became production co-ops. A wild, joyous narcissism took hold in the works of the new Canadian underground, which with few exceptions was more immersed in the experience of making movies than in aspirations to formal radicalism. The New York Filmmakers

---

[41] This film culture also grew out of campus engagements of arthouse fiction films, documentary films, and animated and experimental subjects issuing from the National Film Board.

Co-operative soon established business relations with Willem Poolman's Film Canada, a Toronto arthouse film distributor, and later, with the new-ly formed Canadian Filmmakers Distribution Centre.[42] Filmmakers Stan Brakhage, Andy Warhol, Ben Van Meter and Shirley Clarke were among those whose work was widely seen by Canadian underground filmmak-ers. However, it was not from this growing underground movement, but from the visual arts, that a Canadian avant-garde film emerged. Those who formed the bulk of the Canadian underground film community were, for the most part, unconcerned with matters of concept, craftsmanship and the history and philosophy of art; but visual artists who had estab-lished themselves in painting and sculpture would take up these tools in the service of a more focused program, deeply individual but informed by their sources and training, and by their work in difficult perceptual modes across media. Jack Chambers, Michael Snow and Joyce Wieland, all paint-ers, came to cinema with a fascination for its potential as an art form. Their work would signal a heightened engagement with the difficulties of modernism, assembling a truly vanguard movement, still informal, distinct from the experimental film communities forming elsewhere in Canada.

In February 1969, Adrienne Mancia and Larry Kardish brought a program of Canadian avant-garde films to the Museum of Modern Art in New York. Films by Jack Chambers and Joyce Wieland were prominent among the works shown, having recently received awards at the Canadian Artists '68 competition at the Art Gallery of Ontario, which featured a film component juried by Jonas Mekas.[43] Mekas told Mancia and Kardish that the work of these Canadian filmmakers represented "a finer vibration, a finer density, and a finer matter."[44] Mekas did not mean fine in a purely qualitative sense; these works embodied the subtle and fragile qualities of an art that has enveloped its maker, and yet it was also indirect, elusive,

[42] This marriage of the American and Canadian 'underground' film circuit would be con-summated by a weekend-long marathon of underground films held at CineCity, a movie theatre co-owned by Willem Poolman at Yonge and Charles Streets in Toronto, Ontario, in May 1967. The event, curated by Rob Fothergill and Lorne Michaels (then Lipowitz), would have no equivalent elsewhere in North America, and was a massive showing of major and minor works, a demonstration of Poolman's dedication to avant-garde cinema for the benefit of New York Filmmakers Co-op founder Jonas Mekas, who was wary of working with a commercial distributor. For a fuller discussion of this event, see Stephen Broomer, *Hamilton Babylon: A History of the McMaster Film Board* (Toronto: University of Toronto Press, 2016), 55-57.

[43] In their programme notes, the curators worked from Jonas Mekas's insights into these films, gleaned in his participation in the Canadian Artists '68 exhibition. In addition to works by Jack Chambers (*R34*) and Joyce Wieland (*1933, Cat Food, Rat Life and Diet in North America*), the program featured films by Gary Lee-Nova, Clarke Mackey, Les Levine, Keewatin Dewdney and John Hofsess.

[44] Jonas Mekas, notes, 1969 MOMA flyer, 4.

refined into an absolute objecthood, testing the boundaries of a still-forming sensibility. In those fine densities lay a commitment to telling analysis, to ecstatic experience, to an impulse to transform vision. The films of these Canadian artists had come to represent, by their refinement of form, Mekas's sense of the cinema as an "art of light." The Canadian avant-garde film was made possible by a heritage of difficulty, with its special compound of insights and methodologies.

PART ONE

HOMECOMINGS

In the 1950s, Canada had developed into disparate communities across varied geographies, some on water, others deeply landlocked, of cities, towns, plains unspoiled by human settlement, and cruel, inhospitable territories. It was a nation of coexisting visions and identities, divided in the public consciousness by language and custom. Like America, it was built through Europe's colonial interest in a new world vaguely realizing westward. It had come to mirror American regionalism inasmuch as its Pacific edge eventually met with Asian cultural influence, to the East, its political centre, a region of big cities and dense forests. In between lay a great plain, more a tundra than the Midwest, stretching north to the Arctic, but that tundra was rich with its own regional cultures, marked by labour politics, agriculture and mining. The Canadian occupied the territory between British and American claims and culture. Canada's moral and political philosophies attempted to explain or reconcile this crisis of community, but its art would remain a product of the distances. Artistic communities formed in provincial towns and in the bohemian neighbourhoods in cities, all in the shadow of a great wilderness.

Canadian art, in its early modern form, took that wilderness as its central subject. Emily Carr and the Group of Seven adopted post-Impressionist strategies in their renderings of the varied landscapes of the Canadian wilderness, their heavy application of oils and acrylics annihilating depth and flattening perspective. The drawings of David Milne suggest a further step away from realism, as the represented subject began to vanish into the flatness of the canvas or paper. The Group of Seven, a collective of landscape painters, was formalized in 1920, and in short time would gain a global acclaim unprecedented in Canadian art. Their work would come to define Canadian art by its relation to the wilderness, as witness to harsh and marvellous topographies, and the critical and public regard for their work would emphasize their choice of subject. They succeeded in gaining public favour in spite of a conservative culture, one that met public gallery patronage of modernism with disgust and outrage.[1] With

---

[1] In early-to-mid-twentieth-century Canada, the art establishment was deeply conservative, and modernist activity was met with public scorn. A.Y. Jackson once commented, on the heavy investment of Montreal art collectors in the landscapes of the Hague School, that their homes "bulged with pictures of cows and sheep, windmills and old women peeling potatoes…At a quarter of the price they could have purchased the works of Monet,

the Group of Seven's disbandment in 1932, the living members would be absorbed into a greater body known as the Canadian Group of Painters, formed with members of the Beaver Hall Group, a collective of women painters in Montreal. By the 1950s, the Group of Seven, the Beaver Hall Group, and unaffiliated artists such as Carr and Milne, had begun to fade, not from the public awareness, in which they would maintain their status as the paragon of Canadian art, but from the position of cultural relevance necessary to inspire and extend their movement. Their aesthetics, generally in the service of representation, had become antiquated by late modern aspirations against representation, toward abstract expressionism, the pure forms of post-painterly abstraction and the confrontation and wildness of Neo-Dada.

The more radical stance of Les Automatistes, the Quebecois abstractionists, had ushered the strategies of late modern art into Canada. Post-Impressionist aesthetics had determined the dominant English-Canadian painting of the 1920s and 30s, but Quebecois painters had turned to Surrealism and automatism. In their manifesto, *Le Refus global*, the Automatistes called for "an untamed need for liberation," a liberation of consciousness and the senses that could be achieved through abstraction.[2] This ambition manifested in the spare forms and layered oils of Paul-Émile Borduas and the palette-knife strokes of Jean-Paul Riopelle. Geometric abstraction followed, first with the Plasticien movement which then resonated in the work of Claude Tousignant, Guido Molinari and Yves Gaucher. By the mid-1950s, with the founding of the Painters Eleven, largely under

Cézanne, Van Gogh, Renoir, and many other artists of genius." In the 1910s, Canada's art critics regularly denounced Post-Impressionism as degenerate. Newspaper coverage of the 1913 Spring Exhibition of the Art Association of Montreal shows considerable hostility toward Post-Impressionism, for instance, in the remarks by Samuel Morgan-Powell of the *Montreal Daily Star*, who called it "a fad, an inartistic fetish for the amusement of bad draughtmanship, incompetent colourists, and others, who find themselves unqualified to paint pictures." In 1916, *Saturday Night* art critic Hector Charlesworth led an especially vicious campaign against J.E.H. MacDonald and others for the experimental techniques of Post-Impressionism. The painter Carl Ahrens, a friend of Charlesworth, wrote this statement in the Toronto Star, defending the rejection of modernist aesthetic strategy as a matter of good versus evil: "There are some samples of that rough, splashy, meaningless, blatant, plastering and massing of unpleasant colours which seem to be a necessary evil in all Canadian art exhibitions now-a-days." For a full account of these critical barbs, see Paul Duval, *The Tangled Garden: The Art of J.E.H. MacDonald* (Scarborough, Ont.: Cerebrus, 1978). Such attitudes against modernism would reach even uglier, more destructive and hateful heights in their resonances in the 1960s, when police morality squads began to target late modern art, leading to the criminal prosecution of Dorothy Cameron of the Cameron Gallery in Toronto for her exhibit of erotic art, notably Robert Markle's nudes, as part of the group show *Eros '65*.

[2] *Total Refusal (Refus Global): the manifesto of the Montreal Automatists*, translated by Ray Ellenwood (Holstein, Ont: Exile Editions, 2009).

the aegis of Jack Bush and with inspiration from the German-American abstract expressionist Hans Hofmann, abstraction would be taken up in central Canada, particularly in Southern Ontario and in Toronto specifically. Soon after, in Western Canada, painters experienced a similar shift, away from the lyrical abstraction that had taken root there in the 1950s. In 1959, arising in part from an unfocused national desire for external cultural influence, the Emma Lake Artists' Workshop (Saskatchewan) set to the task of indoctrinating Western Canadian artists, primarily painters, in the contemporaneous late modern styles of New York's schools of art. In the course of a decade, invited workshop leaders would include Barnett Newman, Clement Greenberg, Kenneth Noland, John Cage, Frank Stella and Donald Judd, guiding workshop members in the styles of abstract expressionism, post-painterly abstraction, minimalism, serialism and conceptual art.[3]

Ontario artists were caught between the culturally rich centers of Montreal to the east and New York City to the south. In 1954, when the Painters Eleven formed, an external cultural influence would begin to impose upon the paintings, and later the films and music, of artists in Toronto and London, Ontario. By the early 1960s, artists in these cities were aspiring to the same ends as their counterparts at Emma Lake and in Montreal, forging ahead with vanguard, difficult forms, but with particular emphasis on the resonances of Dada and the formation of an active Neo-Dada movement. In Toronto, much of this activity was concentrated around the Isaacs Gallery and the Cameron Gallery, and was supported by the critical authority of Dada scholar Michel Sanouillet, then a professor at University of Toronto. As these artists began to form their individuated sensibilities, 8mm and 16mm film cameras became newly accessible, and were widely recognized as the tools of a burgeoning independent film movement. Artists would begin to use these cameras, and in doing so would extend a legacy of artists' cinema that had its own roots in early modern movements. The New American Cinema, as promoted by Jonas Mekas, Stan Brakhage and others, was an intimate cinema of diverse aesthetic and political motives, descendent of the 'film poems' made by earlier generations of artists in America and Europe.[4] In this same era, the New American

---

[3] Roald Nasgaard has written extensively on the art that arose from the Emma Lake Artists' Workshops in his comprehensive *Abstract Painting in Canada* (Toronto: Douglas & McIntyre, 2008); but by Nasgaard's own admission, the most comprehensive account of the Emma Lake Artists' Workshops is John O'Brian's exhibition catalogue, *The Flat Side of the Landscape: The Emma Lake Artists' Workshops* (Saskatoon: Mendel Art Gallery, 1989).

[4] P. Adams Sitney's discussion of terminology in his preface to *Visionary Film* (1974) gives an account of the historical usage of the term 'film poem' and its strength as a descriptor of the relation between cinema and poetry. The term was widely used by Jonas Mekas early

Cinema would find an international audience, attracting non-American participants who would take up and expand the language of avant-garde cinema through their individual sensibilities, from the vantage point of their separate cultures. Three Canadian artists—Jack Chambers, Michael Snow and Joyce Wieland—laid the foundation for a Canadian avant-garde film.[5] They were unified in their experience of external cultural influence, and also, in their channeling of the resonances of Dada. Each would depart from Canada to follow individual aspirations. Upon returning, they would come to see Canada with a profound clarity.[6]

Through the 1950s and 60s, the arts were struggling to escape the regressive grip of Canadian culture, but Canadian cinema would largely remain a tool of business, as it had been since the early twentieth century, and of government, as it had become through the formation of the National Film Board (NFB). Within the NFB, an animation division led by Norman McLaren specialized in light, entertaining fare, a kind of visual music, and gained wide acclaim for its enchanting qualities. Later, the collage filmmaker Arthur Lipsett received passing international attention for his innovations in found footage collage filmmaking and for the power of his themes.[7] Such filmmaking would be marginalized in the greater context of Canadian cinema and even within the institutions that made it. When independent filmmaking arrived in Canada in the 1960s, a separate, poetic cinema, rooted in the difficult strategies of late modernism, would begin to emerge.

---

in his career, and the term's significance is discussed in David E. James, *Allegories of Cinema: American Film in the Sixties* (Princeton: Princeton University Press, 1989).

[5] The foundation offered by these three artists is not a conscious, uniform edict, but rather was formed by individual ambitions. But it must be indicated that there were crossings in their experience: all three were represented in Toronto by the art dealer Av Isaacs; all three were roughly the same age, and they shared some common aspects of their political and aesthetic coming of age in Canada in the 1940s and 50s; Snow and Wieland were married, and there is a pronounced interplay of ideas between their work.

[6] By virtue of this argument, one might also consider that the experiences beyond Canada had deeply influenced earlier generations of Canadian artists, for instance, the trench experience of members of the Group of Seven.

[7] For more a fuller discussion of Lipsett's work and his relationship with the National Film Board, see Stephen Broomer, "The Success and Failure of Arthur Lipsett," *Found Footage Magazine* 3 (March 2017): 58-69.

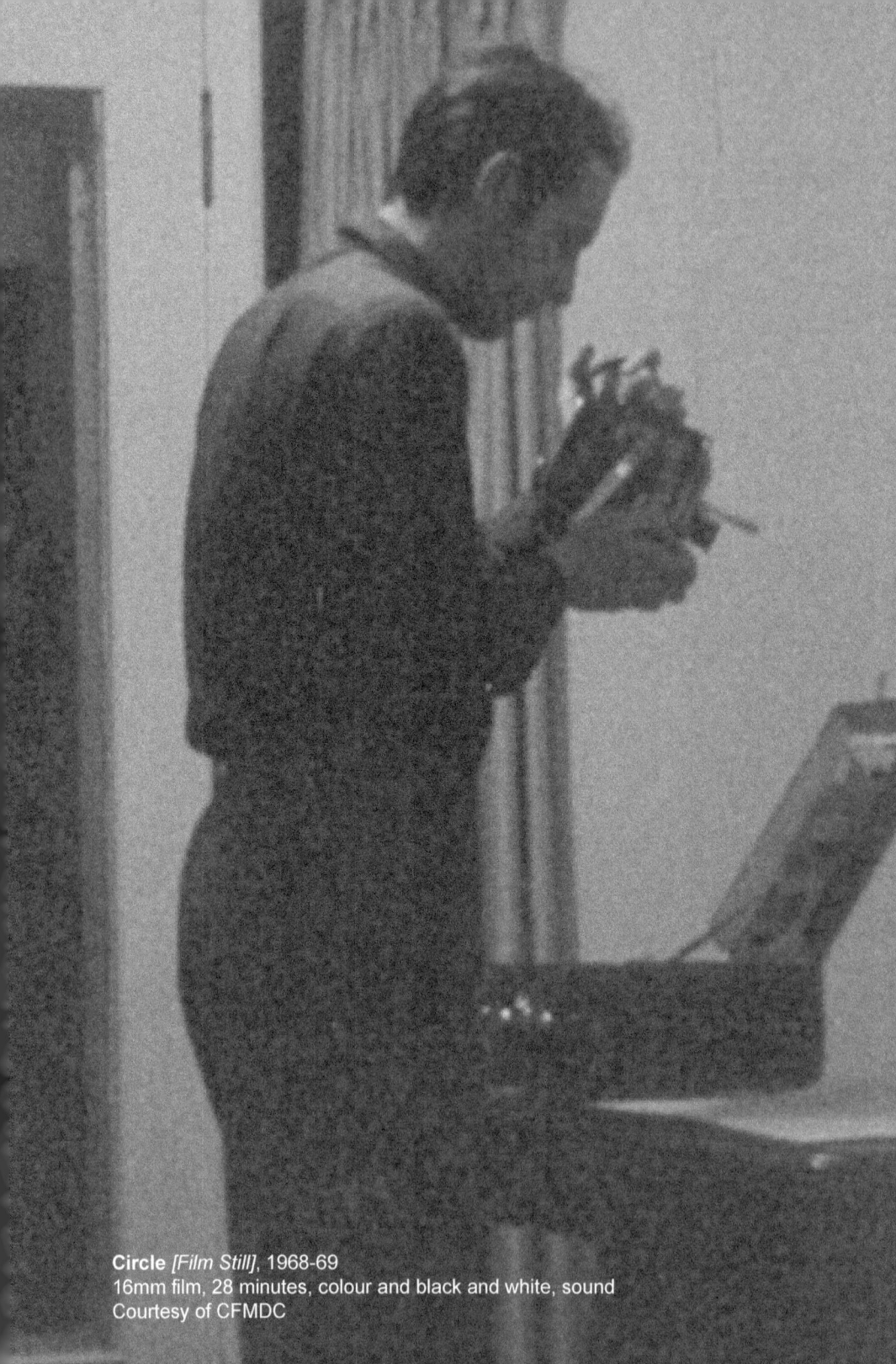

Circle *[Film Still]*, 1968-69
16mm film, 28 minutes, colour and black and white, sound
Courtesy of CFMDC

CHAPTER ONE

Jack Chambers: Gesturing in the invisible

When Upper Canada's first Lieutenant Governor, John Graves Simcoe, was tasked with establishing a capital city in 1793, he chose a site that had long been occupied by Aboriginal villages, flanked by dense hardwood forests. For this geographical feature, his proposal was rejected, but the land would be settled slowly over the subsequent three decades. The settlement would come to be known as London. Although it aped the name of the English capital, London, Ontario had fallen from the nobility envisioned for it by Simcoe, serving instead as the political centre of Ontario's southwest. Thirty years after the village was named, it would be incorporated as a city, and for the remainder of the nineteenth century, London would serve a number of functions, as a spa retreat for the wealthy, a city of industry and then a military centre through the wars. Its economy gradually became dominated by an embarrassment of insurance companies. The city struggled to carve out its own identity in spite of its transient functions, but its Old World namesake overshadowed its daily life: London, Ontario had its own Thames River, its own Covent Garden Market, and street names with British debts, such as Cheapside, Oxford and Piccadilly.

Jack Chambers was born in London's Victoria Hospital in the winter of 1931. His mother came from a family of local farmers and his father was a welder. His art education began in high school under the artist and illustrator Selwyn Dewdney and continued at H.B. Beal Technical School, where he studied with the sculptor and painter Herb Ariss. Selwyn Dewdney, with whom Chambers would develop a close friendship, took his own inspiration from the styles of the Group of Seven, and his interest in art was informed by a lifelong fascination with rock art and other forms of ancient indigenous illustration; one imagines the latter interest might have impressed upon young Chambers the social and historical dimensions of art. Ariss's teachings, on the other hand, belaboured craft and the importance of figurative art. The recent art of the period was increasingly dominated by painterly abstraction, but Chambers was becoming fascinated by the convictions of craft and indoctrinated in a traditional notion of art as a means of representation. London had its own realist art movement, deeply rooted in Romantic tradition, observable in the works of the late nineteenth century painter Paul Peel, whose paintings of cherubic children served as precursors to the domestic subjects that Chambers would himself eventually take up. Even as Chambers encountered these possibilities, he was stifled in his environment, soon seeking a more deeply felt life than he believed possible in London. In 1950, he spent time in Mexico City, returning to London with a lingering restlessness that would soon draw him even further away. Chambers would later come to believe that artists must undertake spiritual preparation for their work. By whatever terms he called it at the time, it was perhaps this need for spiritual preparation that he could not imagine fulfilled in London.[1] Although Chambers recognized a senior art community in London, he had few contemporaries, and against the exotic cultures of elsewhere, his city represented a fate of dispersed creativity, of sign painting and graphic design, for artists of no higher calling than drafting advertisements for insurance companies.[2]

After a year at the University of Western Ontario, Chambers left Canada for Europe, travelling to Italy, Austria and the south of France. His departure was a matter of survival, and began from a "determination not to have forced on [him] what [he] didn't want."[3] He left London in October 1953, in resistance of the "utilitarian, puritanical, indifferent" Canada in which he had grown up, finally settling in Spain in February 1954. He was drawn to Madrid after seeing a Royal Academy of Fine Arts brochure and becoming taken with the paintings of the students.[4] Beginning that October, Chambers undertook studies at the Escuela Central de Bellas Artes de San Fernando, where pedagogical method emphasized a traditional approach to drawing. For the first two years, he drew

---

[1] This notion was fully articulated by the term 'spiritual preparedness', in excerpts borrowed from Jacques Maritain's *Primauté du spirituel* (Paris: Plon, 1927), in Chambers' discontinuous manuscript *Red and Green*, which is in many ways a collage of the ideas of others (artists, mystics and philosophers of perception), printed as Tom Smart, *Jack Chambers' Red and Green: an artist's inquiry into the nature of meaning* (Erin, Ont.: Porcupine's Quill, 2013).

[2] This is an embellishment, but it is how London might have appeared to Chambers in his youth. There was a small realist tradition in London, supported not only by Chambers' mentors Dewdney and Ariss, but rooted in the Romantic realism practiced by Peel, that suggested possibilities far removed from a fate of industrial labour. Chambers' generation would improve the conditions and community of art in London, but from the vantage point of 1953, Chambers had reached the full possibilities for his growth within his hometown.

[3] Ross Woodman, *Chambers: Jack Chambers interview by Ross G. Woodman* (Toronto: Coach House Books, 1967), 3.

[4] On arriving in Spain, Chambers reportedly asked Pablo Picasso's advice on where to gain a formal education in painting. Chambers did not ultimately take Picasso's advice, which was to study in Barcelona.

from statues, and for the next three from life models.[5] Chambers' studies in the figure helped him gain a "sensory education, to develop a sense of proportion and approach."[6] For Chambers, the figure became "an object into which you unload experience," extending his initial training in figuration, under Ariss, from objective realism into an act of greater subjective resonance.[7] Over time, Chambers would take up these matters of objective and subjective representation, tied so closely to the conflicts of naturalism and perception, or of realism and reality. Such ideas would inform the central themes and strategies of his mature work. In Spain, Chambers had sought out a pedagogy uncorrupted by egotism, seeking from his studies a "visible standard that was not made distinctive by personal vision and accomplishment," a standard of craft that would be distinguished by an objective measure.[8] As this measure was met, other aspects of his experience in Spain, beyond the craft of painting, would likewise influence his maturation as an artist.

Chambers underwent, in his words, "a series of births."[9] While he developed his technique and discipline, his style remained inherited due to his emphasis on craft. This is evident in his paintings of this period which, despite the school's entrenchment in pre-modern tradition, bear the influence of twentieth century movements in Spanish painting, the primitive figuration of Joan Miró and Pablo Picasso, the perspectival distortions of Salvador Dalí.[10] As his approach and craft were maturing, other changes in Chambers' life would influence the course of his work. In 1957, inspired in part by the writings of the sixteenth-century Spanish mystic St. Teresa of

---

[5] This description is paraphrased from R. Bruce Elder, "Jack Chambers' Surrealism," in *The Films of Jack Chambers*, ed. Kathryn Elder (Toronto: Cinematheque Ontario, 2002). Elder notes that this approach was vanishing elsewhere in Europe, and as such, represented a form of training with an emphasis on craft that was becoming antique and rare.

[6] Ross Woodman, *Chambers: Jack Chambers interview by Ross G. Woodman* (Toronto: Coach House Books, 1967), 5.

[7] Ibid.

[8] Jack Chambers, *Jack Chambers* (London: Nancy Poole, 1978), 44.

[9] Ross Woodman, *Chambers: Jack Chambers interview by Ross G. Woodman* (Toronto: Coach House Books, 1967), 5.

[10] This influence can be seen in early work such as *Man and Dog* (1959), *Flying Saint* (1960), and *Chinchón Portrait* (1960), all of which have unambiguous debts to Pablo Picasso. The figures in *Man and Dog* and *Flying Saint* are distorted and bent, with exaggerated, stylized, bulbous hands and feet, reminding of Picasso's neoclassical period, for example, the figuration in works such as his *Seated Nude Drying Her Feet* (1921) and *Two Women Running on the Beach (The race)* (1922). In *Chinchón Portrait*, light falls across the face of a labourer to emphasize his sunken eyes, pronounced brow and the pout of his lips, a less macabre and less editorial variation on Salvador Dalí's *La Cara de la Guerra* (1940), with other debts, in its stylization, to the neoclassical and surreal work of Pablo Picasso.

Ávila, Chambers, raised as a Baptist, converted to Roman Catholicism.[11] In 1959, he met Olga Sanchez Bustos, an Argentine woman whom he would later marry, and in 1960, he purchased a flat in Chinchón with the intention of staying. His first solo exhibition occurred at the Lorca Gallery in Madrid in 1961. The work that he had developed in his seven years in Spain was unified by a technical mastery that would become common-place in his subsequent work, but it also uniformly reflected upon the grief and poverty of Francoist Spain, and carried aesthetic debts to Surrealism, debts that would rest beneath the surface of his later work. By the begin-ning of the 1960s, Chambers' development as an artist could no longer be charted in a causal history; the aesthetic that he had developed during his time in Spain would change, but his aggressive mastery of craft had granted him a freedom to explore the perceptual limits of painting. His vast knowledge of Spanish painting styles, and his induction into a Spanish life, served as the initial spiritual preparation for him to undertake his own work, and yet that influence had cast a pall over his work. The changes in his life and the regional aesthetic sensibilities evident in his work signalled his assimilation into Spanish culture, but Chambers still felt an alienation from the land. He had a great desire to belong among the Spanish and in the Spanish landscape. He described that landscape in terms that evoke this desire: "always a beautiful mystery; human odour seemed to reside in it so that a vista of several miles in that clear and machineless light seemed a particle of torso under a microscope. The hills were rubbed bare by wool and hands had touched every inch of them. There was an organism within an organism that appeared as landscape. But I knew I was not inside."[12]

   Chambers returned to London in 1961 to care for his terminally ill mother. What was planned as a short visit would become a permanent return. He reconnected with Selwyn Dewdney and discovered that a re-gional art scene had sprung up in his absence. A Neo-Dada movement was beginning to emerge, led by painter and collagist Greg Curnoe, and though this movement had largely opposite values to Chambers' own—in its crude handling of craft, against formal mastery—it was a movement in which Chambers would find fellowship. Other Londoners with whom he connected included painters Kim Ondaatje and Tony Urquhart, the poet

---

[11] St. Teresa of Ávila authored two seminal texts on prayer, *El Castillo Interior*, or *Las Moradas* (1577), and *Camino de Perfección* (c. 1567). *El Castillo Interior* describes seven mansions, or states, of interior prayer, while *Camino de Perfección* is a method for developing a contempla-tive life (written at the direction of her confessor). Both texts are founded on metaphors of paths, ways and dwellings. The texts present life as a mystical quest, a sensibility that would dominate Chambers' later paintings and films.

[12] Ross Woodman, *Chambers: Jack Chambers interview by Ross G. Woodman* (Toronto: Coach House Books, 1967), 7.

James Reaney and Chambers' former University of Western Ontario professor Ross Woodman.[13] Soon, Chambers' readings in theosophy and late
nineteenth century mysticism would give him the vocabulary to speak of
the resonance of memories that he found in the landscape of Southwestern
Ontario. London provided him with a sense of fate that would reign over
his mature work. He was able to recover a sense of home, observing,
"the seasons uncovered images of myself still gesturing in the invisible."[14]
Incidents recalled from his childhood took on profound dimensions, toward what he termed "the centre of the essential gesture." That latent
content, enclosing past and present, had unfolded in Chambers, and he
would later come to see it, in the writings that consumed his final decade,
as the core of 'Being'. This was "an experience of reality, a revelation, an
experience of an organism within an organism that had accepted me as
its centre."[15] In the brief time back from Spain, Chambers had discovered
that the life he had abandoned in London was more fulfilling for him than
the life he might find elsewhere. He discovered that London, even in its
unapologetic inauthenticity, with its geography of borrowed names and its
stifling, provincial attitudes, was as authentic, as real, as anywhere else, and
that his past there held for him a sense of belonging that he would not find
in Spain. By the time of his mother's death in August 1962, Chambers had
made the decision to remain in London. He returned to Chinchón to sell
his flat and to bring Olga Sanchez Bustos back with him to London, where
they married in August 1963. In short order, they had two children, John
(1964) and Diego (1965).

Chambers' Spanish paintings bear a definite influence from the
Spanish Surrealists, for instance, *Castille Landscape* (1960), in which varied landscapes have colliding, enigmatic perspectives and a mix of rich
and pale colours.[16] By 1961, with *Slaughter of the Lamb*, Chambers' landscapes had become increasingly unreal, in which text, pliant forms recalling marine life and small perfect stones were laid under the horizon of a

---

[13] Slightly younger members of the London Neo-Dada community included the sculptor
Murray Favro (b. 1940), who, along with Greg Curnoe and others, would found the Nihilist
Spasm Band, and Ron Martin (b. 1943), who matured into a minimalist abstract painter
but who, in the mid-1960s, practiced assemblage and painting that had some consonance
with Curnoe, for example, *Regular Price* (1964), which bears a circular form akin to many of
Curnoe's assemblages.

[14] Jack Chambers, *Jack Chambers* (London: Nancy Poole, 1978), 33.

[15] Ross Woodman, *Chambers: Jack Chambers interview by Ross G. Woodman* (Toronto: Coach
House Books, 1967), 7.

[16] Elder specifically situates Chambers' art in the tradition of Veristic Surrealism, a tradition
largely unique to Spanish Surrealism and concerned with the deliberate compromise of an
exacting realism, or in other words, the realist illustration of a dream world. This connects
Chambers' later photorealist paintings to his earlier, more explicit debts to Surrealism.

stylized cosmos.[17] After his return to London, Chambers began to paint from photographs of his subjects, the first steps in developing what would become an overarching memorial theme that would dominate his subsequent work. With *Messengers Juggling Seeds* (1962), Chambers reproduced photographs of his mother and father, in circles inside of circles, as if held in cameos, against an unreal landscape like that of *Slaughter of the Lamb*; the painting extends the colours and textures of his earlier Spanish work, but the figuration is drawn from family photographs, with a heightened realism in contrast to the stylization of his earlier figures. Chambers had found increasingly that photographs became legitimate substitutes for the traditional sitting. By 1962, he had stopped using live models. All that he wanted from the figure, he could get from photographs. Working with photographs allowed him the time to consider the subject, be it a figure or a landscape, held in a fixed instant.[18] Even as these approaches developed in his paintings, he would move in other directions, toward a refined understanding of the interplay between the painting and the photograph. For instance, Chambers had used divisionist strategies in his brushwork, and he would increasingly work in ink on paper with spare pointillist strategies, for instance, in *The Bride* (1963), *Sunday Morning No. 1* (1963), and in the illustrations that accompany James Reaney's *The Dance of Death at London, Ontario* (London: Alphabet Books, 1963). Such strategy would continue in his paintings and preparatory drawings through the following decade. These works show Chambers' fragmentary use of space—the pointillist figures and scenery emerge out of the blankness of the otherwise unmarked paper—and his fascination with the granular makeup of the photograph, a reflection on its base materiality.

In the years following his return to London, Chambers' painting style, now dominated by figures, would become strongly associated with photorealism. He used photography extensively in lieu of life models. The

[17] Other aspects of *Slaughter of the Lamb* might be further developed to implicate Chambers more closely in the styles of radical late modernism that he had, by his admission, neglected in his time in Spain: for instance, his use of direct ('from-the-tube') paints, a technique of Abstract Expressionism, in the form of titanium white and cobalt blue, which depart from the pretense of craft mastery that other strategies in the work suggest, for instance, the mix of realism and stylization in the horizon and the dominant use of contrasting red and green that suggest rigorous attention to colour theory.

[18] For Chambers, the photograph became a correlative of the statue, and though he would explain his use of the photograph to Ross Woodman as a matter of convenience, his subsequent work—which included 'film strip' sequencing in the mixed-media *Regatta* series (1968), a consistent concern with the granularity of photography through the divisionist aspects of his drawings and paintings, the harsh geometric demarcation of frames-encroaching-on-frames, the use of aluminum pigments in his silver paintings—would imply a deeper investigation of the perceptual tensions between painted representation, photographic representation and the sensory experience of the moment.

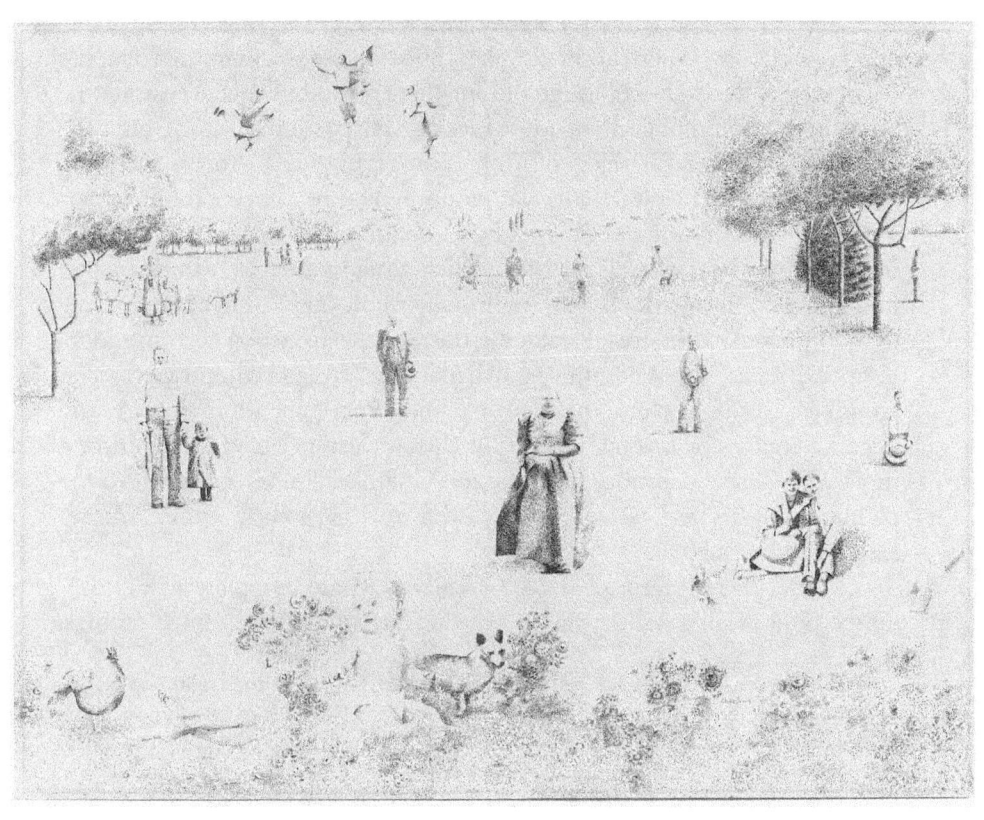

Sunday Morning No. 1, 1963
ink on paper, 56.0 x 71.2 cm, 22 1/16 x 28 1/16 inches
Art Gallery of Ontario, gift of Virginia Hung in memory of Geoffrey Rans, 2006
(2007/34)
Reproduced by permission of the estate of Jack Chambers

photograph served as an "accurate memory object," an ideal description of what he would later refer to as consensus reality, the realm of common perceptions.[19] Chambers would draw from existing photographs, or would take photographs himself.[20] He would never exhibit his photography; what the photograph gave him was a reference image, a description of light, which he could then translate to his paintings. By the late 1960s, he would begin to use mass media images extensively in his silver paintings made with aluminum pigments, for instance, *Three Pages in Time* (1966), *Tulips with Colour Options* (1966) and *Plus Nine* (1968). These works might suggest a resonance of Neo-Dada collage but for their insistent concept, traditional craftsmanship and Chambers' own inextricable presence in the work.

In spite of his relegation of photography to a process medium, Chambers would begin to work with motion picture cameras to make personal films. With cinema, he could pursue an art based in time, without the pressure of generating sales or participating in a market. In this sense, underground films, which were essentially unprofitable, gave him a newfound freedom. As he was developing this work, he pursued corresponding temporal ideas in his painting, particularly in the aforementioned silver paintings, through which the viewer could experience both positive and negative images by passing in front of the canvas; he called them "instant movies."[21] These paintings also marked Chambers' new approach to the picture plane, as vertical and horizontal frame divisions fractured and re-assembled the subject.[22]

Between 1964 and 1970, Chambers would complete five films.[23] These films would resonate with the difficult strategies of his paintings,

---

[19] These ideas are addressed at length in Chambers' three major written works on his art: "Perceptual Realism," *Artscanada* 136-137 (October 1969), 7-13; "Perceptualism, painting and cinema," *Art and Artists* 7:9 (September 1972), 28-33; and his unpublished manuscript *Red and Green*, partially published with commentary as Tom Smart, *Jack Chambers' Red and Green: an artist's inquiry into the nature of meaning* (Erin, Ont.: Porcupine's Quill, 2013).

[20] For example, existing photographs were used in the preparation of *McGilvary County* (1962), *Antonio and Miguel in the U.S.A.* (1964-1965) and the *Regatta* series (1968), as well as a number of commissions. Chambers' own photography is present in all portraits of Olga and their children.

[21] Ross Woodman, *Chambers: Jack Chambers interview by Ross G. Woodman* (Toronto: Coach House Books, 1967), 15.

[22] This effect was most clear in works like *Antonio and Miguel in the U.S.A.* (1964-65), but one sees a similar, yet different, treatment of picture plane in *Three Pages in Time*, in which the subject is not dispersed by fragmentation, but the rhythm of the canvas is offset by banded concentrations of colour that recall the multiforms of Mark Rothko. In that work, elements are not recombined out of a fracture, but assembled out of separate parts, not in a disfigurative collage, but as in the melding of sources in the Neo-Dada assemblage.

[23] In addition to these five films, Chambers also collaborated with artist Greg Curnoe and poet James Reaney on a filmed puppet show, *Little Red Riding Hood* (1967).

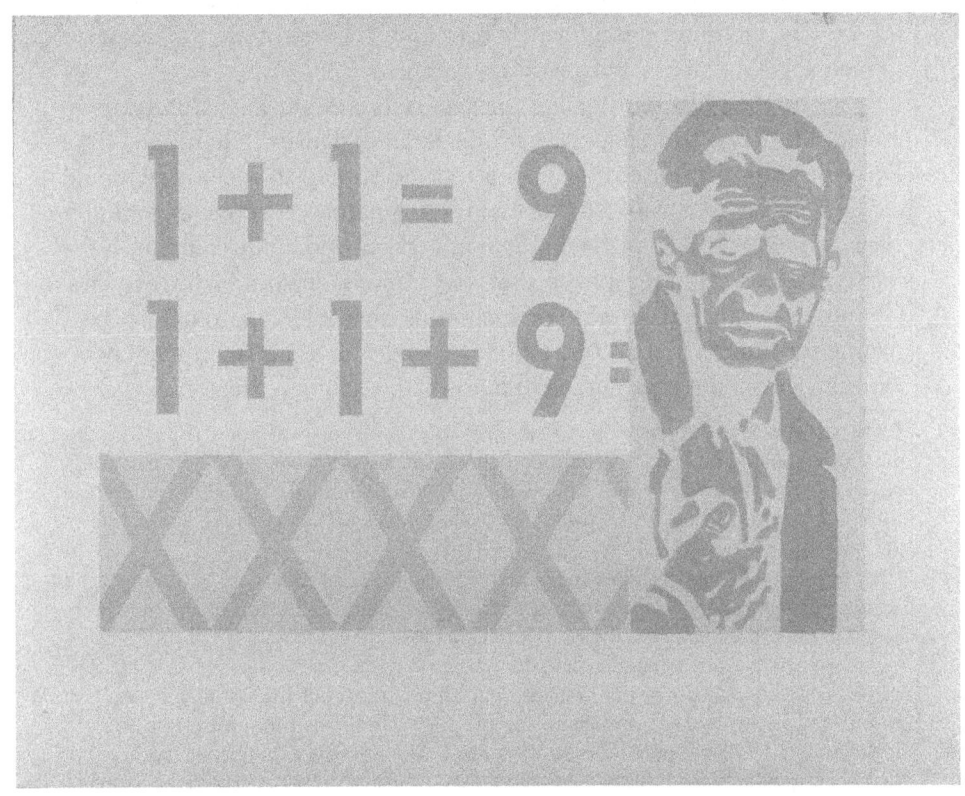

Plus Nine, 1967-68
silkscreen with hand painting mounted on illustration board
25.1 x 37.8 cm, 9 7/8 x 14 7/8 inches
Art Gallery of Ontario, purchase, 1968
(67/25)
Reproduced by permission of the estate of Jack Chambers

particularly his use of fragmentation and collage, his treatment of a subject as an assemblage of particularities, his adoption of found materials and his greater pursuit of a memorial, pan-sensory aesthetic. Like Chambers' paintings, his films dealt with the life cycle, mortality, properties of light and the crisis of photographic representation. In both his paintings and his films, London was cast as a simultaneously paradisiacal and infernal garden. And in this time, the treacherous qualities of nature assumed a particularly fatalistic connotation in Chambers' life and work, when spectres of war and illness hung heavily over him.[24] These broad themes serve to reconcile Chambers' films with his paintings.[25]

In 1964, Toronto gallery owner Av Isaacs put Jack Chambers in touch with the film and television producer Daryl Duke.[26] Chambers wrote Duke seeking distribution for a film that he wished to make that would explore "some aspects of life, death and pregnancy (…) the conception is cyclical: life begins, ends, begins again."[27] He included a treatment in the form of a block paragraph of shot descriptions, separated with dashes. Chambers' treatment shows two aspects that he would discard before completing the film: first, a greater emphasis on death, as his treatment begins with the shrouding of a corpse in a hospital; second, a greater casting of

[24] Much of my analysis begins from Chambers' philosophy of perception, using the mystical terminology of his own unfinished manuscript *Red and Green*. Although Chambers began to write *Red and Green* only after withdrawing from filmmaking, the ideas presented within that manuscript are indicative of ideas Chambers had been pursuing in his art from the early 1960s onward.

[25] My belief that Chambers' films and paintings are unified is in contrast to Stan Brakhage's pronouncement, upon his introduction to Chambers' films in 1977, that the films were acting in opposition to his paintings. His statement was posed to establish the breadth of Chambers' genius, that Chambers had done as much in one medium as he did in another, and was offered in response to a request from Edith Kramer, of the Pacific Film Archive at Berkeley, for his remarks on Chambers. Brakhage's belief that the work is oppositional is certainly a defensible conclusion. One might point to the extremity of accuracy in Chambers' paintings against the cruder constructs of vision in his films, crude in the sense that it was often (though not always) a lyrical and subjective vision, ostensibly in resistance to the objective image. One might also point to the palpable distress of Chambers' films as oppositional to the rapture of the Perceptual Realist paintings that Chambers would begin in 1968. It is possible that Brakhage was referring only to the ecstatic examples of Perceptual Realism, the most iconic of which is *401 Towards London No. 1* (1968-1969), and which, though in continuity with Chambers' earlier works, differ strikingly in tone from the first ventures in photorealism, his drawings, and his silver paintings that largely define his output in the 1960s. Perceptual Realism was a final birth that refined and concealed its difficulty.

[26] Av Isaacs, who at the time represented Chambers through his Toronto gallery, had put together screenings of artists' films that may have served as inspiration to Chambers to take up filmmaking.

[27] Jack Chambers, "Letter to Daryl Duke, January 29, 1964," reprinted in *The Capilano Review* 33 (1984), 20-21.

civic geography, as his treatment frequently discusses the qualities of electric light in the evening, in the suburbs and in the city, and descriptions of buildings and civic landscapes (ex. "street lights shot from rear of car, converging in streaming lines towards centre of frame"). Chambers had anticipated a thirty-minute length for the film, with a recurring subliminal image: a "female figure in low distance running over (a) landscape." Duke would not pursue the film with Chambers. As Chambers undertook developing it on his own, he would scale it down to more modest dimensions. The film, *Mosaic*, would be assembled from fragments that bear a thematic relation. In the park, a woman (Olga) plays with and bounces an infant (John Jr.); an elderly man walks with a cane; a male runner traverses the park's trails. The runner is first seen in close-up shots on his legs, then in repeating medium and wide shots. Olga picks and discards daisy petals which fall onto the corpse of a raccoon. A woman sits in a doctor's waiting room reading a *LIFE* magazine, then a nurse leads her into an examination room where she again waits. A woman travels by bus and sees, from the perspective of the window, a suburban neighbourhood. Women assemble for a baby shower and unwrap gifts. A couple travels by car, the woman in labour, semi-conscious and in pain. Olga kneels with her infant in front of a group of children, breastfeeding as they look on. Initially the scenes abut one another; toward the film's conclusion, long intervals of black isolate the images, seemingly signalling the intrusion of eternity.

The theme of the life cycle runs through *Mosaic*, evident in contrasting scenes of pregnancy and its rituals and of the mundane rites of middle age. Chambers developed the film from 1964 to 1966, and in that time, he painted a series of domestic scenes that involved photorealistic renderings of figures interacting, but which also involved considerable horizontal and vertical fragmentation of the figure, recombined over the picture plane. This reassembly could take the form of the dispersal of a figure in fragments across a canvas (as in *Antonio and Miguel in the U.S.A.*, 1965, or *Stuart Shaw Mixing Red and Green*, 1965), or it could take the form of merging separate compositions (as in *Three Pages in Time*, 1966, *Tulips with Colour Options*, 1966, and in the sequential strip of portraits that run at the periphery of his *Regatta* series, 1968). *Mosaic* is inherently concerned with fragmentation and recombination, a mosaic being a whole composed of bits that combine to create something greater; this in itself parallels Chambers' interest in the recombination of a subject from fragments. That fragmentation appears with the title: as the film begins, the letters are revealed individually: M / OS / A / I, and finally, in full, MOSAIC. As the film continues, fragmentation and recombination soon become the dominant aesthetic gestures, in an intercutting of roughly eight sequences,

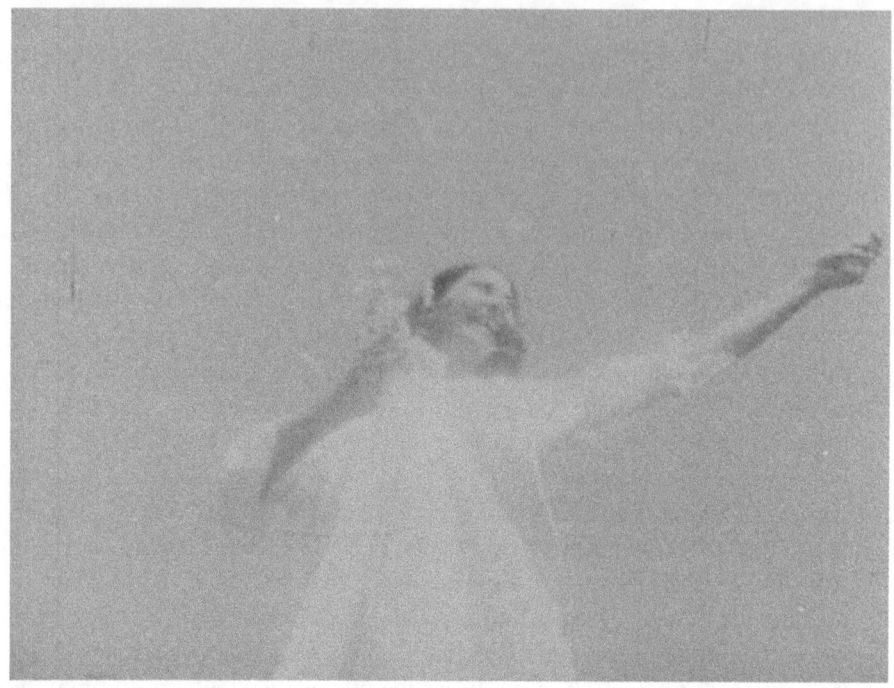

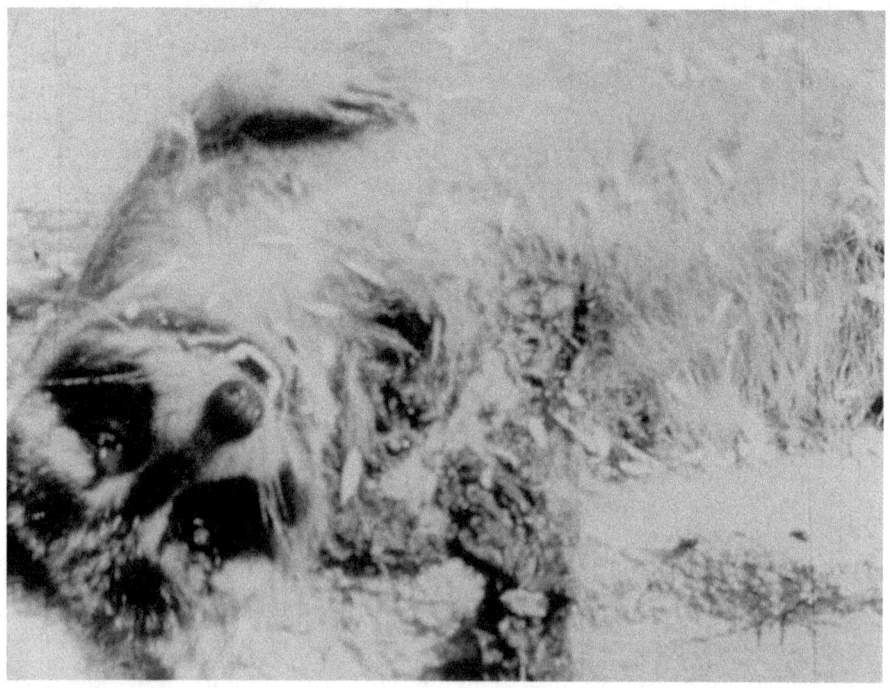

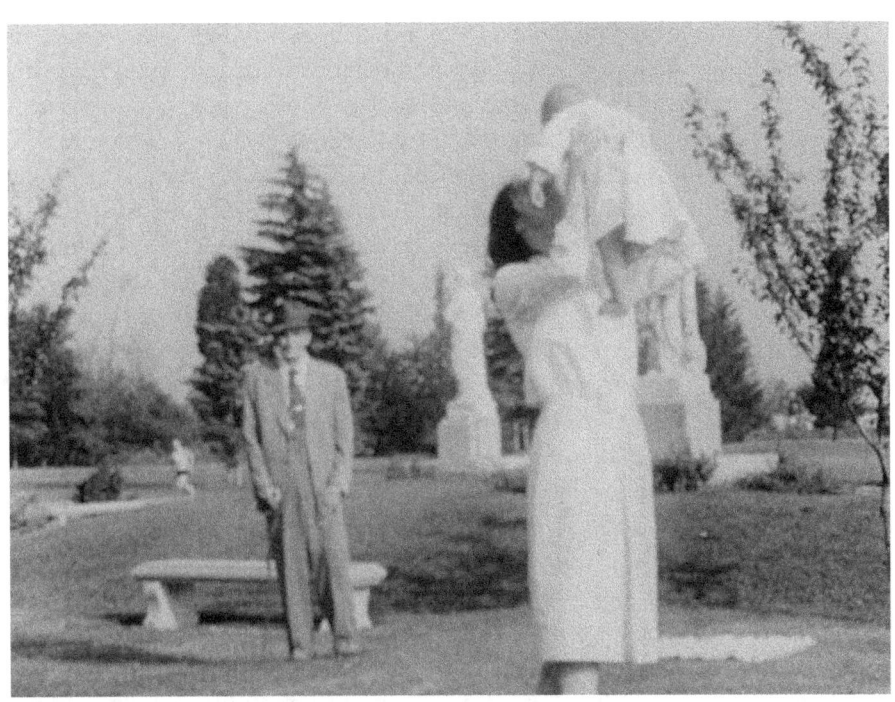

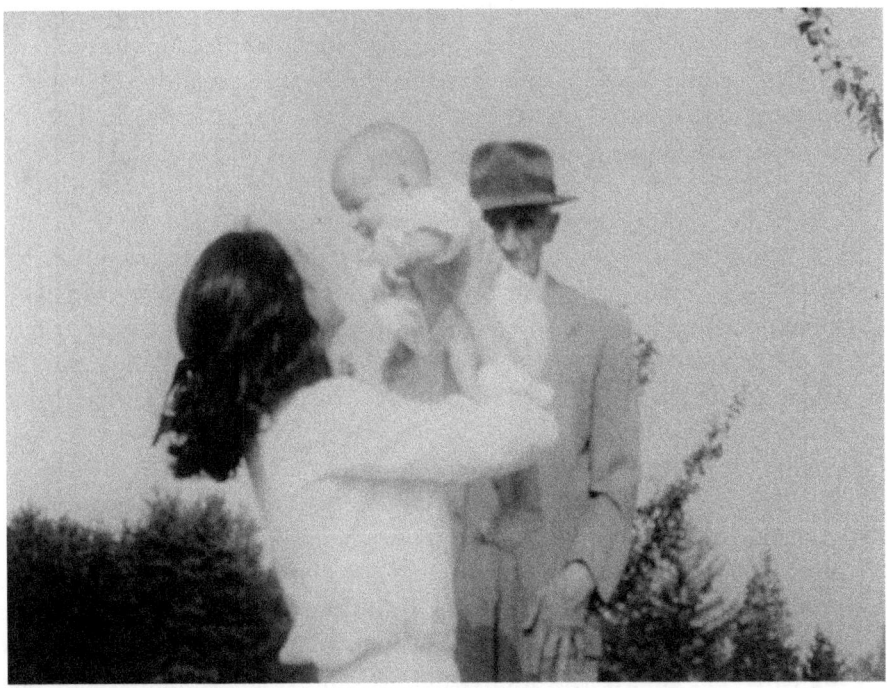

Mosaic *[Film Stills]*, 1964-66
16mm film, 9 minutes, black and white, sound
Courtesy of CFMDC

some seemingly benign and everyday, others confronting the profound experiences that surround pregnancy and birth. Associations build naturally
from one image to another, from one scene to another, in a sequence that is
nevertheless marked by alienation, for intimate scenes keep company with
the most ordinary and distant descriptions of human activity, such as the
clinical scenes in the hospital and the recurring scene of the bus ride. In its
final minutes, the fractures become increasingly pronounced. As the images are divided by black, the sequences are stripped down to an alternation
of Olga throwing flower petals, Olga breastfeeding in front of a group of
children and scenes of a baby shower at which matronly women drink tea.
Black film runs in the interstices between these shots and shot sequences,
emphasizing the intentionality of their spatial and temporal division, defying their fluid recombination.

   Against this editorial fragmentation, Chambers uses compositional fragmentation: perspective shifts from wide, static compositions (for
example, the infant in the foreground with Olga approaching in the distance) to close compositions that suggest an infant's vision (faces distorted
by an upwards angle, magnified by proximity). In the former, subjects are
seen in full—one image of Olga picking daisies, for instance, is reminiscent
of two portraits of Olga both drawn from a shared photographic source,
Olga near Arva (1963) and *Olga along the Thames* (1963). Late in the film, the
four figures—Olga and the infant, the long-distance runner and the old
man—are finally united in the frame, Olga and infant at play, the old man
looking on, the distance runner passing in the background. This precise
composition is placed between two images of unremarkable and seemingly spontaneous capture: first, an upward pan of the hips and chests of
women gathering for the baby shower; second, the expectant father in the
automobile turning the ignition.

   Mosaic is reconstituted out of these fragments as a primitive rid-
dle. Its figures are archetypal, most memorably in the trio of the old man,
the runner and John Jr., as age, maturity and infancy (or even the trinity
of the holy ghost, the father and the son, respectively), and Olga and the
infant as Madonna and child. Chambers uses his reassembled fragments
as illustrations of the mysteries of memory, the wonders of perception and
the life cycle. While its challenge is primitive relative to the films that he
would subsequently make, *Mosaic* serves as a prelude, announcing formal
strategies and themes that would run through his films. Its crude construction may appear perplexing in light of Chambers' commitment to artistic
craftsmanship. With it, however, he went from producing only drawings
and paintings of profound formal deliberation and craftsmanship to making films that gave a false impression of improvisatory photography but

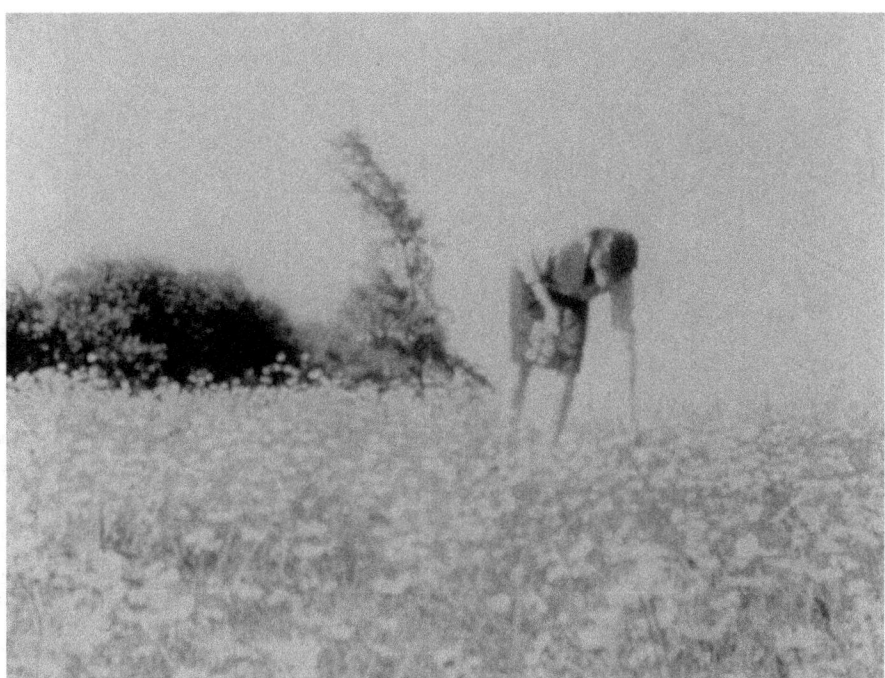

Mosaic *[Film Still]*, 1964-66
16mm film, 9 minutes, black and white, sound
Courtesy of CFMDC

which, in their temporal dimensions, could use sequence and serial juxta-position in a more direct and confrontational manner than his paintings. *Mosaic* carries the marks of its mediation—visible splices, editorial tensions and a general roughness of form—as both object and representation, in keeping with the objecthood of Chambers' photorealist paintings. Such filmmaking offered him an opportunity to build in another direction, without the pressure of producing saleable objects, allowing him to explore his most challenging ideas about art, photography and perceptual experience.

Chambers' next film, *Hybrid* (1967), would serve a more utilitarian end. He travelled to New York in 1966, where he "met with three or four different groups that were protesting America's role in the war [in Vietnam]."[28] The groups loaned him photos and slides of Vietnamese children disfigured by napalm that became the basis for his next film. Along with his rephotography of that material, Chambers would integrate a film on rose gardening that he borrowed and kept from the London Public Library.[29] Such use of found materials would become central to

---

[28] Jack Chambers, *Jack Chambers* (London: Nancy Poole, 1978), 105.
[29] Michael Zryd, "Hybrid as Allegory," in *The Films of Jack Chambers*, ed. Kathryn Elder

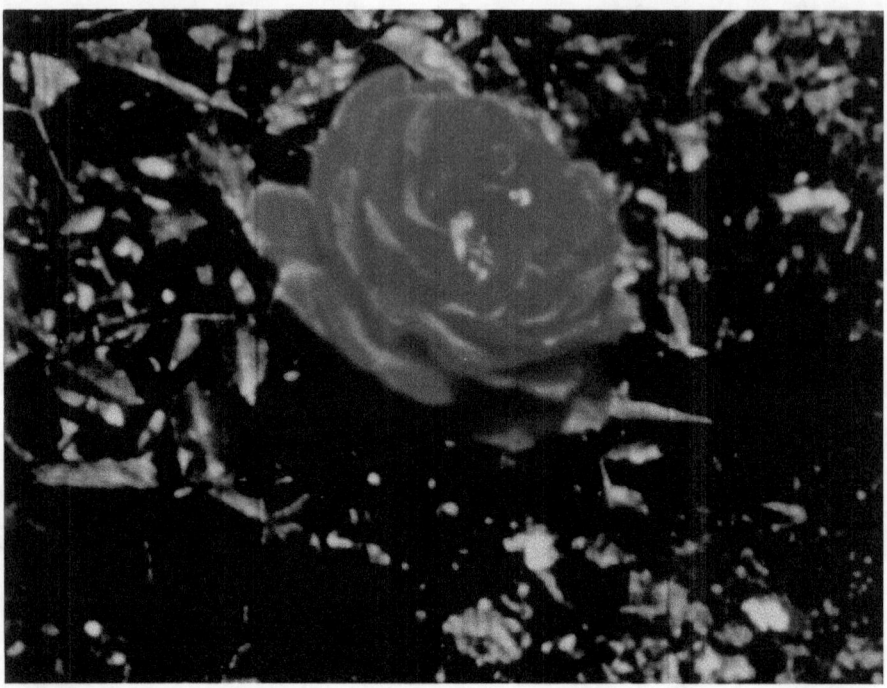

Hybrid *[Film Still]*, 1967
16mm film, 15 minutes, colour and black and white, silent
Courtesy of CFMDC

Chambers' subsequent films, and while mass media images had been a part of his painting process, *Hybrid* is the first instance of such strategies in his films. Of his use of found footage, Chambers told Wendy Michener that he believed old films "should be just like earth that you pick up and use," much like his use of mass media photographs throughout the silver painting period.[30] His use of found footage also allowed him to approach subjects that his own photography could not reach, in terms of both their geographic and social barriers, e.g., footage arising from the Vietnam war, or unique incidents and historical particularities, e.g., the class photos of a drowned boy in his *Regatta* series (1968), and the photographic sources in his pointillist *Sunday Morning No. 1* (1963), a pageant of the living and the dead. But he also used found images as illustrations of life, taken from common and immediate sources. These illustrations could be merged in

---

(Toronto: Cinematheque Ontario, 2002). According to Ross Woodman in an interview with Zryd, "Chambers checked the 16mm film out of the [London Public Library] and cut it up for his film, figuring it would be put to better use and not be missed."

[30] Wendy Michener, "Underground Movies Begin to See the Light." *Globe and Mail*, 6 January 1968, 21.

ways to press the limits of their meaning.

Hybrid is composed of three distinct sections. Each joins footage of horticulture with scenes from the war in Vietnam and the consequences of American aggression against Vietnamese civilians, primarily children. In the first section, the image advances, in hard cuts, through footage of a gardener digging holes and planting bulbs, and stamping soil down with a shovel. He carefully prunes branches and thorns and inspects his irrigation system. Against this, still images are inserted of American soldiers arriving in Vietnam, of the daily life of its agrarian society, and increasingly ominous footage of soldiers in gas masks, an image specific to American aggression and the ambiguous image of invasion, the gas mask concealing their human faces and substituting something menacingly inhuman for their features. The gardener handles shears and a shovel with gloved hands, his routine given macabre significance as the intent of the soldiers becomes clear. The camera lingers on static thorns, then the rose begins to mature in a time-lapse, branches extending and the flower blooming as the camera follows the rise of the plant. Vietnamese families move through trenches and waterways. The horticulturalist sprays chemicals on his rose; a soldier stands in profile with his machine gun. The horticulturalist becomes the soldier, his hose akin to the machine gun; the gardener's shoes resemble the soldier's boots; at the same time, the black and white footage merges the action of his planting with the life of the Vietnamese peasants.

With the second sequence, the implicit violence of the preceding Vietnam war images becomes explicit, as torn bodies and scenes of active conflict begin to emerge. The gardener picks a rose and tears the petals away until there is only a bud. He collects the inner petals into a container. This act of harvesting is held up against images of dead children and children in flight. The inner petals are brushed against images of a dead mother and child. A bulb is carved up with a knife and planted in a pot of soil; Vietnamese children are shown in a hospital. The first section had advanced an interconnection between horticulture and war, as a matter of human supremacy over nature. The soldiers demonstrate their mastery of by conquering and killing their fellow man. This second section furthers Chambers' analogy by focusing on the production and perpetuation of life, both human and plant. By drawing a parallel between the inner petals, which are essentially being engineered, and child victims of bombing and crossfire, he suggests something beyond platitudes of innocence and condemnation of war. It laments the need to impose order and mastery on all things, whether rose or child.

The third and final section of the film extends and concludes this analogy: two elements are contrasted, blooming roses, filmed in time

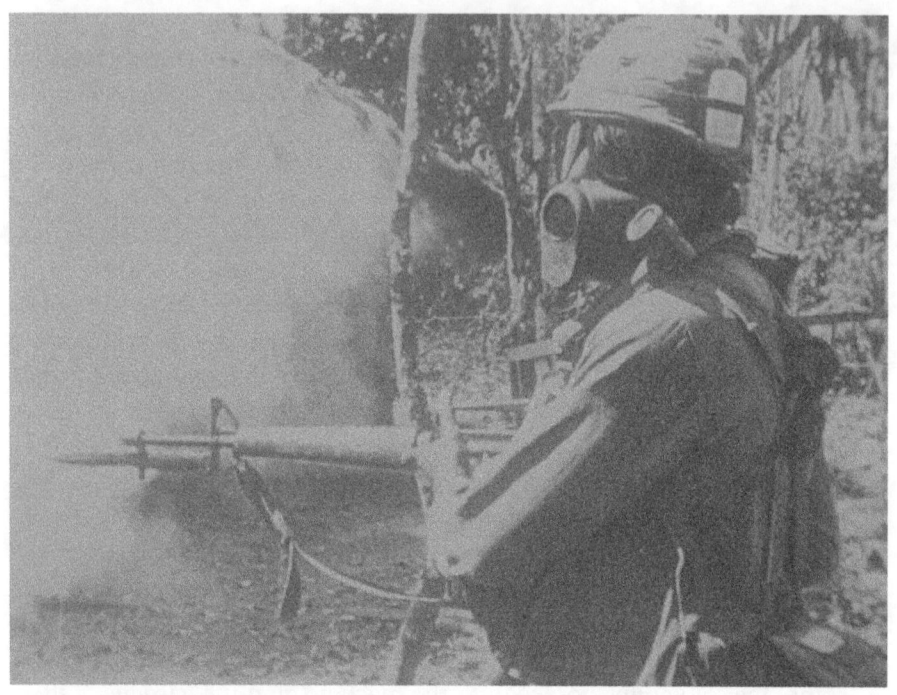

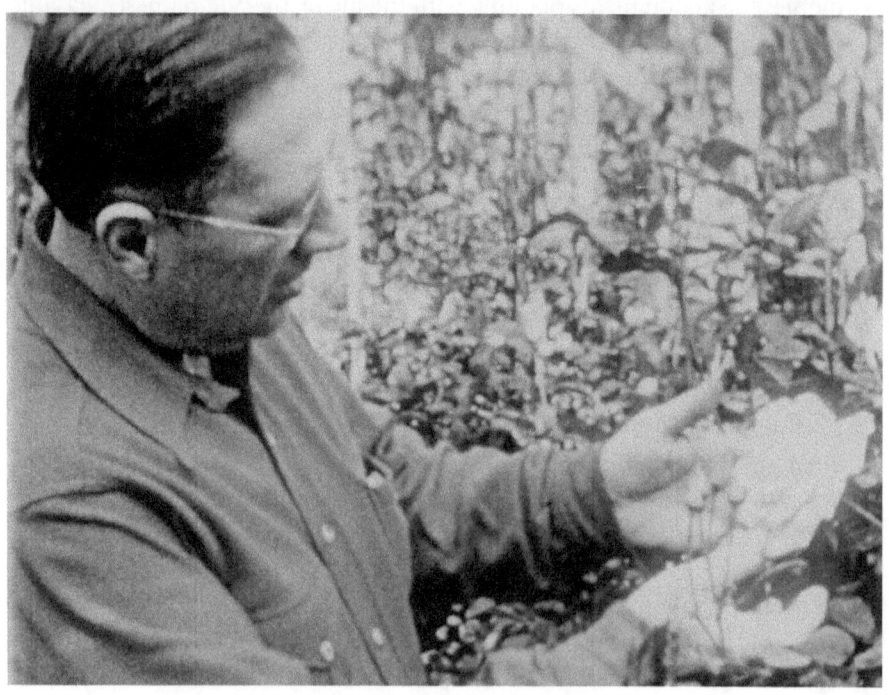

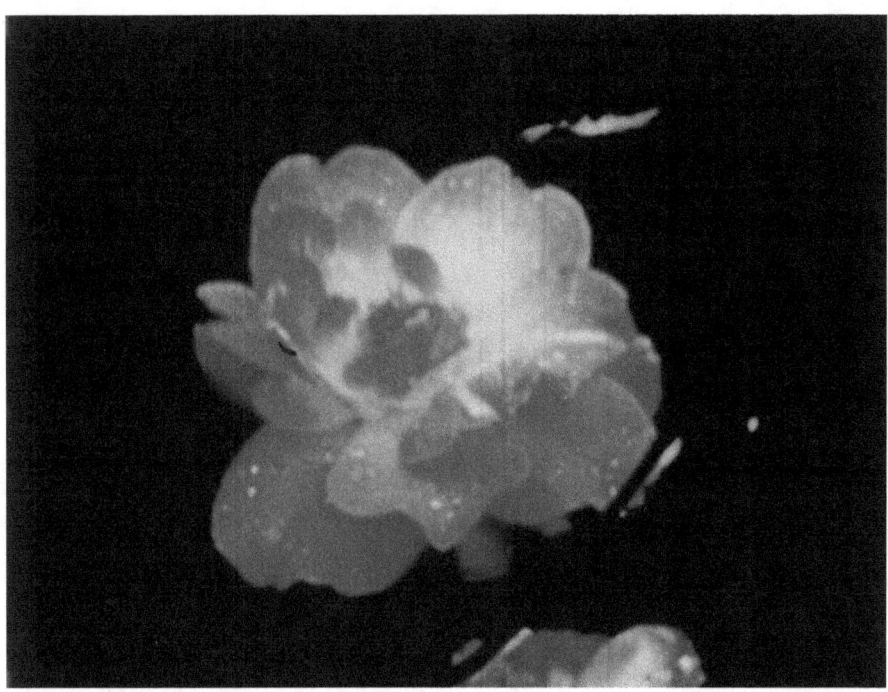

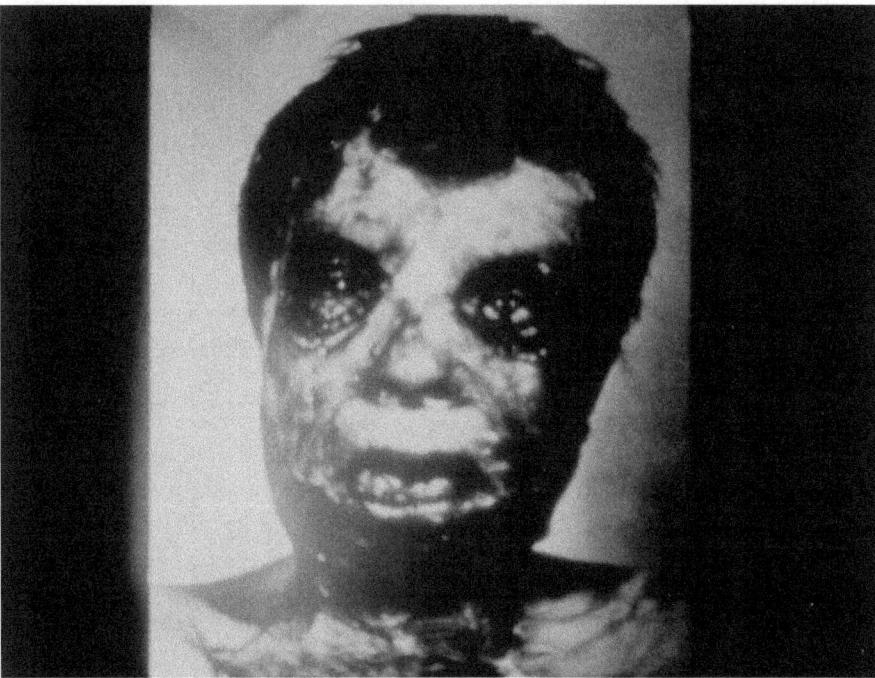

Hybrid *[Film Stills]*, 1967
16mm film, 15 minutes, colour and black and white, silent
Courtesy of CFMDC

lapse as an explosion of luminous reds, whites and yellows, and still images documenting civilian victims of violence and chemical warfare, primarily children. These elements are joined through dissolves, and this gesture—cutting to a bud in bloom, dissolving into atrocities—repeats twenty times, each time restarting by a hard cut, before ending on a rose in bloom. When the roses bloom, they always bloom the same way; the victims' wounds are far more varied, from shrapnel, bullets and chemical burns; to the face, to the chest; some bandaged, some not. The rose petals take on an other-worldly nature in their separation of foreground and background, as their colour strikes out from a black background. This background isolates them, furthering the sterile horticulture of the gardener, but it also flattens them, so that what was intended as an immersive effect in its original context has had its depth annihilated. It plays as a graphic form, a beautiful burst of colour along a flat plane. With the final two victims, the destruction is final: first is a child with the lower half of his face missing and a damaged skull; the second is a face that is completely destroyed, peeling up, eyes loose in sockets, recognizable as human only by virtue of its arrangement, but each feature bent into something alien. The sequence ends with a rose petal unfolding slowly into luminous red.

Mosaic taught Chambers that the fragmentary reassembly that he had taken up in painting could assume a new force in the recombination of film editing. The editorial process served as a natural mirror to perceptual experience and to insight in its ability to break suddenly in another direction; for all that is said of rhythm in painting and sculpture, in time-based forms such as film and music—as in the intervals of poetry—rhythm can take a sudden turn. A composition is not merely redirected but splintered in momentum so that it does not bear trace of what came before it, a fact of editorial sequencing that *Hybrid* resists and subverts. From head to tail, it combines fragments into a binary montage, each resonating with what came before and what follows. *Hybrid* set out with a particular purpose, as political statement, and pursued its subject into new aesthetic territory for Chambers. His paintings had already begun to draw from the photographic archive of a larger society, but he had not done so with moving images, which came with their own set of formal concerns, particularly in the temporal and sequential. Through Chambers' sequencing, *Hybrid* became a work of simile. It represents a difficult aesthetic gesture, one that opens to both simple and complex meanings, holding to an internal contradiction. But it was read in its time as a game of contrasts rather than a work of simile.[31] The sequencing of the two parts, combined with the confounding beauty of colour and form in the final section of the horticulture

---

[31] Matthew Wherry responded to the film in an "autobiographical review," arguing that

footage, could mislead the viewer into the ready analysis that here, beauty is in conflict with horror. This is true, and yet, Chambers is presenting a more tragic agreement between the masterful manipulation of nature and the brutal trials and civilian casualties of war. This agreement assumes a complex and elusive definition, beyond obstacles of ready knowledge and simple meanings, shown here in an alienation from nature and an aspiration toward a total and godly power.

Chambers' integration of mass media images would be central to his next film, *R34*, a study of the London painter and collagist Greg Curnoe during the period in which Curnoe painted *The Camouflaged Piano or French Roundels* (1965-1966), a large mixed media canvas in which the British dirigible R34 appears prominently amidst figures, bright bands of colour and text naming musicians and labelling instruments. The dirigible, which would reappear in other works of Curnoe's, was an insistent symbol of the artist's preoccupation with the history of aviation, a sign of transatlantic westward migration, and by that, of Canadian nationhood.[32] Curnoe identified with Dada, evident in his collages, paintings, and his founding of London's noise ensemble, the Nihilist Spasm Band, who performed on homemade instruments. Where Chambers' paintings and drawings were rigorously traditional in their technique and materials, Curnoe's were crude and spontaneous, teeming with a liveliness that Chambers' work resisted in its isolation of the photographic moment and its entrenchment in memory. But both men were primarily invested in themes of history, memory, community and family. Curnoe's interests tipped toward reflections on a contemporary nationhood; Chambers' tipped toward recognition of the omnipresence of history, the inextricability of the living from the dead, community as necropolis and parade. With community as a common bond, Chambers could create this portrait of Curnoe partly as an impression of Curnoe. *R34* translates Curnoe's

Hybrid offered a binary of "Life-Game" and "Death-Game." Wherry uses these terms to divide the film's central strategy, the juxtaposition of the hybrid rose with the disfiguration of children in wartime Vietnam. The autobiographical basis of Wherry's review quickly emerges, in an account he gives of life on the battlefield during World War Two. His analysis is not concerned with aesthetics, but with treating the work as a social criticism and as a statement of protest. The joining of these images is not as oppositional as 'juxtaposition' would suggest, but rather, an act of analogy and simile. There is at play a simultaneity of life and death, not interplaying as games of strategy, but confounding in utterance. Wherry sees the rose as a symbol of love, its presence a protest against the hatred and senselessness that lies at the root of the competing image. Contra Wherry, in joining the hybridized rose with these deformed faces, Chambers is not merely holding beauty up against horror, but rather revealing the corruption of both games.

[32] The R34 dirigible would be the focus of Curnoe's *Homage to the R34* (1967-1968), a three-panel mural painted for the Montreal airport and later removed amidst controversy, now in the collection of the National Gallery of Canada.

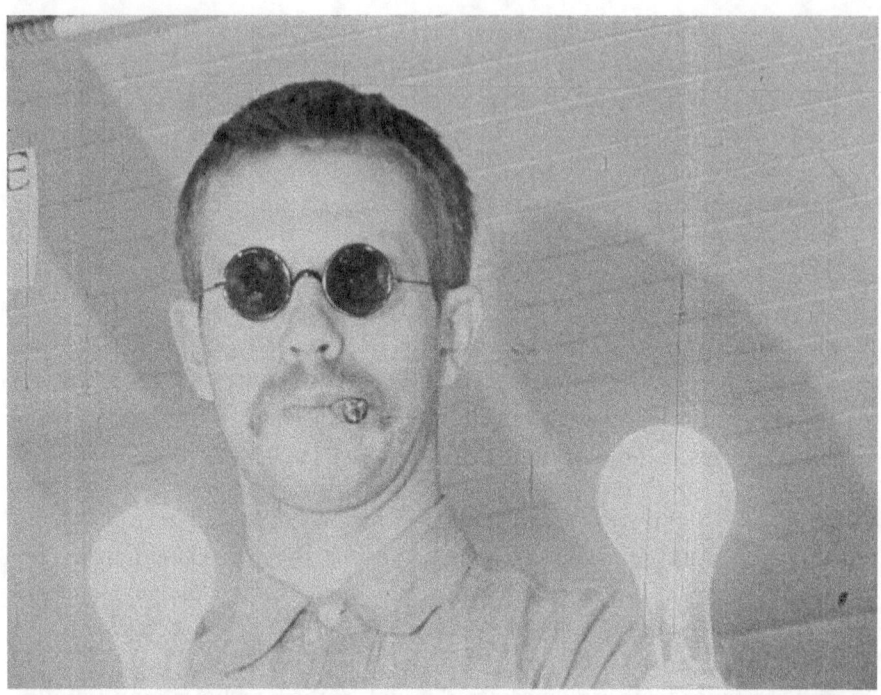

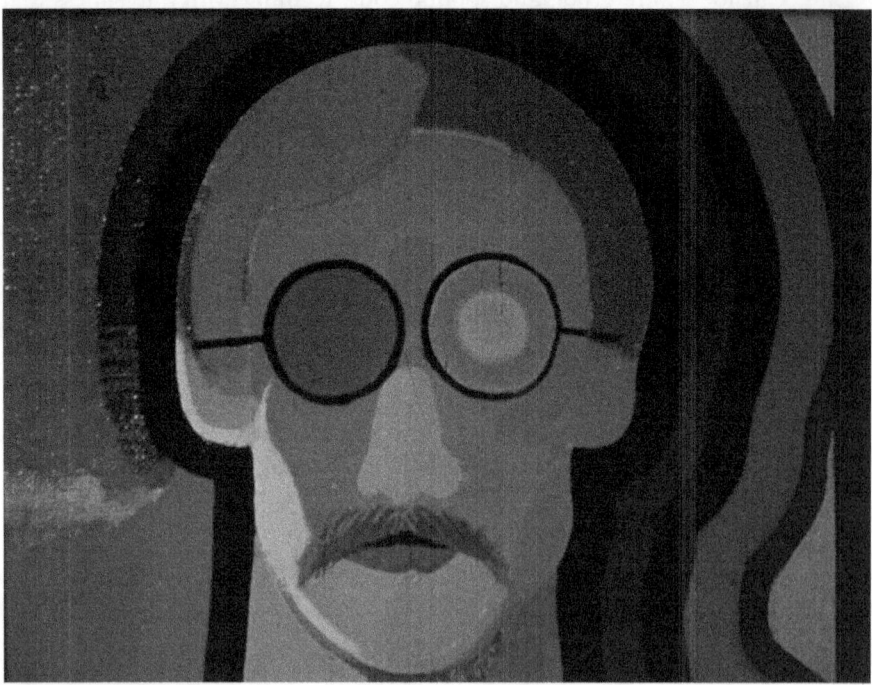

R34 *[Film Stills]*, 1967
16mm film, 26 minutes, colour and black and white, sound
Courtesy of CFMDC

collage aesthetics to cinema but also contains a record of his daily life, its disrupted and interpolating perceptions elevated to the realm of poetry. As he had done in *Mosaic*, Chambers recombines fragments of the everyday into a higher order of symbolic meaning.[33]

Chambers described *R34* as "a kind of self-expressive documentary about someone else." He was drawn to Curnoe as a subject for Curnoe's devotion to art-making. As Chambers later recalled, "Greg was one of the three or four artists in London who had a studio in 1967 and devoted all his time to painting and other related things. When I left London in the fifties no one was painting full-time. Greg was apparently the first one to do so in London and when I returned in 1961 he was the only artist with a studio of his own."[34] In 1961, Michel Sanouillet, a professor of art history at University of Toronto and a bookseller in Toronto's bohemian Gerrard Street Village neighbourhood, had given a talk at the London Public Library and Art Museum titled "Dada's Eye," on the occasion of Curnoe's first solo show, *An Exhibition of Things*.[35] The talk and coinciding show demonstrate that the resonances of Dada had spread and entered Canadian art, that in Chambers' absence, the rich Neo-Dada activity of New York and Paris was resonating in London, Ontario, as it was in Toronto. Chambers' art held a more subtle engagement with the Dada movement, his thoughts already turning to Duchamp's readymades, evident in an essay on assemblage and anti-art published in the London literary magazine *Region* in 1964.[36] *R34* is a portrait of Curnoe that employs Curnoe's own processes of juxtaposition, which comes through in tandem with Chambers' own expressions. The editorial construction of the film reflects Curnoe's assemblages, in both the physical act of editing and the tensions built through rapid editing. *R34* offers scenes from Curnoe's life and Curnoe's statements of his political and aesthetic philosophy, all parts fractured and rejoined into a series of episodes, each bearing incongruities

---

[33] As Chambers' film would take on Curnoe's aesthetics, so too would it influence Curnoe's filmmaking which had started a few years earlier with the unstructured home movie *No Movie* (1965), and which would come to more closely resemble Chambers' filmmaking sensibilities in subsequent years, when Curnoe made *Sowesto* (1969) and *Connexions* (1970).

[34] Jack Chambers, *Jack Chambers* (London: Nancy Poole, 1978), 105.

[35] Denise Leclerc and Pierre Dessureault, *The 60s in Canada* (Ottawa: National Gallery of Canada, 2005), 22.

[36] Chambers' article, "Assemblages, the Found Object and Art" (*Region* 4, 1962, unpaginated), deals in the distance between traditional art and new forms, and argues the necessity of new forms, such as those that emerged through Dada; Chambers is concerned here with the psychology of the artist and their assignment of value to found materials, with an emphasis on Marcel Duchamp's *Fountain* (1917). Later, the Duchamp readymades would figure into the argument of Chambers' manifesto, "Perceptual Realism," *Artscanada* 136-137 (October 1969), 7-13.

and perspectival and symbolic enigmas.[37]

As *R34* begins, colours and vague forms move in soft focus. On the soundtrack, Curnoe describes the Nihilist Spasm Band and its home-made instruments, the description of which will soon find consonance with scenes of Curnoe at work on his assemblages. The credits appear rapidly, listing the title, Chambers, the cameraman Eric Bremner and the Nihilist Spasm Band, who contribute to the soundtrack. The titles repeat in stacca-to rhythms, too fast to be readily comprehended. The image cuts abruptly to a series of Curnoe assemblages in which texts and images are forced into association. Curnoe's collages bear the signs of their process, with glue- and air-bubbles in the paper, the rough marks of his scissors giving the images an air of battlefield surgery. Common elements thread together these assemblages: grids, stars, shapes that evoke badges and flags, prima-ry colours. This introduction announces the form of the film, Chambers' crude, rhythmic assembly corresponding to Curnoe's operations. Curnoe is shown at work on assemblages in his studio, some of which end as boxed, discontinuous topographies. The sequences that follow invoke alternate correspondence and disassociation between language and image, between image and image and between image and sound. It is a vision of work and recreation that unites the process of art with the everyday. Through the coming sequences, the text "HAIR," photographed from an album jacket, is sequenced with an extreme close-up of Curnoe's wife Sheila's hair as she combs it. Images of Curnoe's art are integrated with wedding photo-graphs, scenes of daily life and the environment of his studio.

This montage becomes increasingly discontinuous as more ele-ments are added, an immersion—with only this faint and fast introduc-tion—into the life and ideas of Curnoe, his past, process, art and life in a vacuum of rapid editing. A set of sequences are edited in montage. Curnoe carries a trashcan up a flight of stairs, moving through his studio, adjusting and tidying, and then the studio is shown unoccupied. The Nihilist Spasm Band sets up for a performance. Footage of the 1965 boxing match be-tween Muhammad Ali and Floyd Paterson and the 1966 match between Ali and Canadian champion George Chuvalo is rephotographed from a television screen, edited in montage with Curnoe's paintings of the boxers. Scenes of Curnoe sitting in a rocking chair alternate with an image of a man reclining in a rocking chair; the image flips on its horizontal axis. Curnoe's naïve paintings of vaginas and penises appear, as well as a whirl-igig of a bending nude figure, its spinning implying a gyrating buttocks.

---

[37] As much as *R34* gains a spontaneous appearance by its raw and rapid editorial assembly, it is a conscious result of Chambers' editorial control, as evidenced in his notebooks on the film, which include careful editorial sequencing notes and details of even the film's most subliminal images.

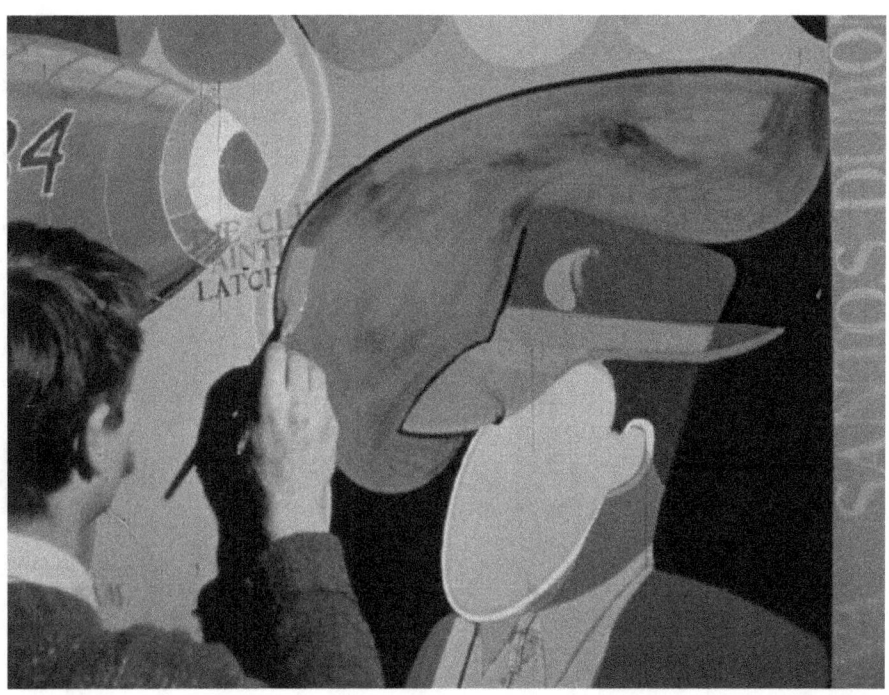

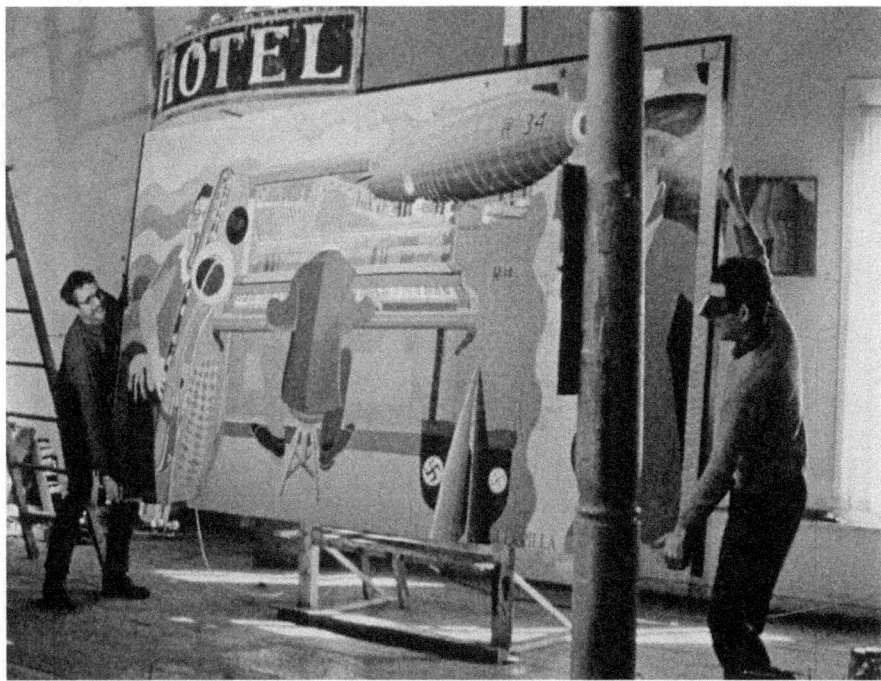

R34 *[Film Stills]*, 1967
16mm film, 26 minutes, colour and black and white, sound
Courtesy of CFMDC

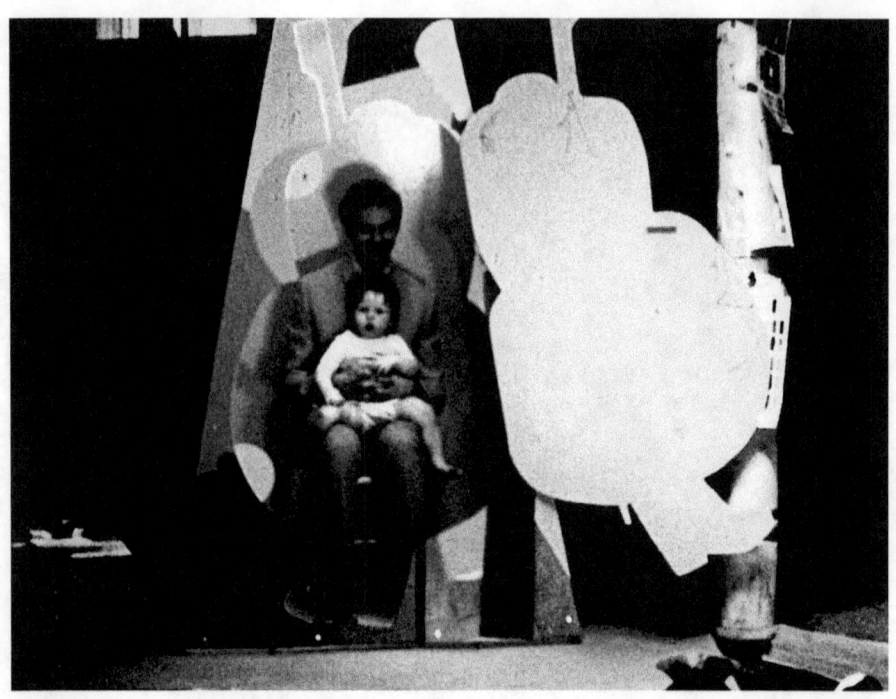

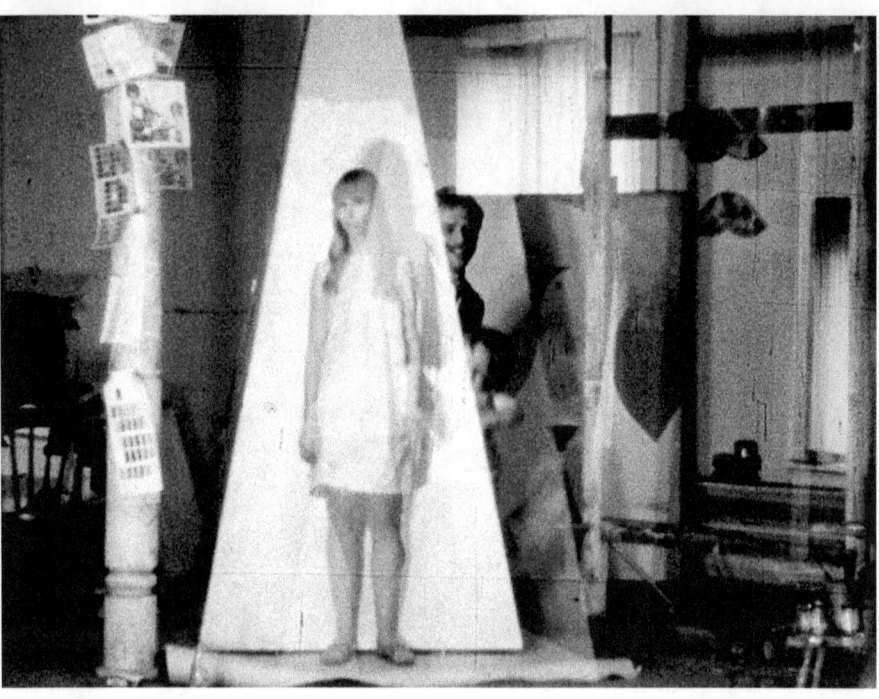

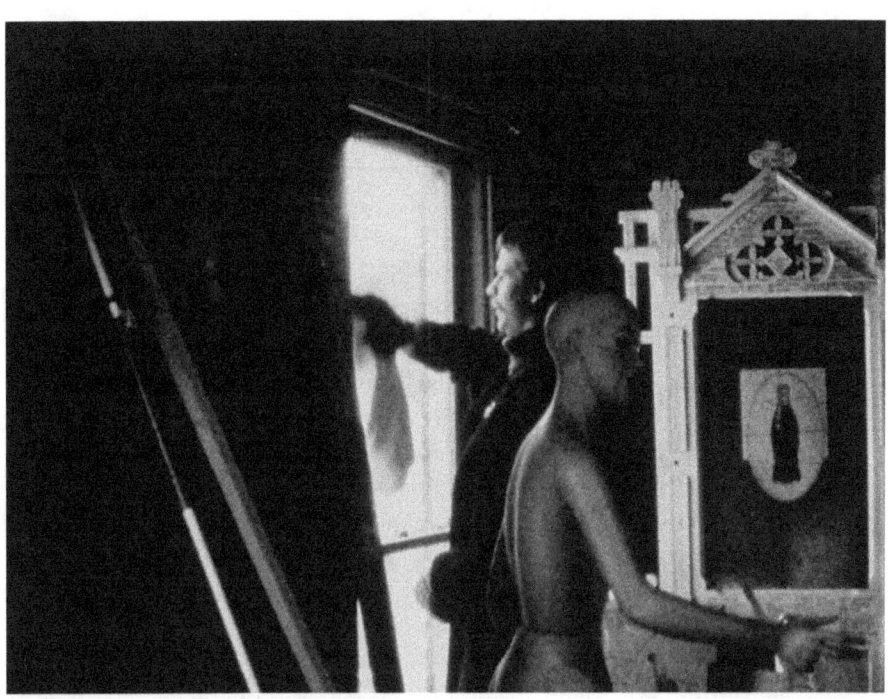

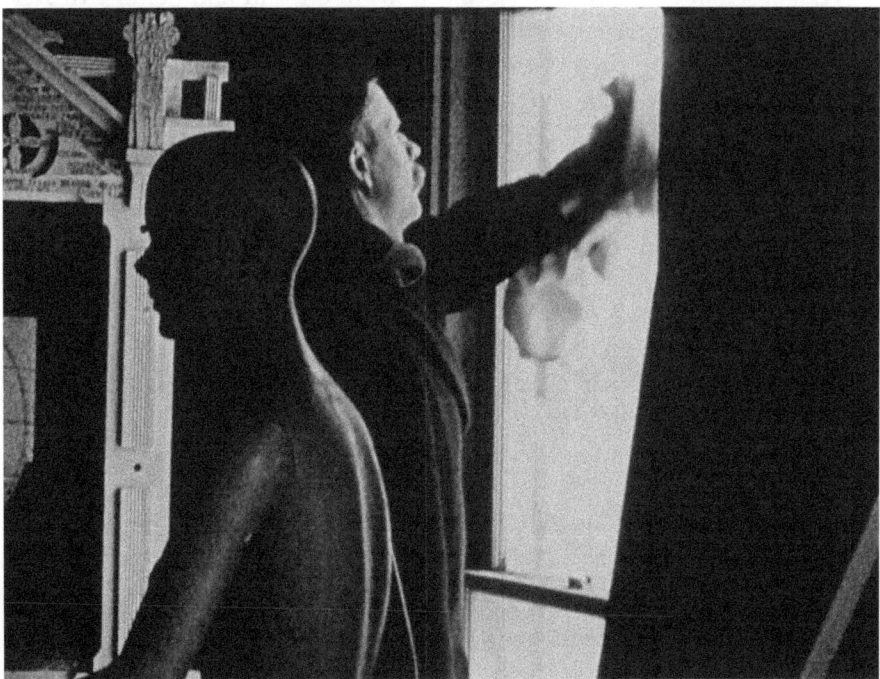

R34 *[Film Stills]*, 1967
16mm film, 26 minutes, colour and black and white, sound
Courtesy of CFMDC

Curnoe, wife Sheila and infant son Owen appear in a double-exposure with a triangular painting. This rapid sequence concludes with Curnoe completing *The Camouflaged Piano or French Roundels* by affixing an antique hotel sign to it.[38]

Mirroring the de-familiarization and serial repetition of Curnoe's assemblages, Chambers flips scenes of Curnoe in his studio on their horizontal axis, so that screen-left and screen-right trade places as these sequences repeat. Black or white interstitials create space and, as in *Mosaic*, emphasize Chambers' editorial fragmentation. At the conclusion of the film, Curnoe's triangular painting reappears, a construction containing a door in the shape of a figure. Curnoe is now seated inside what previously appeared as a two-dimensional form. In keeping with his fascination with aviation, it has become a kind of cockpit. Curnoe's infant son Owen plays on his lap, and the final section of Albert Ayler's *Bells* (1965) plays on the soundtrack. The infant takes on the infant vision seen earlier in *Mosaic*, the camera passing over Greg Curnoe's legs and Owen's face, too near to see clearly, closely identified with the distorted, still-forming vision of a child. The image becomes amorphous and soft, as it was at the outset. The closing image is of a sleeping Owen Curnoe.

With the thematic assembly of *Mosaic* and the binary montage of *Hybrid*, Chambers' films had evinced his interest in film editing. In *R34*, the editorial roughness, both in its physical application (in visible splices) and its staggering rhythms, is the work's defining feature. An impression of Curnoe's private and creative life is fashioned of many elements, some of profound dimension, others, minutiae, from wedding photographs to spent tubes of paint. As an act of portrait and biography, *R34* resembles the Swiss Neo-Dadaist Daniel Spoerri's art book *An Anecdoted Topography of Chance* (1962), in which the artist maps the items spread across a table and diligently details their origins. Chambers portrays Curnoe in an assemblage of details. As Spoerri's book was an act of autobiography, Chambers' film becomes a kind of secondarily-authored autobiography of Curnoe, an impression of voice.[39] Curnoe's assemblages, and the Neo-Dada notion of the assemblage in general, correspond to Chambers' editing in that he fractures and reassembles details, as in his flipping of the horizontal axis.

---

[38] The hotel sign on *The Camouflaged Piano or French Roundels* is one of the more obvious signs of Curnoe's debt to Marcel Duchamp; we see that influence in the way that Curnoe's work consistently repurposes ordinary and everyday images and objects.

[39] While *R34* is more of an act of formal impersonation, one might link this aspect of Chambers' process to Gertrude Stein's *The Autobiography of Alice B. Toklas* (1933), the author's voice masquerading as the voice of the subject, or to the writings of Canadian literary theorist Hugh Kenner, whose studies of Pound, Joyce, Wyndham Lewis and others channeled the subjects' voice as his own.

Late in the film, Curnoe says, "I'm trying to put the whole thing together." This statement has, in one sense, a comic literalism, as so much of the film has recorded Curnoe's electric and woodworking labours in making *The Camouflaged Piano or French Roundels*. The remark also resonates with Curnoe's stated contempt for society, casting him as a thinker of broad application prone to both construction and destruction. The statement also resonates with the film's formal ambiguities, its fragmentary rhythm and alignment, its axial mirrorings, its sense of pieces reconstituted into a new whole. In trying to "put the whole thing together," Chambers is assembling discordant parts into a whole that is this determinedly uncertain portrait. He is pushing toward a perceptual impression of Curnoe rather than a mere document, pushing to the openness of participatory meaning, like that of the assemblage, rather than an enclosure and singularity of meaning, as in the documentary portrait.[40]

In *Mosaic*, the camera was not guided by rhythm; rather, shots were primarily static, composed, the film's energy coming from its editing. The photography of *R34*, like that of *Mosaic*, is balanced between the intimacy of the home movie and documental staging. The editing disrupts, repeats and undermines scenes of the artist at work, fitting them into a sequence with less didactic and rehearsed scenes, as well as with scenes of poetic calculation (e.g., a double-exposed sequence of the Curnoe family standing in front of the triangular canvas). This structure corresponds to the documental nature of the artist portrait and its inbuilt expectation to record process and result, a task at the core of this film but one that is mediated by radical modernist form. The camera moves across Curnoe's artworks, and when in stasis, recording his assemblages, it crops and selects details. In the former instance, the camera's dynamic action is a response to the rhythms of line and form within the painting, much like the American filmmaker Marie Menken's studies of sculptor Isamu Noguchi (*Visual Variations on Noguchi*, 1945) and painter Piet Mondrian (*Mood Mondrian*, 1961). In *Mood Mondrian*, her 'documentation', cropped by intention, gains momentum in editing; the camera performs a similar duty in the opening sequence of *R34*, as various assemblages, seen only partially, appear through the sequence. Another aspect of the camera work that is new to Chambers, but which corresponds to his other usage of found materials, is the rephotography of boxing matches from television. Chambers was treating

---

[40] This impression demonstrates Chambers' engagement with what he would later call "the veil of the human psyche," through which primary processes are expressed (Qtd. in Tom Smart, *Jack Chambers' Red and Green: an artist's inquiry into the nature of meaning*, Erin, Ont.: Porcupine's Quill, 2013). *R34* is his penetration, his glimpse behind the veil of Curnoe's psyche, much as the rest of Chambers' work reveals binaries and dualities that inform his own expressions.

images as raw material, yet another gesture of affiliation with Curnoe and Neo-Dada.[41]

Mosaic and *Hybrid* pursue narrow agendas relative to the staggering scale of their subjects, family relationships and war. By comparison, *R34* retreats from the general subject, shifting to the particularity of the individual; in doing so, it extends Chambers' aesthetic sensibility into increasingly difficult territory. Where his past films, by their subjects, insisted on a relative explication of meaning, *R34* was so intimate as to become vast in the scope of its ambiguity, a work that spoke broadly to creativity, surface and the psychological interior. His earlier films could engage their viewer by universality of theme and by their respective tenderness and outrage, even as more complex inferences lay beneath their surface. *R34* held no direct message; it did not engage the viewer in this way; rather, it dealt out details so particular to Greg Curnoe as to be deeply alienating to the passive viewer, and it did so in a modern form that passive viewing could not accommodate. Instead, *R34* invited the active viewer to construct meaning out of its reconstituted fragments, and so with this film, the viewer's involvement had become increasingly necessary. As Chambers moved forward, his work would emphasize particularities, of place, persona and history, discovering universal potentials for cinema that would allow the viewer to enter into a state of perceptual reverie.

With Chambers' next film, *Circle* (1968-69), also known as *Circle 4*, he would return to the subject of his own domestic life, last considered in *Mosaic*. Much had changed in Chambers' work in the preceding years, not only in his ideas about filmmaking and photography, but his preoccupation with art in a more general sense. His painting had slowed when he began to make films. He had, in the estimation of Ross Woodman, begun increasingly to associate the act of painting with death. Chambers himself spoke of the relief that his silver paintings brought him, in their relation to objects. In the positive-negative transit of those paintings, the object entered into a higher order of reality, fully realized into the world as something dynamic, moving in time, beyond the grip of the painter. For whatever relief the silver paintings gave Chambers, they reflected a deep misery, both in the rage and grief of their subjects and the atmosphere the paint itself created in his studio.[42]

---

[41] The aesthetic of the re-photographed television screen, and the effect of degraded, low-fidelity images marked by visible scanlines, is commonplace in 1960s underground filmmaking, notably Marie Menken's *Wrestling* (1963), who in her accompanying description termed this strategy "TV concrete," akin to musique concrète (the use of found sounds in composition) but also suggestive of the stone-like relief quality of images forged by this act.

[42] Ross Woodman has described the atmosphere as oppressive: "Spraying silver lead-based

The silver painting period was followed by a break from painting activity, during which time Chambers continued to work on his films. By the time he made *Circle*, his ideas about art had shifted away from that grief and outrage, though not away from the gravity of his subjects. He found affirmation through Perceptual Realism, his philosophy of the relation between art and technology that produces, or reproduces, rich perceptual experience. Chambers, unlike his contemporaries in Canadian modern painting and artists' cinema, had a proud investment in realism and had given considerable thought, in his time away from painting, to the distinguishing marks of his own mode of realism. Perceptual Realism, by its barest definition, was an interplay of light, matter and time, a collision of the visible and the invisible, of interior and sensory experience. This theory exalted what Chambers called the "wow" moment, a profound communion between interior experience and perceptual experience that, through gradual acclimation, induces these parts of the self to permeate one another, to perceive "the weaker impulses, the little presences, the whispers that are always there but only recently have become residents of an expanded family awareness."[43] *Circle* has at its centre a study in these ideas, in particular the emergence of perceptual awareness through light, and it joins that study to staged and found materials, framing it in the grammar of his past films, and by extension, to aesthetics closer in spirit to his silver paintings and other works of the mid-1960s.

Where *Mosaic* had offered Olga and John Jr. as icons of motherhood and childhood, *Circle* would turn to the family's backyard, not only as a symbol of familial settlement, but as a laboratory of time and a portal onto the changing seasons. Its perceptions of light and time were made all

---

paint directly from the can onto the wooden panel in an essentially unventilated studio, without using a mask, [Chambers] became increasingly ill, not pausing to diagnose the environmental situation in which he was working or the way he was working. Visiting him in his studio, I was struck not only by an oppressive atmosphere, but by what I felt to be a mounting inner rage as if Jack were constructing the very prison from which he was also determined to escape." Ross Woodman, "The Act of Creation: A Question of Survival," in *The Films of Jack Chambers*, ed. Kathryn Elder (Toronto: Cinematheque Ontario, 2002), 22.
[43] Jack Chambers, "Perceptual Realism," *Artscanada* 136-137 (October 1969), 13. As an expression of inner vision, Perceptual Realism had little if any common ground in philosophy and execution with American photorealist paintings, like those of Richard Estes or John Baeder. The "wow" moment is also distinct from Henri Cartier-Bresson's concept of the decisive moment in photography, for Perceptual Realism connects visual experience to inner vision, while those notions and works in photography and American photorealist painting that deal in the description of moments and the instant of taking are inevitably more concerned with surface, with the isolation of visual interest. Perceptual Realism was, above all, the veneration of visual experience in tandem with the psychological interior, perhaps best observed in Chambers' family portraits that arose out of this period, such as *Sunday Morning No. 2* (1968-1970), *Lunch* (1970) and *Diego Sleeping No. 2* (1971).

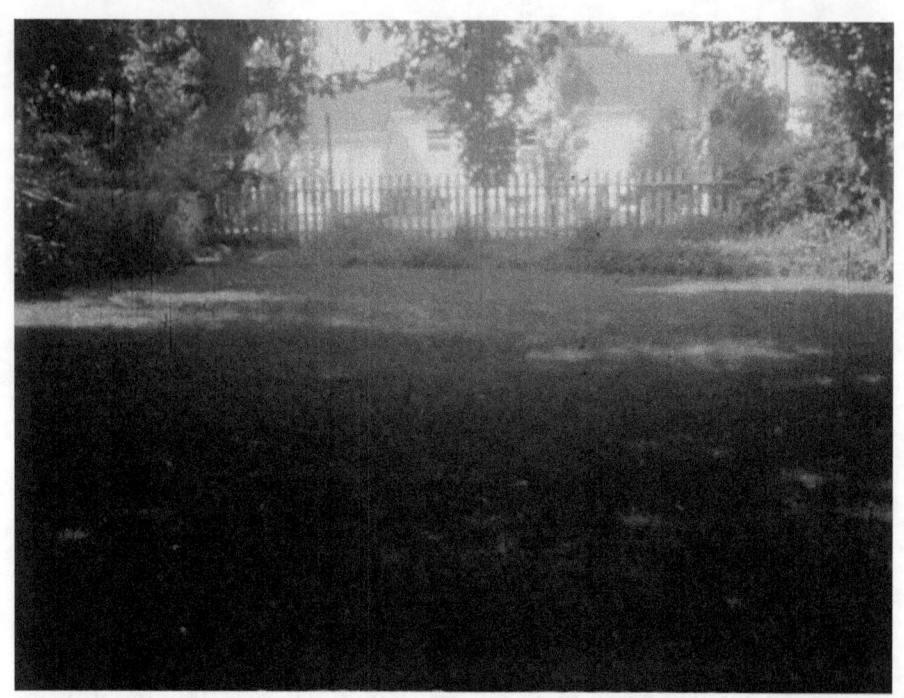

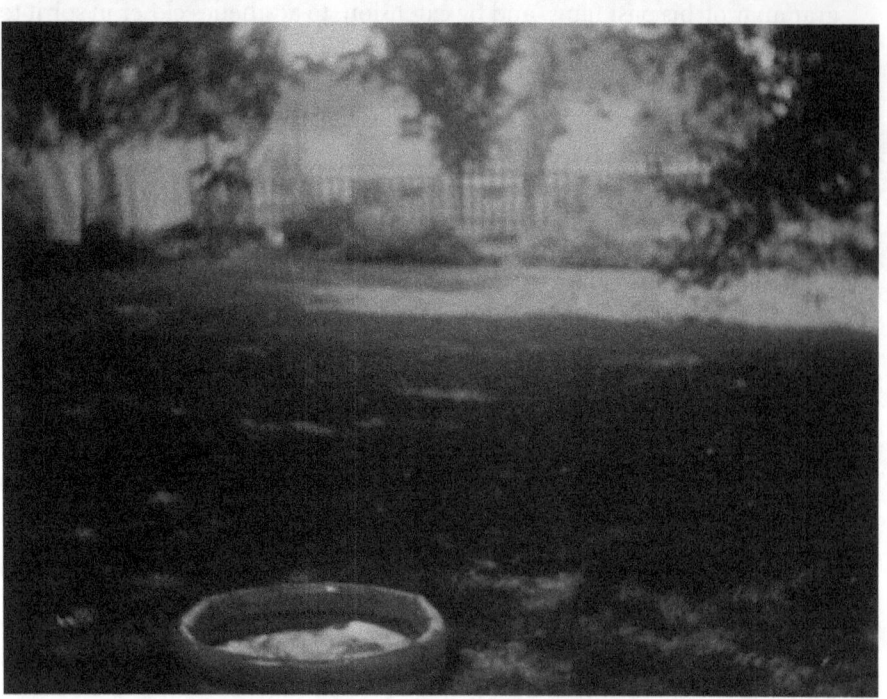

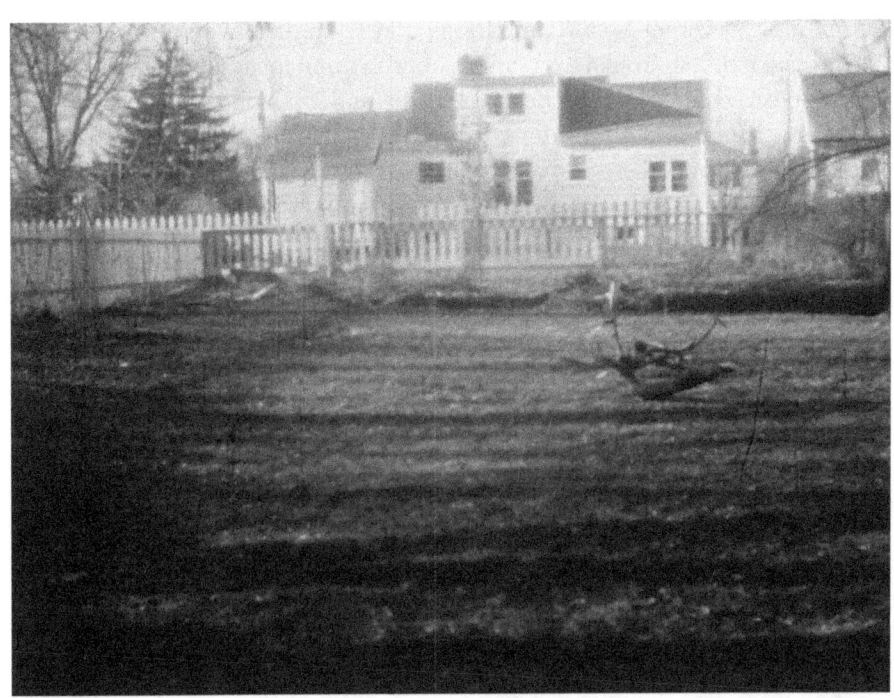

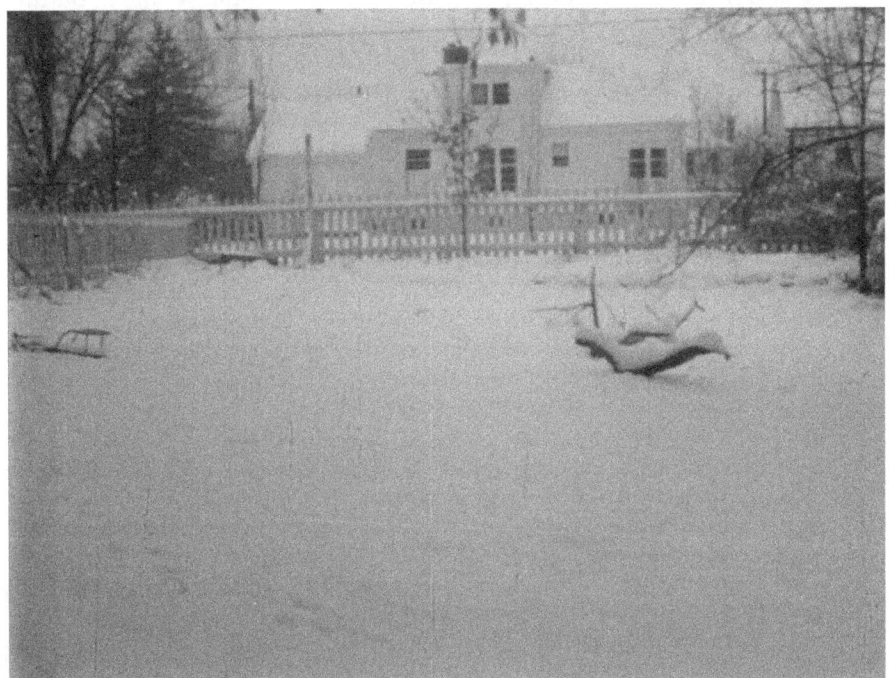

Circle *[Film Stills]*, 1968-69
16mm film, 28 minutes, colour and black and white, sound
Courtesy of CFMDC

the more reverent by the limitations that Chambers would impose upon himself, working from a fixed angle, aperture and focus. This restricted lens emphasized the interplay between space and changing light. *Circle* would assume a complex tripartite structure through which this backyard study would be framed by creative action and records of a broader community. *Circle* begins with a dramatic scene of Chambers filming the credits, alternating camera eye perspective with footage of him preparing and filming with the camera; the film ends with a series of found sequences, culled, it would seem, from television b-roll of labour and leisure in London. In between, Chambers photographs his backyard over the course of a year, through a hole cut in the rear wall of the Chambers family's Lombard Avenue home.[44] As he would later describe it, "The camera was fixed in one position and each day, at the same time each day, it recorded a couple of seconds of the backyard it was pointing at. The aperture remained the same for the year, so the tonal values of one day following another were made visible."[45] This middle and, at 17 minutes, most substantial sequence is a study of reality emerging from light, worked by a predetermined structure, an experiment in the truest sense of the term, and an act of surrender to light and time. Against this, the bookend sequences exert control over the film's form, guiding it beyond the borders of its isolated experiment; they also place Chambers' diurnal ritual in a confounding context, putting it into dialogue with different understandings of space and time: constructed space, historical time.[46]

---

[44] Chambers' experiment, described as such, might be traced back as far as Isaac Newton, seventeenth-century physicist and father of classical mechanics. In 1665, Newton darkened his room and made a small hole in his window shutter. A thin beam of sunlight passes through that hole, and into a prism, and by that prism it dispersed into the colours of a rainbow. Newton deduced that white light from the sun contained all of these colours. Chambers and Newton share a superficial similarity in the execution of their experiments, their observations achieved by similar modes of taming light, but the parallel illuminates a point of contrast between their projects. Newton obtained the first inklings of an essential truth of physics, through an observable phenomenon, and while Chambers is ostensibly looking at and revealing the observable phenomenon of localizations of light through the year, *Circle* as a whole is set to chasing light as spiritual phenomena.

[45] Jack Chambers, *Jack Chambers* (London: Nancy Poole, 1978), 107.

[46] Two precedents in the visual arts that sought similar expressions and knowledge clarify Chambers' experiment in the context of modern art. The root impulse of *Circle*, taken as a study in changing light, could be traced to Claude Monet, and thereby to the origins of the Impressionist movement. Monet, from 1899 until his death in 1926, was occupied with a series of large scale studies of water lilies on his property in Giverny, a project which traced not only the transformation of light and space in time, but also, the artist's own diminishing vision. As Monet's life was ending, and changes in the course of art were taking shape in Europe, Marcel Duchamp executed his *Unhappy Readymade* (1919). With *Unhappy Readymade*, the artist gave his sister Suzanne a geometry textbook, likely Euclid's *Elements*, and asked her to suspend it from a clothesline on the balcony of her Paris apartment, subject to the

The first sequence passes slowly: the camera, its lens at a fixed focus, physically moves toward the title card to bring it into focus. The camera passes over several shapes, a textured stucco ceiling and an overexposed lightbulb, eventually locating Chambers' hand-written credit. The film cuts from this credit to blank drywall, and the camera pans to reveal a light fixture, a door, and finally, a Bolex camera resting in its box. Throughout, the sound of winding clockwork, a fastening, a mechanical motor—the winding, fastening and running of a Bolex's spring motor—play on the soundtrack, along with the faint voices of children. A television set plays a jingle, distorted to obscurity. Chambers himself appears, photographed in profile, unpacks his Bolex camera, winds it, puts his hand under its strap and raises it to his eye. He prepares to film a series of photographs that have been laid out on a table, all depicting the same scene: a lawn, a house, a children's pool, with leaves overhanging the composition. The camera passes over the photographs, its perception altered by Chambers' movements and his adjustments to its focus and aperture, moving nearer to the photograph, transitioning into the next sequence. This prologue establishes a working process unlike Chambers' actual working process, presenting the photograph as an analogue to moving images, as if the instant would give way to the interval. The photograph had given Chambers reference material for his paintings and drawings, but with Circle, the photographic subject, the Chambers family's backyard, now filmed in time, becomes a premonition of his extended experiment. In the opening sequence, the operator's fascination guides the camera eye, but soon the camera will be abandoned to a single, static point of view, open only to the impression of nature. In the film's middle episode, a more rigid system of visual perception would supplant the lyrical and spontaneous limited first-person vision of the camera eye.

The same composition from the photographs, the Chambers family's backyard, now plays out in time, filmed in intervals of four seconds. These images begin in a spring light, which passes through trees with varying density. Shadows are cast on the lawn when the sun is bright, and its shifting angle reveals the ground in fragments. Occasionally this progress is interrupted by days too overcast and black to see, but by the rigid composition, the viewer trusts that the scene remains beneath the darkness. As the scene turns to autumn and winter, the light dims. The fixed compositional

_____

elements, for one year, so that it could "get the facts of life," those facts being a kind of non-Euclidean décollage. This readymade, for its exposure to chance within the parameters of Duchamp's experiment, is an ideal precursor to *Circle*. Duchamp offered an irreverent protest to Euclidean plane geometry, while Chambers treated two subjects that had so consumed him through the 1960s, family and landscape, but both artists were essentially concerned with capturing the passage of time.

elements—the neighbouring house, the fence, the trees—become a graphic form against which variables come and go: a clothesline, a deck chair, children's toys, Olga and the children, the marks of the seasons in bare branches, dead leaves, snow and shadows. The field of vision is cut short by light, and so the house in the background is in varying states of focus, sharply illuminated by the bright winter sun reflected by snow, murky and soft in autumn. The first and final images are of near identical compositions, the fence, the green of leaves and lawn, the white and red of the neighbouring house, changed only by the strength of sunlight. By these images, the cycle of seasons is a closed loop. The 'season word' passes unspoken in the particularities of each of the seasons. Those seasons are taken as a transitory cycle, the beginning and end the only plotted points. As a concept, this experiment metes out an extremity of minimalism, but in practice, the passive action of the artist recording intervals and the bareness of the graphic form reveal the richness of what action does occur. For instance, in one image, Olga leads one of the children into the distance, to the fence line, an image as ambiguously meaningful as any of *Mosaic*'s scenes of Madonna and child. The backyard, mediated by the fixed parameters of the lens, is offered as an expression of inner life, the camera's stare fixed on light and time as subjects of real perception.

The Bolex rests on its side on a table. A light-struck end gives way to the final sequence, assembled from materials taken from the archive of local London television, fragmented and recombined. From a brief shot of running water, we see a series of human activities: a teenaged girl teaches a dachshund arithmetic, rewarding its barked answers with treats; passengers disembark a Canadian National Railway (CNR) train, enter a train station and load their bags into cars; swimmers frolic in a quarry; workers on an industrial processing line transform a long striped coil into hard candies; two children walk through a field; little girls write in the frost on a car's windshield; four children make a giant snow bird and mount the smallest of them on it. At the end of this sequence, birds congregate in the sky. A group of birdwatchers photograph them. Cupped hands open to reveal a bird on its back. As the hands open, it bolts upright and takes flight. Throughout this sequence, a circular impression signs intermittently from the upper right of the frame. It is, by appearance, a hole punched directly in the source footage. In the context of Chambers' film, this hole punch acts as a reminder of the material base of the image itself.

These events, taken individually, are the nondescript viscera of the everyday, the cutting room floor of local news. Here, combined into a discontinuous, apparently heterodox sequence, they become a poetic magnification of that everyday. Their appearance marks a sudden turn,

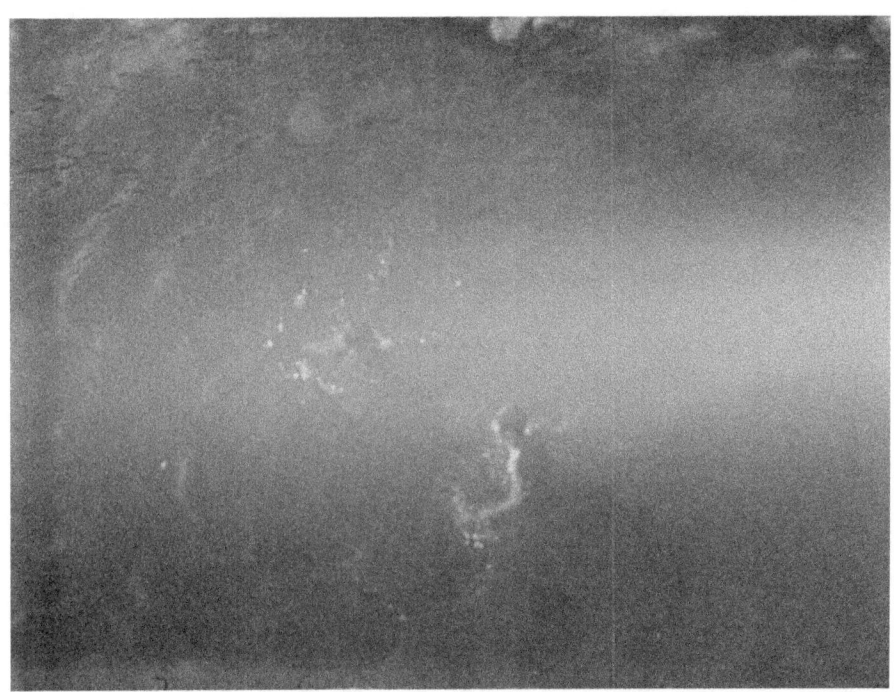

Circle *[Film Stills]*, 1968-69
16mm film, 28 minutes, colour and black and white, sound
Courtesy of CFMDC

extending the themes of the backyard experiment into a realm of wonder. They serve as a transit into the sublime interval of the "wow" experience, a disruption of consciousness and semantic association that, in the act of gathering itself, forms a confrontation with, in Chambers' words, "the Invisible Body," the vital energy that we recognize in the richest perceptual experiences that lie beyond consensus reality, an experience that arrives as an interval and out of which a greater knowledge of real things—and of, in Chambers' words, "gentleness"—emerges.[47]

Hybrid, through its rose gardening footage, had demonstrated humanity's interaction with nature as one strain of the monstrous extensions of technological mastery. With the final sequence of *Circle*, Chambers shows ambiguous interactions between man and animal, industry and fellow man. His judgment on mastery is given through the counting dog, the candy manufacturing, the scenes of recreation, and these speak of a fraught exchange between humankind and environment that is perpetuated in the flow of time. That flow is at the heart of *Circle*, in the permeations and vagaries of light that explicate its middle passage, but which are implicated in all of its parts and which open the work up to the "wow" moment, finally realized in the whole of the associations in the final sequence. Chambers' found footage recognizes his own experience of childhood and maturation in London, now perpetuated by the vessel of universal youth, but it also reveals the bridge between perception and experience, out of photographic descriptions of light that he has fractured and reassembled.

---

[47] This notion of the Invisible Body and the sublime re-gathering of experience has resonance with the disfigurative / recombinational collage that Chambers practiced in his films and paintings through the mid-1960s. While much of Chambers' cosmology was rooted in Roman Catholicism, R. Bruce Elder has made the case (in "Jack Chambers' Surrealism," in *The Films of Jack Chambers*, ed. Kathryn Elder, Toronto: Cinematheque Ontario, 2002), that his ideas of perceptual realism as a rare and heightened experience arising from emanations and energy fields shares much with the sources of the Surrealists. The description I have given here might also be clarified by this description that Chambers himself gives to the "wow" moment that is lurking within the final heterodox sequence of *Circle*, through its action as an assembled whole made from disparate components: "Perception in process is like a sound movie. Suddenly the picture freezes and loses focus. The sound goes. The de-focusing brightens and becomes white light. Then the focus returns, the sound comes back and the film starts moving again. That's a slow-motion version of what happens. The moment of 'white light' is the moment of perception. The frame returning to focus and the first returning sounds are the registration of object-world on the nerves as the senses recover. What the senses record and how and when they record it is an example of creation projecting its pattern on the world. (...) On recovering the senses after the perceptual impact, one feels the stark wonder of the world and the uniqueness of all of its forms. We feel a deep and abiding affection for the physical." Chambers also draws out a description of suspended action from the *Protovangelium of James*, an apocryphal gospel, describing that same vision as it is produced through great paintings. Jack Chambers, "Perceptualism, painting and cinema," *Art and Artists* 7:9 (December 1972), 29-33.

By its tripartite structure, *Circle* takes on the form of the haiku, the intimacy and creative control of its prologue joined to the social and heterodox assembly of its conclusion. These oppositional sequences are bridged by the cutting word, the backyard, the perspective from which the Chambers family perceives nature and the world, broadened by leisure but still insular. In spite of the difficulty of this juxtaposition, *Circle* bears the Romantic aspirations of much of Chambers' art. Chambers held Romantic notions of art even from his early development in London. Those ideals were furthered in his mastery of the figure and his studies in classical tradition, even as they were compromised and enriched by the vanguard strains that emerged elsewhere in his work. Chambers was never so concerned with the past as to be struck blind to the powers of modern movements, so deeply marked were his silver paintings by stylistic resonances with Neo-Dada, and his abstract landscapes by the formal strategies of Abstract Expressionism. But an essential, immutable Romanticism was present in the memorial gesture of so much of his work, in the attempt to reconcile his life with his environment and its history. Romantic ideals made strange company with modern impulses. Chambers' dedication to the glories of perception, and to discovering the universal in the particular, may at a glance cast him against aesthetic difficulty. For so many modern artists, difficulty was a series of faults and fractures that collapsed aged notions of man reconciled with his emotions and environment, a conciliation that was impossible in the modern age. Romantic idealism would not gather up the talismanic depths of dense modern allusion or the modal enclosures of modern aesthetics. And yet, that idealism, which for Chambers takes its final form in the philosophy of Perceptual Realism, was, in his last films, corresponding with his most allusive and tactical difficulties. His strategies of compositional and editorial fragmentation, jarringly contradictory visual conceits, and the mythic implications of the everyday, advanced a London-centric universe that could simultaneously affirm and subvert itself. From that ambiguous vantage point, Chambers could translate his life, a spiritual and poetic quest for meaning, into work that concurrently held ready and complex meanings, drawing on the difficulties of modern perception.

When Jack Chambers left London in 1953, it was provincial, far from paradise. By the early 1960s, a newfound liveliness and radicalism in the art scene made it possible for him to return to the city, but it was the resonances of childhood memories that compelled him to stay. Those visions of his youth "gesturing in the invisible," implicated his past in his present and future, his permanent return fated. In his early films, Chambers rediscovered London as paradise. It was not an ideal paradise of justice and love, but a compromised paradise where a natural order, in the lifecycle and the circulation of the year, rigidly governed over all things. Spectres of violence and a mastery of man over man were cast far from London but their menace resonated there, and against that the Chambers films pose family, community and creative action. With his next and final film, Jack Chambers would further enclose the distance between province and paradise.

Michael Snow in **Peggy's Blue Skylight** *[Film Still]*
Joyce Wieland, 1964/1986
16mm film, 12 minutes, black and white, sound
Courtesy of CFMDC

CHAPTER TWO

Michael Snow: Signs and Silhouettes

Michael Snow was born in Toronto in 1928, the son of an Anglophone father, a civil engineer and surveyor, and a Francophone mother who loved languages and music. Raised between English- and French-Canadian societies, Snow's dual heritage formed the bulk of his cultural experience, and was complemented by a fascination with the senses. His father's partial and later total blindness, arising from a workplace accident, stimulated Snow's interest in vision, and his mother's attraction to language would similarly guide his passion for sound and music. In Snow's own words, "the two most important things in my life were that my father went blind when I was 15, and that my mother loved music."[1] In his youth, Snow took up painting, drawing, writing and music, but even then he did not cast rigid divides between these pursuits, allowing the activity of one to inform another. An interdisciplinary sensibility is evident in the early painting *Jazz Band* (1947), a bizarre and elastic depiction of a septet in which the environment, figures and instruments share a common plasmaticness.[2]

As the son of an affluent family, Snow attended the prestigious Upper Canada College and afterward pursued a formal art education at the Ontario College of Art (OCA). His studies there had emphasized design, but with a Bauhaus model of interdisciplinary foundations, by which the curriculum guided him toward painting and sculpture. Snow shared his paintings with his teacher, John Martin, who encouraged him to read the books of artists' writings issuing in the Documents in Modern Art series, edited by Robert Motherwell and published by George Wittenborn. Through this, he came to study the work of Paul Klee, who would become a major influence on his development as an artist.[3] His most pronounced

---

[1] Manny Farber, "The Arts: Farewell to a Lady," *Time* (Canadian Edition), 24 January 1969, 17.

[2] In much of the work that immediately followed, Snow used jazz, as improvisation and liberation, as a subject or to inform structure. Later, his work would involve free jazz musicians such as Albert Ayler and Roswell Rudd, and he would be a founding member of the improvisatory Canadian Creative Music Collective, or CCMC.

[3] Joe Medjuck, "The Life & Times of Michael Snow," *Take One* 3:3 (January-February 1971,

debts to Klee were in works such as his *Wall Panel* series (1951–52) and *Still Life: Red Goblet* (1952), in which geometric forms, distorted from perfection by pliable lines, are dissected, fitted together, in a style recalling Klee's work in the Bauhaus period, for example, *Red/Green Architecture (yellow/violet gradation)* (1922). In Snow's paintings from the mid–1950s, the application and density of paint, pronouncement of line, billowing of forms, evident in works such as *Reclining Figure* (1955), recall Klee's mystical-abstractionist work of the 1910s; and the line, naïve figuration and frontal portraiture of *Georgine* (1954) and *Colin Curd About to Play* (1953), in which faces are rendered with features tilting across a round plane that comes to a pointed chin, have debts to Klee's portraits and figuration, such as *Senecio* (1922), in which a human face is assembled out of gradating and bounded colour contrasts, the face subdivided by a series of curvilinear forms and ninety-degree angles.[4]

Shortly after completing his studies at OCA, Snow undertook travel throughout Europe, which exposed him to both the historical roots and modern vanguard in painting. This early immersion would inform his later decision to shift away from the business of graphic design and toward the calling of art. After his return to Toronto, Snow was hired by the firm Graphic Associates, an independent animation company founded by former NFB animators Jim McKay and George Dunning. His first Toronto show of drawings at Hart House in 1955 had impressed Dunning, who had brought him on board the fledgling company.[5] Graphic Associates would ultimately disband in 1957, but for the short time it was in operation, the company had a lively staff of artists such as Warren Collins, Graham Coughtry, Bob Cowan, and Snow's future wife, peer and collaborator Joyce Wieland. At Graphic, Snow would make his first film, *A to Z* (1956). Snow described the film as a "cross-hatched animated fantasy about nocturnal furniture love. Two chairs fuck." The film holds a tenuous relationship to his later films and art, coming as it does almost a full decade before his next finished film, but it does bear relation to his work in other media at the time, for instance, the pliable, elastic forms of the dinner set; the comedy of personified action, the furniture anthropomorphized into ecstasy; and the rhythm of those ecstatic motions, their punctuations, in continuity with visual music films, such as Norman McLaren's contemporaneous *Blinkity*

---

published April 1972), 7.

[4] These debts would carry on in Snow's other figurative paintings in this period, such as *On the Hero Myth* (1955) and *Young Girl* (1955).

[5] In a show of Canada's puritan, anti-modern sensitivities, Nathan Phillips, then-Mayor of Toronto, demanded that those same drawings be removed, deeming them "offensive." This incident is elaborated in David Kilgour, *A Strange Elation: Hart House, the First Eighty Years* (Toronto: University of Toronto Press, 1999), 57.

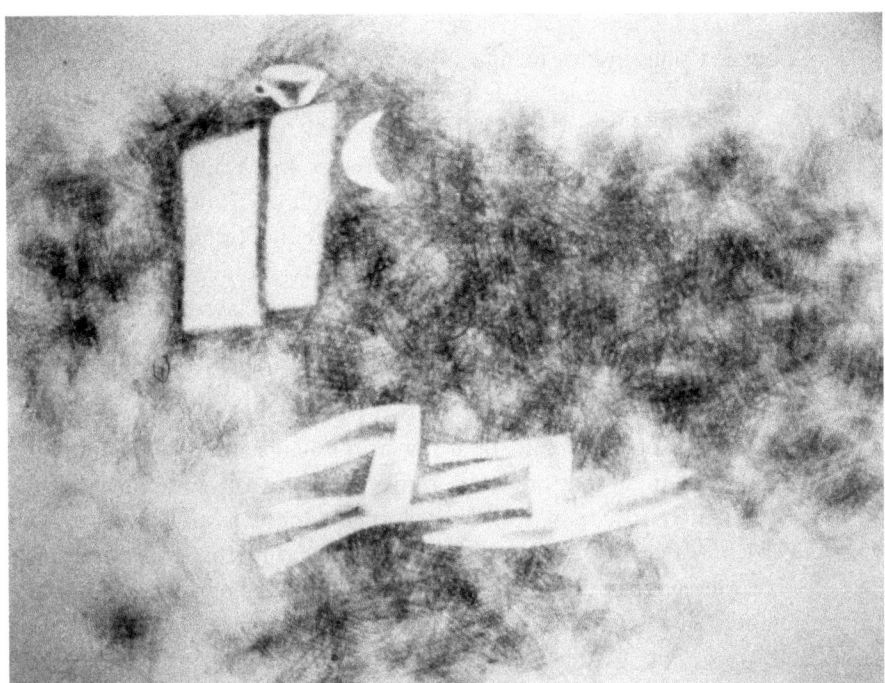

A to Z *[Film Still]*, 1956
16mm film, 7 minutes, colour, silent
Courtesy of Michael Snow

Blank (1955), which shared Snow's rhythmic affinities for modern jazz, though little else. The choice of subject mirrors Snow's contemporaneous painting *Table and Chairs No. 1* (1956), in which the overlapping silhouettes of a table and two chairs make a stark, flat, black form against a red background, painted in visible strokes showing through to a black base. In its spatial execution, *Table and Chairs No. 1* is unlike *A to Z*; in the latter, blue ink cross-hatching and depicted action gives the subjects a dimensionality that is absent in the former. The film also demonstrated Snow's transgressive comic sensibility, descended from the absurd shocks of Dada, which would become an enduring mark of his style.

Snow's involvement in improvised music began in his teenage years and by the late 1940s had developed into a vocation. From 1948 to 1950, Snow spent several weeks each summer in Chicago, serving as an informal pupil to the boogie-woogie pianist Jimmy Yancey and jamming with, among others, Cootie Williams, Buck Clayton and Pee Wee Russell. Yancey would serve as a key influence on Snow's aesthetic sensibilities in general, for his sense of vamps, motifs, and wild, mechanized action.[6] Years later, while at Graphic, Snow would divide his time, off the job, between painting, drawing and performing as a pianist in Toronto's traditional jazz ensembles such as Ken Dean's Hot Seven and later, after Graphic dissolved, the Mike White Imperial Jazz Band. But Graphic also provided Snow with an early exposure to film, a medium that would become increasingly central to his work through the 1960s. In addition to *A to Z*, Snow made a number of short films in collaboration with Graphic coworkers Joyce Wieland, Graham Coughtry, Warren Collins and others: *Tea in the Afternoon, A Salt in the Park, Assault on Grenville Street* and *Hamlet*.[7]

In September 1956, Snow and Wieland married in a small civil ceremony at Toronto City Hall.[8] In coming years, the couple would at times exhibit their work together in two-person shows, both channeling Dada in their approaches to painting and collage, their work ultimately diverging as their styles became more determinedly individual. When in subsequent years Snow would develop statements about his activity as a painter, his ideas were pitched between radical aesthetic gesture and a deep knowledge of commercial design, both under the influence of Dada and situated in an awareness of the implications of insignia and signature. In Snow's thought, formal radicalism and commercial branding could correspond; in the late 1950s, his painting was becoming increasingly radical, while his 'day job' kept his attention on commercial design. As the films of Graphic's staff demonstrate, this workplace was another venue for joyous expression. As Snow had found peers and companions at Graphic and was fostering some of his experience in the practical manifestations of commercial art, he maintained a serious commitment to his work as a painter, and was building his reputation in the Toronto art scene. To that end, he joined the original group of artists represented by the Isaacs Gallery in 1956.

Av Isaacs had grown up in Winnipeg, Manitoba, the heartland of Canadian red politics. It was perhaps that exposure to class and labour politics that had led him to study Political Science and Economics at University of Toronto. Isaacs began a framing and art supply business in 1950, and soon his shop would become a commercial gallery specializing

[6] Michael Snow, "Michael Snow Musics for Piano, Whistling, Microphone and Tape Recorder, 1975," in Louise Dompierre (ed.), *The Collected Writings of Michael Snow* (Waterloo: Wilfred Laurier Press, 1994), 175.

[7] The dates on these films are a matter of some speculation. An illuminating account is provided in Iris Nowell's *Joyce Wieland: A Life in Art* (Erin, Ont.: Porcupine's Quill, 2001), which describes their content and rightly positions Warren Collins as the instigator of these collaborations; however, Nowell's dates for the production of the films and the closure of Graphic Associates are not reliable.

[8] Jane Lind, *Joyce Wieland: Artist on Fire* (Toronto: Lorimer, 2001), 103.

in modern art. He proved to be a champion of new and difficult forms as he gathered his first stable of artists—Snow, Graham Coughtry, William Ronald, Gerald Scott and Robert Varvarande—later expanded to include Wieland, Chambers, Robert Markle, Gordon Rayner and Tony Urquhart, among others. Isaacs' role went beyond sales and representation, as his gallery became a focal point in the local and national modern art communities, hosting poetry readings, concerts and groundbreaking shows.[9] Between the Isaacs Gallery, its neighbor the Cameron Gallery, and the Librairie Française, the Gerrard Street Village bookstore of Dada scholar Michel Sanouillet, a generation of Toronto artists would receive an informal education in the styles of late modernism and would build platforms for their own radical practices.[10] Michel Sanouillet would serve as a central guide to the Dada movement and a champion of its resurgence among painters in New York, Paris and Toronto. A leading expert on the original Dada movement of 1916 to 1924 and a friend to Marcel Duchamp, Sanouillet had published the first collection of Duchamp's writings in 1959, *Marchand du sel* (Paris: Le Terrain Vague), and had, through his years in Toronto, engaged young artists in that movement, many of them members of the roster of the Isaacs Gallery, their own work already emerging from a mix of the comic, lively, dissatisfied and uncertain vicissitudes of modern life in a mode of perceptual challenge and distress.

With the closure of Graphic Associates in 1957, Snow focused on his painting full time. Both he and Wieland had begun to move in the direction of Neo-Dada. Snow's work no longer bore an obvious debt to Klee. It became increasingly abstract, still painterly but rough-hewn, using cardboard and plywood in lieu of canvas. He began to make sculptural works such as *Colour Booth* (1959), a standing corner, narrow, ninety-degrees at its base, dark blue with yellow bands painted vertically from its midpoint up, recalling the zips of Barnett Newman's zip paintings. In 1959,

---

[9] The Isaacs Gallery had a public program of artists' films in February 1964. Participating artists included Snow, Wieland, Bob Cowan, Graham Coughtry, Louis de Niverville, Arthur Lipsett, Al Sens, George Gingras, Carlos Machiori and George Dunning, a mix of artists working in late modern idioms and career filmmakers working within the institutional mechanisms of the National Film Board and the CBC. Where Wieland, Snow and Coughtry represented the former, Machiori, Sens, Dunning and Lipsett represented the latter, with figures like underground filmmaker Cowan falling somewhere in between.

[10] This community originated in the Gerrard Street Village which had developed in the mid-1950s, a Toronto cousin of New York's Greenwich Village, which would stand as the centre of the city's avant-garde jazz, art and poetry movements through to the late 1950s when an expansion of Toronto General Hospital annexed the village. Isaacs started his first gallery here in 1955 as the Greenwich Gallery. For further discussion, see Stuart Robert Henderson, *Making the Scene: Yorkville and Hip Toronto in the 1960s* (Toronto: University of Toronto Press, 2011).

Snow's use of geometric forms and space showed the influence of abstract expressionists such as Newman and Robert Motherwell, with firm geometry, often in the form of paper collage, serving as fixed forms under spontaneous brushstrokes. Snow's work dealt increasingly in the relation between paint and other materials, integrating paper collage and adhesive tape. In Snow's painting *Two* (1960), linear form, present in the impression of a rectangle, is revealed by a loose application of paint, strokes moving outward from the rectangular stencil, forming an oblong circle. The Klee influence remained, but the work that Snow would develop through 1960 would emphasize the demarcation of the frame, a self-consciousness of painterly activity and obscure programme, evident in *Green in Green*, *Years* and *Lac Clair* (all 1960).

Of these works, *Lac Clair* was a breakthrough achievement, a dense, pale blue painting composed in pronounced brushstrokes, flowing on a slight curve. There is no other guide to its orientation within the image, as adhesive tape runs in a repeating pattern from each corner, demarcating the frame and placed in such a way as to give the work a rigid symmetry.[11] At the same time that his painting became abstract, Snow was honing his relation to realism and the photograph. This is most evident in *Drawn Out* (1959), a work of twenty-two charcoal-on-paper drawings, based on a diptych photograph of a murderer and his victim taken from an old newspaper. Twenty-one of these illustrations are portraits of the murderer Alan James Grierson, each one marked by absences, partially filled silhouettes, including and excluding features such as his nose, eyes and mouth. Each illustration was in a markedly different style. In the first image, Grierson is rendered by the conventional expectations of realism, his visage resembling the source photograph, and likewise, in the final image, his victim Molly Brown is rendered realistically. She is never subject to these variations that turn the photograph into a series of changing impressions, reassembling Grierson's face in pieces to mirror his compromised humanity. This is not mere gradation through the features of Grierson but

---

[11] It is also worth noting another relation between *Lac Clair* and one trait found in allusive abstractionist painting: the title is programmatic, suggesting a subject. Many of Snow's other titles of the period had not been so much suggestive as indicative of formal construction (for example, *Blue and Purple Drawing*, *Painting Un-Foldage*, *Between*, *Title*). By 1960, programme in the form of allusive titling had clarified the relation of Snow's painting to exterior experience, for instance, showing debts to jazz, with *Green in Green* (1960), an abstract description of colour relation within the work but also an allusion to Bill Evans's composition "Blue in Green" from Miles Davis's album *Kind of Blue* (Columbia, 1959); and Snow's *Blue Monk*, its title taken from a Thelonious Monk composition first recorded for the album *Thelonious Monk Trio* (Prestige, 1954). Snow's allusions did not begin and end with jazz; consider the literary debt of *Notes from the Underground* (1959) to Dostoyevsky, or the historical debts of *Petrograd 1917* (1958), an allusion to the February Revolution.

a catalogue of recognizable styles of art and portraiture. They bear marks of primitive and naïve movements, of Cubism, Surrealism and Dada, one in cross-hatching, another in a style that recalls bas-relief. Some bear the boundaries of the frame while others allow the face to dissipate into the paper. These variations recall Pablo Picasso's 1957 suite of variations on Velázquez's *Las Meninas*. Even by its grave nature, the work took on the form of play, punning on Grierson's face, but also bearing an earnest rumination on photographic accuracy and truth.

From December 20, 1961 to January 9, 1962, the artist Richard Gorman held a show of local manifestations of Neo-Dada at the Isaacs Gallery, featuring work by Gorman, Snow, Wieland, Curnoe, Rayner, Dennis Burton and Arthur Coughtry (Graham Coughtry's brother).[12] This would prove one of the rare group shows to announce the presence of a Canadian Neo-Dada. Michel Sanouillet wrote that this show indicated "a healthy reaction against a lethal form of stuffy conservatism which has pervaded most of this country's artistic circles."[13] While Neo-Dada thought and expression is inextricable from Snow at all stages of his art from 1957 onward, and the legacy of Dada informs so much of his aesthetic philosophy, by the winter of 1961, his work had already begun to depart from the dominant aesthetics of that movement. He would confront realism and representation, adopting an inclusive attitude toward form and content, and that inclusiveness would become a dominant characteristic in his mature work.[14]

Snow wrote poems and texts sparingly, but one early text, "Title or Heading" (1961), served as a free form statement of his ideas about art that included aphorisms, descriptive expressions and lists of influences from Gustave Flaubert to Art Blakey. It was an inventory, a mode of speech, rife with enclosures and allusions, a declaration of art as "Difficult Entertainment," and it began with a statement of Snow's process that would declare the most enduring and difficult character of his work: "I make up the rules of a game, then I attempt to play it. / If I seem to be

---

[12] Donnalu Wigmore, *Isaacs Seen* (Toronto: University of Toronto Hart House, 2005), 158.

[13] Michel Sanouillet, "The Sign of Dada," *Canadian Art* 78 (March/April 1962), 111.

[14] The notion that Snow's work is inclusive of various forms comes first from Snow himself, in "A Lot of Near Mrs.", in which he writes: "My work is inclusive not exclusive, puppetry, choreography. I'm not so interested in making a lot of paintings, sculpture etc. as finding out what happens when you do such and such a thing" (18); but to speak of this as an inclusive aesthetic that simultaneously endorses realism and abstraction comes from R. Bruce Elder's writings on *New York Eye and Ear Control* in *Image and Identity: Reflections on Canadian Film and Culture* (Waterloo: Wilfred Laurier Press, 1989). Inclusivity is one of the central modal difficulties of Snow's work, which arrives at a time when so much modern and postmodern art demands that artists and critics take sides between oppositional and ideologically exclusive manifestations of form and content.

losing I change the rules."[15] These ideas of difficult entertainment and the flexible game would achieve most vivid application as Snow began, in subsequent years, to develop films and happenings, work that could play out in time and that would take as the variables of its games perspectival enigmas, clarity of forms and visual and verbal puns. Snow's relation to punning, mass culture and modal tension (between artwork, perception and context) would evolve his work further, away from painterly abstraction and toward the reproducible gesture of postmodernity, toward the self-conscious manufacture and repetition of the icon.

In late 1960, Michael Snow developed what would become the enduring sign of his work through the 1960s, a cardboard figure in the shape of a woman mid-stride. He would later write that this resulted after several years of "worrying about where the figure is or could be or would be."[16] The Walking Woman, as he would call it, was first cut from cardboard, creating a positive-negative stencil that Snow would use to initially reproduce the work, and as a model for later stencil reproductions of varying scale. The figure's contours would remain fixed, or else, elasticized in a consistent way, but it was cast on many surfaces, on paper, wood, canvas, cardboard, even a car door; and in many media, including acrylic, enamel, ink, spray and oil paints. It was a symbol synonymous with Snow and yet anonymous, an icon of marketing, manufacturing, commercial culture, and was itself aware of these traits, assuming a semi-ironic presence within that culture.[17] It was also an expression of pure form, a stylized silhouette that could be repurposed, a mark of continuity in varied styles and environments, to exhaustion. Snow would cast it unsigned on lampposts, subways, buildings, and it became his signature, or as he would pun, his

---

[15] Michael Snow, "Title or Heading," (1961) reprinted in *The Collected Writings of Michael Snow* (Waterloo: Wilfred Laurier Press, 1994), 13.

[16] Michael Snow, "A Lot of Near Mrs." (1963) reprinted in *The Collected Writings of Michael Snow* (Waterloo: Wilfred Laurier Press, 1994), 19.

[17] The complexity of the Walking Woman, as a sign caught between marketplace and aesthetic radicalism, and its ultimate implications, recalls Donald Kuspit's discussion of Pop Art's devotion to the empty signifier and to the ideology of capitalism, as well as the way in which Andy Warhol and Jasper Johns used repetitions of mass images, the celebrity portrait and the American flag respectively. The Walking Woman works parallel the Pop Art movement, and they are the next evolution in Snow's art, in continuity with his Neo-Dada and abstractionist periods. They assume some similarity with both Warhol's and Johns' acts of repetition in ideology, or at least inasmuch as they resist the social commentary that might be assigned to them by critics and audiences who search for inherent comment, rather than form, within the works. Such works are a declaration, not that anything can be art, but that art need not have its meaning dictated by anything beyond its own values; that beyond its formal values, a work might contain thematic ambiguities that could not be resolved with any certainty in surrounding discourse. This is especially true of Walking Woman works of 1964, dealing explicitly in perspectival distortions, such as *Hawaii* and *Five Girl-Panels*.

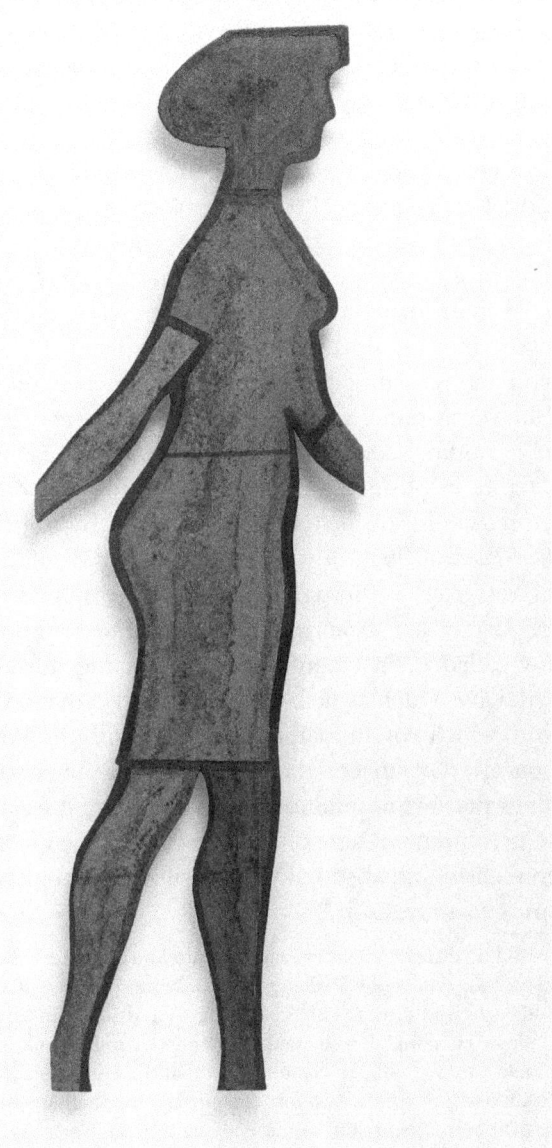

Spring Sign, 1961
oil, weathered on plywood, 155 x 49 x 3.5 cm, 61 x 19 5/16 x 1 3/8 inches
Art Gallery of Ontario, Gift of Norcean Energy Resources Limited, 1986
(86/54)
Reproduced by permission of Michael Snow

"trademark." This lost art, like much of the Walking Woman work, was rooted in the Dada gesture, continuing from the found objects that Marcel Duchamp had exhibited in New York forty-five years earlier. The Walking Woman would serve as witness to and central object in a continuous evolution in Snow's art from 1961 until 1967. The presence of the figure allowed Snow to challenge any expectations an audience might bring to his work as regards realism, figuration and classical perspective. For example, in the distortion of *Touched Woman* (1961), in which the figure is fragmented by paper folds; *Forty Drawings* (1961), one of several works in which repetitions of the figure reveal anamorphic distortions and variations, following in the line of *Drawn Out*; the painting *61-62* (1962), in which a pair of Walking Woman forms are then filled by colour differentiations that divide the figure into an abstract composition, departing from the figurative dimension and returning to Snow's Klee influence; the figure is slowly realized in the seven-panel sequence of *Clothed Woman (In Memory of My Father)* (1963); another sequential work of the same year, *Olympia* (1963), renders the figure in positive and negative stencil, in photographic detail and in styles recalling Pop or the Neo-Classical. By the time that Snow made *Five Girl-Panels* (1964), in which the Walking Woman is repeated on five canvases, distorted as through a funhouse mirror, by width and height and angle, the figure had been realized in painting, sculpture and as 'lost art', as Snow called it, in environmental stenciling throughout Toronto and New York City. Much as Jack Chambers had come to see the figure as "an object into which you unload experience," with the Walking Woman, Snow had conceived of an icon that could serve as the prison-house of art, a series of lines that were simultaneously limiting and freeing, and a path toward a greater understanding of the relation between form and content, and between realism and abstraction. The silhouette could suggest realism and yet, as pure form, resist it.[18]

---

[18] In Snow's period of transitioning between Toronto and New York, he began to write a statement to clarify aspects of the Walking Woman works that he felt were being misunderstood by audiences and critics. This statement, "A Lot of Near Mrs.", continued the punning of "Title or Heading" but focused on matters of representation and meaning. It was more combative than "Title or Heading," in that the earlier piece was posed to declare certain forms and sources, its own form of punning resonating with Snow's painting, and announcing the comic sensibility of the Walking Woman works. With "A Lot of Near Mrs." Snow was less concerned with playful declaration than with introducing critics and audiences to the potential meanings of a significant and focused body of recent work, to disabuse them of interpretations he believed to be incorrect or reductive, and to declare his movement across media. The resulting text offers expository statements, still often punning, that gave considerable insight into Snow's use of the figure and his relation to real things. Perhaps the most definite statement in the text is this: "My subject is not women or a woman but the first cardboard cutout of W.W. I made." This is an explication of his distinction between form and content, and of his rendering of the Walking Woman as icon rather than

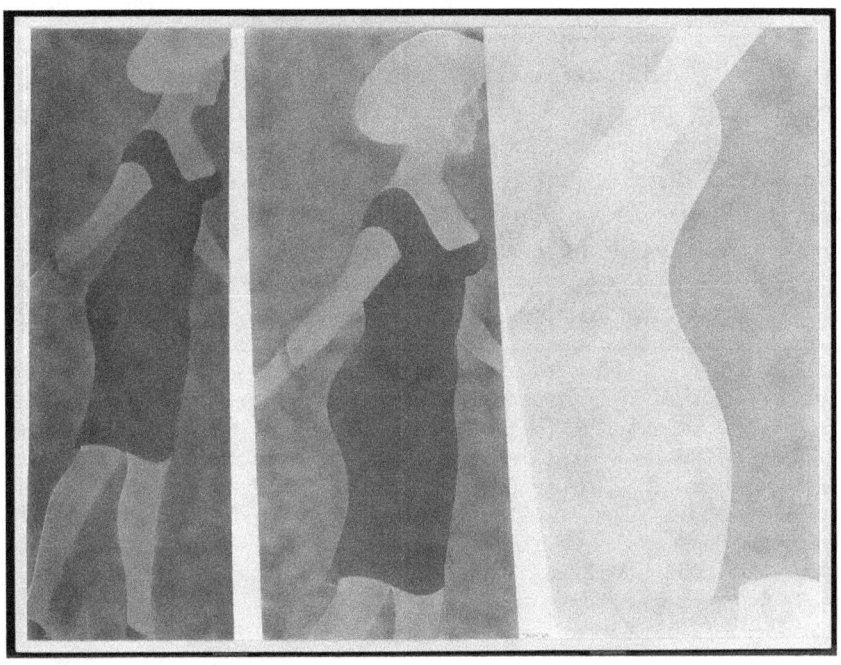

Test Focus Field Figure, 1965
spray enamel on canvas, 152.4 x 203.2 cm, 60 x 80 inches
Art Gallery of Ontario, Purchase, Corporations' Subscription Endowment, 1966
(66/10)
Reproduced by permission of Michael Snow

At the same time that Snow's work was moving in the direction of the Walking Woman, Snow and Wieland were planning a move to New York City. Snow would later tell Joe Medjuck that his reason for going had been "to get out of me what I hoped was there."[19] He believed that the energy of New York would draw out all dormant abilities, that it would make new things possible, an intention that mirrored the role of the Walking Woman, which was essentially an organizing principle for formal radicalism that challenged Snow to work around the parameters of the icon, and in doing so, to draw out from him and refine a total vocabulary of form.[20] Snow would later describe New York as "a sampling of everything good and bad everywhere," and there, Snow and Wieland received greater exposure to contemporary movements.[21] They would befriend others who, like them, had come under the influence of Dada and Surrealism and were wrestling with the experience of making radical art and poetry, chiefly, Jonas Mekas, Ken and Flo Jacobs, and Paul and Jo Haines, among others.[22] Soon after arriving, Snow would begin to work in film again, with *Walking Woman in New York*, a project first discussed in winter 1962 as a collaboration with filmmaker Ben Park and TV presenter Hugh Downs. Not many details are

---

stand-in. Snow reveals, in his reflections on real things, a deep debt to Marcel Duchamp, for instance, in this statement that suggests a relation between Snow's thinking on art and the *Unhappy Readymade* (1915): "Use time: outdoor exposure for one month: weather woman Jan. 1 to 31. Weather report. (...) in the process show the path of the model." On the relation between abstraction, realism and subject, he writes, "An 'abstract' shape can be sexier than a representation of a (beautiful) breast but neither are sexier than a (beautiful) breast," a claim that the purpose of art is not to supplant the experience of reality but to give rise to experience and sensation that is, in the resistance of realism, as distinct from real things as is realist representation itself.

[19] Joe Medjuck, "The Life & Times of Michael Snow," *Take One* 3:3 (January-February 1971, published April 1972), 6.

[20] In this context, the Walking Woman becomes the flexible game, a fixed form that is subject to acts of recontextualization, and that is encoded with process instructions, but despite those instructions and fluctuating contexts, the artist may spontaneously change the rules.

[21] Kay Kritzwiser, "What's So Special About New York? Ask an Artist." *Globe and Mail*, 15 April 1967, 13.

[22] The influence of Neo-Dada is common to Mekas and Jacobs, apparent in their sense of a living community and of the agency of art, to which end, of the two, Jacobs puts those ideas into practice with films such as *Little Stabs at Happiness* (1960) and *Blonde Cobra* (1963), both of which are raw in construction, improvisatory and mysterious, and defiant to order. Later, Jacobs would depart from these ideas, but the rough material awareness of these early works would stay with his films. Mekas, on the other hand, embraces the anti-art aesthetics of Dada and Fluxus as a thinker, but not as a filmmaker, as he began to advance an elegiac body of work in the resonances of Romanticism. Of all of Snow and Wieland's friends in New York, it was the poet and sound engineer Paul Haines whose work most strongly resonated with Neo-Dada, by its fragmentary construction, its cooption of idioms and images out of everyday experience, surreally recapitulating the everyday into foreign syntax and minimal expression.

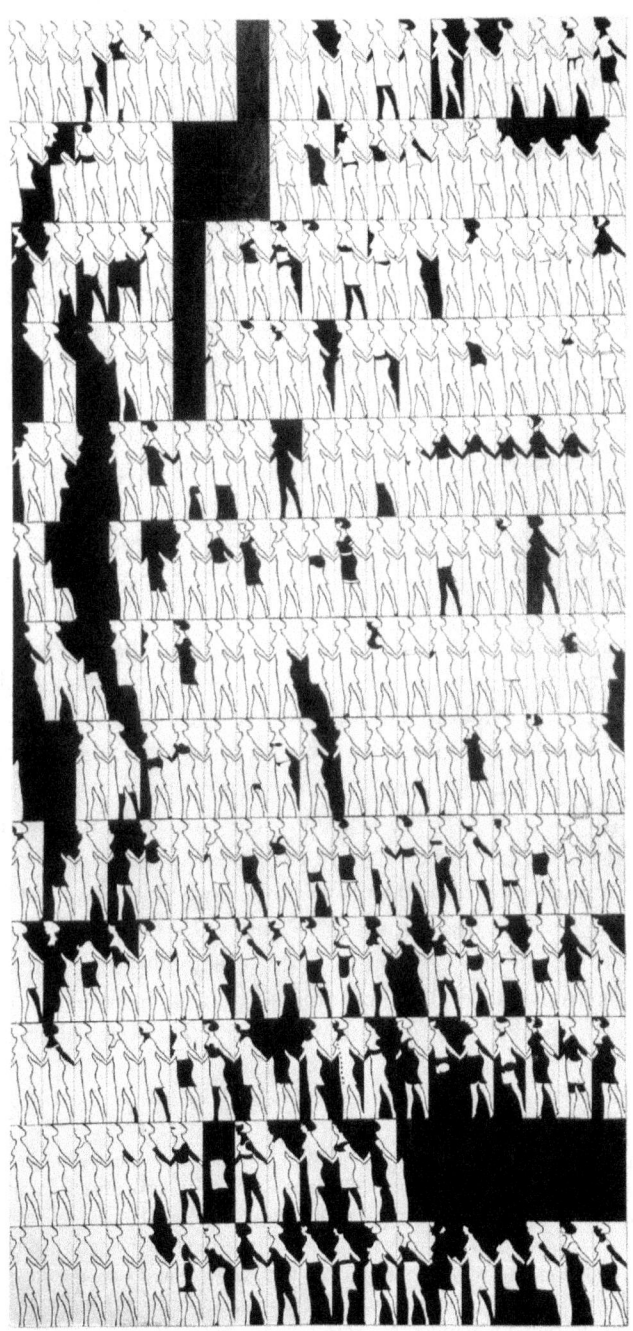

Encyclopedia, 1965
ink on printed reproductions, 245.1 x 118.1 cm, 96.5 x 46.5 inches
Art Gallery of Ontario
Courtesy of Michael Snow

known of the film's content, but Marcel Duchamp, to whom Snow and Wieland were introduced by Michel Sanouillet, was to appear on camera. *Walking Woman in New York* was conceived for television and art house theatres, and it was to be a non-narrative film in which the Walking Woman icon was sighted around New York. Asked at the time why he wanted to get into films, Snow replied, "I don't. It's just another way of using the walking woman."[23] Although the film would never be completed, the idea of making a film that would serve as a vehicle for the Walking Woman stayed with Snow, and the process of working with film became more appealing.

Much as the Walking Woman was inspiring Snow to carry on his painting in the mode of Difficult Entertainment, it, and the influence of his and Wieland's New York social circle, was also drawing him toward underground cinema. In New York, Snow and Wieland had been exposed, via their friend and former Graphic Associates coworker Bob Cowan, to the work of George and Mike Kuchar, twin brothers whose underground films such as *The Pervert* (1963) and *Sins of the Fleshapoids* (1965) parodied melodrama and established the camp aesthetic. They were also exposed to the films of Jack Smith, specifically *Flaming Creatures* (1963), an explicitly gay work, equal parts shocking, repellent and joyous, which was immediately seized by the police on charges of obscenity. These charges hit close to home as Snow and Wieland's friends were directly involved in this work, as exhibitors, distributors, allies and collaborators with Smith. At a screening the following year, police seized the film again, and arrested Ken Jacobs and Jonas Mekas for exhibiting it. Some strata of New York society were just as threatened by modern art as stuffy, conservative Toronto where, within a year, gallery owner Dorothy Cameron would be arrested for exhibiting Robert Markle's nude drawings. Against this climate of censorship and suppression, the films of Smith and the Kuchars represented freedom, and what is more, these films had made filmmaking seem a possible and worthwhile activity.[24] The film community in New York City, and

---

[23] Arnold Rockman, "Same Woman, But In All Shapes and Sizes." *Toronto Star*, 6 July 1963, 26.

[24] For its liveliness and its explication of material illusion, much of the New American Cinema bore a resemblance to the Neo-Dada performance art of the era. For instance, John Cage's *Theatre Piece No. 1* (1952), a proto-Neo-Dada performance piece, brought about a confrontational experience that, in its assembly through multiple media, distinguished the work produced from the action and minds that produced it. As the Neo-Dada formed in New York City through the 1950s, it arose from the idea that art and life were distinct but connected, that existing confrontational impulses in art, even the material consciousness inherent in work that distinguished expression from meaning, was a false confrontation, that the necessary artistic gesture of the present moment was to ask Cage's question, "which is more musical: a truck passing by a factory or a truck passing by a music school?" Out of this mentality came the formation of intermedia and Fluxus, with its emphasis on performative

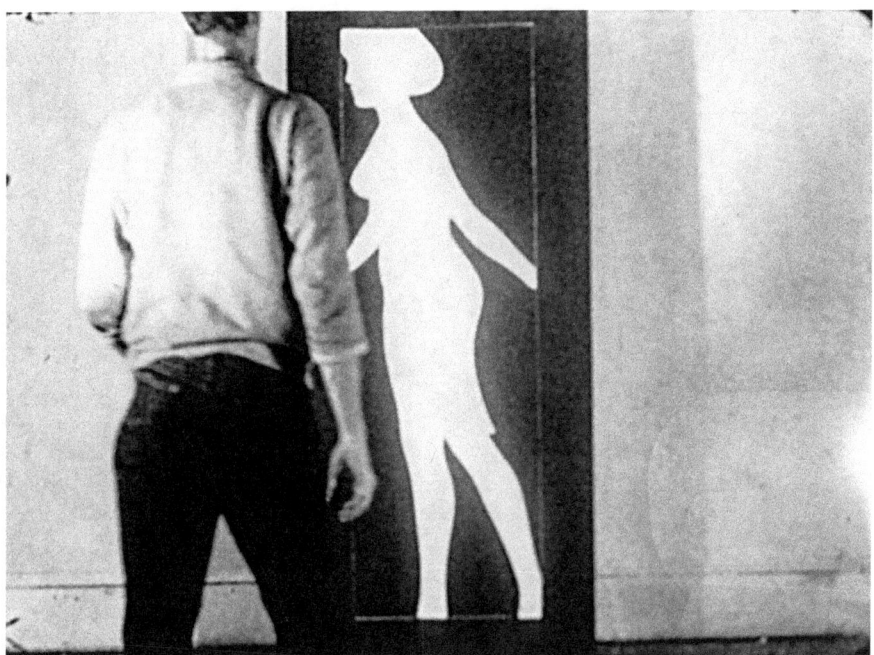

New York Eye and Ear Control *[Film Still]*, 1964
16mm film, 34 minutes, black and white, sound
Courtesy of Michael Snow

in particular this lively group of personal and satirical underground film-makers, revealed to Snow that cinema still had diverse artistic application, and that like painting and sculpture, it held unmapped territory for him to explore.

In 1964, Snow was commissioned by Ten Centuries Concerts in Toronto to make a film. That film, *New York Eye and Ear Control*, would act as a prelude to the aesthetic concerns that would dominate his filmmaking through the remainder of the 1960s. It would signal a coming change in his work, a shift away from the iconographic activities that he had pursued around the Walking Woman, and yet it would also be an essential part of the Walking Woman series. The earlier film project with Ben Park, *Walking Woman in New York*, had collapsed. By Snow's account, this was because the enthusiasm with which Park had initially approached the project had waned. Park's original ambition was to make an artistic film that

---

manifestations and happenings. For example, the happenings of Allan Kaprow emphasized spontaneous situations and audience participation. This formed the basis for the Neo-Dada of the New American Cinema as seen in the films of the Kuchar Brothers, Ken Jacobs and Jack Smith.

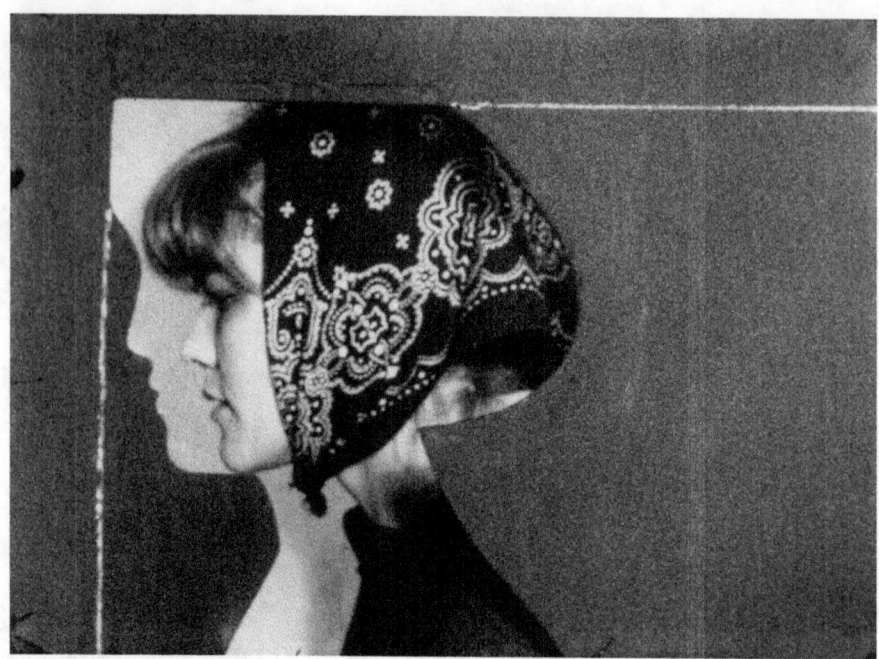

New York Eye and Ear Control *[Film Still]*, 1964
16mm film, 34 minutes, black and white, sound
Courtesy of Michael Snow

would be palatable to a television audience. *New York Eye and Ear Control*, the film that Snow would make with some of the same ideas, had elements of material self-consciousness uncommon even in avant-garde film at the time, elements that remain incompatible with the mass audience. Snow wrote of the collaboration with Park that it seemed "to concern itself with the poetry of the juxtaposition of the static and the dynamic, absence, presence, development of events for capture..." and *New York Eye and Ear Control* would be haunted by his icon accordingly, occupying compositions, sometimes announced, sometimes hidden.[25]

If *Walking Woman in New York* had been posed around the loose narrative structure of a day-in-the-life of the icon, that mission continued in *New York Eye and Ear Control*. The Walking Woman travels from rustic, natural settings, shorelines and woodlands, to the city, largely empty in early morning. The icon is insinuated into nature, on beaches and in forests, alternately stood upright and laid flat on the ground, obscured in trees, stood among rocks on the shore, and in one witty image, stood in water

---

[25] Michael Snow, "A Lot of Near Mrs." (1963) reprinted in *The Collected Writings of Michael Snow* (Waterloo: Wilfred Laurier Press, 1994), 18.

on the shoreline, walking on water. The figure is reversible, black on one side, white on the other, mirroring the black and white of the film stock. The camera rides through a forest wildly, trees becoming abstracted by motion and speed, their original form evident in silhouettes as sun breaks through them. The camera slows as it approaches the Walking Woman in the woods, then starts again. It ends up in New York City, entering over bridges. Trumpeter Don Cherry stands on a sidewalk as a car approaches and slows. He waves to the camera, gets into the car and departs. The title is photographed in fragments of awnings and signs, broken down into individual letters. Cherry arrives at his destination, exits the car and enters an apartment. The black Walking Woman is stood in front of a series of buildings in New York. In a long shot, light and smog overtake the image in a gauzy blur. Back on the beach, the white Walking Woman is stood against rocks on the shoreline. The Walking Woman becomes a graphic form when laid flat, but when stood, becomes both graphic form and a part of the landscape, blending with her surroundings. Sand and water wash over the Walking Woman, laid on the shoreline. The white Walking Woman is set on fire and burns against an otherwise black set, burns against a background of white light, until all that remains is her ashen impression. After its day out, the icon retires to a studio, where, now in the form of a cut-out silhouette, the icon is filled by real women.[26]

Snow would describe this work as an attempt to make a film in which sound and image had equal weighting, neither one subservient to the other. The sound component of the film is a group improvisation performed by Albert Ayler (tenor saxophone), Don Cherry (trumpet), John Tchicai (alto saxophone), Roswell Rudd (trombone), Gary Peacock (bass) and Sunny Murray (drums). For this session, Ayler's trio (Ayler, Peacock and Murray) was supplemented with Cherry, strongly affiliated with Ornette Coleman's Atlantic quartets, and Tchicai and Rudd of the New York Art Quartet. Their faces also make up the penultimate sequence of the film. The band arrives in their recording space and each member is filmed in a frontal portrait. As the film ends, two figures, a black man and white woman, are seen having sex, embracing nude, in a bed with white sheets. The Walking Woman has entered reality in the literal representation of the woman. And yet, the notion and function of that icon, as

---

[26] This sequence has direct correspondence to Snow's *Carla Bley* (1965), a photo-collage portrait of the composer posed as the Walking Woman, but it also corresponds to the variations on the fill of the figure that had come through the Walking Woman works of 1963, such as *Olympia*. In the paintings, the Walking Woman silhouette is 'filled' by representations of women, stylized in the various idioms of representational painting. By contrast, the film and photograph might be taken as documentation of a direct interaction between icon and woman.

a positive-negative suggestion of form, one side black, the other white, is also present in the interplay of black and white forms, in skin tone but also in illumination and shadow, in all aspects of this final episode. This final sequence is at once image and theme, graphic form and realist form.

New York Eye and Ear Control begins with a text by the poet Paul Haines; in Snow's writings, he indicates the role of this text as an indicator of the flatness of the screen: "Start with Words. Words flat on screen which is Flat. Words don't have much visual space unless you're asked to see that."[27] The text, therefore, not by its content but by its presence, announces the role of the screen as a flat plane. The viewer is confronted by this, but indirectly, without context and without instruction to connect this idea with the rest of the film. The film invariably casts the flat form of the Walking Woman into three-dimensional space, spaces occupied by the dramatic, shifting surfaces of nature (sand, rock, forest), and the flat planes of civilization (street signs, buildings). There is little editorial mediation in what follows, as one roll leads to another, with light-struck ends bridging the sequences. The aperture changes on the same compositions, indicating that each camera roll contains several exposures of the same shots. These strategies distress the conventional realist expectations of cinema, as the camera rolls play against the artifice of film editing, and bear the marks of their material base, process and construction. As a document of Snow's artistic activity, in the context of activity with which he identified (the free jazz of this ensemble), *New York Eye and Ear Control* was profoundly difficult, alluding to his sources and his prior work, placing it in a context where parallels (between his Walking Woman activity and free jazz) were not comprehensible or immediate, and in disorienting sequence, the relation between one episode and another forged by physical editing alone and not by logical, causal transition. Snow could build perceptual puzzles in film, and extend to cinema the most difficult ends of his art, the work developing around puns, disjointed sequence and self-referentiality. The film was perceptually distressing, dense, fortified against ready interpretation, and yet, it remained as vibrant and witty as his work in other media.

When *New York Eye and Ear Control* premiered at Ten Centuries' season finale in April 1965 at the Edward Johnson Building, home to University of Toronto's Faculty of Music, it inspired a massive walkout from angry, confused patrons. A local newspaper headline read, "300 flee from far-out film."[28] The premiere in New York inspired similar hostility, with the audience throwing popcorn at the screen. Gerard Malanga,

---

[27] Michael Snow, "Around about New York Eye and Ear Control." In *The Collected Writings of Michael Snow* (Waterloo: Wilfred Laurier Press, 1994), 25.

[28] Ralph Thomas, "300 flee from far-out film." *Toronto Star*, 5 April 1965, 22.

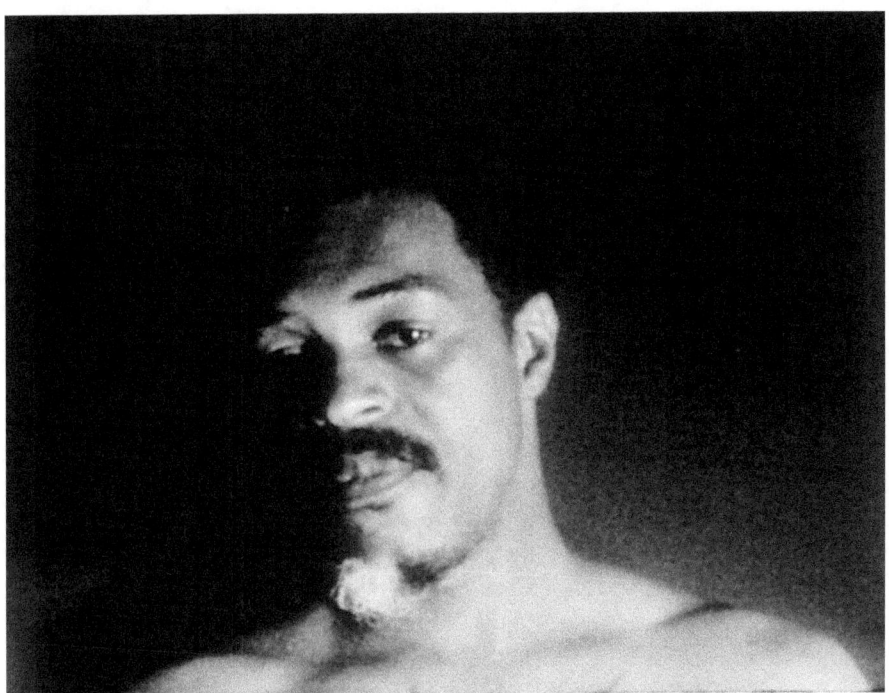

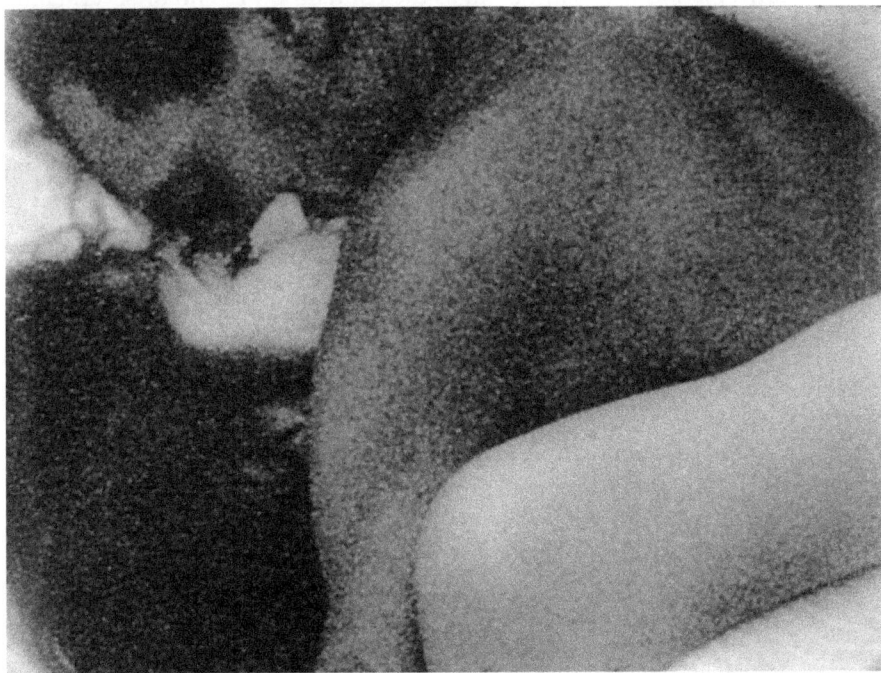

New York Eye and Ear Control *[Film Still]*, 1964
16mm film, 34 minutes, black and white, sound
Courtesy of Michael Snow

despite his enthusiasm for the film, charged that it could not have been made when Michael Snow said it was made because of its formal correspondences to Andy Warhol's *Screen Tests* series (1964–1966). While this correspondence could be taken as derivation or dismissed as coincidence, it might best be regarded as a sign of the common disposition of Snow and Warhol toward structural transparency and choice of subject, that both were essentially devoted to the repetition of the icon, but to different ends: Warhol to the emptiness of experience, Snow to the richness of forms. In a statement that Snow wrote about the film, "Around about *New York Eye and Ear Control*," it is clear that he did not see his method, what P. Adams Sitney would later name structural film, as clinical. Snow connects *New York Eye and Ear Control*, in the abstract, to the authority of experience ("James Joyce could legally pun because he had the Background [...] Who has the foreground?"); to ecstatic experience, in a long digression dealing with emotional response to art; to the Difficult Entertainment of jazz and its ascension toward freer forms; and to the classical idea of art and its aspiration toward scientific declarations of form. This connection is stated but not directed to any evidence of the film itself. It is only an impression that forms around the film. The statement reveals that the primary concern of the work is not the image as an isolated thing, or as a thing put into conversation with sound, but as the contemporary end of several lines of thinking, around race, art, authority, rhythm, presence, and the spatial and temporal relations between language, image, representation and real things.

Snow would follow *New York Eye and Ear Control* with a 3-minute 8mm film titled *Little Walk*. It was to be projected onto "a flat white cut-out screen in the shape of the Walking Woman," and consisted of "images variously fitting or overflowing the curvy contours of the feminine screen."[29] All that remains known of the film's content is its forced uniformity to a sculpted screen. His next extant film, *Short Shave* (1965), has its origins in Snow's happening *Right Reader*. In *Right Reader*, Snow sits and mouths along with a tape recording advertising an exhibition of his work; he reaches to a pile of cards on a nearby table and, one by one, holds them up in front of his face, within a suspended picture frame. While *Right Reader* commented on film language and technology (among the cards are a zoom, fades, changes of focus, etc.), *Short Shave* would adapt this premise to a different end, obstructing the representational certainties of the photographic portrait. It begins with Snow with a full beard, mysteriously shaved clean by way

---

[29] Max Knowles, "Michael Snow: A Filmography," reprinted in *The Collected Writings of Michael Snow* (Waterloo: Wilfred Laurier Press, 1994), 64. Note: Max Knowles is a pseudonym Snow took in order to write about his own films.

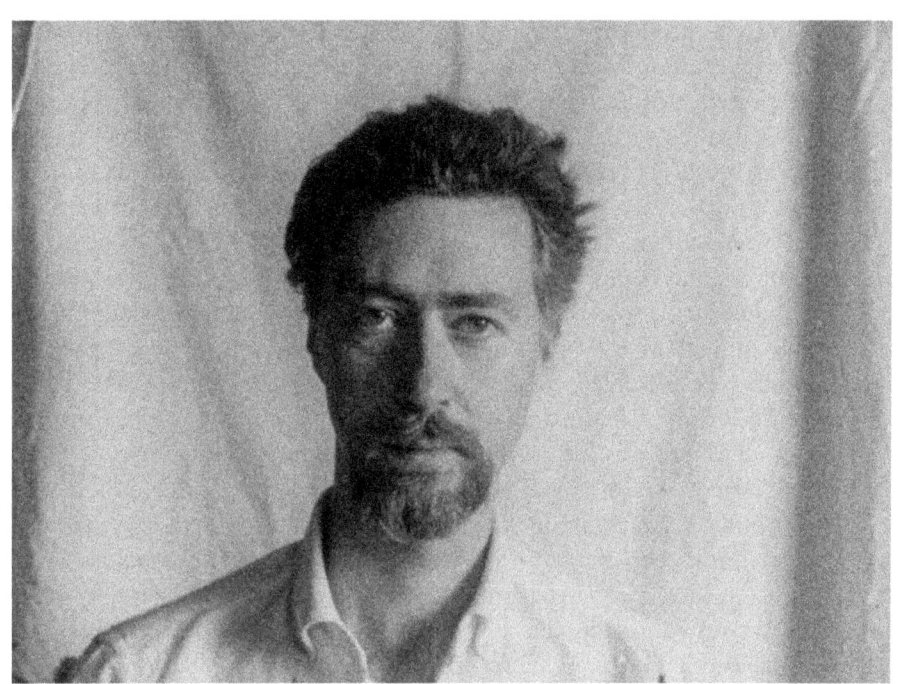

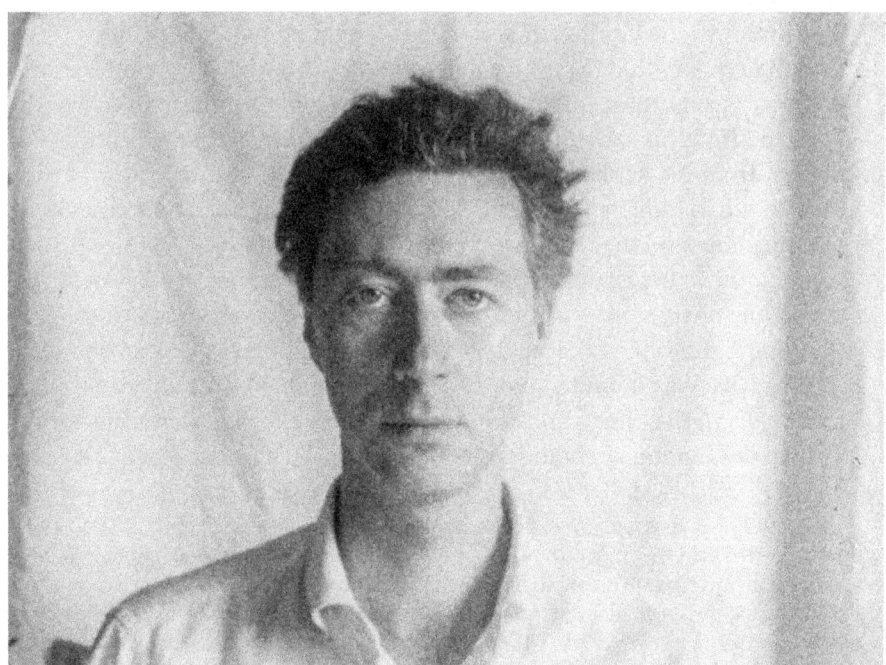

Short Shave *[Film Stills]*, 1965
16mm film, 4 minutes, black and white, sound
Courtesy of Michael Snow

of stop motion photography. Snow then conceals his face with a sheet of textured plexiglass. *Right Reader* presented aspects of self-portraiture, both in the presence of the artist on stage and in the inventory that the voice and the cards presented. With *Short Shave*, Snow produced a self-portrait in which he reveals obstacles to perception even as he uses them to transform a frontal portrait into its obtuse shadow. The parallel between *Short Shave* and *Right Reader* was definite and intentional, but *Drawn Out* (1959), Snow's series of charcoal drawings of the murderer Alan James Grierson, had also foreshadowed the work. Like that series, *Short Shave* demonstrated Snow's fascination with an essential mutability of composition. In *Drawn Out* that mutability was formal, a series of impressions of styles, while in *Short Shave*, the variations of the portrait were created by material obstructions, the former alluding to art history, the latter to material reality.

New York Eye and Ear Control and *Short Shave* directed Michael Snow's efforts toward filmmaking, but they were also direct extensions of his work in other media. As Snow had said in 1962, filmmaking itself did not interest him, but he was interested in observing the effect of creative action within various media. Filmmaking began to open up for Snow as he realized that cinema could reflect the impulses of his various activities across photography, painting, sound and sculpture, and that the material and temporal dimensions of cinema could serve as a stage for wit and punning. Snow's next film, *Wavelength* (1967), would be shot in his studio loft on Canal Street. With it, Snow established a new approach to compositional and conceptual rules, an approach that extended from his earlier work in film, and from his earliest interests in sound and vision, but which was also distinct from his work in other media. His experiments were now becoming specific to film, its material being, its temporality, the boundaries of its picture plane and the cinematographic apparatus itself.

Snow began work on *Wavelength* in December 1966. As he described it, "I set up my camera at one end of my 80-foot loft and began shooting right to the other end," a gesture effected by way of a zoom lens. The camera was mounted at a high and wide angle, surveying the space, the focal length rising from wide to telephoto, following that trajectory to its final destination, a photograph of waves on a wall.[30] The idea had come

---

[30] Kay Kritzwiser, "Artist Michael Snow Wins Prize for Movie." *Globe and Mail*, 3 January 1968, 10. The photograph of waves was also used in Snow's wave sculpture, *Atlantic* (1967), a grid of thirty images (six horizontal columns, five vertical rows) of similar photographs of waves. The variations in these images were slight, always detectable by the variations of two phenomena, the fluctuations of waves and the corresponding fluctuations of light. *Atlantic* is complementary to *Wavelength*, which deals in a similar subterfuge, a work that appears to be structured by a regimented code but which is actually host to variables (in *Wavelength*, the zoom as conceived and the zoom as executed, with all drama and material viscera included; in *Atlantic*, the grid, which by its form presumes similarity, or at least, forces a fixed form,

to Snow throughout 1966, and after considerable thought on what film could offer him, he came to the idea to make "a summation of my nervous system, religious inklings, and aesthetic ideas."[31] Eventually, he settled on this shape, the zoom and the loft, to create a work of perspectival enigma, a game piece with structural parameters and an inventory of his aesthetics. Snow would come to imagine the work as dealing with "the beauty and sadness of equivalence"; by this, he might indicate a cosmic sense of equivalence in which a series of interactions play out, between the action and the space, between the conical passage of the zoom, the frustum shape of the action and the ultimately flat canvas of the film plane and projection screen. Such interpretation of this equivalence would also resonate in the marriage of sound and image in the work, which as with *New York Eye and Ear Control*, privileged neither one nor the other. That soundtrack was an electronic sound, a sine wave, one iteration of the titular wavelength, which like the zoom passes from its lowest pitch, 50 cycles per second, to its highest, 12,000 cycles per second, through the course of the film's length. Sound and image function as glissando, raising, narrowing, a contrast to the crescendo structure of a work that passes down a plotted path.

In Snow's descriptions of *Wavelength*, he discusses the central action as being punctuated by four human events. Those events are both mundane and dramatic, and are made equivalent by the apparent ambivalence with which the zoom regards these events. A woman enters the loft with two movers, carrying a cabinet; the same woman enters again soon after with another woman; they close a window, sit together drinking coffee and talking, listen to a radio that plays the Beatles' "Strawberry Fields Forever," and then they leave; a man enters and collapses; a woman enters and phones to report the man's apparent death. These four dramatic events are divided by aesthetic events: the frame is not demarcated by any fixed parameters, but there are details that gradually vanish as the zoom slowly and subtly passes forward, for example the strip fluorescent lighting that runs along the ceiling; the four tall windows that define the composition; and the view of the outdoors that is alternately visible and invisible depending upon a given exposure. Non-human events include sudden superimpositions; solid colours appear over the composition, stripping the space down to its graphic form, the windows showing strongly and the rest of the space fading to solid, flat form; there are positive-negative inversions, light leaks and aperture shifts.

---

onto something that is wild and unpredictable, and that speaks not only to nature and the apparatus but to the interval, to time itself).

[31] Michael Snow, "A Statement on Wavelength for the Experimental Film Festival of Knokke-le-Zoute," *Film Culture* 46, reprinted in *The Collected Writings of Michael Snow* (Waterloo: Wilfred Laurier Press, 1994): 40.

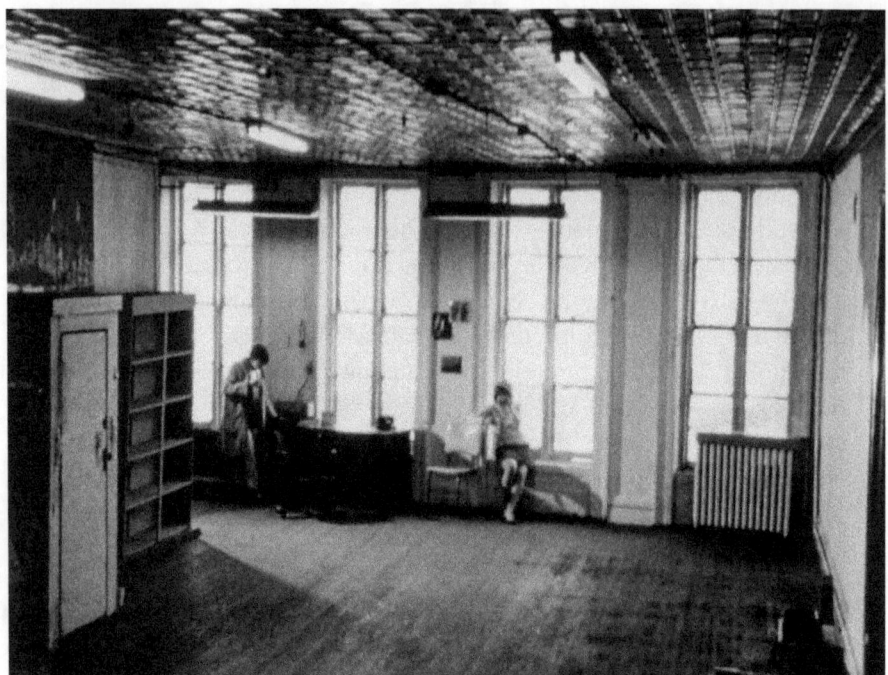

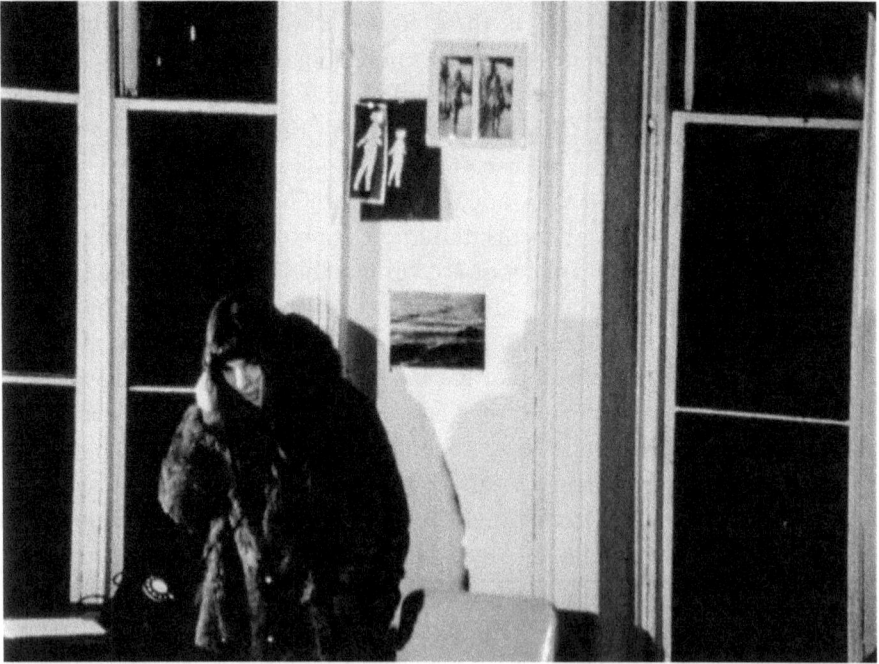

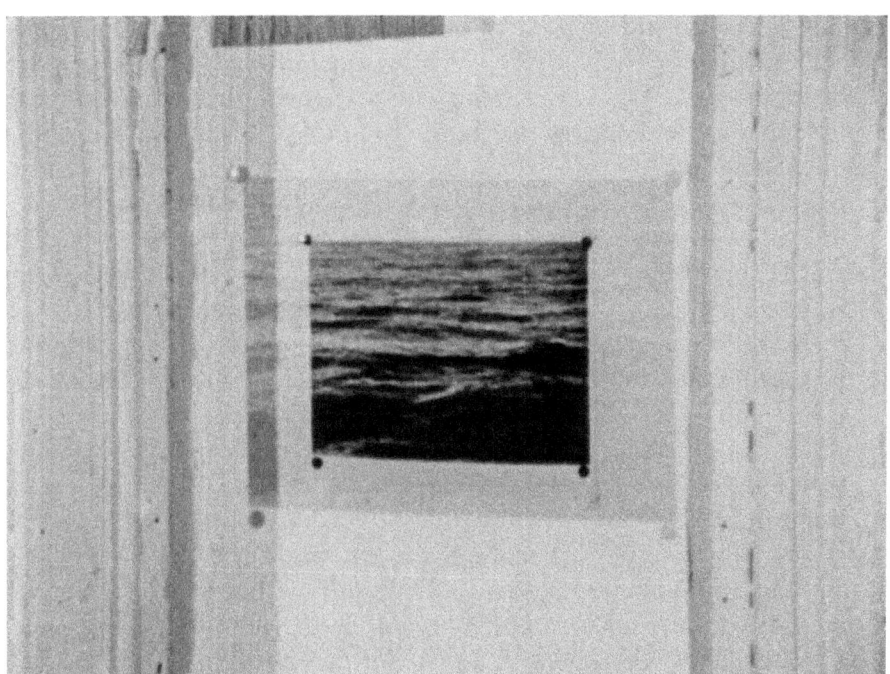

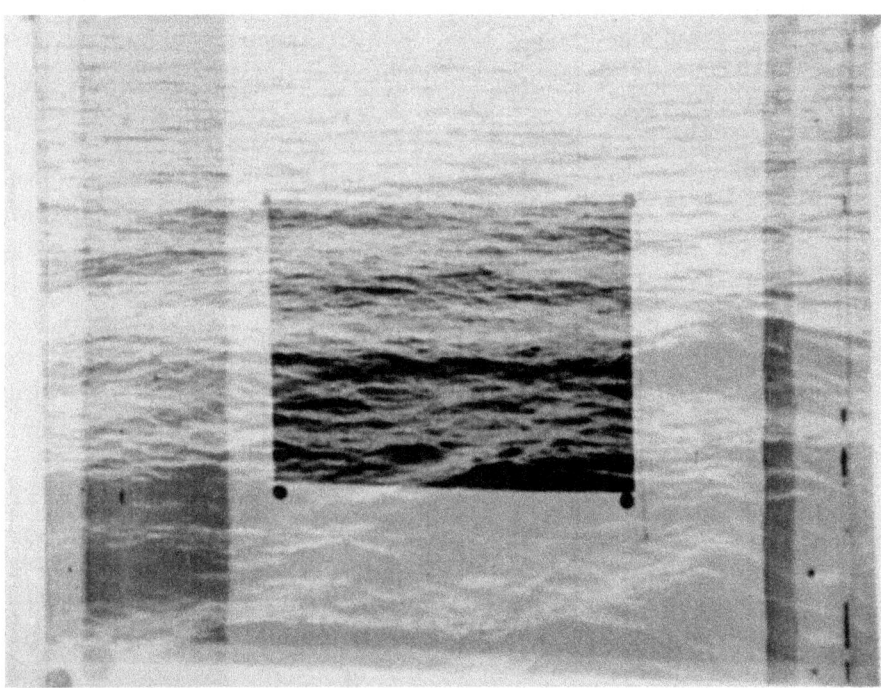

Wavelength *[Film Stills]*, 1967
16mm film, 45 minutes, colour, sound
Courtesy of Michael Snow

As the human activity culminates, roughly thirty minutes into the film, the trajectory of the zoom becomes obvious. The photograph of waves on the wall comes into focus, is exposed clearly, and the zoom extends until it overtakes the frame. Eventually, this image, like others throughout the film, is double-exposed, with still waves of another scale superimposed on the earlier wave images. *Wavelength* insists upon a structure of equivocal expressions: sound to image, space to eye, event to event, and finally, movement to stasis. Snow aimed to create a "definitive statement of pure Film space and time, a balancing of 'illusion' and 'fact'."[32] Down the barrel of his lens, *Wavelength* becomes the apotheosis of film space and time, space and time becoming plastic material into which events can be inserted, in which spatial and temporal events can echo and overlap, and where compositional values can be altered, in colour saturation, positive and negative interchange and a slow but unremitting plummet from first frame to last.

Through the period leading up to and including the Walking Woman works, Snow's expression, 'Difficult Entertainment', had seemed an all-encompassing descriptor of the late modern and postmodern modes in which he was operating. Pleasure was wrestled out of the Difficult Entertainment of modern art, but modern works were not so dense that their pleasure was entirely elusive. This was true of Snow's Abstract Expressionism-influenced paintings (contemporaneous with his statement) and of the perspectival and textural richness of the Walking Woman variations. *New York Eye and Ear Control* and *Short Shave* followed on this, in an 'entertainment' medium, and in the case of the former, the heights of its challenge were evident in the wild, hostile reactions with which it was met. If the allusive, self-conscious difficulties of modern and postmodern art constituted, in Snow's cosmology, difficult entertainment, *Wavelength* was especially particular about its difficulty. It was more dense than what had preceded it, not only in Snow's work but in avant-garde film in general, and despite its chaotic, overlapping assembly, *Wavelength* was built around a set of minimalist binaries—what is perhaps meant by Snow's use of the term 'equivalence'—that were downright alien, even to a modern audience.

This work challenges its viewer to reconsider all that they believe about the medium that they are observing, but the greater challenge of the work arrives in its connections to other media, to vision itself, and as an inventory of ideas all parcelled in one incessant, overarching gesture. The film is crowded by narrative action that may form yet another equivalence, activity to non-activity, human event to non-human event, and these actions, despite their drama, cannot redirect or interrupt the zoom. *Wavelength*

---

[32] Ibid.

could be described, in barest terms, as 'a long zoom', but Snow's ambition was to summarize, among other things, his nervous system. This is felt in *Wavelength*'s fundamental contradiction, that its content is so much richer an experience than any description can suggest; it is not reverie or reflection, nor does it, as 'a long zoom' may suggest, inflict or meditate on boredom. Rather, it is the natural extension of the energy and punning wit of Snow's paintings and writings. Here a long interval of continuous action assembles and clarifies artifice and allusion, challenging its viewer to experience a foreign nervous system, a personal aesthetic history and a spiritual mode of interrogating space that, against all of the conciliations of the film's equivalences, cannot be reconciled with the material constraints of the image.

Wavelength represented a point of departure in avant-garde film, for though there had been filmmakers working in such modes—works which would come to be called the 'structural' film and among which *Wavelength* would stand as a foundational work—the film style that Michael Snow pursued from *New York Eye and Ear Control* onward was essentially his own invention, struck between lyrical and structured composition, an interplay between the improvising mind and the rational machine. There had been far more mechanized works of 'structural' film predating Snow—the extended exercises of Andy Warhol: *Sleep* (1963), *Empire* (1964), *Blow Job* (1965)—works built around one-shot composition, emptied of meaning and human autonomy, a disavowal of the creative act of looking. Warhol's films were the paragon of visual disinterest, and in pursuing that, achieved a remarkable emptiness, emptying the world and human activity of meaning, transforming the world seen into graphic form, the world as a long wait. Warhol's films were cynical and final and above all conceptual. In Parker Tyler's words, these films "[don't] mind not being watched."[33] By contrast, Snow's films were rich with compositional and sonic enigmas, and if his experiments were long, it was because they contained the energy of labour and process (for example, in the 'camera roll' construction, marked by light leaks, of *New York Eye and Ear Control*). By means of those energies, the lens became a tool for visual construction, and the beholding eye was enchanted to look for long intervals. The experience of *Wavelength* led Snow to consider himself as a "time-light-sound poet," an artist for whom the medium of film had become primary, for its ability to encapsulate his thinking about multiple strands of perceptual experience.[34] Film would

---

[33] Parker Tyler, *Underground Film: A Critical History* (New York: Grove Press, 1969), 222. It might also be said, as a point of comparison between Snow and Warhol, that equivalence was an important act (however, of ambivalence) in Warhol's aesthetics. His *Chelsea Girls* (1966) is cast on two screens, as if to say, if you look at this, you might as well look at that.

[34] Michael Snow, "Letter from Michael Snow," *Film Culture* 46, reprinted in *The Collected*

allow these aspects, dispersed in his other work, to be gathered in tandem. It would allow him to develop new ideas about space that would cross over into his work in other media, as the density, spirituality, sensual stimuli and material consciousness of this body of work would unify it with the difficult strains found in late modern and postmodern poetry, painting, dance, sculpture and all other media and would enrich its situation in a broader context of art, rather than reduce it to a concept only relevant to cinema.

Snow would follow *Wavelength* with another long-form minimalist experiment, <—> (or, *Back and Forth*, 1968), but between *Wavelength* and *Back and Forth*, he would make another short film, *Standard Time* (1967), to serve as a sketch for the latter. The action of *Standard Time* is limited to a few changing gestures, oscillating between various directions of camera movement, bounded, reversing and repeating. As it begins, the camera pans continuously about a room in Snow and Wieland's Chambers Street loft. The camera revolves as if mounted on a turntable. There are dark corners in the room, and light changes throughout subsequent takes. There are cuts, and on each cut, the experiment restarts. The movement alternates as leftward and rightward pans, stopping one direction to move to the other. The back and forth movement of the camera is bounded by particular objects, for instance, a stereo receiver. The span is narrow and, as the pan speeds up, the movement begins to distort and obscure forms that have now become familiar. The camera returns to a continuous pan, then changes direction. There are more false starts. As the light in the room changes, darkens, the forms that are being altered by the speed of the pan change too. The left and right pans become shorter, and then the camera makes a simple pan that, through hard cuts, keeps repeating. After a cut, the camera begins to move up and down: up to Wieland on a bed, down to the legs of the tripod; up to Wieland on the phone, above to the ceiling. These gestures repeat, staggered by edits, the content changing each time. Other occupants are revealed within the home: a cat, a turtle. The turtle's appearance is a comic epiphany, a symbol of slow movement glimpsed amid these rapid, mechanized movements. Eventually the camera movement speeds between stations with enough force to abstract the subjects. The pan becomes continuous again, right to left. Wieland walks across the room. The pan moves with her and continues past her.

With *Standard Time*, Snow's interest in camera movement as a means of achieving abstraction re-emerged. The frustum passage of *Wavelength* is not so invested in abstraction; it resists the realism of its photography through colour saturation and the superimposition of various stations of that zoom, but the zoom itself is a trajectory, a slow and precise

Writings of Michael Snow (Waterloo: Wilfred Laurier Press, 1994): 43.

rendering of space, not an agent of abstraction but an agent of material self-consciousness. The nearest forerunner of optical abstraction in Snow's filmmaking was *New York Eye and Ear Control*, in which lens abstraction is created by driving through a forest, trees and sunlight spilled across the lens, forms passing at a faster rate than the lens can perceive. In *Standard Time*, speed of movement again causes abstraction, as the pan and tilt amplify, eventually switching between the bounding stations so quickly that forms come too fast to tender realist representation. As with the Walking Woman, the work introduces this action as a continuity, the pan repeating, continuing, restarting, but the construction made from this continuous action is subject to variation, and what is more, the repetition of camera movement gradually introduces subtle variations in itself, in its speed and its relation to motion blur, much as the Walking Woman variations gradually impacted on the shape and scale of the icon itself.

The panning action finds a parallel in the flipping of a radio dial, which scans through noise, half-utterances, truncated deejays, news and music. *Standard Time* could be mechanized and yet true to this aspect of visual phenomena, and this phenomenon could extend, by mechanical, automated execution, into aesthetic realms of mechanized sight that barely resembled human sight, the slow survey of the lens tracking from left to right or the tripod head craning up and down, here at speeds and consistent execution (through handling of the apparatus and through editing) impossible to the body, to the eyes, to the neck. The perceptual challenge of *Standard Time* lies not only in its relation to visual construction—its audience's vision a frail, surveying tool against the mechanized eye of the camera—but to the gesture that carries vision, to stagger and stutter, further fragmenting perception by the suggestion of a sudden turn, the redirection and repetition of action that forms a visual construction that ascends beyond our bodily experience and eyesight. *Standard Time* was a sketch for *Back and Forth*, which would take such visual constructions to a new mechanized and ecstatic extreme, and which would serve as a masterful extension of the binaries of *Wavelength*, image and sound sandwiched by human and mechanical gestures. But *Standard Time*, by its own virtue, posed these gestures, in the rough, in dialogue with a complex idea of time, its titular 'standard time', normal time, measured time, which is at once human and mechanical, fluctuating and fixed, a term of manifold, ambiguous, contradictory meanings.

Back and Forth was filmed at Fairleigh Dickinson University in Madison, New Jersey, in July 1968. Snow had been invited to attend a month-long seminar, along with a number of other artists including poet Emmett Williams, drummer and composer Max Neuhaus, painter and performance artist Allan Kaprow, sculptor Richard Serra, film and video artist Jud Yalkut and others, all of whom would appear in the film. Where *Standard Time* had established the varying tempos for pan and tilt motions that Snow would again pursue, *Back and Forth* returned to an idea of space that Snow first arrived at with the original Walking Woman cardboard cutout, the paired opposite, fitted puzzle pieces, of the stencil and its fill. Almost all of the action in the film occurs within a ground-floor classroom, the door of which opens onto a summer day. However, the film begins outside of the classroom, to the side of the building, which bears four windows, each divided into two frames, the reverse of which will become familiar to the viewer through the course of the film. A man passes, edited in staccato, and exterior cuts to interior, a classroom with a chalkboard and a set of chairs, near the front of the building. An apparently vacant space is to the right of this, with windows and a wall. The relation between exterior and interior here is a direct inversion of space, like the stencil and fill of the Walking Woman, an impression and its silhouette, positive and negative. Dramatic actions occur in the space, but throughout, the camera makes two movements repeating ad nauseam. The first, which forms the bulk of the film, is a back-and-forth pan that is bounded by the chalkboard and chairs to the left, windows to the right. The camera pans from one composition to the other and back, slowly at first and building in speed.

Dramatic actions begin to occur within the space, all of which seem to reflect the repeating pan: a man draws a double-headed arrow on the chalkboard; a woman sits shaking her head; a woman speaks, giving explicit description to the camera movements: "Back and forth, to and fro, hither and thither, hither and yon." Occasionally, a person will walk, inside or along the perimeter of the building, seen through windows, and the camera will change its pace to follow, rhythm becoming variable, timed to events dispersed across the composition. A metronome sounds, not always in rhythm with the image. The pan is continuous and consistent, interrupted rarely by an elliptical cut that displaces it. With each motion it stops and settles for a brief moment at its left and right ends. The speed will suddenly decrease, the pan will stutter; a custodian sweeps the floor, staggering with his broom forward out the door; a man and a woman play catch, but with a cut they disappear; a man and woman kiss and hold one another; figures come and go in sudden edits. The classroom is transformed by gathering students in the vacant space at the right end of the pan. Some look out the windows. The pan follows to the empty classroom and back. A playful fight breaks out among the gathered students, and then, in a cut, immediately ends. It starts again, the opponents laughing, and is again interrupted. An observer, serving as a referee, calls it a draw.

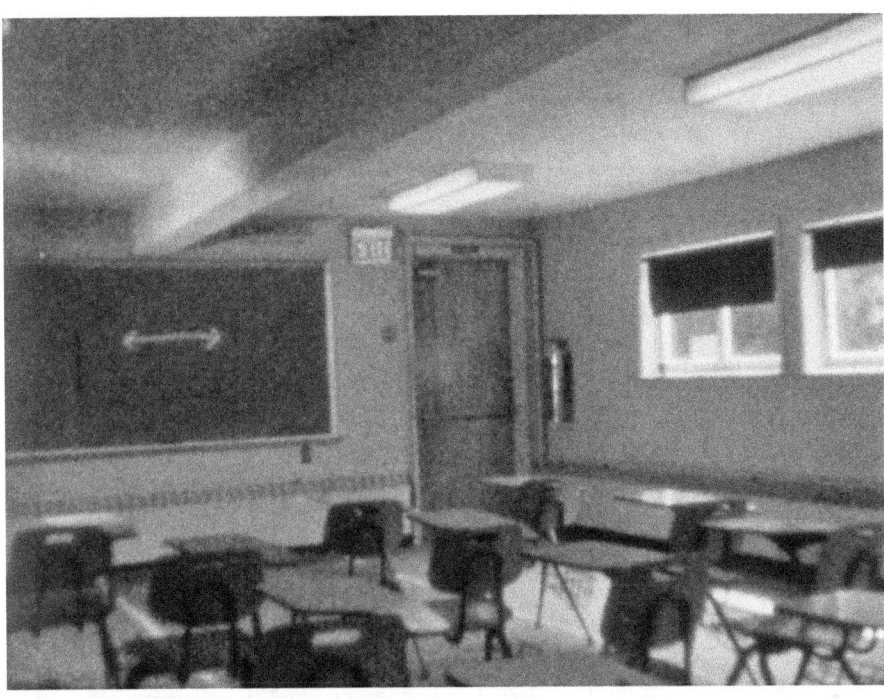

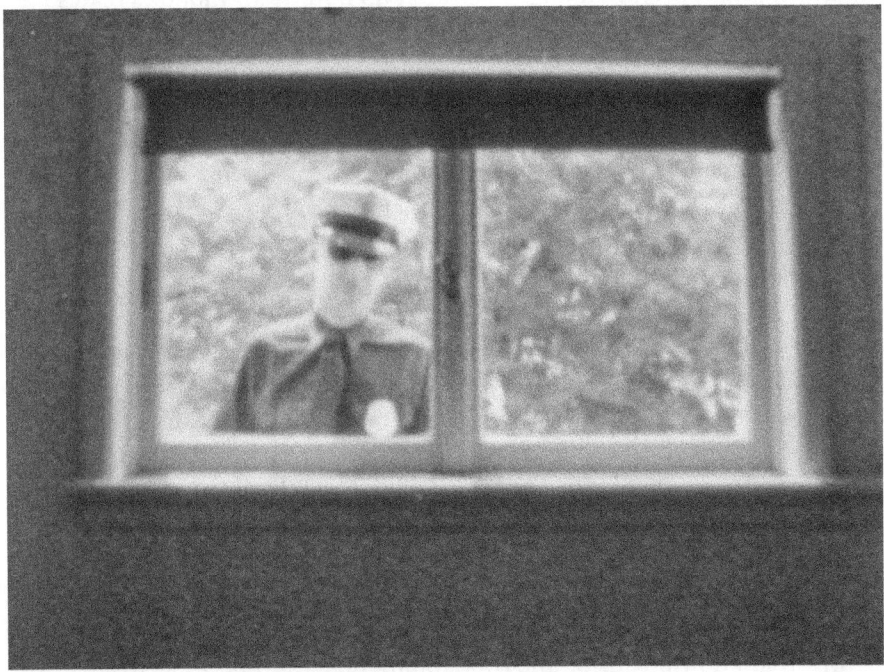

Back and Forth *[Film Stills]*, 1968-69
16mm film, 52 minutes, colour, sound
Courtesy of Michael Snow

The empty or sparsely populated classroom represents one form of focus, the party represents another—the classroom holds rapt attention, while the party is a crowded gathering, of dispersed attention. The pan becomes increasingly swift, with brief interruptions, returning to the original state of the empty classroom. In a long, unpeopled sequence, the left-right pan anchors to the left, stopping, and then stabbing out to the right, boomeranging back to the left. This alternates, coming to a full stop right, while to the left only reaching and then suddenly springing back from its boundary. The swiftness of the movement begins to abstract the image, as speed causes the space in between stations to lose definition. At its most extreme, the features of each end of the composition overlap by optical phenomena rather than material mediation, anchored by streaks of daylight and artificial light bouncing off the school desks. The film becomes a transit of light between two stations. It becomes impossible to gauge the gesture's relation to time, as the early, clear motions and the tic-toc of the metronome had established false rhythmic instructions. The pan has been interrupted on occasion, but now it has derailed itself, in a motion so rapid as to erase the panning gesture.

As in *Standard Time*, the camera, now repositioned in front of a window, tilts rapidly, frenzied, up and down, at the same high speed at which it had been panning. The rapid up and down motion creates lines of light that recall the Barnett Newman-inspired zip forms that appear in Snow's abstract paintings and sculptures, but his abstraction here arises from photographic reality, the action bounding between the abstraction of high speed and the realist rendering of low speed. The camera passes from a ceiling light down to the silhouette of a window with sunlight repeating the windowpane's form on the ground; in between is the window itself, glimpsed in precise frontal composition. Day passes and the sun's position changes; as this happens, the speed of the tilt gradually slows. The motion occurs between two stations, the bounds of the tilt clearly marked by black electrical tape on the floor and ceiling. A security guard comes over and looks in through the window, his walkie-talkie heard on the soundtrack. The metronome continues to sound in the background, but the tilt is moving at a fraction of its speed, resetting from the top and moving down, stuttering. A false ending occurs, as a text card appears that lists the setting, performers, technology and distribution information for the film, but then the image resumes, this time with the pan occurring at different speeds, double-exposed, the windows forming a ghostly horizontal passage. The tilt enters over this, and some of the layers are reversed or upside-down, causing the overlapping images to become symmetrical, casting over this final passage the abstract provocation of a Rorschach ink blot. The dramatic actions and human interventions repeat in fragments—the staged fight, the security guard in the window, even Snow's descriptive text—the image and its reversed, upside-down double colliding so that the light from the windows now riddles the full image, until the whir of the pan, laid atop itself, becomes a blur of simultaneous movement and stasis, a shimmering center of activity that never diverges sharply from its anchor, a central mass of abstracted light. The two continuities of camera movement—the pan and the tilt—have converged into this final variation.

If *Wavelength* had been, by a reductive distinction, an act of camera movement still in the shadow of realism, in *Standard Time* and *Back and Forth*, the camera was geared toward a further joining of realism and abstraction. These films dealt in the abstraction of photographic reality, which has its own specific traits, such as blur and distortion, that are given shape by lens, speed of movement, aperture and subject. In the coda, Snow superimposes the results of the two motions, creating contrapuntal movement, a polyphony that, like *Wavelength*'s equivalences, ends in a mysterious simultaneity of movement and stasis, the shimmering mass of light. But complementing its abstraction, *Back and Forth* also deals with binaries of space that extend the relation between cone and canvas in *Wavelength*; here, interior and exterior, fill and stencil, figure and setting, form a poetics of impression or relief. The brief image of the building's exterior informs the depth of its interior, an illustration that even in this unexceptional building, a plain classroom carved, as a void, out of a greater environment, space is the protagonist of architecture. The back and forth motion of the pan takes on the form of a pun, a head shake: it becomes Michael's No, a refusal of the depth of the space, a refusal that transforms that space, by the fury of its shaking head, into flat abstraction. The up and down tilt becomes an affirmative nod, an admission of the depth of the photographic image, which, as a picture of the real, extends out through the window in fleeting glimpses, as the nodding motion passes between two bends that give the interior depth, outward from floor to wall, inward from wall to ceiling.

By the end of the 1960s, Michael Snow's work in film had shifted dramatically. In the course of little more than two years, he had parted from the Walking Woman and taken up axial movement and lens distortion as the central aesthetic device of his films. His film activity reflected the spatial and compositional values that he would pursue across the arts, which constitute not so much a departure from the Walking Woman works as a maturation of that activity. At the heart of this activity were repetition and the game, advancing continuities that are subject to variation. The repetition of the Walking Woman represents one height of difficulty in

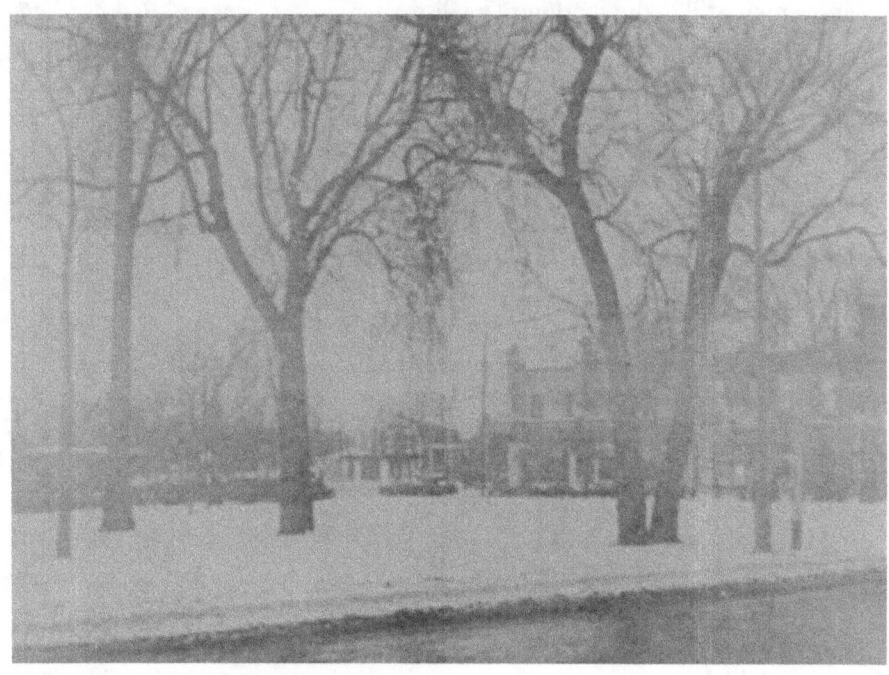

One Second in Montreal *[Film Still]*, 1969
16mm film
26 minutes at 16 frames per second or 17 minutes at 24 frames per second
black and white, silent
Courtesy of Michael Snow

Snow's work, perceptually difficult in its insistence on a particular mode of pleasure. The repetition of the icon became the repetition of the gesture. The icon had been at once gesture and sign, but now having shed the sign, there came a deeply individual expression, informed by Snow's influences, his roots of repetition—the geometric figuration of Paul Klee, the boogie-woogie vamps of Jimmy Yancey, Pablo Picasso's *Las Meninas* suite. These were Snow's ideals, his aesthetic origins. By 1970, Snow was producing work unlike any seen before. He was giving an illustrative definition of Difficult Entertainment, the film's shape fixed into new expression, riddled with thematic parallels, enigmatic figures and gestures, ending in a mysterious vision. Snow had become so individual that his aesthetics could move fluidly, in the free grammar of radical difficulty.

The suite of works that Snow began with *Wavelength* comprised a comedy of forms, but they also held to aesthetic themes that further defined his relation to duration, perspectival enigma, the interplay of sound and image, and realism. Each work expanded on gestures that were, by description, simple: a zoom, a pan and a tilt. These movements, which joined visual composition to temporal experience, were subject to material interruptions, such as superimpositions, colour saturation and elliptical editing. This challenged the perspectival integrity of the work, undermining the instructions for vision that the camera movements implied, contradicting the regimentation of the image by making it subject to improvisation. Throughout this work, sound and image had a correlation, neither one dependent upon the other but both enacting contrapuntal equivalences: in *Wavelength*, of glissando to crescendo; in *Standard Time*, the pan of a radio dial to the trigger of a visual edit; and finally, in *Back and Forth*, the system of metronomic time to something far more elastic, the metronome tock subdividing visual rhythms that were guided, in part, by visual interest. Its project was not so much to resist realism, but to regard it as a modality that film could adopt, and that the temporal and compositional aspects of film could interrogate and interfere with. *Back and Forth*'s inclusivity, in its exchange between the real and the abstract, challenges entrenched presumptions of perspective and of what constitutes an enriching aesthetic experience. Snow was accommodating the photographic apparatus and its mimetic relation to reality, but his work was also situated between media, pursuing an agenda of improvisation, perceptual distress and fragmentation. Where other movements in avant-garde film had attempted to tame the camera lens so that it would mirror and extend the artists' eyes, Snow, by imbuing his compositions with all manner of his experience and simultaneously stripping his technology down to essential gestures, had conceived the lens as a mechanized, all-seeing eye, which was not really an eye at all, but an agent of difficult experience, an aesthetic far removed from both the absent mind of Andy Warhol and the intimate eye of Stan Brakhage, removing parallels between human sight and mechanical vision. Snow's centrifugal, mechanized lens would evolve further in the coming years, but he would follow *Back and Forth* with two films that advanced different aspects of his work and that, on their surface, served a more utilitarian function, acts of taking inventory, one meditating on time, the other on perspective.

With *One Second in Montreal* (1969), Michael Snow sought to form a pure relation between duration and image. He selected a series of, in his words, "bad offset-printing images" he had made years earlier for a competition to erect monuments in Montreal parks. They were "bleak photographs of parks and public spaces."[35] The photographs are unexceptional; Montreal becomes an anonymous snow-covered city. The spare figures that turn up in these images are engaged in the dull everyday of walking and waiting. However, the dull and ordinary fact of the image becomes mysterious as the procession wears on, as these ordinary scenes are magnified by their duration, forcing the viewer into a deeper consideration of the content of ordinary scenes. In a gradual acceleration, the parade goes by. The twenty-six photographs are re-photographed to film, taken out of the static experience of their medium and put into a dialogue with time. The images pass as in a slideshow. They linger at first, until about half of them have passed, and then they begin to move faster, speeding to a final image, each image given greater significance for the time spent in reflection on preceding images.

One Second in Montreal bears the same structure of elastic rhythm as does *Back and Forth*, as the images decelerate immediately to a slow speed, and then begin to accelerate. Both films have a centre point where their time folds in on itself. *Back and Forth* gradually speeds up and then slows down, while *One Second in Montreal* does the inverse. The compositions are, by their origins, utilitarian, but when offered for extended contemplation, something greater emerges out of them. It may be that Snow has discovered the false profundity of duration, that duration forces the viewer to search for meaning where no meaning is intended, and this becomes, in the lapsing time of contemplation, something genuinely profound. These photographs do not depict a sentimentalized environment or a social history. They are the debris of art, derelict of intentions of authorship, and yet, recast as a fixed temporal experience, they suit Snow's conception of time as a vehicle for difficult experience. He elongates time in such a way

[35] Scott MacDonald, *A Critical Cinema 2: Interviews with Independent Filmmakers* (Berkeley and Los Angeles: University of California Press, 1992), 68.

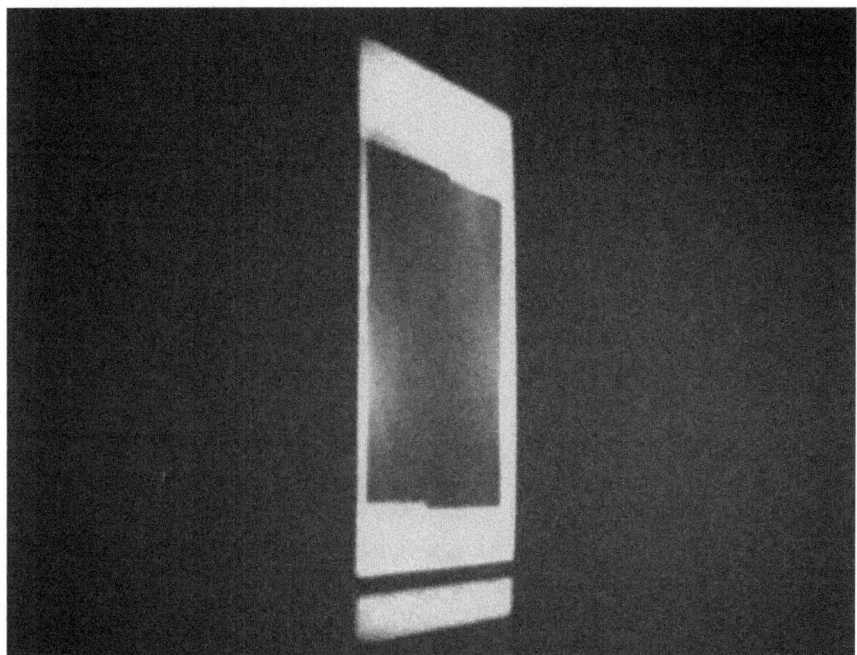

Side Seat Paintings Slides Sound Film *[Film Still]*, 1970
16mm film, 20 minutes, colour, sound
Courtesy of Michael Snow

as to conceal rhythm, so that the viewer becomes unaware of the film's metric constitution, only that the duration of each image is somehow uncommon.[36] This buried rhythm becomes more evident in the acceleration, as the rhythmic qualities of film editing slowly begin to resemble more accessible, less difficult durations. Snow is not interrogating his own images; rather, he is creating the circumstances for an interrogation by deceleration and acceleration. In that interrogation, the viewer discovers the poetry of the procession, giving a studied look to casual composition, and upon becoming accustomed to this deceleration finds the process changing. The poetry is gained by a search for the monumental, which, in light of the original purpose of these images, becomes an elaborate pun.

---

[36] Snow recalls, in an interview with Scott MacDonald, Yvonne Rainer's description of this experience of duration: "Yvonne Rainer told me one time that she got very, very fidgety as the shots got longer and longer, and was really mad. And then, when they started to go fast and the film ended, she was really mad that it ended. She wanted more." Rainer's remarks illuminate the way in which Snow's work acts on an audience, engaging and disengaging attention to the specific end of fascination and rapture. Scott MacDonald, *A Critical Cinema 2: Interviews with Independent Filmmakers* (Berkeley and Los Angeles: University of California Press, 1992), 68.

For his next film, Snow would translate his recent painting activities to film, and in doing so, extend the comedy of forms and of perception that he had taken up in his recent film work. *Side Seat Paintings Slides Sound Film* (1970) was made for the occasion of Snow's first retrospective at the Art Gallery of Ontario. The film features projected slides of paintings with spoken descriptions, played back on a tape recorder of variable speed, the images seen by a viewer who is seated at an angle, forcing the image to appear not as a rectangle, but as a parallelogram, introducing visual distortions akin to anamorphosis. The sound slows to a lower pitch, the image darkens until it is black, and the film takes on a kind of boredom, attention dispersed between sound and vision, but also disengaged. Later, the voice speeds up and the image brightens, again to an extremity, the slide reproductions of paintings never quite seen, mediated by perspectival distortion and several generations of translation between media. Snow characterized the film as "a recycling, a conversion which, by employing the illusion of temporal alteration which film and sound recording have made possible, becomes a completely new experience."[37] His distortions are achieved by the machines in play: the aperture of the camera, the beam of the slide projector and the variable speed dial of the tape recorder combine in comic unity. The distorting beam, photographed at an angle, fails to accurately render the photographs; the camera's aperture closes and opens too far, failing to accurately render the beam; and the tape recorder stretches the pitch of the voice out of the range of clarity. All three machines operate in tandem, obscuring the source images and their factual details, including dimensions and dates of origin. All act in the service of interference, to implicate the viewer of the film in the structured inattention of the film itself. This distance of media, the concealing of one within another within another, is reminiscent of the reproductions of Peter Paul Rubens' paintings in Diego Velázquez's *Las Meninas*, a work that contains Velázquez's assistant's reproductions of another artist's body of work. Snow's film becomes a container for the reproductions of his work, but it is also an act of reflection on the act of reproduction and on the communication of a body of work, the former evident in the unintelligible image, the latter in Snow's comic first-person performance of disengaged spectatorship.

One Second in Montreal and *Side Seat Paintings Slides Sound Film* follow in continuity from the structural approach that Michael Snow began to refine with *Wavelength*, but they also clarify ideas, subtle in prior work, that would gain traction in his coming work. One idea, in the case of *Side Seat*

---

[37] This description has been printed, as a remark from Snow, in the LUX distribution catalogue.

Paintings Slides Sound Film, is distortion of the subject so that it becomes an unresolvable enigma, contesting realism by twisting the subject, known to be a representation of reality, in this case a photograph of a painting, into further abstraction. In the case of *One Second in Montreal*, Snow stretches the experience of an indistinct composition to assume a profound, and profoundly ambiguous, significance. In both cases, as with the axial films, these films engage the viewer in the construction of meaning, placing demands on them to participate, suspending them in a state of unease far more confounding than those of Snow's prior films.[38] These works demand that the viewer earn the difficult pleasures of this experience, which puts to them open questions of the nature of time and perception. These films serve as an immediate precursor to the concerns of depth and plane that would dominate Snow's next major film, *La Région Centrale* (1971).

Snow's work had become progressively more challenging through the course of the 1960s, and while New York as a setting and the colleagues he found there had enriched and shaped his art, the difficult extremities of his filmmaking would soon take purchase in Canada and expand to an epic scale. Snow's aesthetics were an engagement with the toughest obscurities of the modern and postmodern projects in art. His works of mixed-media abstraction drifted to his prevailing icon of the Walking Woman, and from there, to the axial and perspectival concerns of his mature work. The Walking Woman allowed Snow to take up an inclusive position between aesthetic and theme, form and content, and his art was filled with puns, paradoxes of form and riddles of perspective, each work conscious of its construction, a puzzle and an invitation. Upon retiring the icon, Snow's pursuit of difficult perceptual experience was freed to move deeper into material self-awareness, at the same time casting a greater investment of self, as each work became an inventory of his ideas across media, as a 'time-light-sound' poet.

After several years of splitting their time between Toronto and New York City, Michael Snow and Joyce Wieland made a permanent return to Canada in 1971. The transition was gradual, each maintaining studios in both cities through the late 1960s, and Wieland spending the better part of 1970 in Ottawa preparing a major exhibition of her work. The couple had long since taken separate but related directions in their art. For Wieland, a critique of Canadian nationalism, based in myth, ecstasy and tactility, and posed between irony and sentimentality, would form the central base for her creative activity. For Snow, a return to Canada meant a

---

[38] It may even be argued that these films were nearer in continuity with *New York Eye and Ear Control* and *Short Shave*, in that they involved a direct translation from one medium to another, and in their act of integrating Snow's work in other media, something that, for all of his gestural inventory, was not true of *Wavelength*, *Standard Time* and *Back and Forth*.

new plain to test the physics of vision, a reflection on compositional space, the boundaries of horizon, the absence in a landscape. Both structural and expressive impulses would push Snow's aesthetics further, with his next film, toward an ultimate expression of vision, in the Canadian wilderness, the mechanized all-seeing eye of the camera becoming the very eye of God.

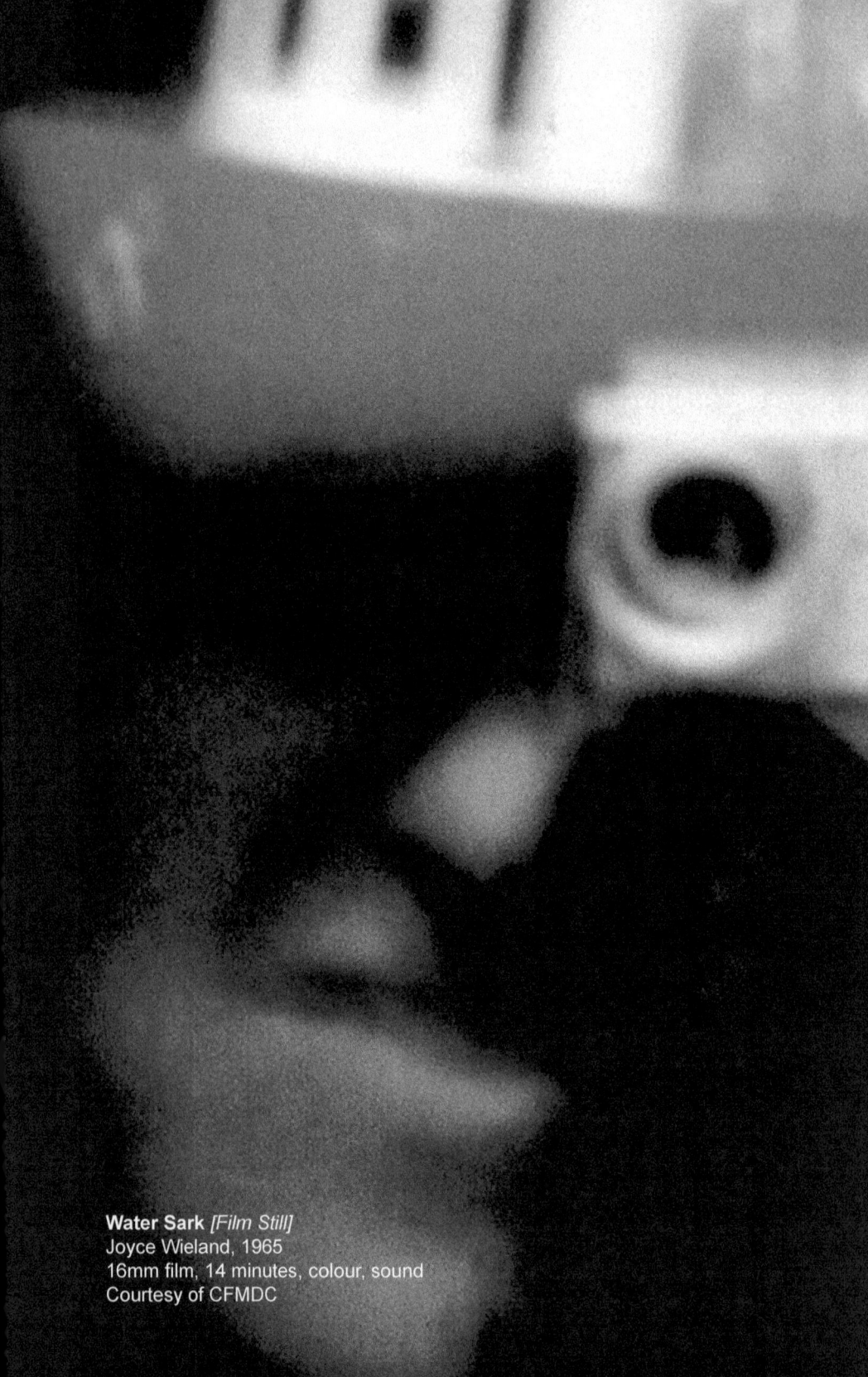

Water Sark *[Film Still]*
Joyce Wieland, 1965
16mm film, 14 minutes, colour, sound
Courtesy of CFMDC

CHAPTER THREE

Joyce Wieland: Ars Longa, Vita Brevis

Canada's sovereignty arrived slowly, from initial European explorations and settlements in the sixteenth-century through to its confederation in 1867. Its evolution was a struggle between language, customs and staked territories. Settlers faced inhospitable seasons and dangerous terrain as they assembled their new culture. Susanna Moodie became an icon of both British colonial settlement and of Canadian settler womanhood for her book *Roughing it in the Bush*, published fifteen years before the country's confederation, and the regard for Moodie's account as something exotic betrayed an inscribed puritanism in British and Canadian culture. Canadian women would gain some advocacy through the National Council of Women of Canada, formed in 1857, only a decade before confederation, and by the end of the nineteenth century it pursued a campaign to upgrade the status of women, albeit without pursuing the vote.[1] Eventually, in 1918, in tandem with movements elsewhere in the west, Canadian women gained the right to vote in federal elections. A female nationalist would see two things arising in the era of confederation: a slowly forming critique of hegemony and gender inequity, and a growing pride in Canada as an autonomous presence, a nation that formed slowly but was now assured in its cultivation of citizenship and patriotism. Against this history of slowly evolving gender equity, Canadian women painters began to emerge. The first to achieve recognition engaged with romantic styles, but by the twentieth century, when modern movements arrived in Canada, female painters would form a minority among those who would pursue and expand the new vision.[2] As modern art struggled into Canada,

---

[1] The National Council of Women of Canada, an organization still in place today, held a contentious position in the transit from the nineteenth to twentieth centuries, arguing for recognition of the communal role of women rather than lobbying for withheld rights, like the vote, to be bestowed. Their causes aimed to upgrade the status of women through 'transcendent citizenship', a citizenship that posed women as a moral influence over men, and by that, rationalized that the vote was unnecessary. Their platform has, in the interim century, become more progressive, but its resistance to the suffragette movement reveals a conservative, puritanical bent present throughout the evolution of Canadian society.

[2] The earliest among Canada's female painters to achieve some recognition were Mary Ella

any acclaim for it was directed primarily to the Post-Impressionist paintings of the Group of Seven, but it was also present in the work of other artists, such as the Post-Impressionist Emily Carr and the geometric abstractionist Kathleen Munn.[3] In these modern movements, there was a pronounced lack of female painters, who for the most part were ignored or at the fringes of discussion in Canadian art criticism, much of which was hostile toward modern art. In order to pursue the most difficult ends of art in Canada, a woman would endure twofold discrimination and exclusion, both for her gender and for the direction of her calling. Modern art represented the newfound and elaborate pleasures of the perceptual challenge that came with freer forms. The expressive potential of gesture, unhindered by the straits of realism, was not isolated from the senses but of the senses. This art stemmed from a critique of the faculties, a position that first formed around the effect of the art itself and which also, most evident in the transit into the postmodern, could turn to critique history and society.

Joyce Wieland was born in 1931, the daughter of working class English-Scottish immigrants living in the Trinity-Bellwoods neighborhood, a low-income immigrant community in Toronto's west end. By age 11, both of Wieland's parents had died. She lived through a series of upheavals, moving with her elder sister and brother into precarious arrangements, struggling through debt to achieve financial security.[4] As a teenager, Wieland studied art at Toronto's Central Technical School, gaining a high school education that emphasized commercial-industrial skills. There, she encountered women artists for the first time: among the faculty were sculptor Elizabeth Wyn Wood and painters Virginia Luz and Doris McCarthy.[5] Wieland took classes in dress design, through which she learned figurative drawing from McCarthy, a graduate of the Ontario College of Art known for her abstract landscape paintings. At McCarthy's urging, Wieland

---

Dignam and Laura Muntz Lyall, contemporaries born in the mid-nineteenth century, both working with sentimental subjects in styles that mirror nineteenth-century Dutch painting. This work of sentimental realism had no visible influence over the work of Canadian moderns, who, like Dignam, Lyall and their contemporaries, had developed styles and technical vocabulary out of the influence of European and American movements.

[3] Despite the present regard for them as pioneering figures in Canadian modern painting, Emily Carr did not receive significant recognition for her art until very late in her life, and Kathleen Munn's debts to Cubism made her a target for Canadian art critics resistant to modernism.

[4] The pains of the Wieland children are described extensively in Jane Lind, *Joyce Wieland: Artist on Fire* (Toronto: Lorimer, 2001). Lind's precise accounting of the family's hardship, down to the minutiae of bills and earnings, characterizes the situation of the Wieland family as dire.

[5] Jane Lind, *Joyce Wieland: Artist on Fire* (Toronto: Lorimer, 2001), 56.

enrolled in the school's Fine Arts stream, where she would first develop a technical knowledge of drawing and painting.[6] Wieland came to understand the purpose of art as a force for both creative and social expression, influenced by an atmosphere of class unrest. She devoted her creative energies to building a skillset that would help her find employment, but her early experiences of art making and the experiences particular to her class and gender would later inform the directions of her painting and filmmaking.

In her final year of high school, Wieland attended a labour strike at Eaton's. The event would prove a formative introduction to the grim realities of labour politics. Her experience on the line would further strengthen her identification with the experiences and trials common to workers, suffering at the hands of an elite business class and struggling, much as Wieland and her siblings had struggled, for stable work and a living wage. She would recall in later years the frightened faces of the marching workers, but ultimately, it was the collective, collaborative action of the strikers that would leave the deepest imprint on her.[7] Wieland's mature work would come to echo that action of collective resistance and outrage, a great unity in the service of justice. Her childhood anxieties about work and domestic life, coming of age as she did in unstable circumstances, found consonance in the politics of labour. This vision, of the personal in the political, would later emerge as an insistent theme in her art. To make art was to engage in another form of labour, likewise worthy of collectivity and protest. A cartoon found in one of Wieland's journals shows a male and female, drawn as a highly stylized cartoon, as dwarfed rotund forms. They hold signs that read "Ars Longa, Vita Brevis," the Latin translated to English on accompanying signs, "Art is Long, Life is Short."[8] Her protestors declare art eternal, a classical idea but one best explained, in the context of modern art, as finding the universal in the particular.

---

[6] An early portrait, *Untitled (portrait of Chris Karch)*, c. 1948-49, of housemate Chris Karch, betrays an interest in, or at least, knowledge of, the technical execution of realism, the figure seated at a slight angle, offsetting the shadow on his turtleneck sweater. The portrait demonstrates an engagement with the technical precision of realist painting, knowledge of light and shadow, and, by the flush of Karch's face, a superior skill at rendering skintone. This painting, made toward the end of Wieland's high school education, shows a technical knowledge of traditional painter's craft that could be overlooked in critical considerations of her abstract or stylized works, but which also broadcasts her prodigious knowledge of traditional composition.

[7] Wieland would later describe the experience: "Everything looked grim, and it was the middle of winter and those people were walking up and down and looking scared and there were a bunch of students watching." Qtd. in Jane Lind, *Joyce Wieland: Artist on Fire* (Toronto: Lorimer, 2001), 55.

[8] This image is reprinted in Jane Lind, *Joyce Wieland: Writings and Drawings 1952-1971* (Erin, Ont.: Porcupine's Quill, 2009), 129.

Wieland's engagement with fine art also developed outside her formal education. Growing up in Toronto, she had seen the collection of the Art Gallery of Toronto (renamed the Art Gallery of Ontario in 1966), and a trip to New York City to visit galleries in the late 1940s found her in Rockefeller Centre, in awe of its murals. She attended screenings of the Toronto Film Society, a community group interested in advancing the cause of artistic filmmaking.[9] In 1949, they invited the Dada artist Hans Richter to screen *Dreams That Money Can Buy* (1947), a Surrealist feature film in which a man becomes a dream merchant upon realizing that he can sell psychic projections, or 'dreams', summoned by a mirror in his apartment. Richter made the film in collaboration with artists such as Max Ernst, Fernand Léger, Man Ray, Marcel Duchamp and Alexander Calder, his collaborators crafting the 'dreams' for the film. To Wieland, it was an early introduction to the possibilities of film as art, and to Dada and Surreal aesthetics as a living force as powerful as they had been in the 1920s. At the time, there was no Canadian cinema to speak of, save for the educational and animated films issuing from the National Film Board as an alternative to the Hollywood film. The Film Society screenings of European narrative art cinema and films by Richter and Maya Deren introduced the city to the artistic potential of filmmaking. For young artists like Wieland, the experience connected this medium with the aspirations and forms of the other arts struggling into modernity.

Wieland's training at Central Tech had prepared her to assume a position in the design workforce. In 1948, she was able to secure a job designing packaging with ES&A Robinson, and she remained there for five years.[10] When she left, she took freelance jobs in the design industry and also began to design greeting cards. In 1954, she took up regular work at the animation firm Graphic Associates. Her time there would be short, with the firm closing little more than two years later, but in that time she met her future husband, Michael Snow, and began to make films communally with the rest of the staff. By the time that she and Snow married in the fall of 1956, they were both committed unequivocally to their art practices, working at the heart of a loose Neo-Dada community to build something new, in a city with a history of closed, exclusive art scenes, from the Group

---

[9] The Toronto Film Society's most significant achievement in relation to avant-garde film came in the early 1950s, when it brought Maya Deren to Toronto to show a retrospective of her work. During the course of her visit, she collaborated with members of the organization on a film she would later disown as unfinished, *Ensemble for Somnambulists* (1951). The history of the Toronto Film Society has been recounted in detail by John Porter, "Maya Deren and Hans Richter in Toronto," *The Funnel Newsletter*, November-December 1983.

[10] Jane Lind, *Joyce Wieland: Artist on Fire* (Toronto: Lorimer, 2001), 64.

of Seven to the Painters Eleven.[11] The narrow channel of Toronto art in which Wieland, Snow, and their friends and contemporaries found themselves would in coming years be challenged, bent into a form more accommodating for confrontational and dense modern and postmodern art. The work of Jack Bush and his peers, with their debts to Hans Hoffman and painterly abstraction, had tamed Toronto audiences to celebrate them, if more as a movement than as individuals. That same audience would now face work that was lacking in common values of beauty and that followed in the psychic collage of Joseph Cornell's boxed assemblages and the precise mess of Robert Rauschenberg's combines, toward raw expressions of a different order.

Wieland had spent much of her time in high school drawing comic strips and writing journals. They survive today to reveal common experiences of youth, for instance, a longing for romantic love, but they also demonstrate an instinctual critique of such longing.[12] Ideals of love would take on a greater thematic design in Wieland's character, in her abstract paintings that were messy and dramatic in their sexuality, in paintings and installations that spoke explicitly of brotherhood and love, and in the repetitions of valentine card hearts and lipstick traces that would, in her mature work, become synonymous with her ironic expression of nationalism. Her work was not naïve, but indirect; even as she mastered the symbols and gestures of sentimentality, she cultivated a rich sense of irony. Her art could not be taken by its surface, whether of sentimentality or mere whimsy and joy, because that surface masked the work's greater investment in which whimsy and joy were a subversive force. Just as Michael Snow would construct an open, adaptable, neutral form with the Walking Woman, Wieland would adopt stylized hearts and lips, cutting and pressing them in series, made ironic by their malformation, by their presence in fine art, by their allegorical indirection. As her work matured and she experienced personal crises, these ironies would likewise mature, becoming more pronounced and grim, even as these symbols became increasingly earnest in their sentimental declaration.

When Graphic Associates shut down some months after their wedding, both Wieland and Snow took on odd jobs in the design industry

---

[11] This idea has its roots in an interview given by Snow to Jane Lind, in which Snow remarks that the Painters Eleven, despite its ushering in of abstraction, was just "another scene," in the tradition of landscape painters and other groups that had restricted the possibilities of Toronto art by defining it in a narrow way.

[12] Jane Lind has published a collection of Wieland's journals, *Joyce Wieland: Writings and Drawings 1952-1971* (Erin, Ont.: Porcupine's Quill, 2009). Lind has elsewhere, in *Joyce Wieland: Artist on Fire*, written that these records demonstrate longing for romantic love as learned through popular culture and commercial images.

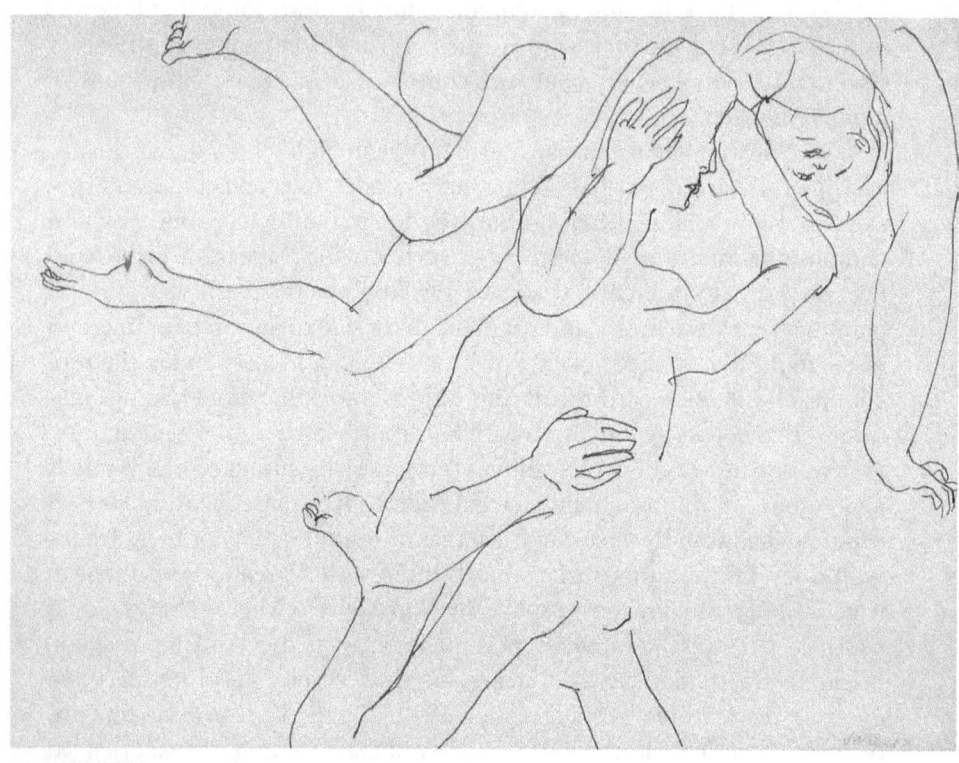

Lovers, 1956
ink on wove paper, 21.5 x 27.9 cm, 8 7/16 x 11 inches
Art Gallery of Ontario, Gift of Betty Ramsaur Ferguson, Puslinch, Ontario, 1998
(98/640)
Reproduced by permission of the National Gallery of Canada

while devoting their free time to their painting activities. Early drawings of Wieland's that survive show a combination of enigmatic perspective and cylindrical figuration. Her work through the 1950s used a variety of materials, for instance, *untitled (heartgame)* (1956) combines red ink and charcoal on a torn piece of notepaper; elsewhere she was using crayon and paper collage. Her work of the mid-to-late 1950s, and in particular the evolution of her figuration, included a series of oil on canvas paintings. In *Green Lady* (1956), Wieland paints an amorphous form that takes on the position of a seated figure. The figure is reduced to a series of abstract shapes, creased by faint black lines down its centre, all forms serving the purpose of flattening the image and annihilating conventional figuration, a resistance to realism. In two canvases, *Morning* (1956) and *Myself* (1958), the subjects are recognizable as abstractions of the figure, the former with debts to Malevich, two figures realized by an assembly of circles and rectangles; the latter a self-portrait less concerned with geometry than her contemporaneous paintings, more a work of expressive brushwork and strategic coloration. Her interest in the figure turned to programme-informed abstraction such as *The King & Queen* (1960), an enigmatic assembly of forms against a pale blue background, roughly forming three abstract figures. Her new embrace of abstraction placed large, amorphous forms, often partly obscured by the boundaries of the canvas, in fields of gradated colour. This was true of *Time Machine* (1959) and *Time Machine Series* (1961). *Redgasm* (1960) continued these forms, distortions in a red-pink colour, and was followed by the violence of *War Memories* (1960), a scattering of circles in red. The programme of these works group the experience of orgasm and menstruation with that of wartime, signaling a cornerstone of Wieland's art, the simultaneity and co-penetration of intimate and universal experience.

In 1961, Wieland would begin to pursue mixed media collages such as her *Summer Blues* series. Like Snow, her work shifted from the influence of abstract expressionism to Neo-Dada. With these assemblages, Wieland departed from oil-on-canvas work, returning to the fluid material repurposing of her earlier work in paper collage. Her integration of objects and her use of paper collage extended the forms of her abstract paintings, but now her work would integrate refuse and markers of common experience and mass culture. In *Summer Blues – The Island* (1961), spent cardboard tubes, some creased and bent, combine with electrical tape, a piece of paper cut into the shape of a crescent moon and a crude encaustic to form an image that is at once topography and horizon. The materials used in the work are the refuse of mass culture, but they do not turn critically on mass culture; rather, they bear enigmatic perspective, primitive and chaotic representation or evocation, and an intimate and memorial presence beyond material introspection. Her Neo-Dada influence was most pronounced in *The Clothes of Love* (1961), with roughly cut rectangular fabrics—marked by ink and paint in a manner resembling colour field painting—strewn on a clothesline within a tall wooden frame. Of Wieland's work in this period, this piece has the strongest ties to Robert Rauschenberg's combines, an ordinary sight recast as something alien.[13] It is not only a collage of materials but of styles, with the textiles, crudely stained and painted, suspended across a rectangular frame, the upper region of which is a dense and subtle abstract painting of dark blues concealing black charcoal lines, the lower region empty, showing through to the gallery wall. Like the Rauschenberg combines, *The Clothes of Love* employed real things, arranged and altered, to combat realism. Its difficulty was particular to its time, the markers of process placing the work far from the illusion of figurative realism, as strange in 1961 as Marcel Duchamp's *Fountain* had been in 1917; its difficulty, like that of *Fountain*, was an enduring one that posed open-ended relations of cultural valuation, objecthood, purpose and meaning. When Robert Fulford wrote on it in the *Toronto Star* in 1962, he described *The Clothes of Love* as "a flung-together collection of cloths [...] open to the widest possible variety of interpretations," and nothing more.[14] Wieland's work passed from abstraction, and its young material traditions, through to a confrontation with real things, drawing forms and shapes out of reality and, in a primal act, blending them into unresolvable mysteries. In a statement on the collage *Heart-On* (1961), speaking on her obscurity, Wieland said "it's good because no one has to know it. It just might come up some day that these things exist. It is good to have mystery because people want to explain everything."[15]

In short order, Wieland had developed a number of complementary aesthetics. Her oil paintings dealt with abstract forms and, increasingly, with erotic evocation. Her mixed media collages were not merely wild for their multi-dimensionality and bare confrontation with the surface and presence of the art object, but for their integration of objects that were memorial to both the individual and the crowd, that turned them into scrapbooks of experience. By the time Wieland and Snow began their

[13] Wieland's relation to Neo-Dada might be best demonstrated through a parallel: *The Clothes of Love*, which manipulates real things in such a way as to confront the nature of art in itself, has much the same technique and effect as Rauschenberg's *Monogram* (1955-59), a mixed media work in which a taxidermy goat is placed on top of a canvas, a rubber tire around its waist, a tennis ball on the canvas by its rear. Both *Monogram* and *The Clothes of Love* are assembled from multi-dimensional mixed media components that challenge conventions and uniformities.

[14] Robert Fulford, "Wieland," *Toronto Star*, 2 February 1962, 30.

[15] Iris Nowell, *Joyce Wieland: A Life in Art* (Toronto: ECW Press, 2001), 224.

move to New York City, Wieland was fluidly combining these aspects of her work, as in *Time Machine #2* (1961), a Red Ensign emblazoned in the centre of a black canvas, offset by a pale tan pool, a clockwise form etched around it, with numbers assembling at the bottom. As Snow was beginning his Walking Woman variations, Wieland was pursuing an almost opposite path to the same end of material consciousness, her gestures less structured in their repetition, her work more autobiographical and personal, and at the same time, largely unconcerned with graphic form, invested instead in texture, perspective and presence as vehicles for obscure, ambiguous meaning (as in *The Clothes of Love* and the *Summer Blues* series). In Wieland's poetics, conventional representation would act against the expressive possibilities of art, as her own representational interests had moved so far from the erotic drawings of Matisse-like figures that had occupied her in the 1950s, going toward an obscure programme that assembled a familiar unfamiliar out of painted abstract shapes and paper cut-outs, some likewise abstract, others crude series of symbols (the valentine heart, the lipstick trace). Soon she would shift to the stylization of the cartoon, figures drawn from comic strips and greeting cards. Such cartoon forms, bulbous and rounded with loose, curved lines for details, would appear frequently in the figurative painting that she would pursue through the remainder of the 1960s.

When Wieland moved to New York City in 1962, Wieland's painting had only recently taken on mixed media forms. While she would continue to be represented in Canada by Av Isaacs, and through the Isaacs Gallery would participate in regular shows of new work, Wieland would begin to work in film. Wieland's immersion in the New York art community further introduced her to the rough and spontaneous fringes of cinema. In her first year in New York, screenings of Jack Smith's *Flaming Creatures*—and the consequent arrest of Jonas Mekas and Ken Jacobs for exhibiting it—affirmed the wild and difficult pleasures of avant-garde cinema, a sometimes camp cultural critique joined to an exposé of inner life. George and Mike Kuchar, who had become collaborators of Wieland's friend and former Graphic Associates coworker Bob Cowan, also served as a prime example of artists for whom cinema represented freedom of form rather than commercial enterprise. The grammar of film was expanding, and forms as disparate as those of the Kuchar Brothers and Jonas Mekas were not merely coexisting but implicated in a brotherhood of aesthetic freedom. Freedom of form rested on the surface of these practices, their difficult pleasures to be wrestled by the delights of perceptual enigmas and allegorical indirection, by the freedom of wit and satire or love and joy which in itself was a shelter from the despair and hopelessness of critical neglect, poverty and persecution. Cinema could also hold pure motives concerning expression, relative to the competition for wealth in the city's gallery scene. Like Jack Chambers, who achieved a purity of expression in his films, making art without a saleable result in a medium at the margins of critical assent, Wieland would find freedom from the pressures of New York gallery representation, balancing her filmmaking with new painting activity that was still gaining recognition in her native Toronto.

Wieland had placed love and its symbols at the centre of her work, in her use of valentine hearts and lipstick, but also in her erotic programme and with her long-standing series of drawings of *Lovers*. That love was not a naïve declaration, but an increasingly ambiguous comment, manifested in misdirection between sentimentality and irony. In 1963, when Wieland discovered that she was infertile, this misdirection would become more pronounced. Love, brotherhood and the body would become enduring symbols in her work, signaling fracture, disappointment and absence; though these ideas had been present in her earlier work, they would expand in the wake of this experience, her ironies revealing deep torment and gallows humour, her sentimentality increasingly earnest, her art falling between these traditionally incompatible positions. Adopting a posture of naïve, uncritical joy and love, Wieland could conceal a more personal and profound confrontation with the menace of nature and the earth's critters, both animal and human. The gratuitous platitudes that formed across her work were simply a veneer masking insights formed by grief and pain. It was in this misdirection that her mature work achieved profound difficulty: it could simultaneously offer earnest sentimentality and winking irony, in a devastating combination and to the ambiguous end of coexistent, incompatible meanings.

Elizabeth Kilbourn, reviewing Joyce Wieland's 1963 solo exhibition at the Isaacs Gallery, acknowledged references to both the comic strip and the film strip in the sequential action of Wieland's paintings, the latter made explicit in a series titled *Homage to DW Griffiths*.[16] In Wieland's paintings, sequential action is governed by horizontal grid forms (*Car Crash*, 1963; *Sinking Liner*, 1963; *Sailboat Sinking*, 1965; and many others) and vertically stacked panels (*Sailing on the Bay*, 1963). All of these paintings involve events made mysterious by fluctuations of perspective and by ambiguous interim movement between panels, concealing action.[17] The film strip was most explicitly referenced in two paintings from 1963. *The First Integrated Film with a Short on Sailing* runs two sequential strips, one horizontal (of a

[16] Elizabeth Kilbourn, "Art and Artists." *Toronto Star*, 23 November 1963, 36.

[17] In the twelve-compartment oil on canvas grid *Nature Mixes* (1963), a hand gradually turns into a flower, and then to a penis, like a furious act of masturbation, the hand and penis divided by what, in Georgia O'Keeffe's kitsch aesthetic, became a surrogate for the vagina.

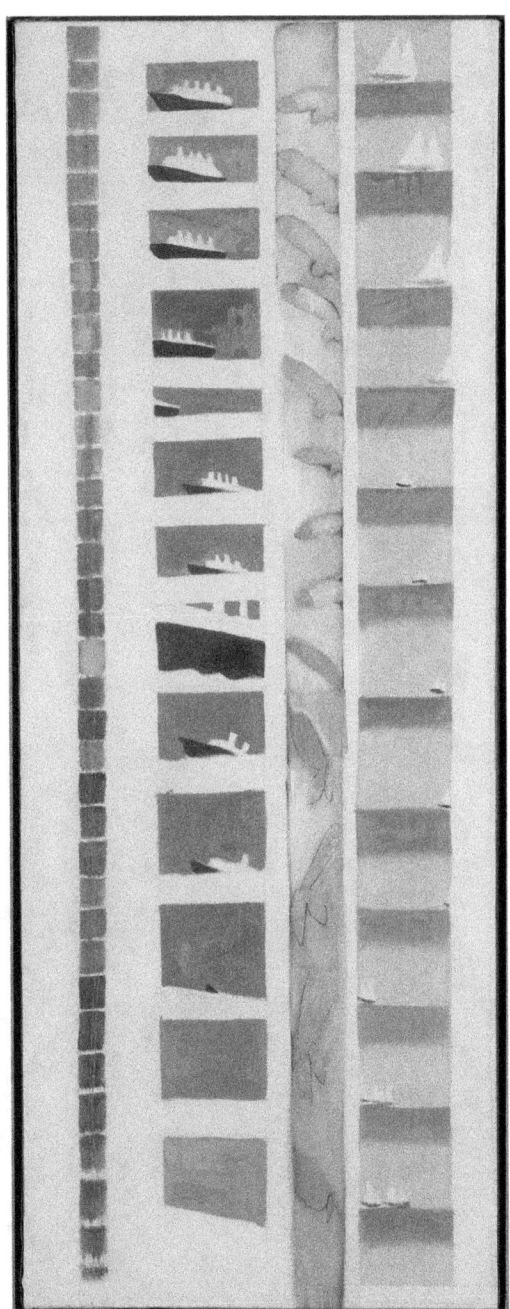

Flick Pics #4, 1963
oil on canvas, 106.6 x 40.8 cm, 41 15/16 x 16 1/16 inches
Art Gallery of Ontario, Gift of Morton and Carol Rapp, 2007
(2007/429)
Reproduced by permission of the National Gallery of Canada

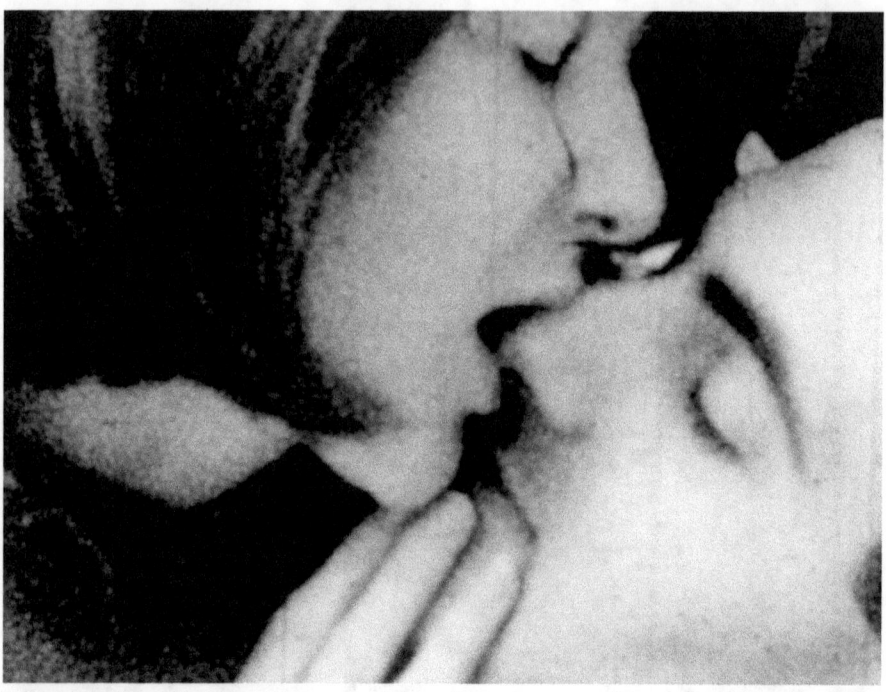

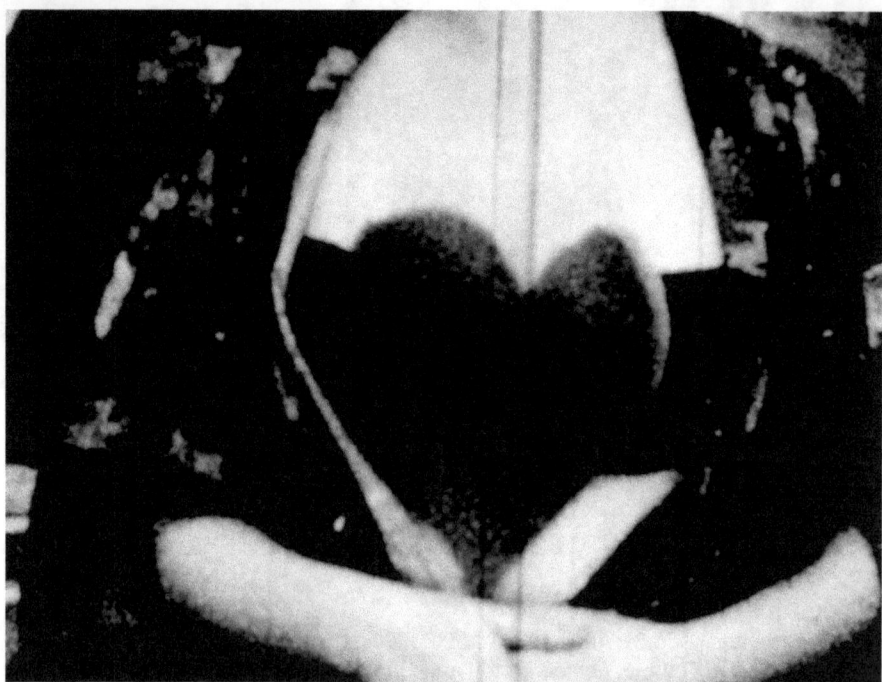

Larry's Recent Behavior *[Film Stills]*, 1963
16mm film, 17 minutes, colour and black and white, sound
Courtesy of CFMDC

sailboat) and one vertical (of a white woman and a black man kissing). *Four Films* has a series of four vertical strips: one of alternating red and pink solids; one of an ocean liner sinking into a white sea; a narrow strip unmediated by frame lines featuring a series of cartoon phalluses; and finally, one of a sailboat, each frame changing the dimension and presence of the subject. Although the sequential aspect of Wieland's work would naturally lead to the expectation that her films would be grounded in sequential relations, as she began to make films, her work would be less concerned with conscious editorial construction. Her first films would more closely resemble her assemblages, raw, crudely fit, drawing from the Neo-Dada strain of her work, which suited her assimilation into the New York Underground.

Out of her exposure to the New American Cinema, Joyce Wieland would make her first film, *Larry's Recent Behavior* (1963). The film, influenced by Jacobs and the Kuchars, would introduce certain concerns that would mark Wieland's later films, chiefly her interest in political iconography and obscurantist form. The body of the film is a series of vignettes, most marked by intertitles introducing the sequences in one or two words (for example, dance, drums, feet, and most obscurely, 'manus felicitus'). The titular Larry's aberrant behaviours (picking his nose and tasting his fingers, licking jam from women's fingers, smelling feet) were inspired by the nervous illness of a friend. The film therefore bears an obscure personal programme, shifting from the particulars of Larry's behaviour and into Wieland's vision of American culture and her interest in John F. Kennedy, in the wake of his assassination.

The actor contorts his face, exaggerating joy and disgust, as he performs Larry's behaviors. He plays with soft fabric hearts, making them beat, chewing on and spinning them. His activities (picking his nose, smelling feet) are held against scenes of other figures: Sylvia (Sylvia Margret Rose) pops her pimples in a mirror until blood streams from the lesions; Michael Snow dances with a cat; Wieland herself sits with her dress open, a construction paper heart across her chest; Snow eats and drinks sloppily, food spilling from his mouth. Sylvia kisses Larry's nose; he licks jam from her fingers, to her protests, her expression struck between horror and pleasure. In the film's final sequence, Larry gives mugging, ambiguous expressions, intercut with images of a flaccid penis. Wieland lies in bed, reading Vogue, in a raccoon-skin cap. A close-up on her eyes cuts to a brief image of Napoleon Bonaparte, and from there, to images of John F. Kennedy. Scenes of Kennedy and his family, rephotographed from magazines, show the president as an ideal of American manhood and the first family an ideal of the American family. On the soundtrack, a distorted recording of the Chiffons' "I Have a Boyfriend" (1963) is sped unnaturally so that the

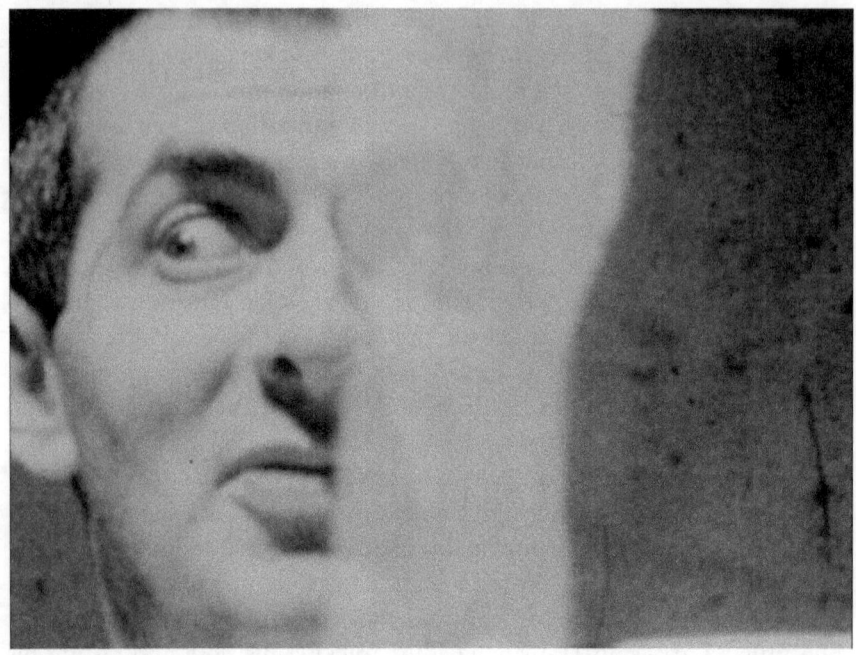

Larry's Recent Behavior *[Film Still]*, 1963
16mm film, 17 minutes, colour and black and white, sound
Courtesy of CFMDC

words are barely comprehensible. A cat wrestles with the American flag, and a model boat appears in soft focus and compositionally fragmented, the hull a looming soft form. Finally, paintings of sailboats are rapidly intercut with the flaccid penis. A concluding title is superimposed over Larry, as he chews on a soft sculpture of a heart.

Although the film deals, on its surface, in the comic miming of a nervous condition, ultimately, it is about love, among men and women, and between the individual and the state; of the former, the unconventional passions of Larry and Sylvia, and the family of Wieland, Snow and their cat, form one vision of love, as something spontaneous and even disgusting, in step with the wild loves of Ken Jacobs and Jack Smith's street theatre performances. The second and more complex matter of love, idealization and nationhood, comes with the arrival of Kennedy, accompanied by the song that Dallas radio had been playing at the time of his death, a song made painfully ironic by the presence of Kennedy in American culture as an icon of manhood, idealized boyfriend to the nation's women. Canada plays no explicit role in the work, but Kennedy is Canada with different vowels. Wieland's regard for Kennedy suggests admiration and longing, compromised in the fleeting glimpse of Napoleon as the Kennedy sequence starts, casting the fallen hero of American statesmanship as master strategist and conqueror.[18]

Larry's Recent Behavior announced certain formal difficulties particular to film. It begins with a prologue in which a rapidly sped-up and incomprehensible recording of voices plays under a projected image of Larry, mugging and contorting his face, sped up by way of stop motion photography (pixilation). The projection is rephotographed in straying composition, in and out of focus, and objects pass in front of the beam: a valentine heart cut from construction paper, a cat, and Wieland's hands performing shadow puppets. This opening sequence foreshadows several aspects of formal difficulty that will enter the film later, in fragmentation and obscurity of sound and vision. As she began to work in film, Wieland discovered these ways to assemble film form in a perceptually distressing way, grotesque and comic vignettes punctuated by images and sounds that were disconnected from the staged sequences. Wieland referred back to ideas that had dominated her paintings and assemblages, such as the distorted figure and the raw marks of construction, and these gestures further situated the film in the discourse of Neo-Dada.[19] For example, the valentine heart soft sculptures have a strong relation to other works of New York Neo-Dada such as the soft sculptures of Claes Oldenburg; however, while

---

[18] Napoleon is a minor figure among the icons that Wieland would use in her art, adopted in the late 1950s after she read Emil Ludwig's *Napoleon* (Garden City, New York: Garden City Publishing Co., 1926) and became taken with him for his consolidation of power, coming as it did by the force of his class mobility as he rose up from the Corsican underclass to become the Emperor of the French. Jane Lind has speculated that Wieland's interest in Napoleon was due to this, her desire to simultaneously transcend and embody her impoverished origins. In Wieland's "Josephine's Last Letter to Napoleon," she writes, "Many people chastise Napolean for killing people needlessly but, how hard it is to do good without being bad" (in *evidence*, n.d., unpaginated). This statement, not so much an act of apology or justification as an admission of the ironic compromises that come with power, suggests how Wieland came to view contemporary figures in North American politics, in particular John F. Kennedy and Pierre Trudeau, idealized and powerful figures who, like Napoleon, were formed of contradictions.

[19] Wieland's collages and drawings had often used the form of the valentine heart. This icon entered her work of the early 1960s, with works such as *Hart News* (1961), in which a series of blocks and semi-circular forms make red and pale blue impressions around serial repetitions of red valentine hearts, some stenciled, others more inexact, given fluctuating dimensions against white paper. With *Heart-On* (1962), the heart form was painted in oil on linen. By the time that Wieland made *Larry's Recent Behavior*, the heart form had departed from two-dimensional illustration and had become a multi-dimensional trademark, in the form of the cardboard cutout as well as the soft sculptures seen in the film. The heart form would be integrated into Wieland's painted constructs *Cooling Room II* and *Young Woman's Blues* (both 1964), and *Larry's Recent Behavior* demonstrates the ways in which this form was coming off the canvas.

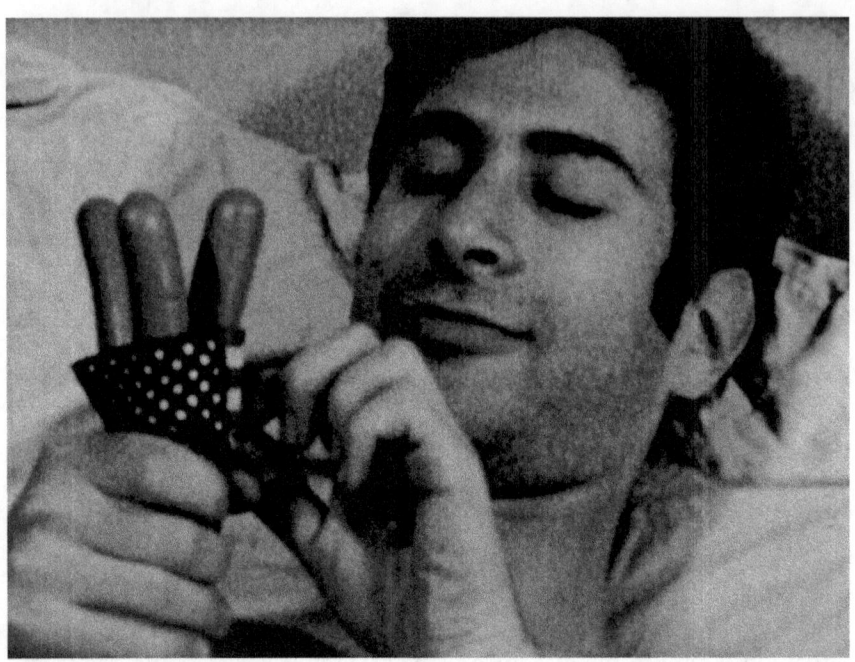

Patriotism *[Film Still]*, 1964
16mm film, 4 minutes, colour, sound
Courtesy of CFMDC

Oldenburg was creating representations of real things, realized in crude paint and at comic scale, Wieland was drawing the commercial symbol of romantic love, a graphic icon that conveyed an idea, and not a form drawn from reality. The sailboat and tall ship, persistent subjects in Wieland's sequential paintings, are likewise integrated into the film, either as non sequitur or, as a tall ship may be, a symbol of colonialism.[20]

Wieland followed *Larry's Recent Behavior* with another film in the same comic vein. With *Patriotism* (1964), she would stage a short scene, in a style recalling Norman McLaren's *Neighbours* (1952), combining stop-motion and live-action photography in the service of metaphor. It features a

---

[20] Wieland's use of nautical and aeronautic imagery is tied to her sequential canvases, often as a representation of catastrophe, even as they also reflected her newly stylized figuration. The tragic cartoon faces of *Ill Fated Crew of July 6 1937* (1963), bound in portholes that become cameo mementos, extend the sequential nature of Wieland's nautical paintings, but are also a rare early example, alongside an earlier collage work, *Laura Secord Saves Upper Canada* (1961), of allusive programme, an idea that would come to be of increasing importance to Wieland as her work became strongly identified with Canadian history. The figures are grotesquely exaggerated, like figures that populated her journals, illustrations and contemporaneous paintings such as *Clues* and *Fine Foods* (both 1963).

simple series of actions: a man (David Shackman) sleeps in a bed, his figure partly covered by a white sheet. Hot dog buns assemble out of thin air on his bed, advancing like an arrow in a march across his stomach, circling around to occupy the space next to his pillow. Shackman yawns, turns and sees them, with a look of disbelief. They overtake his face, march out of his armpits and perform strategic formations around a miniature American flag napkin. The napkin strokes each hot dog, in a sexual motion, destroying and sweeping away the buns. In an act of war, the napkin consumes all of the hot dogs, and then retreats under the covers. Shackman wakes up with a look of discomfort, reaches underneath the covers and pulls out three hotdogs and an American flag napkin. He gathers them up, smells them, and the film ends with him holding them in the napkin, grouped as a bouquet. The film's simplicity, relative to the unwieldy structure of *Larry's Recent Behavior*, could disguise its ambiguity. Its performance of American patriotism, and patriarchy, as a destructive, consuming, assimilating force is unambiguous, but Shackman, as happy, sleeping witness, is an ambiguous, unallied subject at the centre of the film, both victim and victor.

Having completed two films in the comic vein of the New York underground, Wieland turned, with her friend Betty Ferguson, to making a film using 16mm found footage.[21] Much as Jack Chambers had used found footage in *Hybrid* to advance a vision of the barbarous exchange between humanity and nature, Wieland and Ferguson used materials, culled from the refuse of commercial and educational-industrial films, to form a darkly funny parable, *Barbara's Blindness* (1965). A blind child wears surgical bandages over her eyes. Her bandages are shorn away and she regains her sight. This process is interrupted by images of atomic explosions, Buster Keaton, flowers blooming and tribal dances. These visions appear in reverse, turned upside down and in photographic negative as malformed visual pleasure, or, in the case of the most menacing images, as ironic contradictions of the glory of the child's newfound vision. The child, wandering through a meadow to smell and pick flowers, has her actions intercut with elephants charging through and decimating a forest, her bounding joy akin to the blind force of a stampede. In a long sequence that serves as

---

[21] Betty Ferguson was at the time married to Graeme Ferguson, one of the founders of IMAX, who had also been a member of the Toronto Film Society. The Fergusons had met Snow and Wieland in Toronto, but had moved to New York shortly before them. This would serve as Wieland's first substantive work in found footage filmmaking, and it was the birth of Ferguson's practice, which would continue through the 1970s with *Telephone Film*, *Airplane Film* and *Kisses*, all films which delivered what their titles suggested, serving as catalogues of images assembled in witty formation. Much like Wieland, Ferguson's experience of the Depression had influenced her desire to rescue film materials that were being thrown out by television stations, and so, for Ferguson, the repurposing of film materials was about finding a second life for refuse.

a further analogy for recovered sight, a woman emerges from padded dirt, her stone-like features making her a Golem, her eyes sealed by dirt. She staggers in the sunlight, her expressionless face frozen between ecstasy and suffering. She finds her way to a river where, stumbling through reeds, she submerges her body in water. A series of further images, taken from other contexts, extends this setting: a woman looks out on a lake; a man saves a drowning woman from rushing water; a fight between a man and a child occurs on a boat; an alligator sinks into water, intercut with an infant wading. Crowds of chickens are intercut with crowds of men. The film takes as its central device a series of cuts, establishing early on that the cuts are going to have logical cohesion. It then resists those instructions, with non sequitur digressions, logical pairings that are divorced from surrounding material or images that serve as comical exclamation. The film ends with a prolonged exchange between a man and a young woman, her weeping into his chest, on board a ship. Their eyes search the viewer, the gaze of the camera, as if waiting for direction.

Barbara's Blindness has many aspects to its authorship that, by evidence of their later work, could be readily assigned to Ferguson, who would go on to work exclusively in found footage filmmaking. However, the elusive and decentered meanings and false instructions demonstrate Joyce Wieland's ideas as to the innate mystery of vision and the importance of obscurity. Further to Wieland's contribution, the editing advances almost exclusively disjunctive pairings, extending Wieland's distinct sense of irony. The title of the film is spelled out in braille, hands passing over it, an image of tactility, yet also a declaration of obscurity, the embossed letters encoding a different or absent meaning for the fingers rather than the eyes, the irony of a repurposed linguistic system made meaningless to its own blind audience. Wieland and Ferguson appear in four frames between the titles and the film body, their eyes blocked out with black construction paper. The difficulties of Larry's Recent Behavior and Patriotism in their political ambiguity, programme obscurity and, in the case of Larry's Recent Behavior, the aggression of its disorientation as well. With Barbara's Blindness, difficulty shifted into another mode, of literacy, the anticipation of coherent structure, here undermined by an unhinging of film's grammar, pairing a sentimental parable of eyesight returned to the ironic grief of eyesight 're-deemed'. Logical inference, between two or more alternating passages, creates a comedy of recognition, but it can suddenly be turned by the illogical comedy of the non sequitur. This essential oddness is perhaps best felt in the intrusion of African tribesmen and Lon Chaney's gruesome Phantom of the Opera, intercut with paradisiacal scenes of a child frolicking along a garden wall. The compositional fragmentation of Wieland's sequential

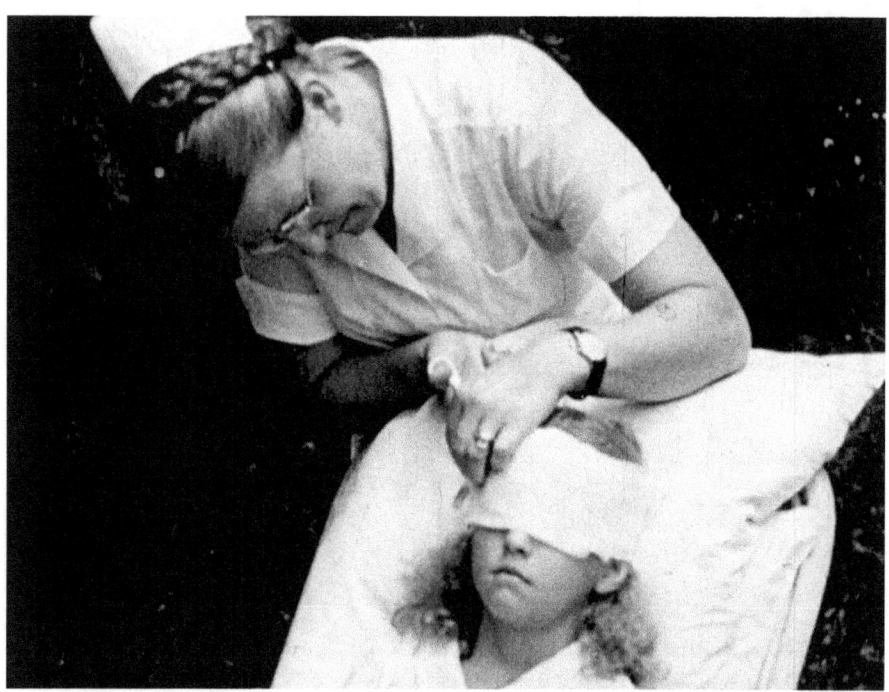

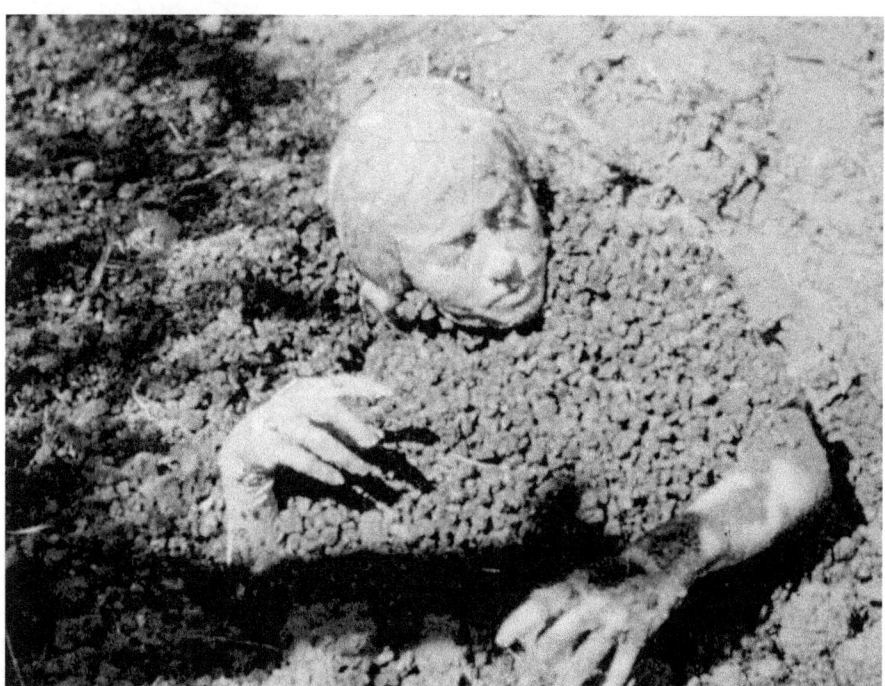

Barbara's Blindness *[Film Stills]*, 1965
16mm film, 16 minutes, colour and black and white, sound
Courtesy of CFMDC

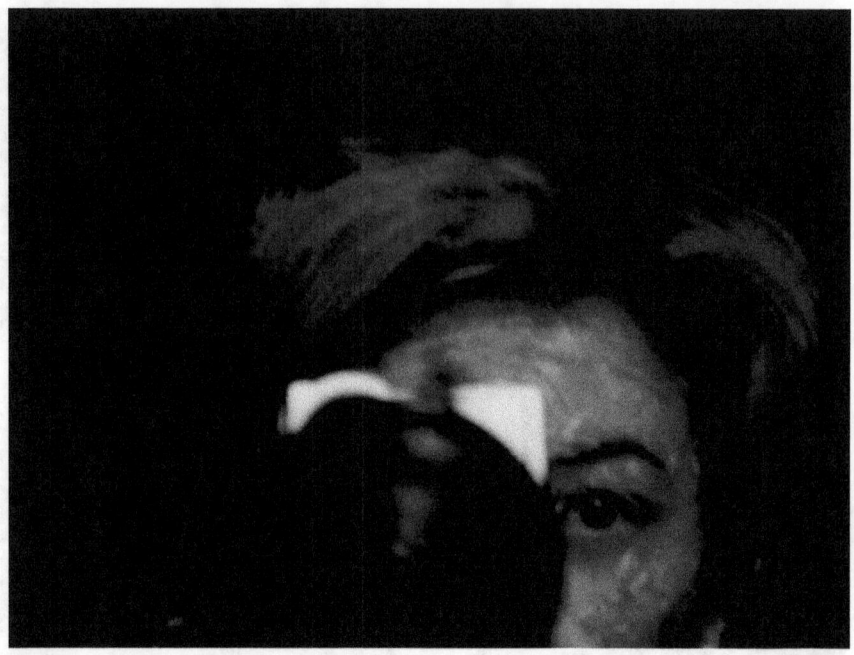

Water Sark *[Film Still]*, 1965
16mm film, 14 minutes, colour, sound
Courtesy of CFMDC

paintings is not present in *Barbara's Blindness*, its parts assumed from the conventional compositions of commercial or industrial cinema; instead, the film subverts the logic of film editing itself, giving way to fragmentation of theme and of meaning. The ready meaning of *Barbara's Blindness* finds a blind child, the viewer's alter ego, discovering vision as darkest comedy. A more complex meaning comes from the destabilization of the film's subject, the miraculous experience of vision, eventually settling instead on the image itself, as a kind of blindness; its grammar, a kind of braille; and the ironic, obscure comedy of its sightlines.

With her next film, Wieland would depart entirely from narrative programme, instead using the camera to reveal an elastic and intimate vision of her home. This work was not an unanticipated redirection, but rather evolved slowly and concurrently with her other underground films.[22] *Water Sark* (1965) would resemble Wieland's diaries, as a flow of spontaneous observations, but it was also a constructed performance in

---

[22] This evolution can be seen in Wieland's diary film *Peggy's Blue Skylight* (1964), completed in 1986, more intimate and sentimental in tone than the concurrent *Larry's Recent Behavior* and *Patriotism*.

which, on one level, the artist interacted with a set and props, on another, the whole space and its contents interacted with controlled angles of light. In a note accompanying the film, Wieland wrote, "I decided to make a film at my kitchen table, there is nothing like knowing my table. The high art of the housewife. You take prisms, glass, lights and myself to it."[23] The credits are superimposed over an image of a round paper lantern lamp-shade covering a hanging light bulb, its form resembling that of a breast and nipple. The lantern begins to ripple outward in circular currents, its image a reflection in water. Wieland films a set table under the light. She holds a piece of mirror over the table with one hand. In the mirror, the light appears, as do Wieland, her Super 8 camera and the paper lantern above. The light swings, changing the angle of light on the table's con-tents. The lampshade's reflection expands and contracts in the surface of a water glass. The mirror allows Wieland to guide the light around the set table, and that light wavers along water glasses, trays, plants and pots. The mirror is murky, distorted, more so as water is added to make it wet. The mirror makes symmetries as Wieland holds it to flowers and the water glass, bending it to create perspectival anomalies, the water glass stretched against the flat surface of the table, the paper lantern suddenly and ag-gressively striking down at the glasses by way of its reflection. Water fills the glass as a motif, but the rest of the sequence lacks motivic structure, symmetries always creased by the wide angle of the lens, the eye almost always aware of the distance between a real thing and its reflection. The fluctuating light changes the rendered colour of the plants, along a scale from deep reds and greens to the white limits of exposure. Exterior light comes through a window, obstructed by a pink filter.

The mirror is visibly wet. Wieland's exposed breast is wet with water, and its image is wetted further through its reflection, by the drop-lets forming on the mirror. Wieland, in a shower cap, films her reflection over a bubbling horizon of water. The environment is composed of sharp geometric forms, and as she begins to film through a prism, it is revealed as the same table, the same window. A red and white toy boat is suspended above a bowl of ice, and the pink filter is stood between the camera and the table, with Wieland photographing through and around it. She wears an ill-fitting rubber globe, of smooth plastic, which makes her hand a blunt instrument. She holds it to the camera. The toy boat sways back and forth. Wieland films through a magnifying glass, further distorting the toy boat and her own form, water streaking the glass. She magnifies her cat as it

---

[23] This quotation is attributed to 1963, the year that Wieland began work on *Water Sark*, first given in Hugo McPherson, "Wieland: An Epiphany of North." *Artscanada* 158-159 (August-September 1971), 22.

licks its lips. She films herself and her neckline through the magnifying glass, and holds the magnifying glass up to her eye and mouth, filming in fractured steps so that transitional movements of the mouth are annihilated.[24] She rests the toy boat on her forehead, still filming her reflection. In the final image, her bare fingers splash at water in a bowl.

The film features music and sound by Carla Bley, Ray Jessel and Mike Mantler. The soundtrack includes percussive sounds evocative of water and pots, mixed with the modes of free jazz that Bley and Mantler would pursue as founding members of the Jazz Composer's Orchestra.[25] The soundtrack features, among other elements, elastic percussion, possibly sounding from the interior of a prepared piano; the rapid tapping of dead piano keys; and faint harmonic whistles from the highest register of Mantler's trumpet. The sound reinforces the domestic presence of the work, at times sounding like the incidental sounds of a meal being prepared, or of a table being set or cleared, taken to a comic extreme. The film is so interior an image of home that images of its primary beholder, Wieland, are constantly reflected into the lens, making *Water Sark* less an environmental portrait or performance, more a work of introspection. The film opens with a simple disorientation, the paper lantern gradually betraying itself as a wet reflection, in rippling, circular waves, but this establishes a false instruction, assuming the film will be made up of reflections that subvert space and objecthood. Each succeeding sequence deals instead in surface, angles of light and the forms of real things, and each sequence lays plain the tools that create these enigmas, the filter, the mirror, the swinging light, all shown clearly for what they are. The film is therefore torn between an interior experience that shirks dimension and perspective, that uses the 'water dress' of its title to distort the image, and an exteriority that reveals the depth and dimensions of this domicile, its contents and inhabitants.

Wieland later described *Water Sark* (1965) in conversation with filmmaker Hollis Frampton as "[resembling] the drawings that I did for the ten years preceding that film. It was an extension of those drawings.

---

[24] Such self-portraiture would take on increased significance in three later works, the lithograph *O Canada* (1969) and the embroidered *O Canada Animation* (1970), in which a sequence of lips form the syllables of the titular Canadian national anthem, and the film *Reason Over Passion* (1969), in which Wieland, again filming her own reflection, mouths the Canadian national anthem in a manner recalling the lithograph.

[25] Ray Jessel, who had known Snow and Wieland in Toronto and lived in New York concurrently, became a successful composer of mainstream Broadway shows, beginning with *Baker Street* (1965), a musical about the life of Sherlock Holmes. He later collaborated with Richard Rodgers on *I Remember Mama* (1979), and wrote and produced for mainstream American television through the 1970s and 80s contributing to *The Carol Burnett Show*, *The Love Boat* and *Head of the Class*.

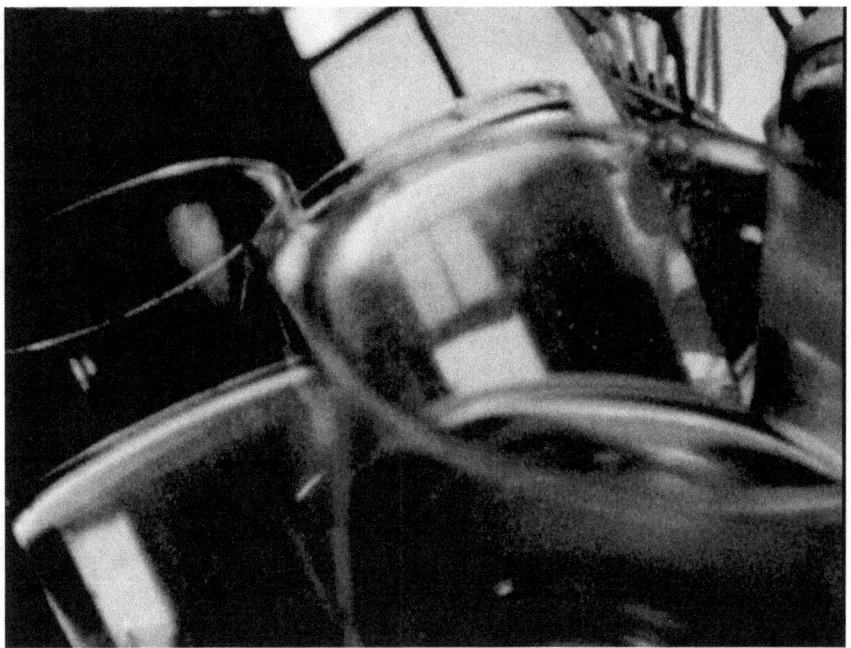

Water Sark *[Film Still]*, 1965
16mm film, 14 minutes, colour, sound
Courtesy of CFMDC

It was a drawing film."[26] In those drawings, such as her *Lovers* series, the figure was never aspiring toward a wholeness of form, was instead made of loose lines, hands and eyes left incomplete, a torso or head or leg left open by truncated lines, with multiple figures joined together by these fissures. Her style turned later to figurative forms drawn from greeting cards, rotund cartoon figures that likewise emerged only partly from the plane of the paper, broken lines rendering the figure incomplete, like the drawings of penises that seemed appeared in her notebooks. In *Water Sark*, lines fluctuate with droplets and streaks of water and with aperture fluctuations that overexpose the image, causing it to vanish into the clear plastic of the film and muddying the definition of surrounding forms. In addition to the film's aesthetic origins in the line work of Wieland's drawings, there are definite consonances of subject: for example, in *Woman Amusing Herself* (1955), a figure kneels in a skirt, her breasts exposed, her face splintering into two halves as if facing a mirror; she holds a small hand mirror away

---

[26] Hollis Frampton and Joyce Wieland, "I Don't Even Know about the Second Stanza," transcribed and prepared for publication by R. Bruce Elder. In *The Films of Joyce Wieland*, ed. Kathryn Elder (Toronto: Cinematheque Ontario, 1999), 172.

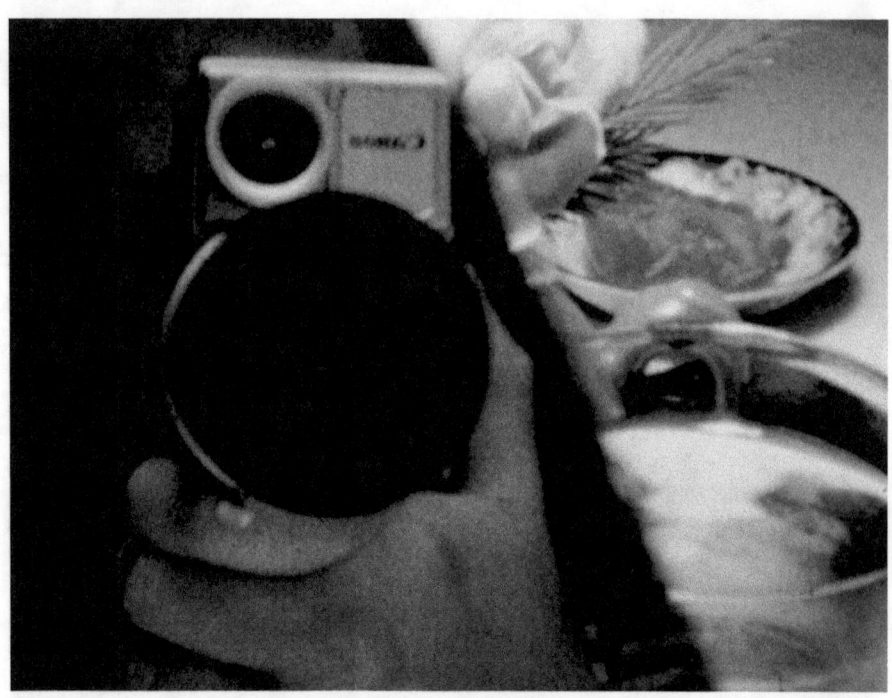

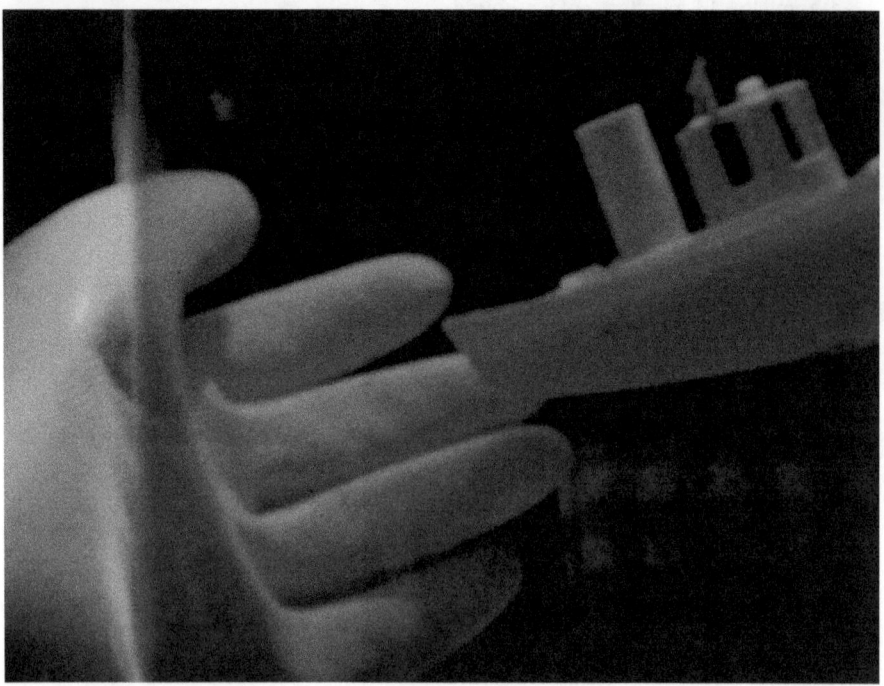

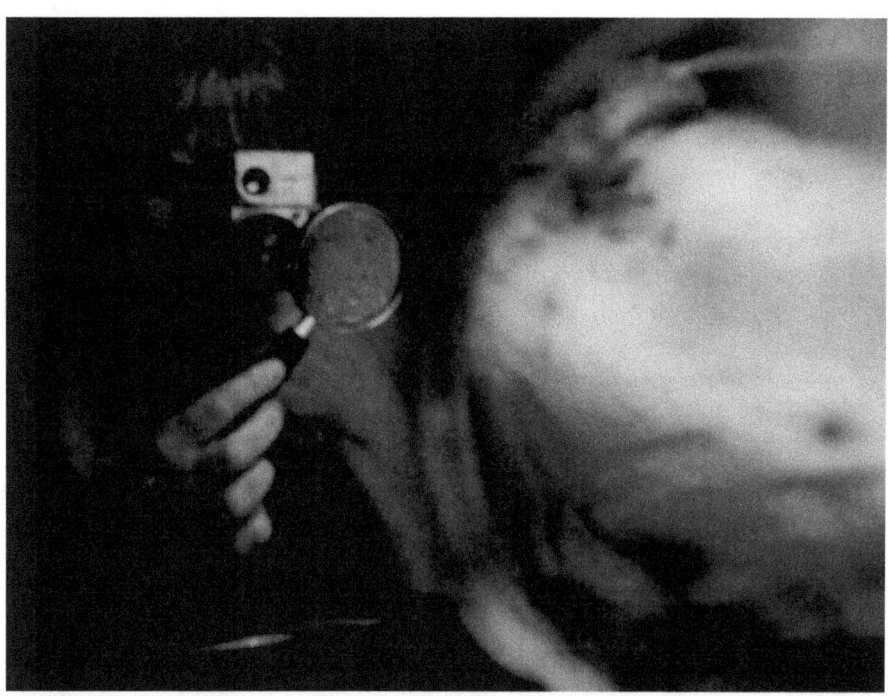

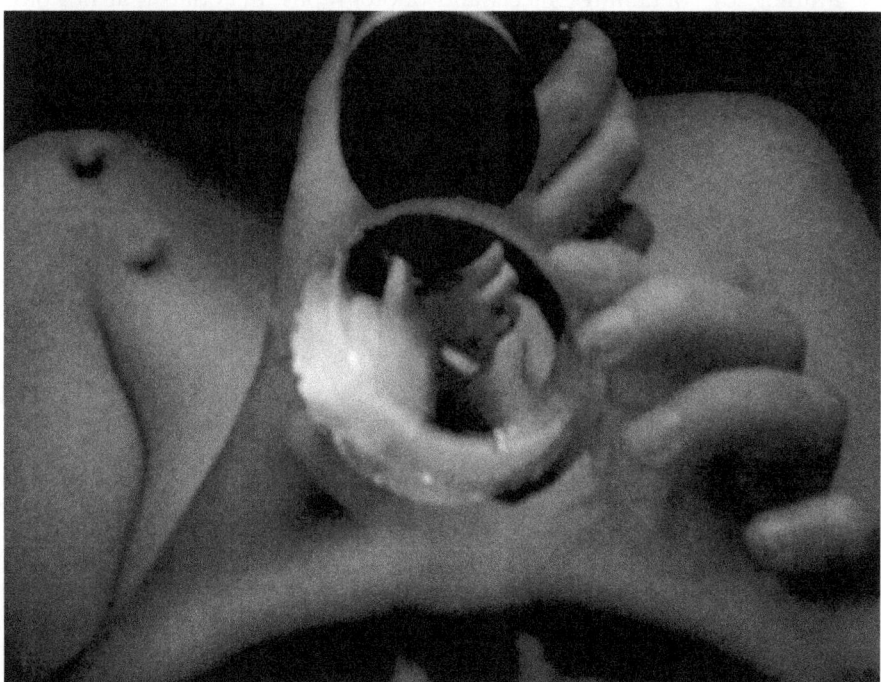

Water Sark *[Film Stills]*, 1965
16mm film, 14 minutes, colour, sound
Courtesy of CFMDC

from her side; this figuration, of the face splitting as if against a mirror, continues in *Lovers with Curly Hair* (1955). *Water Sark* also deals in elastic fluctuations of form, as the table, its contents, and the nude self-portrait are all subject to recomposition through lenses, whether the machined lenses of the magnifying glass or camera or the chance lens of the water glass. This recalls later entries in the *Lovers* series wherein figures fluctuate in dimension, referencing idols of human figuration from the artists' mannequin to the Venus figurine, an elasticity of form that is also present in Wieland's sequential paintings and drawings involving cars, boats and phalluses.

Wieland's accompanying note on *Water Sark* concluded that it "is a film sculpture, being made, while you wait," an ironic borrowing of the language of advertising.[27] Wieland's treatment of light in *Water Sark* would continue with a body of sculptural collage work, what Frampton would call tactile icons, a part of her 'para-cinema' work, work resembling or occurring alongside her films. This para-cinema, hanging assemblages that she called 'stuffed movies', had debts to her earlier mixed media collages, but also resulted from her interests in sequential arrangement and in harnessing light, the work posed in a direct lineage from her sequential paintings and her films. Her 'stuffed movies' made use of plastic forms, from inflatable waterproof swim paraphernalia to tinted plastic bags, arranging, framing, or containing objects and photographs, materials that not only situated the sculptures with the Neo-Dada uncanny of Claes Oldenburg, but which also allowed them to interact with light in a manner specific to the material being of soft plastic, light lured to their crumpling surfaces. *Stuffed Movie* (1966) consists of five pale green and orange bags, hanging vertically, containing, among other things, American and Canadian flags, mass media images, toys and small banners, each object coloured by the plastic bag that envelops them. Other hanging assemblages that explicitly address cinema include *War & Peace, 8mm Home Movie* (1966), in which familiar images from Wieland's work—self-portraits, boats and flowers—are suspended from a blue circle and yellow triangle; and *D. W. Griffith and His Cameraman Billy Bitzer* (1966), a diptych in green and pink soft plastic, portraits of the men sewn in pink into the centre of reflective plastic squares. Other hanging assemblages were not so aimed at cinematic context but dealt with Wieland's concerns over nationhood, labour, the body and spirituality, both individually and in combination. *Patriotism* (1966) consisted of flags—the British Union Jack, the Canadian Maple Leaf and the American Star-Spangled Banner—arranged as a body, the Canadian flag divided and extended in cruciform. The torso contains photographs of

---

[27] Hugo McPherson, "Wieland: An Epiphany of North." *Artscanada* 158-159 (August-September 1971), 22.

voluptuous lips in bright orange plastic, placed as a glowing heart.[28]

The 'stuffed movies' would continue through 1967 and 1968, to a different end – first, in the minimal, comic scale of *Don't Mess with Bill (for Anita and Sylvia)* (1967), its title taken from the Marvelettes, its form a phallus with a black heart pinned to it, anchored by a magnifying glass; in *Home Work* (1967), a series of variable plastic forms with photographic contents, shaped into a flat graphic form recalling a potted plant; and later, in the explicitly nationalist critique of *Puerco de Navidad* (1967) and *Confedspread* (1967), both of which prominently feature the Canadian flag and extend Wieland's use of this material to a larger scale, the soft plastic's light effects met by obscure programme, their critique masked by the pleasure of their forms. As she began to work with film again, concerns of light, plasticity and form continued but gained new dimensions. The trajectory of radical experimentation in New York underground film had changed. Snow had completed *Wavelength* and was beginning his axial films, and Hollis Frampton had likewise begun a series of films aggressively fixated on the material construction of cinema itself. Wieland, for her part, had already made films aware of their material being, the physical roughness of *Larry's Recent Behavior* and *Barbara's Blindness* following in the aesthetics of Neo-Dada, the light fluctuations of *Water Sark* using the clear base of the image to transform line, but her work, despite its rhythmic construction, did not yet bear a material reflection on time itself. Upon returning to filmmaking in 1967, Wieland would further define her relation to time. The raw and spontaneous structures of her earlier films would now turn to signification itself, and to the nature of time and temporal experience. She, like Snow, would remain an emissary of what the critic Robert Rosenblum had called, in coining Neo-Dada, the "vital neo-Dada spirit," vitality itself an agent against the deadening intellectual distance that would infect the structural film movement.[29] Wieland's films would continue to retain both

---

[28] Other assemblages of this year include *N.U.C.* (1966), an acronym that may stand for 'no use crying', a soft plastic heart, made from the stars of an American flag, suspended from a green soft plastic circle with a reflective red dollar sign emblazoned on it. *Home Art Totem* (1966) is a series of shapes, including circles, windows, hearts, tubes. Its images include a photograph of the pattern of her *Square Mandala* quilt (1966). It was a work in which creative and domestic labour becomes a series of colourful signs in heterodox sequence. Finally, *The Space of the Lama* (1966) has some consonance with the work of Jack Chambers in Wieland's cooption of old photographs, retaining their monochrome against the pallid orange and blue of their soft plastic backing, in four vertical bags: the face of a child, the background shorn away, below it a series of photographs: one of the earth from the moon's surface and a crescent moon cut out of soft plastic; below that, an unexposed film strip tied into a ribboned bundle of curves; and finally, a dark circle in a blue bag.

[29] Rosenblum's remark is in response to the work of Jasper Johns in a 1957 show at the Leo Castelli Gallery in New York. Robert Rosenblum, "The Castelli Group," *Arts Magazine* 31:8, May 1957, 53.

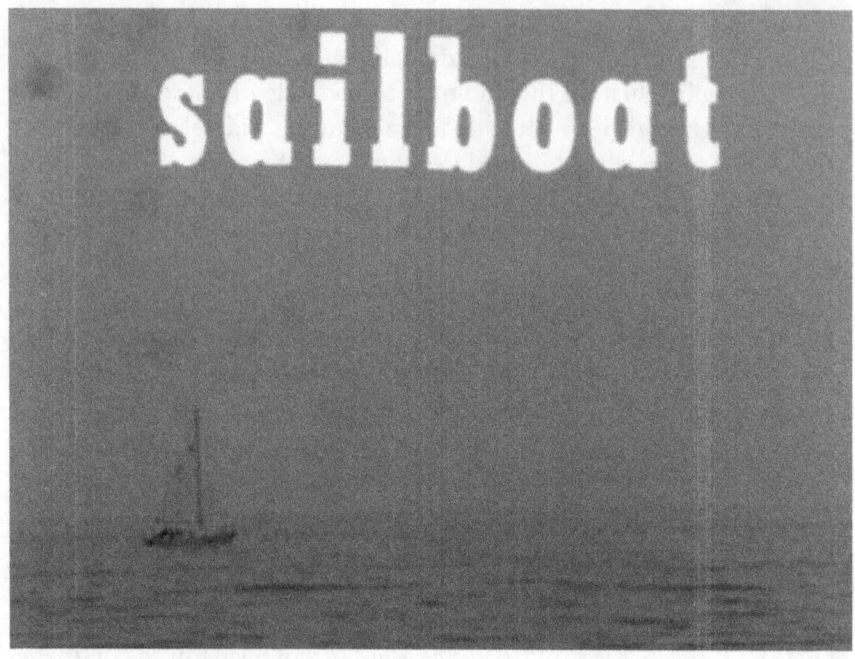

Sailboat *[Film Still]*, 1967
16mm film, 3 minutes, colour, sound
Courtesy of CFMDC

her surface fascinations with nautical themes, labour and nationhood; her aesthetic interests in light, enigmatic sequence, perspectival distortion and the marks of process; and as her work continued, it would deal in the most intimate and personal aspects of her life, her embrace of the role of house-wife and her anxieties over the body and the absent family. They would also extend the central dichotomy of her work, of coexistent sentiment and irony, enclosing content, form and personal expression.

Sailboats, tall ships and ocean liners had appeared in Wieland's paintings from 1963 onward, and in all of her preceding films save for *Patriotism. Sailboat* (1967), her first film to be completed after 1965 and the first to arrive in the aftermath of her para-cinema sculptures, was a sin-gle composition, of minimal activity, extended in ten repetitions. Wieland described the film as such: "This little Sailboat film will sail right through your gate and into your heart," an oblique reference to the gates of the camera and projector, the frame itself. A sailboat snakes left to right across a horizon, the word 'sailboat', all in lower case, emblazoned at the top of the screen in white letters. Throughout, harsh ocean sounds play on the soundtrack, in keeping with the day's murky, overcast light, which has cast sea, sky and sailboat in a uniform blue monochrome. The boat crosses the frame three times before a bather interrupts the shot, in the left fore-ground, marching toward the horizon, disappearing at the bottom of the frame. After some fluctuation of scale, the boat grows more distant, shrink-ing on the horizon, but the sea and the text remain the same. The sailboat will cross the full horizon seven times, and then, in three final movements, it will pass from the centre of the composition to the right.

The joining of actions, of the sailboat passing in full, in part, and the one human obstruction, demonstrate Wieland's new interest in the temporal dimension of film, its ability to repeat and elaborate on simple actions and to fracture activity, in order to magnify rhythms: the bather's brief interruption assures the viewer that this is not a loop, but it also shows that Wieland, in her process, has left room for the unexpected or impro-vised. The text is omnipresent, isolating this object from the sea and sky, identifying it as the central focus of the image, even as the colour of the sea and sky bleed into it. Like her earlier paintings of similar subjects, *Sailing* (1963) and *Sailboat Sinking* (1965), the subject gradually changes scale and, as in *Sailboat Sinking*, is mediated by something placed between vision and object (in the case of the painting, it is a porthole; in the film, it is text). The omnipresence of this text is a difficult gesture: it runs the full course of the work, against the conventions of film titles, but it also forces an as-sumption of the relation between image and text, reinforcing the sailboat as an inescapable central figure, and the word's prolonged presence and demanded attention taxes the purpose of the word and its meaning, by extension, language itself, a divorce of signifier and signified. These tem-poral and structural strategies can only describe the film's trajectory and its play on meaning, its relation to time and logic, and not the presence of light and line. *Sailboat* is a dense vision of the sea, in this regard a far cry from the sequential paintings that Wieland had made of sailboats, where the graphic form of the sailboat, in red, black and white, fluctuates in scale between edits, on a blue sea. In *Sailboat*, the overcast day shrouds the boat in fog, and as the distance widens, the sailboat itself is reduced, from a fully realized vessel into a bare triangle.

It was an act of material self-consciousness to set this little sailboat to sail through the gate, repeating its signifier, at twenty-four frames-per-second, to exhaustion, until the meaning of the word and the form of the boat had become dulled in their exchange. But Wieland's games of lan-guage and meaning would achieve a more puckish form with her next film. In *1933* (1967), another single-shot film, the image looks down on a busy street and the exterior of a restaurant. The camera is positioned looking out of a window, seeing the activity in the street through the bars of a fire

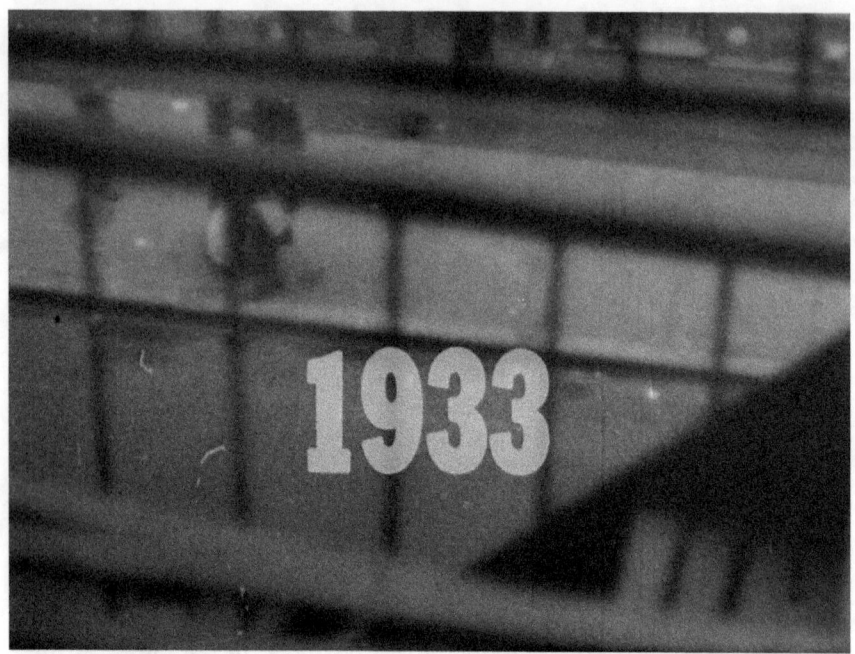

1933 *[Film Still]*, 1967
16mm film, 4 minutes, colour, sound
Courtesy of CFMDC

escape. The number 1933 is superimposed over the image in white text, the text appearing for fifteen seconds at a time, roughly once per minute. The filmed image alternates with sections of white. Wieland performs the soundtrack, a mouth organ sounding discordantly against chords hammered on a piano. This music plays when the photographed image plays, but is replaced with the hum of an empty soundtrack during stretches of white. The sound is only this, dissonance or silence, the dissonance standing in for the bustling sounds of street life, the silence signaling the film's material being, its natural silence, a hum. Wieland would describe *1933* as "a speeded up shot out of a window/repeated/evoking the feeling of 1933/walking/window/repeat." This image, of or around 1933, is held against the blank frame and its silence, its depiction of street life coming under the influence of text that forces an assumption. Michael Snow explained the presence of this text as an evocation rather than a definition: "1933. The year? the number? the title? Was it (the film) made then? It's a memory! (i.e. a Film.) No, it's many memories. It's so sad and funny: the departed, departing people, cars, streets! It hurries, it's gone, it's back! the film (of 1933?) was made in 1967. You find out, if you don't already know, how naming tints pure vision."[30]

The image is ambiguous, unlikely by its composition to have been made in 1933, and the figures and vehicles pass too quickly to fix in a particular era. The number given, as implied in these two statements, is a suggestion rather than a fact, or simply an element that exposes the presumed exchange of word and image and the viewer's suggestibility. The number forces the assumption that this image of bustling street life, taken from an obscure angle, is of another era. Wieland's use of this number then raises questions about the nature of film itself, all images being of the past, their distance from the present dependent upon context and language, variables that hold the power to subvert. The relation between vision and context had been a consistent interest of Wieland's from her programmatic titling of her paintings of the early 1960s to her filmmaking activities and stuffed movies. The stuffed movies had joined disparate parts into a common form, placing into dialogue icons, drawings and mass culture symbols that held no logical cohesion. Likewise, the image and text formed disparate parts in *1933*, the image questioning the number's role, as a date or some other value, the number forcing an assumption of the image's role, as an evocation of or a picture of an increasingly distant past.

In her time at Graphic Associates in the mid-1950s, Wieland had begun to draw directly on blank film. These filmstrips were later incorporated into her early assemblages, and by the mid-1960s, Wieland would use similar techniques, applying fabric dyes directly to the film plane in her filmmaking process.[31] This technique first occurs in *Barbara's Blindness*, in which stretches of the film have been painted over. Her interest in these strategies culminated in *Handtinting* (1967), a film assembled out of outtakes from a black and white Job Corps documentary which Wieland had shot in 1965 and 1966, showing the recreational activities of poor women in New York City.[32] *Handtinting* shows women dancing, preparing to swim and then swimming, clapping, laughing, smoking and waiting, some with

---

[30] Qtd. in Hugo McPherson, "Wieland: An Epiphany of North." *Artscanada* 158-159 (August-September 1971), 22. It has subsequently been used as a descriptive text for the work in distributors' catalogues.

[31] R. Bruce Elder has pointed to this as a natural transition of Wieland's material concerns in other media to cinema. The ways in which she uses dyes on the film plane reinforce this claim and demonstrate the rich interchange between media in Wieland's work. However, it also bears noting that Wieland was aware of the painted films of Storm De Hirsch (*Peyote Queen*, 1965) and Stan Brakhage (*Eye Myth*, 1967, among others) that would inspire many to take up painting and drawing on film.

[32] Wieland became involved in the Job Corps documentary through another Canadian expatriate, Sylvia Davern, who was commissioned to make the documentary for the Xerox Corporation, with the intent of broadcasting it on television. Kay Armatage, "Kay Armatage Interviews Joyce Wieland." *Take One* 3:2 (November-December 1970), 23.

rapt attention, some bored. They speak and sing but there is no sound. None of these actions are shown in full; they are fragmented into a terminal state of mid-action. This gives the film a nervous energy, as these fractured gestures are punctuated with black, which like the clear leader of *1933*, suspends the image, in this case to reinforce that the images will not assemble into a logical sequence. Wieland intercuts shots that have been dyed green, pink, orange and blue. The dye has been inconsistently applied, so that its watermarks remain on and between the frames, revealing the film's material being, the dyes resting on the surface of the image.[33] It is another wet dress, but unlike the droplets and wet mirror of *Water Sark*, the dyes cannot alter lines or refract light; they can only form other mysteries on the surface of the film, in their lack of coherent colour-relation and their loose communion with the images underlying them.

Wieland's earlier work of 1967 had indicated deference toward generating conventional rhythmic structures through editing, in the repeating vessel of *Sailboat* or the alternating sequences of *1933*. With *Handtinting*, she worked with rhythmic punctuation, forged by rapid cutting, an editorial form that was essentially musical. The film is silent, but the images come in uttered rhythm, spaced out with stretches of black, taking on the rhythmic dimensions of music or speech, with the black serving as rest or silence. Even that black is punctured, literally, by holes punched by sewing needles.[34] The act of building visual rhythms in silent film was long-since common in the American experimental cinema, its greatest apostle being Stan Brakhage, whose work achieved what he believed to be innate rhythms of vision. Unlike that work, *Handtinting* uses extensive motifs and punctuations, among them flipping the film so that images repeat with their horizontal axis reversed. Its structural conceits act against the innate rhythms of vision, advancing instead a rhythmic system of cinematic artifice. Its broken, mid-action gestures and its tints inhabit the same frames, the underlying images synchronizing with the overlaying colours, and yet, tint and action remain independent from the other. The film's title prioritizes the tinting as the central act of the filmmaker, but the film itself is a more complex treatment of form and content, with cinema verité and water-marked, saturated colours simultaneously occurring, joined by an overarching rhythm.

Joyce Wieland's alternately durational and fragmentary approaches to rhythm would combine in *Cat Food* (1967), in which a cat consumes

---

[33] R. Bruce Elder, *Image and Identity: Reflections on Canadian Film and Culture* (Waterloo: Wilfred Laurier Press, 1989), 262.

[34] Wieland's choice of tools—fabric dyes and sewing needles—also implicate the film in a women's craft tradition, much like her quilts of the same period such as *The Square Mandala* (1966), *The Camera's Eyes* (1966) and *Film Mandala* (1967).

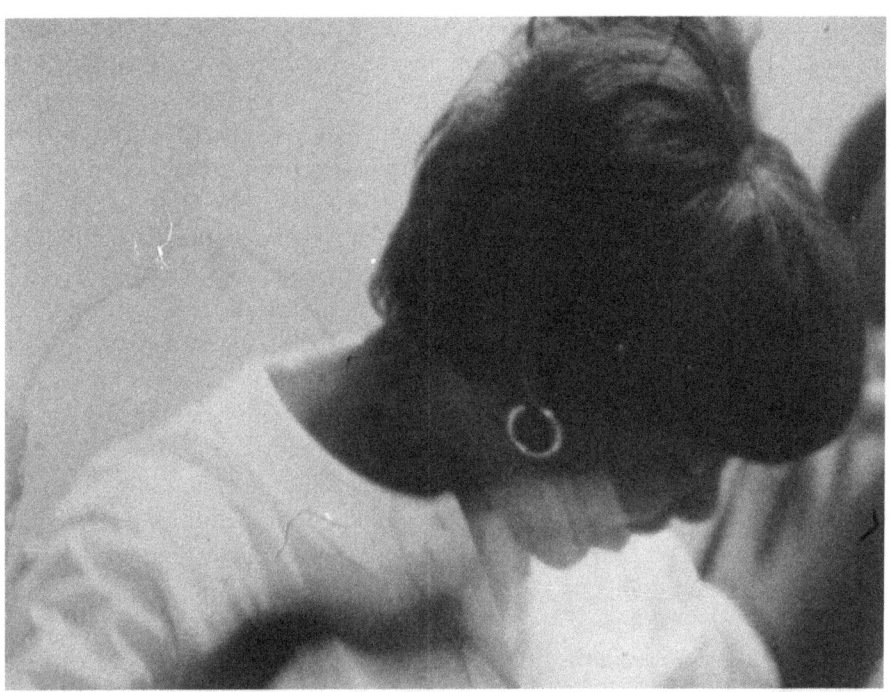

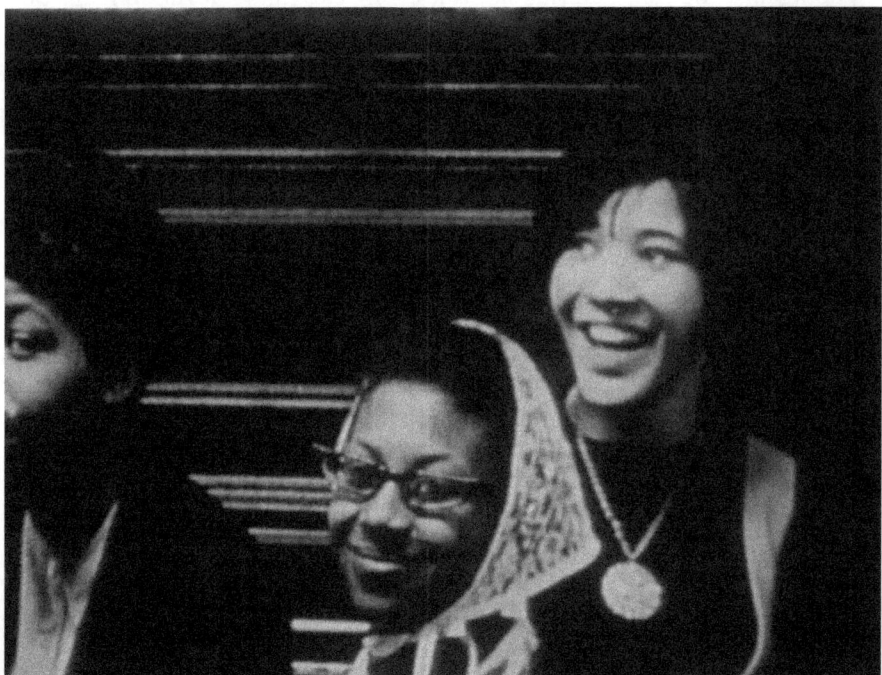

Handtinting *[Film Stills]*, 1967-68
16mm film, 6 minutes, colour, silent
Courtesy of CFMDC

several fish over the film's thirteen-minute length, its activity broken down and rearranged to pitch its consumption as an ambiguous metaphor. The set is again Wieland's kitchen table, now with a white tablecloth that will, as the film goes on, become stained with viscera. The cat sleeps on this white sheet and gradually stirs. A sardine (eyes, scales and all) is on the table, next to a glass of water. What follows is filmed in elliptical edits: the cat gnaws on the fish; the fish, another of Wieland's phallic symbols, is slowly eaten away; the course of the meal breaks from chronology as the amount of fish consumed fluctuates between cuts; the fish is substituted, alternating between the sardine, a rockbass and an unidentified frozen fish. The camera's speed changes, altering the exposure. The pale underside of the fish and the paler fur of the cat lose definition and become pure light, merging with the white of the tablecloth and wall. The cat's eating is sped comically by a low frame rate. Eventually, the eating slows, and the image darkens with the changing speed. The film continues the editorial fragmentation of *Handtinting*, as time is not chronological but constructed around visual interest and rhythm. The composition, aperture and speed fluctuate, as if Wieland is punning on 'scales', the scales of the fish, the scale of the composition and the scales of technological rendering (camera speed, aperture) fluidly oscillating. Late in the film, the camera is held right up against the fish, entering its scales. The cat gnaws at the remains of a fish head, but with an edit, the fish becomes whole again.

The temporal aspect of *Cat Food* is subject to the visual interest of the event itself, continuing the departure of *Handtinting* from the temporal structures of *1933* and *Sailboat*. It might be presumed from the title, and the near-immediate commencement of the meal, that the film will last for as long as the activity lasts, a performance piece, a minimalist act of documentation. Hollis Frampton's response to the film illuminates the relation between its temporal structure and content. He writes of "the projector [devouring] the ribbon of film at the same rate, methodically," the action of the cat forming parallel to that of the film projector, the cat's chomping incisors analogous to the projector's intermittent mechanism.[35] To view the film in this way, one must presume that the ribbon of film, devoured by the projector, is being given a rhythm matching the gnawing of the cat, but the film also contradicts this statement, as the cat's activity is broken

---

[35] *Film-Makers' Cooperative Catalogue*, no. 5 (New York: New American Cinema Group, 1971), reprinted in *On the Camera Arts and Consecutive Matters: The Writings of Hollis Frampton*, ed. Bruce Jenkins (Boston: MIT Press, 2009), 191. Frampton is not alone in viewing the eating in *Cat Food* as methodical, a convenient interpretation as it allows the film to become analogous to the same concerns as *Patriotism*, coming as it did in the time of the Vietnam War, with the cat serving as a metaphor for American aggression in her subsequent film, *Rat Life and Diet in North America* (1968).

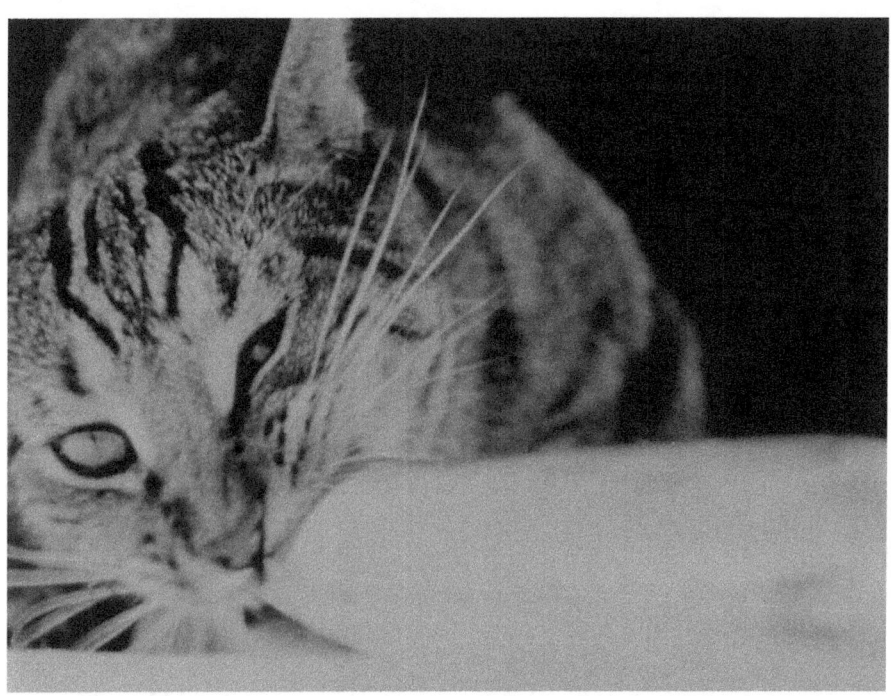

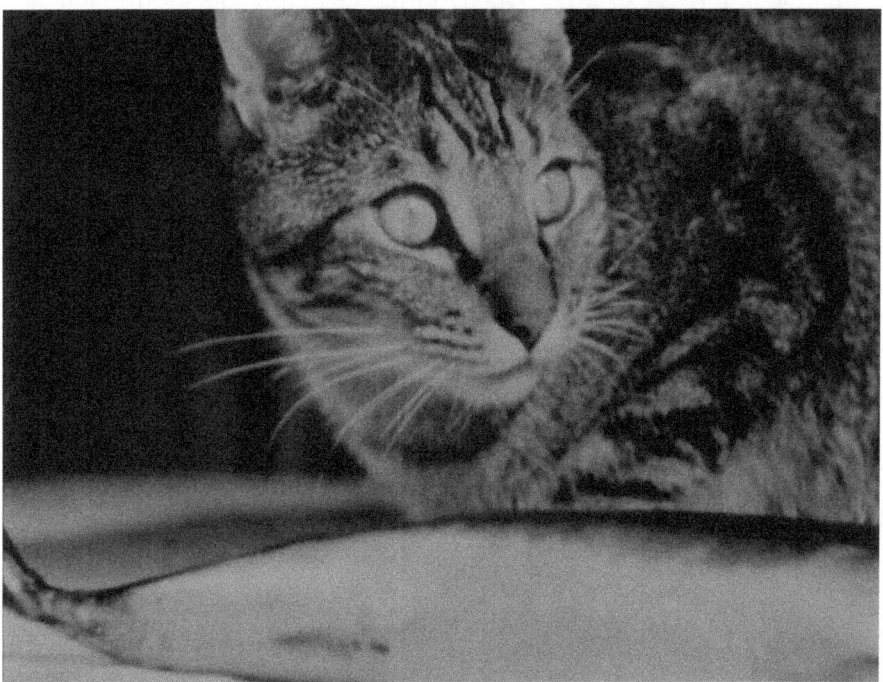

Cat Food *[Film Stills]*, 1967
16mm film, 13 minutes, colour, sound
Courtesy of CFMDC

down into morsels, some of intense focus, others of boredom and indifference, a waning activity that, rather than reduce interpretations of the film
that would cast the meal as an allegory for the American role in Vietnam,
or for the more general relation of predator to prey, enriches such interpretations, the cat's progress one of diverse annihilation.[36] The temporal
relation of one to the other is not so narrow, as the cat's activity is based in
a looser and more improvisatory engagement than that of the machine to
the filmstrip. *Cat Food* deals in the reordering of experience, the cat's and
the eye's, so that all action is in flux: the cat's empty and full stomach, the
fish's eaten and whole form, even the speed of the cat's chewing. The film
ends with the sardine being eaten, the cat chewing on it off screen, so that
what of the fish is visible moves seemingly of its own accord. This was a far
funnier and unexpected bridge between image content and media, as the
film's elastic editing mirrored the viewer's focusing and waning attention,
mirrored in editorial suggestion, rather than the projector in its ceaseless
eating of the film itself.

The films that Wieland made in 1967 were not explicitly political. She had found, by extending the aesthetics of *Water Sark* into a realm
of temporal experimentation, a way for her aesthetic ideas, apparent in
other media, to be realized in her films. With *Wavelength*, Michael Snow
had found a way to invest wholly in the medium, coming to see it as a
vehicle for 'time-light-sound' poetry, a means of encompassing his various
activities, in happenings, music, painting, photography and sculpture, in
a single pursuit. Wieland was likewise, and concurrently, discovering that
cinema could tie together her various interests, in tactility (as in her quilts),
in sequence (as in her paintings) and in light (as in her 'stuffed movies').
The work also began to distinguish her sharp wit, as it had appeared in
her paintings, and revealed the dichotomy of sentiment and irony, as in
the collision of form and content in *Handtinting*; the wistful descriptions
that accompanied the difficult formalism of *Sailboat* and *1933*; and in the
simultaneous loving portrait, ambiguous comment and structural comedy
of *Cat Food*.[37] However, while her films were no longer dealing with explicit

---

[36] Leila Sujir has advanced the argument that the film is an analogy for the Vietnam War,
arguing that the cat is a metaphor for American force, an idea that is reinforced by its subsequent role in *Rat Life and Diet in North America* (1968), and in conversations between Sujir
and Wieland, circa 1987.

[37] The 'loving portrait' was an important aspect of Wieland's work in this time, in the
oblique *Larry's Recent Behavior*, in her unfinished film *Peggy's Blue Skylight* (completed in 1986),
her unfinished film later known as *Patriotism 2* (a portrait of Dave Shackman), and in the
expanded cinema happening *Bill's Hat* (1967). Izabella Pruska-Oldenhof has argued that
by such portraiture, in particular, that of *Peggy's Blue Skylight*, Wieland was gathering up
her family, made up of friends and fellow artists. Among those who would appear in these
films were Michael Snow, Jo and Paul Haines, Ken and Flo Jacobs, Jack Bush, A.Y. Jackson,

political content, as had *Larry's Recent Behavior* and *Patriotism*, Wieland was engaged in politics, and there she likewise held to the strange contradiction of earnest sentiment and irony that had been a thread in her life and work.

In March 1968, Wieland, along with the playwright Mary Mitchell, contrived a fake expatriate movement for Canadian Prime Minister candidate Pierre Trudeau, and named it Canadians Abroad for Trudeau. Her fondness for Trudeau first formed in earnest, out of respect for his liberal positions on revisions to the criminal code. She was enchanted by his masculinity, as she had been by her semi-ironic idols Napoleon and Kennedy before him. She would later become disenchanted with Trudeau, as the chasm between their philosophies became increasingly apparent, but at the time that she was making *Rat Life and Diet in North America* (1968), her first film to deal explicitly in Canada as a political entity, she was thinking of the surface idealism of the new Canadian left; the need for radicalism to combat environmental and social injustice; and the contradictions of Canadian centenary nationalism, at a time when the country was increasingly estranged from its own customs and culture.

With *Rat Life and Diet in North America*, Joyce Wieland would continue her photography of critters, in this case, cats and gerbils (the titular rats). The film was, on its surface, an allegory for a radical left underground, persecuted by a totalitarian regime, with gerbils as political prisoners and cats as totalitarian predators. The film arose from Wieland's concerns over the psychological effects of crowding, the fatal implications of crowding in American society and the social-environmental gap between American and Canadian philosophies.[38] The cats observe the gerbils in their "political prison," a mesh-screen cage. Superimposed text announces the date ("1968"), and, much as text had tinted vision in *1933*, subsequent text cards give anthropomorphic meaning to the scurrying of the gerbils, for example, "They plead for their freedom." The gerbils move in the red crosshairs of a rifle's scope. The Jazz Composer's Orchestra plays on the soundtrack. In the allegorical frame of the text, the gerbils' ordinary sauntering is coloured as frantic, fearful action, under the reticule eye of the cat. The trailblazing gerbil freedom fighter Skaag Mitchal flees, in a comical non-event: a gerbil dashes over a wood-paneled deck. Thus commences an exodus of gerbils, a montage in which the rodents are seen struggling in water, with flames superimposed over them, their actions made desperate when their rapidly breathing nostrils are intercut with flames and cats' eyes. Now refugees, the gerbils use American flags as

---

Timothy Leary, Judy Lamarsh, Jean Sutherland Boggs, Larry Zolf, Jackie Burroughs, Zal Yanovsky, Stuart Broomer, Doug Pringle, Michaele Berman and Jacqueline and Ben Park.

[38] Jane Lind, *Joyce Wieland: Artist on Fire* (Toronto: Lorimer, 2001), 159.

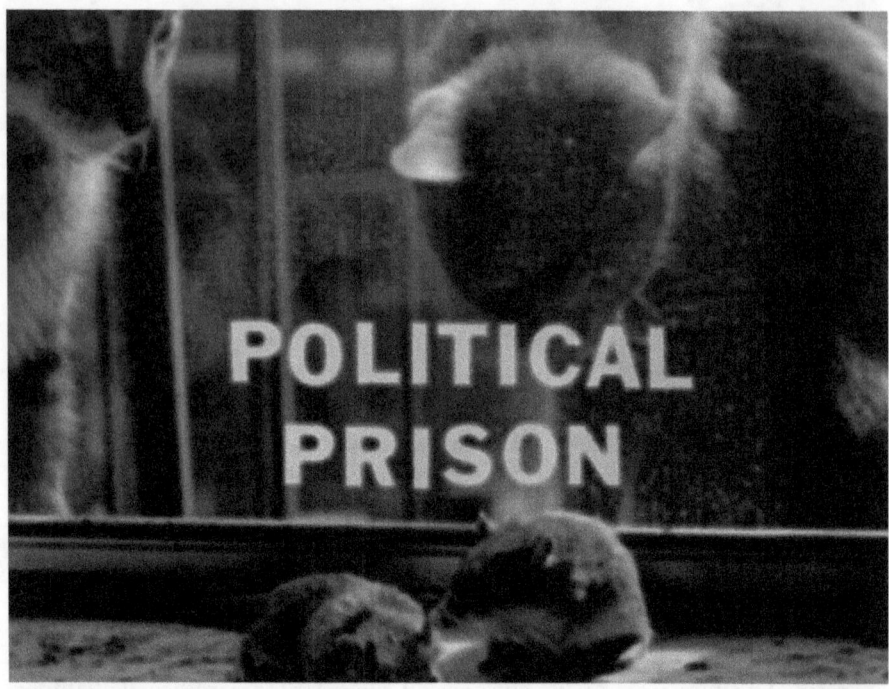

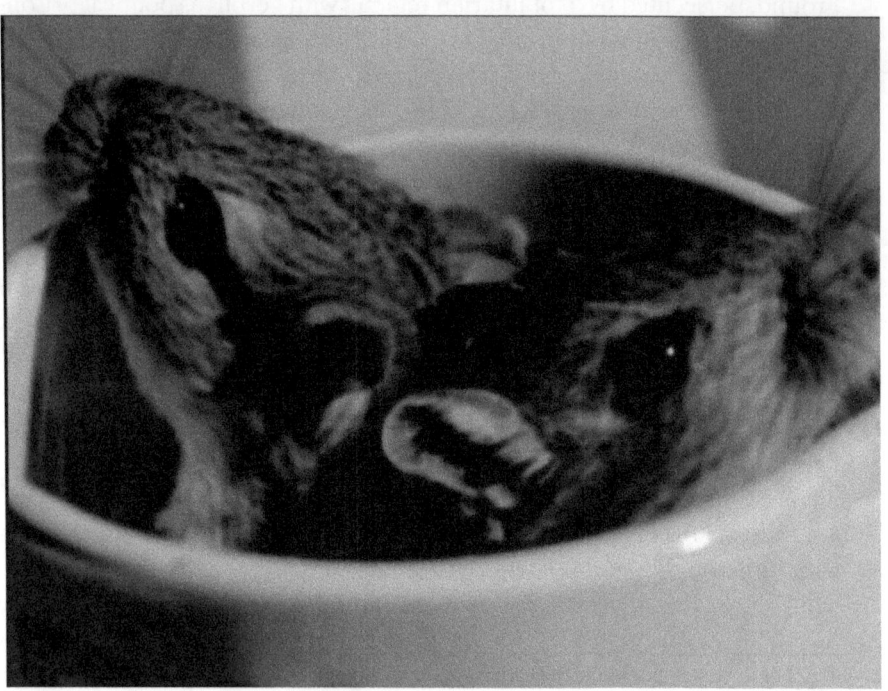

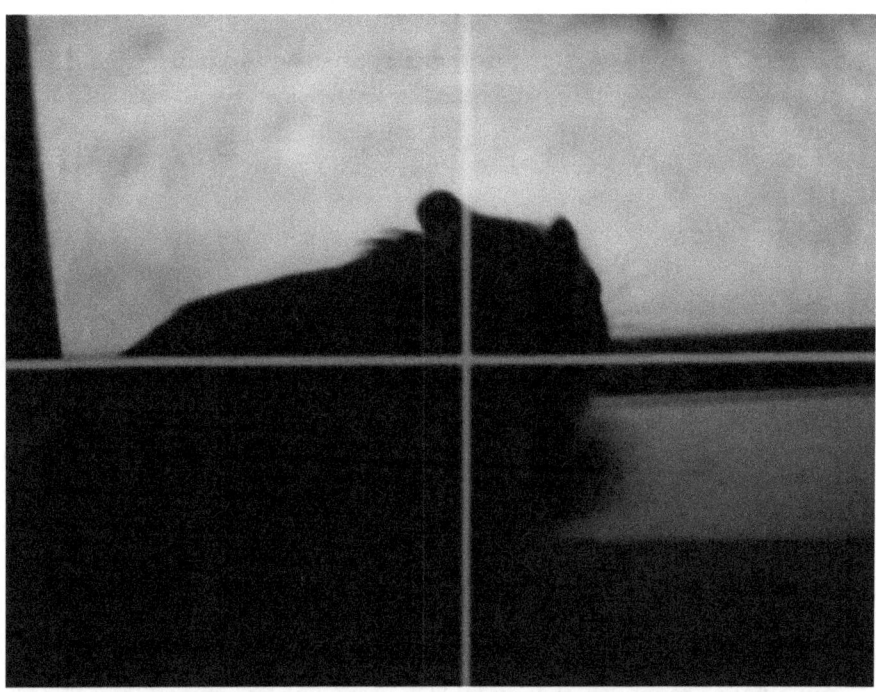

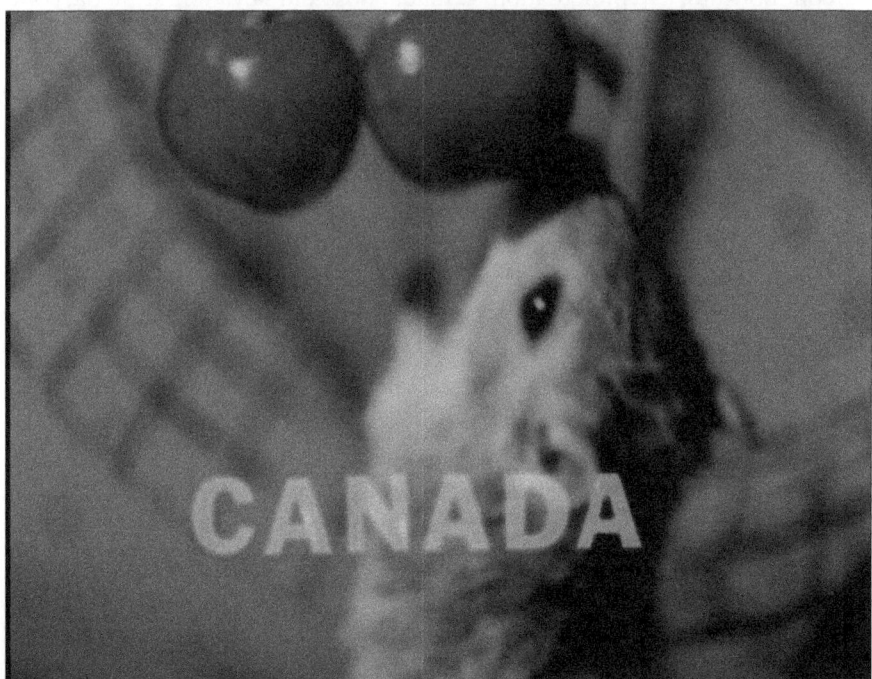

Rat Life and Diet in North America *[Film Stills]*, 1968
16mm film, 16 minutes, colour, sound
Courtesy of CFMDC

blankets, which they chew at. With the introduction of Skaag Mitchal, the allegory becomes less general and more particular to Wieland's combined personal and political thinking: named for Michael Snow, Skaag Mitchal resembles, as an allegorical figure, Front de Libération du Québec (FLQ) leader Pierre Vallières, who had been imprisoned in New York for his political activities.

The text describes the gerbils' subsequent adventures: they travel to the Upper Hudson Region; they occupy a millionaire's house (again, Wieland's kitchen table) where the gerbils eat at a modest tea set, made mammoth by their small stature, the scene scored with sentimental violin music in the vein of Stéphane Grappelli; and finally, they are welcomed to Canada by Monsieur Waterhole, a pun on Pierre Trudeau, trou being French for hole, d'eau being French for water. An American flag is rolled up to resemble a phallus and pressed against a Canadian flag, laid flat. In keeping with this male imposition on female Canada, text exposes Canada as "72 per cent owned by the U.S. Industrial complex." The gerbils take up organic gardening, and Wieland's macro photography finds them chewing on lush green grass, a sign of their newfound prosperity. Text tells that they "raise more grass than they could possibly use," and also gives punctuating reminders that no DDT is used. The text repeats "CANADA" conduplicato, as a punctuation; Canada, host and salvation; Canada, compromised refuge. It appears that the gerbils have found sanctuary from the tyranny of the cats, demonstrated by scenes of luminous grass, of a cherry festival and harvest, performed by gerbils who, in a frenzy, eat cherries and flowers and run on miniature exercise wheels. Even as their activities change, the gerbils' behaviours change little; they remain, like the cat in *Cat Food*, driven by dumb consumption, their actions tinted by the text. A final sign of peaceful, horticultural activity, the "flower ceremony," finds the gerbils eating flowers as the Beach Boys' "Vegetables" plays. Text tells that they've learned "to swing like their great leader ... Monsieur Waterhole ... and worked with him to buy back Canada." In a coda, "the CIA reads in Newsweek that Canada is 3 per cent communist," and they invade Canada. As the image ends, the sounds of a struggle play: a man yelps, guns pop and doors are broken in. This final comic gesture is also the ultimate realization of the film's underlying anxieties and, in spite of its whimsy, its grim implication: that the invasion will be more a whimper than a bang.

Rat Life and Diet in North America extended naturally from Joyce Wieland's past experiments. It combined close-up photography and wide-angle compositions with rich overexposure to create fissures between subject and light source; with text that was used extensively to build allegory;

and with editing that revealed both the environment and the narrative at a rhythm that paralleled the frantic scurrying of the gerbil refugees. The wide-angle compositions gave the gerbils a figurative resemblance to the rotund, comic strip figures that had appeared in Wieland's sketches and paintings through the mid-1960s, and other aspects of the photography, including exposure and an emphasis on deep reds and greens, likewise recalls the forms and palette of Wieland's paintings. Where Wieland had used text to the end of signification, extended to meaninglessness (as in *Sailboat*) and, more playfully, to tint vision (in *1933*), text is integrated in *Rat Life and Diet in North America* in an act of continuous allegorical broadcast. It extends from both *Sailboat* and *1933*, the allegory and anthropomorphic descriptions similarly tinting vision, but it also creates associations, assigning human meaning to the instinctual acts of the gerbils. Finally, the piece is edited in continuity with Wieland's earliest work. As with *Larry's Recent Behavior* and *Barbara's Blindness*, the film held subtle but meaningful insertions in its editing, notably, a recurring image of Che Guevara's corpse on display with Bolivian troops gathering around it, a non sequitur but also a potent sign of Wieland's disgust over dehumanization, the pains of rebellion and the fatal silencing of rebels; however, the film also uses editing to disorient, making the intimate scale of the gerbils' perspective discontinuous, and the text, which is edited to repeat certain expressions in cycles without an organizing principle, the act of repetition itself becoming ecstatic and systematized utterance, a cheer or anthem.

The interplay between sentimentality and irony in Wieland's work was nowhere more apparent than in *Rat Life and Diet in North America*. The endearing faces and movements of the gerbils would inspire sentimental naivety and were offered with an implicit love for their cuteness. And yet, that cuteness, however sincere its rendering, was a Trojan Horse for the more substantial causes of the work, an environmental and emancipatory protest against the corruption of North America. In this context, the film becomes a work of Socratic irony, its naivety a vehicle for outcry, its central device the allegory, used in a manner conscious of the two sides of the film's narrative. On one hand, it is a story in the vein of Beatrix Potter's fables such as *The Tale of Peter Rabbit* (1902), but on the other, it is contained within an unsubtle, yet encoded critique of totalitarianism, closer in spirit to George Orwell's *Animal Farm* (1945). In this way, the film posed an ontological difficulty far more disorienting than the parcelling of simple and complex meanings that had come in Jack Chambers' *Hybrid* and Michael Snow's *Wavelength*. The film gave false instructions by its whimsy and cuteness, as if to provoke dismissal from cynics, and even with its more complex references decoded, even with its stance stated directly, this binary, of the sentimentality of its anthropomorphism and the irony of its allegory, might eclipse the overarching gesture of the work. It is a portrait of freedom from tyranny that offers an alternative to the strife and crowding and fear of modern life, a goal achieved by bravery, altruism and collective rebellion. This aspiration is evident in the intimate scale of the film, rendering this moral vision of freedom is vulnerable to sudden, surprising defeat.

Rat Life and Diet in North America encapsulates several strands of Wieland's thinking about Canada, as home, as female and as liberation. While the film serves the didactic role of criticizing the exploitation of Canada from within, in terms of commerce and industrialization, and the threat of American influence, this results from a sense of ecological and spiritual panic, one particular to Wieland that joined her personal homesickness to more general and timely cultural anxieties. The domestic collaboration of Wieland and Snow had manifested in her films by her adoption of the role of housewife, the kitchen table serving as her studio.[39] Their marriage was strained as their work and lifestyles moved in different directions and they grew apart. In her films, Wieland had pursued a comic and political agenda from the outset. She was drawn to cinema as a mode for intimate expressions, inspired by the Kuchar Brothers and Jack Smith, and the comic and political undercurrents of her life shaped her approach. When she began to turn to temporal modes of formalism in 1967, filmmaking came to encapsulate her thinking across media. After five years in New York, her work was turning more insistently toward her position, not as housewife, but as an expatriated Canadian witnessing the violent rebellion of the FLQ and the crisis of Canadian nationhood, all in the vacuum of the country's 1967 centenary. Like the feminist patriots of 1867, Wieland could see the nation, forming slowly, as it had a hundred years prior, and now even unwinding at the interference of American cultural and industrial imperialism. The advancement of women, a likewise slow evolution, was still stunted, shy of true equality in a nation that Wieland viewed as female. Her critical, patriotic vision would turn toward political statement, but her statement would remain indirect, obscure, fortifying its

---

[39] Although Wieland and Snow had appeared in one another's films—Wieland in Snow's *Wavelength, Standard Time* and *Back and Forth*, Snow in Wieland's *Larry's Recent Behavior*—they would collaborate as artists on only one film. *Dripping Water* (1969) was a long take of water dripping from a tap onto a porcelain plate. Wieland would leave the instructions to "Play sound loud." The film captured the serenity of a phenomenal collision, between the water droplets, the ceramic plate and the steel sink. It was a union of separate strains in their respective practices. Snow had begun to work with long takes and extended duration, and so the work, by its temporal aspects, resembled the minimalist dimensions of his work and happenings; Wieland's films of 1967, with their concerns for not only duration but repetition, and her principle subject of domestic life and housework, influenced not only the choice of subject but, like Snow's prior work, influenced the film's relation to time.

truthfulness against the singular meaning.

PART TWO

THE ABSOLUTE FILMS

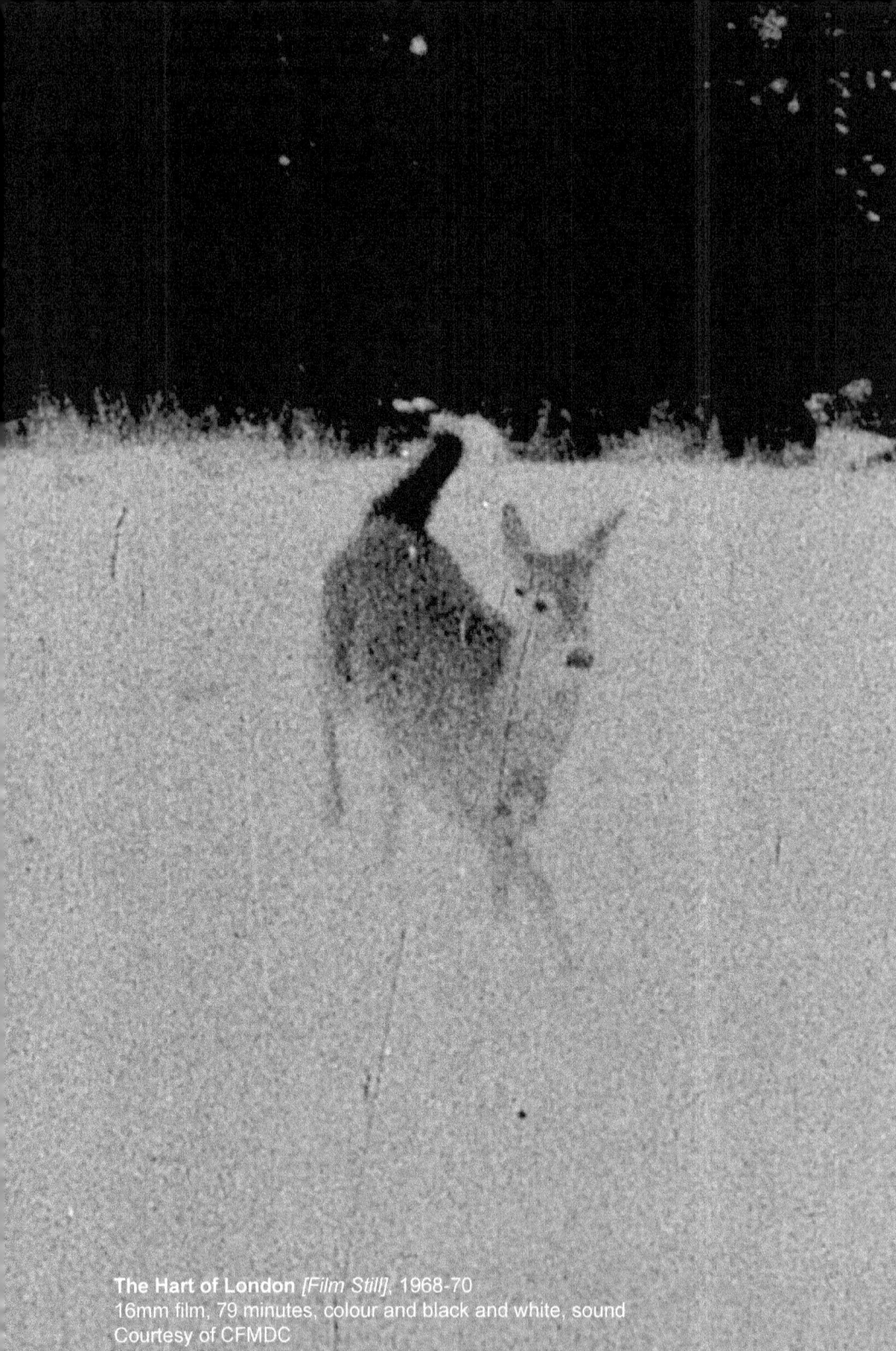

The Hart of London *[Film Still]*, 1968-70
16mm film, 79 minutes, colour and black and white, sound
Courtesy of CFMDC

CHAPTER FOUR

Careful Symmetries:
Jack Chambers' *The Hart of London* (1970)

By the time that Jack Chambers began to make films in 1964, he had already undergone a "series of births," as he had characterized them, through his training in Spain. There he had cultivated an individual approach to painting, measured by an objective standard of craft. After his return to Canada, his style continued to evolve. His homecoming to London, Ontario, had signalled further development of the memorial and sensual ambitions of his art, and more births would follow, some through his initial engagement with photography, others after he was diagnosed with leukemia in 1969.[1] His early films were technologically primitive, compositionally and sequentially masterful impressions of his life, philosophy and environment. This work, and the impulses that had simultaneously emerged in his painting activity, gave way to his final film, *The Hart of London* (1970). It would serve as an ultimate reckoning of his apocalyptic vision of man at odds with nature, a film of cosmic and spiritual immediacy, a reverie of childhood and fatherhood. *The Hart of London* dreams, not in the conceits of *Mosaic*'s trinity of early, middle and late life, but in a freer stream that fastens those stations to the evolution of the spirit; it symbolizes a tragic current in modernity, not through the binary analogues of *Hybrid*, but by the menacing and universal implications of local newsreels; it documents, not in the narrow particulars of *R34*, but by the wider scope of social history; and it passes in instants, not only in the circulation of loss and rebirth found in *Circle*, attendant to the past, but toward a union of joyous and suffering witness remembered, a hesitant stare forward from its present moment.

---

[1] Chambers had been ill through much of his adult life prior to his diagnosis, for example, when he contracted pleurisy while living in Chinchón, and in the damage wrought to his breathing by the atmosphere of his studio during his silver painting period. While the presence of death and despair in his work was partly inherited from Spanish art and from his Catholicism, his fascination with death as a theme predates his illness, traced to a possibly apocryphal anecdote of his having been arrested for breaking into a London mortuary as a teenager, presumably in pursuit of a close encounter with death.

The Hart of London marks the culmination of formal and social concerns that had dominated Chambers' earlier work as a painter and filmmaker. It results from Chambers' heritage of difficulty, which first arrived for him in the gulf between the plasticity of painting and the dimensional depth of photography and filmmaking, and which matured in its merging with his mystical notions of poetic sensory intuition, his embrace of multi-tiered perception and his devotion to perceptual mystery. This film would be the final evolution of this branch of aesthetic difficulty in Chambers' art, as the paintings that followed it would adhere more strictly to his philosophy of Perceptual Realism, a pursuit of sublime vision that dealt in a more mystical difficulty, and that was not so fortified and obscure as his preceding work had been. The Perceptual Realist paintings were concerned with the exaltation of perceptual experience, with vision as an entrance to a greater interior chamber of the senses, an extension and departure from the obscurities of the works that presupposed them. These works were open to engage the casual viewer.

Paintings such as *401 Towards London No. 1* (1968-69), *Victoria Hospital* (1969-70), *Lombardo Avenue* (1972-76) and the *Sunday Morning* series (1968-1977), contrary to their meticulous form, were primitive riddles. But they were most celebrated for their extremity of technical skill that approximated realism, in a manner distinct from the kitsch of contemporaneous American photorealism.[2] Their form had the superficial integrity of the photograph, but they were essentially painterly, their textures created with marble dust and rabbit fur that altered the plane of the canvas and augmented the multi-dimensional presence of the work, bodies and spaces rendered in the distinct compressions of a lens' focal length. Their presence, the true content of the work, would in Chambers' view be a communion of artist and spirit, or God, the artist as the eye, the spirit in the landscape, the suburban street, or the interior of the Chambers family home. So startling and visceral was the viewing of a Perceptual Realist canvas that their allusions and other referential difficulties became elusive, further masked by the potential relation of the work to the ready pleasure of the Romantic landscape, that narrow passage of aesthetic disavowal by which the Post-Impressionists would come to be embraced in the popular imagination.[3] These paintings represent a height of rendered reality, an

---

[2] For a fuller discussion of Chambers' work in relation to American photorealist painting, see Chapter 1 fn43. It is central in addressing the effect of Perceptual Realism to distinguish it from kitsch 'hyperrealist' paintings by artists such as Richard Estes and John Baeder who, despite a superficial relation of skill, exemplify the disparity between Jack Chambers and other artists who pursued photorealist painting in his time.

[3] Just as Chambers did not fit easily into the American hyperrealist movement, he did not fit easily into a lineage of romantic landscape painting, although romantic landscapes are

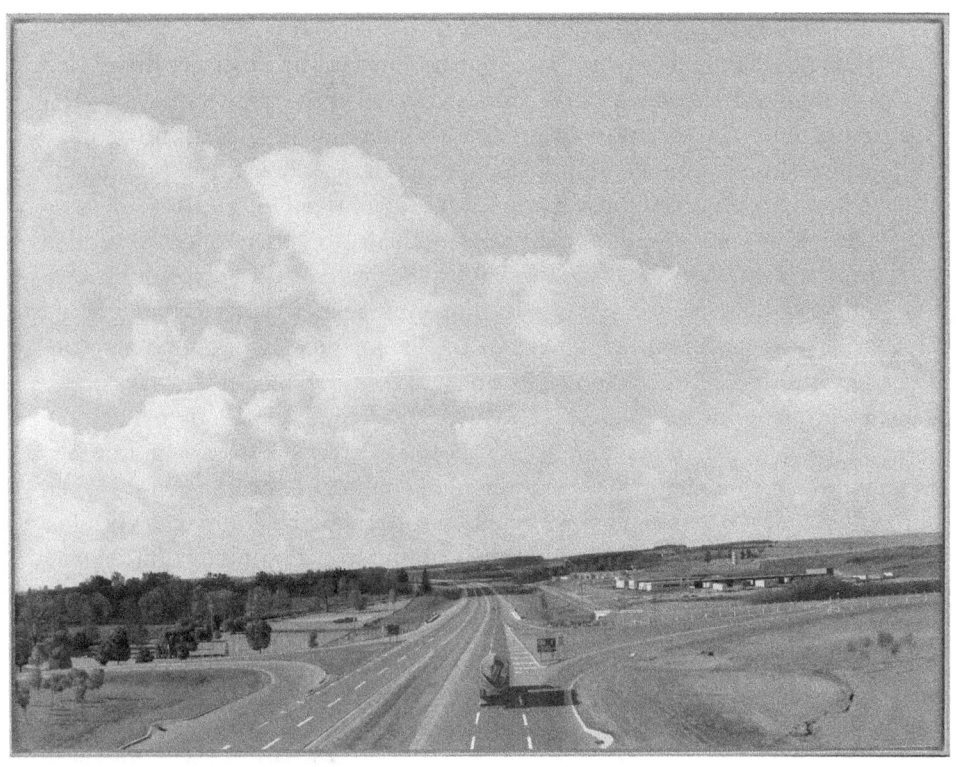

401 Towards London No. 1, 1968-69
oil on mahogany, 183 x 244 cm, 72 1/16 x 96 1/16 inches
AGO, Gift of Norcen Energy Resources Limited, 1986
(86/47)
Reproduced by permission of the estate of Jack Chambers

endorsement of the real and a disavowal of the perceptual falseness of realism. Perceptual Realism allowed Chambers to further brand his work in its relation to reality, to cultivate a philosophy, at the dispensation of the obscurities and rage that had marked his earlier work.

A Perceptual Realist painting was offered as an elevation of the camera's mechanical description, be it of a figure or a landscape, but the work was as much about time, not only the interval of vision unfolding— as opposed to the suspended action of the distilled moment, the 'still life' that had haunted Western art—but the interval in which profound perceptions are encountered. What Chambers called the 'wow' moment of Perceptual Realism was an artifact of temporal perception, a moment when sense-comprehension is disrupted and must be gathered up again.[4] Chambers provoked those moments through his paintings. His sources included the past that informed that moment, the elastic interval of that moment, the distance of memory from the present and a profound knowledge of the relative impotence of moments lacking such temporal frames. The work itself was ultimately one of disrupted perception that is reconfigured, that permeates and is permeated by experience. The stakes in this work are spiritual. Chambers wished to celebrate glories of perception, and what meant more, to redeem perception, from the quotidian, from the impotent moment, from the spiritual alienation of the modern observer. This was the redemption of reality itself. He arrived at this work after his most sinister period, out of the oppressive atmosphere of his studio, filled with the fumes of aluminum paint, with which he made his silver paintings. The silver paintings had used fractured perspective and plane divisions and, in their most dramatic engagement with time, affected a

---

among the best known Perceptual Realist paintings. In the Canadian context, much of that tradition was influenced by Dutch painting with motives and skillsets distinct from those of Chambers. As audiences acclimated to Post-Impressionism, by disregarding the alien nature of its form and focusing instead on the more standard fare of its content, the Group of Seven and associates formed the context for Canada's modern landscape painting, a context which Chambers steadfastly resisted by working in portraiture and social scenes, and which the presence of photorealist technique already resisted, for the fine density of its forms, and for an appearance that could be presumed inherited from older Spanish styles and pre-modern notions of precise representation.

[4] Chambers describes this as such: "Perception in process is like a sound movie. Suddenly the picture freezes and loses focus. The sound goes. The de-focusing brightens and becomes white light. Then the focus returns, the sound comes back and the film starts moving again. That's the slow-motion version of what happens. The moment of 'white-light' is the moment of perception. The frame returning to focus and the first returning sounds are the registration of object-world on the nerves as the senses recover. What the senses record and how and when they record it is an example of creation projecting its pattern on the world." Jack Chambers, "Perceptualism, painting and cinema." *Art and Artists* 7:9 (December 1972), 31.

positive-negative transit in their viewing, so that as the viewer passed, an image was actively transforming and transformed by time. Some of Chambers' images were plundered from mass culture, others from his own life, and the work integrated photographic renderings with design text in an overt critique of media and society, specifically, society's cruel skill at reducing extremities of love and hatred, joy and tragedy, to a neutral base-line. Against the falseness and indifference of mass culture, Chambers' silver paintings were indignant statements of his position against the de-valuation of perception. This position would be tempered and refined into Perceptual Realism.[5] This sinister work constitutes another tier of what Chambers called the spiritual preparation of the artist.

On January 20, 1968, the *London Free Press*'s Bill Webster announced in his column that Jack Chambers was making a new film. His headline announced, "Underground film on London planned." This film would be about life in London, Ontario, and through Webster's column, Chambers was placing a call for snapshots from Londoners, "of any vintage and any quality."[6] In a follow-up column, Webster gave the address for submissions, adding that Chambers would "make his film directly from the material he receives and title it, *Heart of London*."[7] Chambers repeated this request on local television and radio. He also achieved access to "all the TV footage shot by the local station since it went into operation" 15 years earlier, in 1954.[8] Chambers travelled to Madrid, Orense, La Touza, Sevilla, Huelva and La Antilla, in September and October of 1968, shooting footage for

[5] The last of Chambers' sinister paintings came in the same year as *The Hart of London*, for example, the *Regatta* series and *Grass Box No. 2* (1968–1970). His paintings of the late 1960s bore his skill for realist representation, but also demonstrated his use of firm line as a tool for compositional fragmentation and of the rhythm of images within images. In his work that dealt with compositional divisions, the photorealist representations were increasingly rendered as photographs, on boxes, in strips, and as if taped to a wall or pinned to a board. His approach to realism had much in common with Wieland's sequential paintings, inasmuch as fragmentation reimagined the images as component parts of something else. Where in Wieland's work, that 'something else' was the illusion of 'real time' in moving images, Chambers cast the photo as a memento occupying the greater reality to which he devoted his Romantic style. With the Perceptual Realist paintings, this relation finally matured into a simultaneous rendering of the craftwork of realism and Chambers' own Romantic ambitions, joined to provoke the exalted moment of perception.

[6] Bill Webster, "On Entertainment: Underground Film on London Planned." *London Free Press*, 20 January 1968, 43.

[7] Bill Webster, "On Entertainment: Back to Heart of London." *London Free Press*, 22 January, 1968. 27. The working title *Heart of London* is not Webster's error; it is spelled as such in Chambers' own notebooks and correspondence held at the archives of the Art Gallery of Ontario.

[8] Ross Woodman, "London: Regional Liberation Front." *Globe and Mail*. 13 December 1969, 27. It was, presumably, from this arrangement or from an earlier, similar arrangement that Chambers secured the footage that appears in the final section of *Circle*.

what would become *The Hart of London*. The homophonic title had, as Bill Webster had indicated in spelling it 'heart', implications that this work would reach the irreducible core of the city, and drew the parallel of architecture as metaphor for interior being, as in St. Teresa of Ávila's seven mansions of the soul. The hart of the title was the city's heart, its central organ and life essence, and it was also a literal hart, a deer which, as the film begins, wanders into the city, becomes trapped, disoriented, ensnared by suburban fences, and is consequently captured by hunters, placed in a metal holding fence and killed. All of this action, from the deer's terrified galloping on the outskirts of the woods to its execution, was captured by television cameras and would be integrated by Chambers into his film, as its prelude, the declaration of a theme.[9]

The term hart was already antique when Chambers began his film, replaced widely by the terms deer and stag. His choice of this word, and of the deer as icon, is not limited to homophonic punning, but rather drew from his knowledge of the deer's symbolism in medieval Christianity.[10] In the medieval hunt, the hart was a prized game, and by pursuit of it, hunters participated in an allegory for Christ's ordeals. The process of the hunt was elaborate and ritualized: an expert huntsman would track the hart and identify its lay. A party would then assemble, and dogs would be positioned along a path to serve as relays. When the quarry was sighted, a chase would begin, and finally, when the hart could run no longer, the leader of the hunt would make the kill. The hart's carcass would be subject to 'unmaking', a dissection ritual.[11] For its agony, the hart became a symbol of Christ, an allegory that was reinforced in Christian mythology. For example, the Christian martyr Saint Eustace was said to have undergone conversion after seeing a crucifix suspended from the antlers of a hart.[12]

---

[9] This event, and in particular, the newsreel source footage, was also used by Chambers in his painting *Hart of London* (1968).

[10] As further evidence of Chambers' intentional use of the hart as an allegory for Christ, his notebooks describe an original opening sequence wherein Christ arrives at the Chambers family home. The deer sequence becomes a substitute for this scene.

[11] This description of the medieval hunt is informed by an account given in Anne Rooney, *Hunting in Middle English Literature* (Woodbridge, Suffolk: Boydell & Brewer, 1993).

[12] The story of Saint Eustace, in which the hart serves as an instigator of conversion, might further testify to Chambers' film and its role in the greater allegories of Chambers' life. As a General in the Roman army named Placidus, Eustace was on a hunt when he experienced an ecstatic conversion. A vision of a crucifix appeared to him, fixed between the antlers of a stag. Eustace subsequently converted himself and his family, and changed his name. After this, he suffered a series of calamities, like those of Job. His faith was tested through poverty, the death of his servants, the kidnapping of his wife by a seaman and of his sons by a wolf and a lion. Despite his grief, Eustace did not lose his faith. His family was restored by the endurance of his faith, but he was consequently condemned to death by the Emperor Hadrian for refusing to make a pagan sacrifice. As in Eustace's trial of faith, Chambers'

People of the middle ages believed that the hart could live for hundreds of years, and that a mature one could therefore be several hundred years old, the beast host to the wisdom of witness. In their superstition, medieval folk also believed that a bone in the middle of its heart prevented the hart from dying of fear.[13] The imagined hart, for its age and endurance, was a symbol of immortality. Choosing a modern-day slaughter of the hart as his central metaphor, Jack Chambers would embark on a work of environmental, moral, spiritual inquiry into the dread character of the present.

As he was in the midst of making the film, Chambers learned that he had terminal leukemia. In the ensuing decade he would fight it, and survive far longer than had been expected. Our knowledge of this might lead to the conclusion that the work itself was formed by his diagnosis, that its grieving and angry confrontation with mortality and its lamentation of the sins of man and of modernity result from his awareness of his own mortality.[14] But *The Hart of London* also continues the sinister topics and aesthetic assembly of his earlier films and paintings. It represents the apogee of the work that he had pursued throughout the 1960s, with an eye to death gained in his Spanish conversion, and in its use of film time and sequence, with its calculated editing and visible roughness. Chambers had known terror in Spain, embodied in the predators that stalked the suffering Picasso-like figures of his paintings of the late 1950s. They were the specters of illness, poverty and indifference. Such beasts gave form to the stalking menace of modern convenience and complacency that Chambers had seen first in provincial London's resigned imitation of life. In the mid-1960s, he spoke out against the grave effects of chemical warfare in Vietnam and the inhuman practices of the American armed forces. In an act of environmental morality, he confronted the compromises dealt to the land by sophisticated agricultural practices and aspirations toward technological mastery. These moral stances would become urgent as he assumed his role as a father. The grief and rage of Chambers' film came from

---

faith, which is simultaneously Roman Catholic and more broadly encompassing, endures this lamentation of the miseries and terrors of the world.

[13] Much of this account of the mythological significance of the hart is condensed from a more detailed account found in Boria Sax, *The Mythical Zoo: An Encyclopedia of Animals in Myth, Legend, and Literature* (New York: Overlook, 2013), 141-149.

[14] This claim has been advanced widely, most recently in Mark Cheetham's *Jack Chambers* (Toronto: Art Canada Institute, 2013). It is important to state Chambers' diagnosis as an influence on the film, but to regard it as the key to the film supports the mistaken belief that *The Hart of London* is merely a set of stages on the Elizabeth Kübler-Ross chart of grief, that ends with the Perceptual Realist paintings as 'acceptance'. To view Chambers' work in such a trajectory is a disservice to him, to his most difficult works of the 1960s, and to the profound and complex pleasures of the Perceptual Realist paintings, the power of which is too often treated in step with the low ambitions of American photorealist kitsch.

something greater than his own doom, more encompassing even than the individual causes of his grief. His overarching concern was with the denigration of life and of perception, and the aim of *The Hart of London* was not merely to illustrate suffering, but to redeem perception through new and old myths. It joined a haunting vision of his life, his perceptions and his rituals, to an anonymous, unconscious record of his hometown, a stage for paradise and inferno.

A Field of Ghosts

When he returned to London in 1962, Jack Chambers had been convinced to stay by the traces he saw of himself as a child "gesturing in the invisible." Chambers had come to believe that the energies of the past lingered in the present, that all activity in the present occurs in a field of energy formed by the ghosts of an all-encompassing past. This field of energy contained the lacuna of the past, energies of a scale more intimate than the scope of cultural memory, and this energy gave purpose to the present, as a station in the history of man. Later, when Chambers undertook readings in Theosophy, Gnosticism and Spanish mysticism, he would find corresponding ideas and integrate them into his philosophy of Perceptual Realism.[15] In *The Hart of London*, he would represent this energy field, the ghosts of the past serving as an extended opening chorus, in a dense silver cast, the anonymous polyphony of London, Ontario's home movies and photographs, bridging the slaughter of the hart, with its mythic dimension, to intimate scenes from the Chambers family's life, and finally, to a series of dreams, a reverie culled from London's more recent past. Chambers, in describing the social aspect of his process, wrote that he had "received thousands of snaps and thought of the film as a municipal team effort."[16] Chambers had transformed those snaps into an evocation of William Butler Yeats' *spiritus mundi*, the primal mass of images and symbols out of which rough beasts emerge.

As the film begins, the deer has strayed into the city and is trapped by fences. Chambers describes this event: "The deer had leapt several fences to get there and was too exhausted from his efforts and his fright

---

[15] Many of these ideas are elaborated in Tom Smart, *Jack Chambers' Red and Green: an artist's inquiry into the nature of meaning* (Erin, Ont.: Porcupine's Quill, 2013), "Sight and Vision," 49-64, and "Down and Up," 67-88. Chambers' mystical sources include Madame Blavatsky, and his concerns around spiritual unity, entropy and rendering the invisible form his sense of the need for essential, unresolvable mysteries. This magical thinking, which was devoted to betraying the mystical ends of perception, was the most implicit aspect of Chambers' difficulty to remain through the Perceptual Realist paintings.

[16] Jack Chambers, *Jack Chambers* (London: Nancy Poole, 1978), 107.

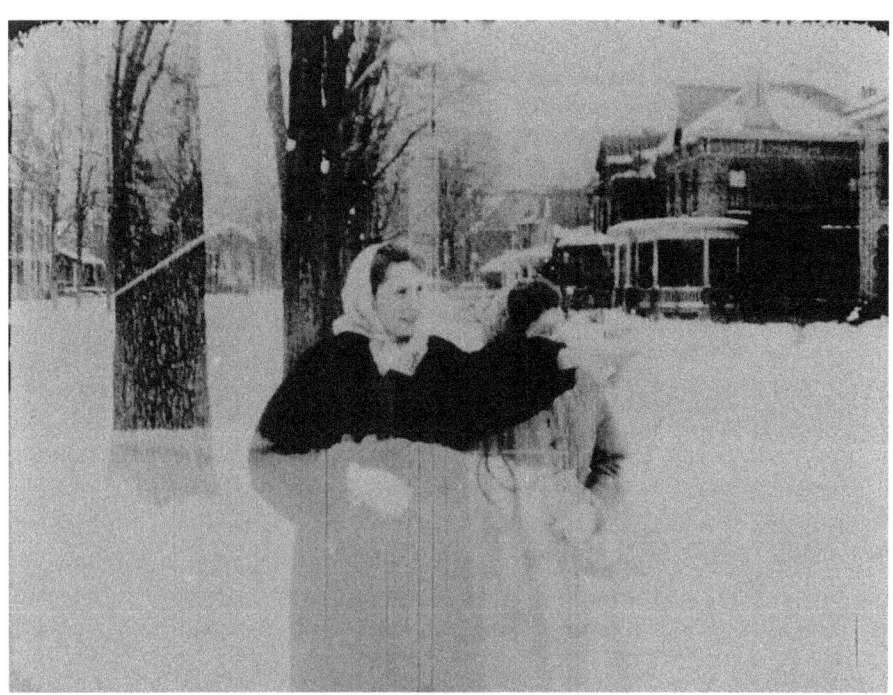

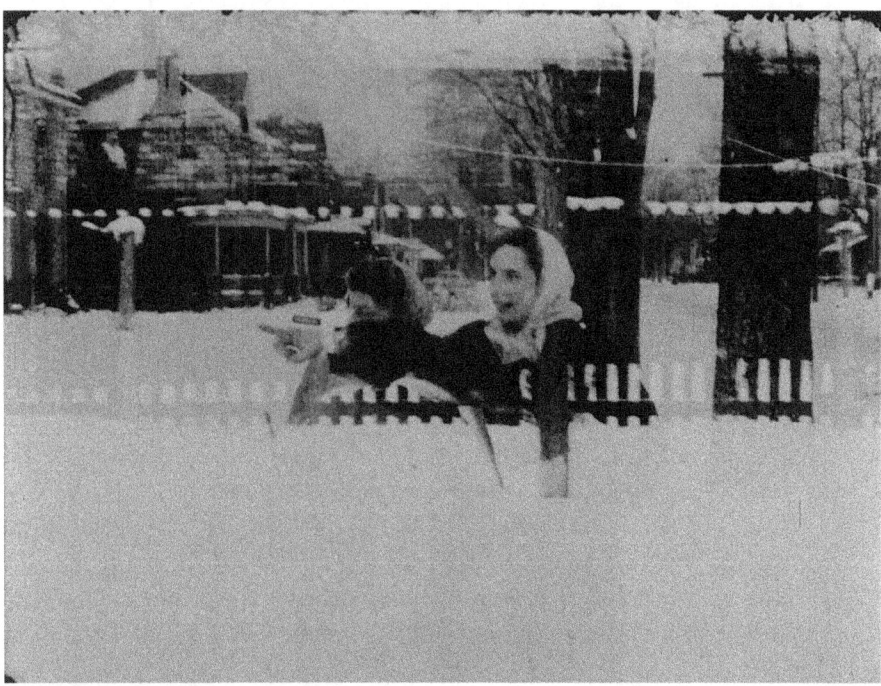

The Hart of London *[Film Stills]*, 1968-70
16mm film, 79 minutes, colour and black and white, sound
Courtesy of CFMDC

to jump further. The police brought in ropes and harnessed him, then he was transferred to a wired enclosure, name unknown. The deer had been wounded by his frantic leaps, by the wooden fences and the shock of it all, and a huntsman was called in to finish him off."[17] The deer gallops through farmland. It moves toward the camera and is overtaken by a negative inversion of the same scene. The deer runs through a meadow and stops as if alerted to a sound. On the soundtrack, water passes in reverse, an alien sound that is further obscured by the long gaps of silence between rushing waves. Hunters load shotguns. The images are flipped so that left and right orientations are inconstant, and this horizontal exchange emphasizes the entrapment of the deer. When these images are flipped horizontally and superimposed, they form menacing symmetries in which forms visibly part from the center of the composition in fields of snow. Superimpositions begin to assemble, apparently at random. The camera passes through a neighborhood of middle-class bungalows, a traveling shot running over a static shot of a house's facade. Men gather hunting equipment. As one exits his car, the camera seems, by means of superimposition, to be simultaneously behind him and in front of him as he passes through himself. This maze of bodies is punctuated by an image of two women walking. One holds her arm out and points off-screen. The transparent deer gallops over this image of the women and over the fences that further box in the beast. The wooden fences pass through one another in superimposition, one tracking to the left, the other to the right, creating another strange horizontal tension. The town has become a cage, and this cage is finally laid over the hunters themselves as they gather in the road. The image becomes much denser and grey, in photographic negative, still multiply superimposed, faint traces of representational images emerging from that haze. The men are binding the deer's legs. A game warden is petting its head and stroking its ears, calming and preparing it as they carry it to its enclosure. A hunter aims his rifle through the mesh tangle of the enclosure and fires. The deer's body is glimpsed, a faint impression in silver. Like many images that will follow, it appears simultaneously positive and negative, which positions the images ambiguously between two poles, tempering the white and black to resemble the aluminum pigments of Chambers' silver paintings. The inverted waves on the soundtrack persist.

In his earlier drawings and paintings, Jack Chambers had given form to his field of resonant energies, in the parade of the living and the dead, where figures taken from the photographic archive assembled alongside the artist's contemporaries.[18] With its second sequence, *The Hart of*

---

[17] Ibid.

[18] This is most apparent in the drawings in which Chambers uses the white of the paper as

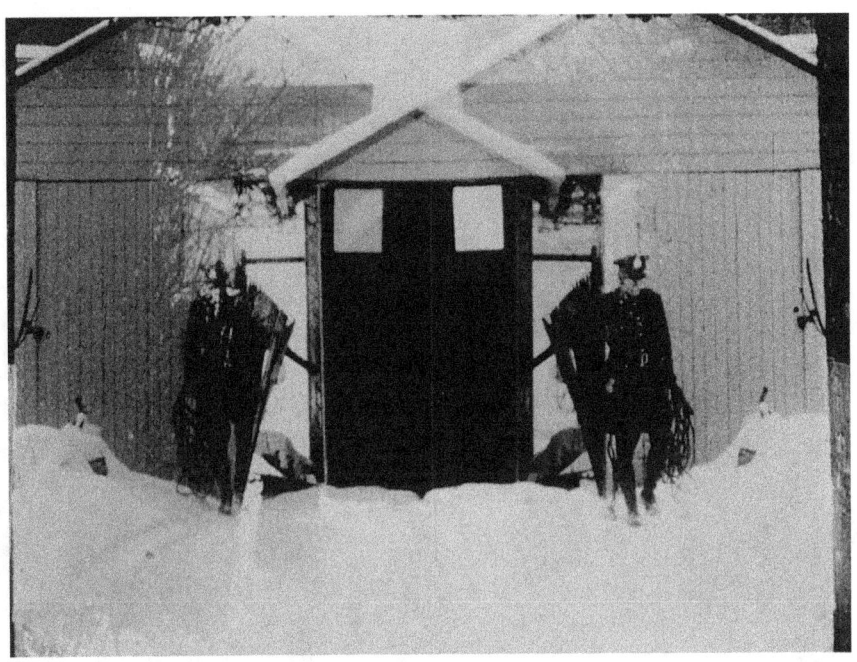

The Hart of London *[Film Still]*, 1968-70
16mm film, 79 minutes, colour and black and white, sound
Courtesy of CFMDC

London would mark Chambers' final attempt to illustrate this field of energies in explicit representation, a stream of the everyday photographic records of London, Ontario assembled as a silver chorus. Chambers
writes that, following the deer's slaughter, "the film then resurrects some
historical Londoners in negative footage. Their historical footage of the
city is brought forth in overlapping negative and positive exposures of the
same images until gradually, by repeating themselves, they synchronize
into clear positive pictures of the present."[19] The image is edited in steady
revelations, too dense and rapid to be intelligible at first, and gradually,
out of its murky silver cast, a faint impression of human figures, animals
and landscapes comes into view. Plants, homes, commercial buildings, fac-
tories, the river, roses and wolf carcasses dragged through the snow by
hooks, all appear in silver and black. Although these images are drawn
from photographic records, the human figures bear the aged or cherubic

---

an unoccupied, negative space, for example, *Sunday Morning No. 1* (1963) and the illustrations from James Reaney's *The Dance of Death at London, Ontario* (London: Alphabet Press,
1963).

[19] Jack Chambers, *Jack Chambers* (London: Nancy Poole, 1978), 108.

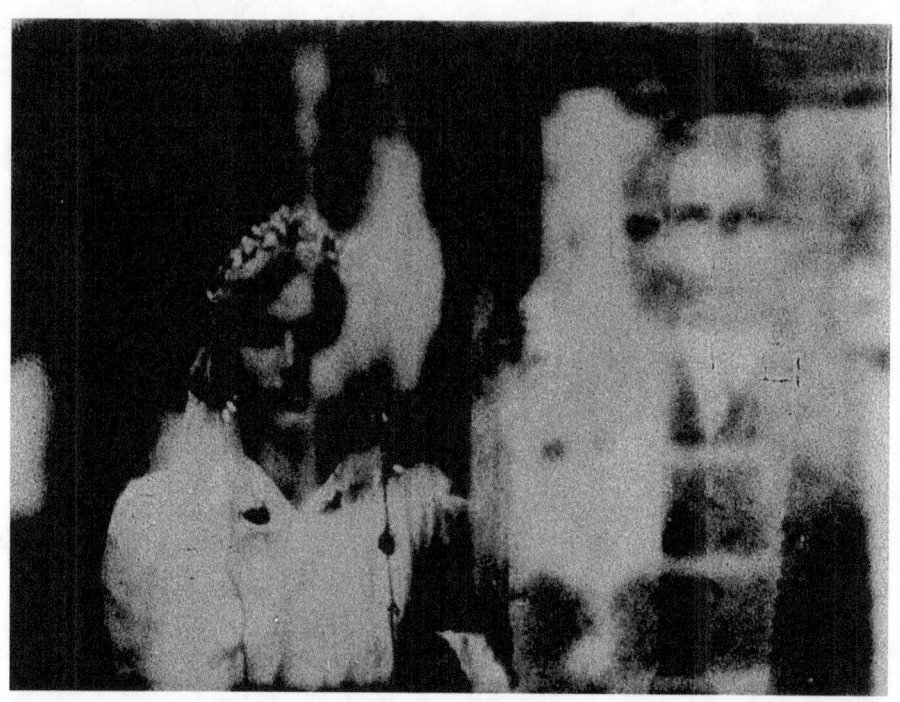

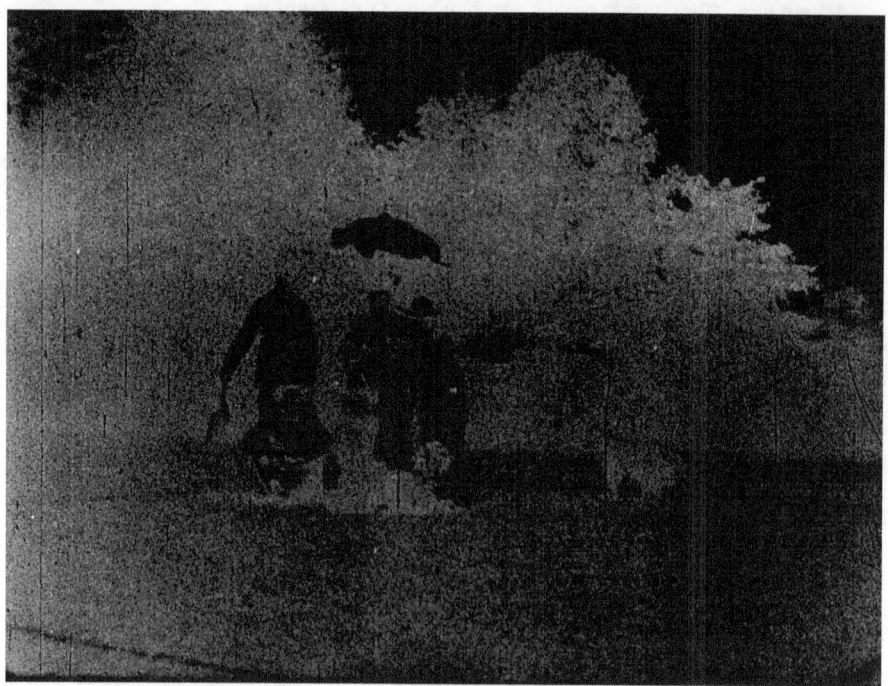

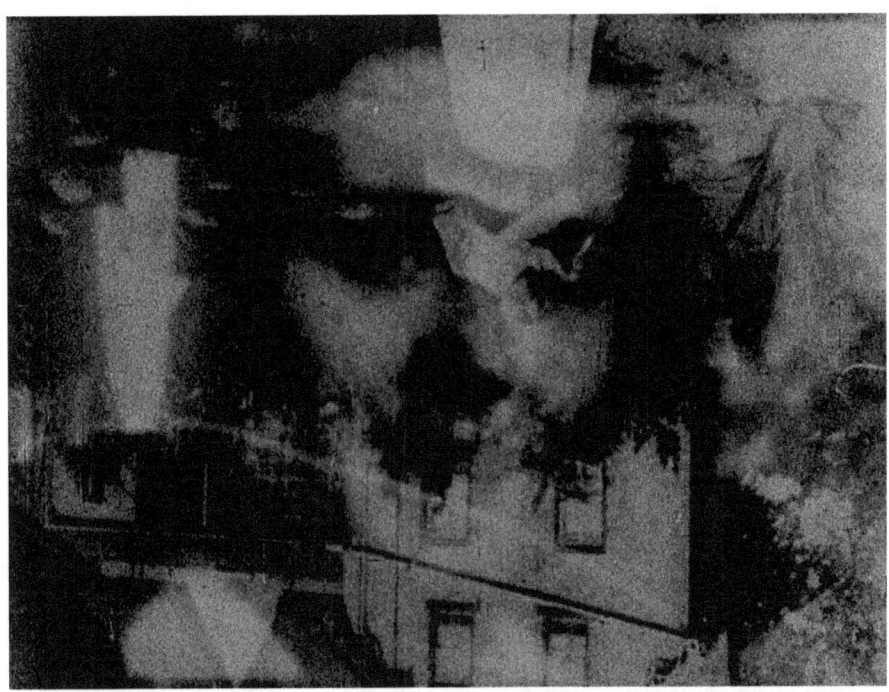

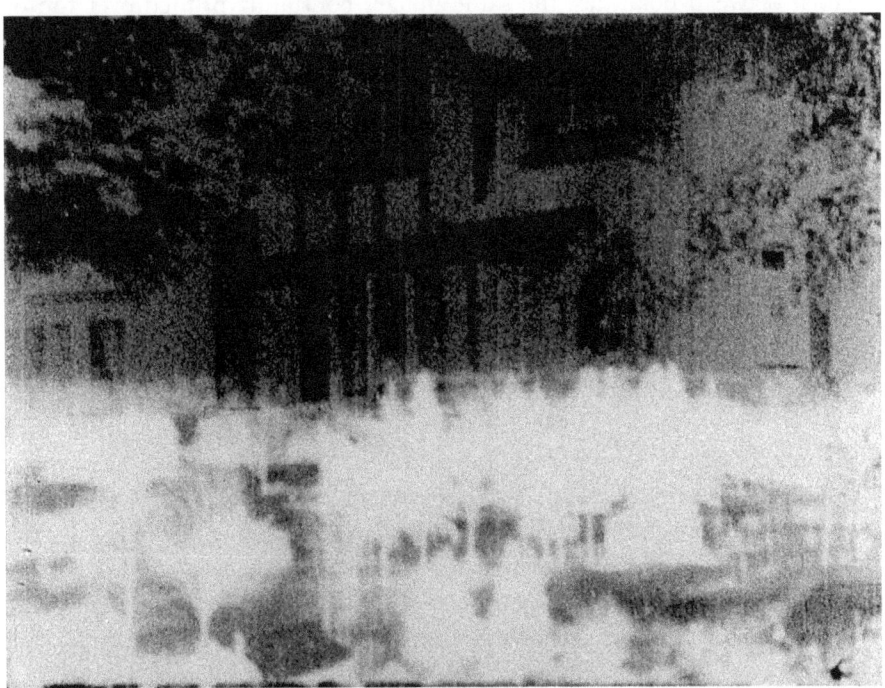

The Hart of London *[Film Stills]*, 1968-70
16mm film, 79 minutes, colour and black and white, sound
Courtesy of CFMDC

faces of Chambers' paintings, his standard exchange of culling images from the archive cycling back on itself as these resurrected presences begin to resemble his work. As the image moves into a section of dense photo negative, black patterns come and go in rapid editing that seems to accent their granularity. A face, a street, a boat, a car: these shapes emerge, but the details are stymied by the silver and black, declaring the narrow palette of the work. Even when the image begins to take on a collision of negative and positive, the density and the strangeness of the composition (with images flipped and even upside down), turns it into a continuously heterodox collage, an arrangement of black emulsion which, by virtue of the double-image and of positive-negative simultaneity, has become abstract, advancing in a steady tempo tempered by slight movements within the image, the loose and overlapping edits of superimpositions.

The eye searches for referents as the silver chorus conceals the images in superimpositions. Scenes of domesticity, civic labour and scenery evolving through the decades all play, all drained of context, passing only as component parts of the silver chorus's vortex. London is an old city, by the age of English Canada, and for its age it has a long record of conflicts with nature, as farm acreages were replaced by housing for a growing population. The energies of these conflicts are present, in vision torn between polarities, the same images constantly printed over top of themselves, a few frames apart so that one becomes a relief shadow of the other, forming symmetries and faint impressions of an evolving society out of the faces of the past. As the sequence nears its end, identical positive and negative images of a construction crew working on a city street are printed over one another. This makes the images unstable, as the polarities shudder within the figures and buildings, the energy field finally achieving its most romantic illustration that at the same time joins and thereby reveals the role of physical elements forming the sequence. The silver chorus of historical images is a manifestation of the obscurity of the common field of perception and a testament to the mysteries of perceptual phenomena and individual vision in the tide of history. The scenes struggle for the reality at their root, which is one of transcendental-agrarian farm labour, industrial labour and domestic continuity. Chambers writes, quoting Teilhard de Chardin, that "[w]e live at the centre of the network of cosmic influences as we live at the heart of the human crowd or among the myriads of stars, without, alas, being aware of immensity."[20]

The silver chorus sequence is a confrontation with that immensity, concealed in the vacant landscapes of so many of Chambers' Perceptual

---

[20] Qtd. in Tom Smart, *Jack Chambers' Red and Green: an artist's inquiry into the nature of meaning* (Erin, Ont.: Porcupine's Quill, 2013),

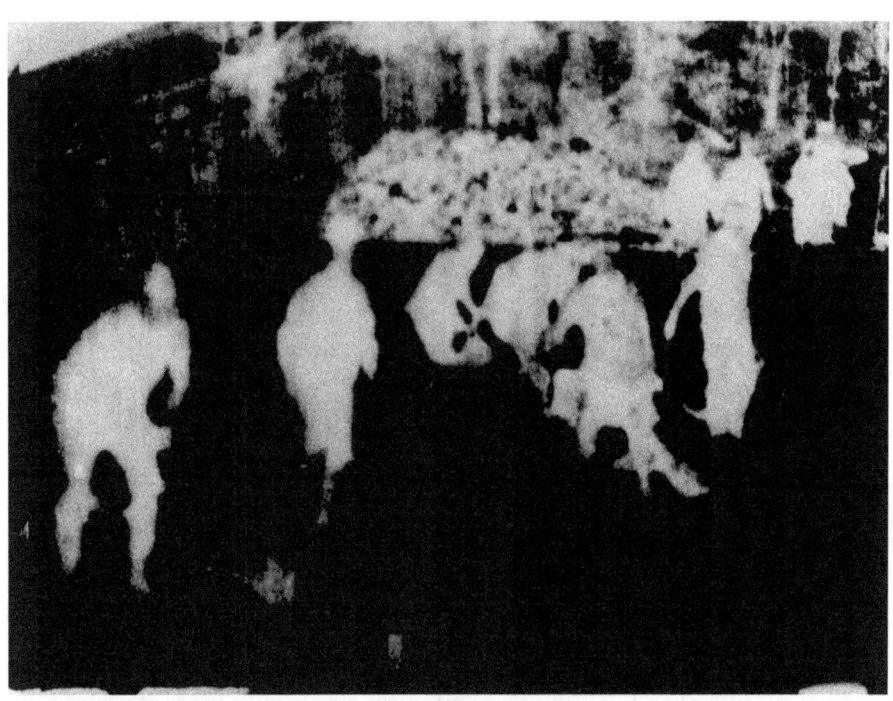

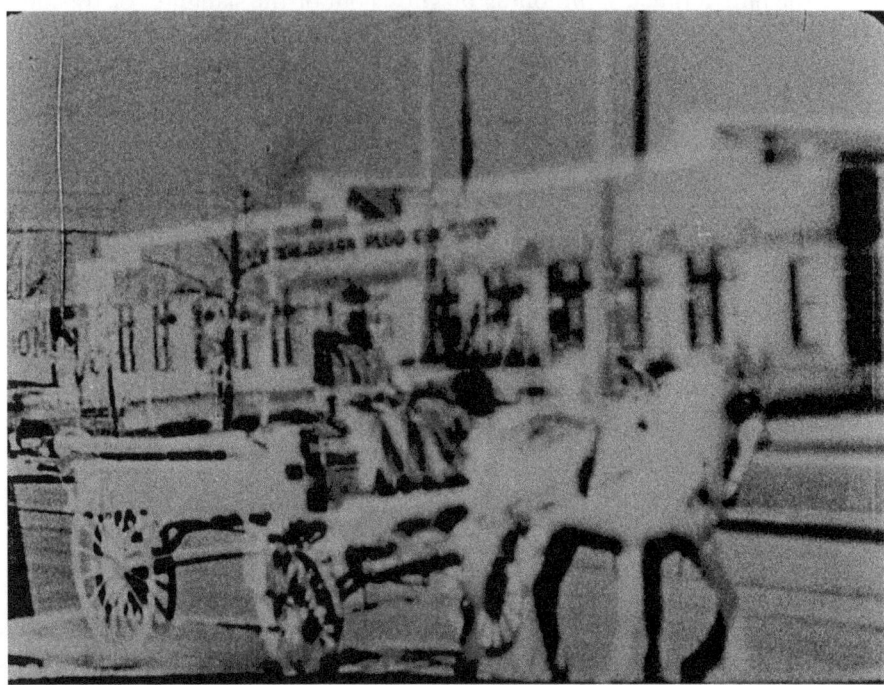

The Hart of London *[Film Stills]*, 1968-70
16mm film, 79 minutes, colour and black and white, sound
Courtesy of CFMDC

Realist works. It represented the communal end of Chambers' spiritual unity. Chambers' simultaneous positive and negative vision prefigures his later declaration: "I want to take hold of what is usually taken for granted around us, so to effect a 'being there' whose presence presses on me the alternate possibility of its absence."[21] The relation of the negative and positive images to one another is one of presence and absence, and the coexistence of both at once is therefore a wholeness, albeit one that is compromised and fractured by its resulting vibrations. The silver chorus poses coexistent renderings of the same reality, with the strangeness of photographic negative that pushes all detail of all matter to an ashen pale, lacking the reassurance of the photographic positive. The negative is the revelation of the image's process and construction, the material root of a scene as its alien mirror.

The silver chorus treats civic history, and society itself, as an energy that gives thematic unity to many strands of life in the region; but it is a history without explication, without instruction, with a simultaneous ambiguity and particularity. It could be anywhere like London, and yet it could be nowhere else. This is simply 'past', an assembly of energies built to such density that its meaning can only be related by recognizing it not as distilled historical time, but as a temporal gesture in the greater structure of the film, a timed summoning of ghosts out of the slaughter of the hart. The sequence as a whole takes on the religious and social significance of a harvest. This harvest gives way to shots from Chambers' own camera, slowly realizing fresh images, of Olga, John Jr. and Diego playing in snow banks, in a field with the horizon of a tundra, and by a garden gate. These scenes are superimposed with images of leaves and the branches of trees. On the soundtrack, the running water that has been playing backwards now runs forward, in measured bursts separated by silence, while in the image, a river rushes rapidly in reverse. The glimpse of running water that had bridged the second and third sequences of *Circle*, a simple but subliminal platitude, symbolic of flow, is here distorted in time, running backward and then forward. *Circle* demonstrates a cyclical time that, even as it recognizes the repetition and continuity inherent in a cycle, acknowledges time's forward momentum. In *The Hart of London*, vision is shuttled between past and present events, and even as time endures in cycles, history's lingering energies guide and shape a present moment that is ever referring to its past.

The Hart's Unmaking

With *Circle*, Jack Chambers had developed the film's structure around a

---

[21] Ibid., 115.

sudden turn. The garden gave false instruction, acclimating the viewer to a superficial understanding of the film as documental, or to the more complex recognition of it as a spiritual record disguised in the conceits of a science experiment. When the scenes from newsreels compose the final episode, they arrive in the form of familiar documentary conventions broken into heterodox and incomprehensible order. Their thematic resonance was buried so that it had to be wrestled out of the sequence, a line of indirection and multiplicity triggered by a brief shot of running water. *The Hart of London* would likewise pivot around a shift from one mode into another, growing richer and more ambiguous as the film passed out of the silver chorus and into a collision of personal and pilfered visions that, like the final sequence of *Circle*, was incongruous, disorienting and best understood as reverie. This modal incongruity would allow Chambers to set his myth, of the slaughtered hart and the mass resurrection, against records of his city that become the dream of his city, as well as scenes from the more intimate scale of his family life.

The visual obscurities of the silver chorus give way to more legible images, Chambers' aforementioned "clear positive pictures of the present." Farmers till soil with horse-drawn equipment, a bird's eye camera surveys flooded farmland, a child is taken out in a canoe and bodies frolic in a quarry, a shot familiar from *Circle*.[22] This sequence is interwoven with close-up images of leaves, branches and bubbles in water. The camera passes over leaves, fading to a close up of a child's sleeping face, his eyes shut, his lips parted. A menacing pair of shears cut aggressively at thick grass. As the first reel ends, a gardener perches at a hedge with his shears, which along with the scenes of flooding farmland, recalls Chambers' earlier themes, from *Hybrid*, of man's attempts to exert mastery over nature. As the second reel begins, a child's eye, blinking but mostly shut and possibly shifting in sleep, is superimposed with a spout of water. His eye opens wide as the superimposed image surveys windowpanes, leaves, a wooden floor, a medicine bottle. Water runs beneath images of this child playing with toy trucks, another consonance between the water lapping on the soundtrack and water imagery in the picture. The parts of the child (a foot, a hand, a penis, teeth) are paired with the torso of a man and the eye of a cow. This sequence is one of exalted intimacy, the camera moving in and out of focus as Chambers moves his fixed-focus camera nearer to the subjects. In close-up, the child cries and laughs. This intimacy soon gives way to

---

[22] This is not the only recycled image in the film; the shattered Vietnamese face that closed *Hybrid* also appears again in the silver chorus, a suggestion that contrary to Chambers' instructions for understanding the sequence as a municipal effort, it contains images consumed from beyond the city limits, which foreshadows later sequences of international news footage from the Middle East.

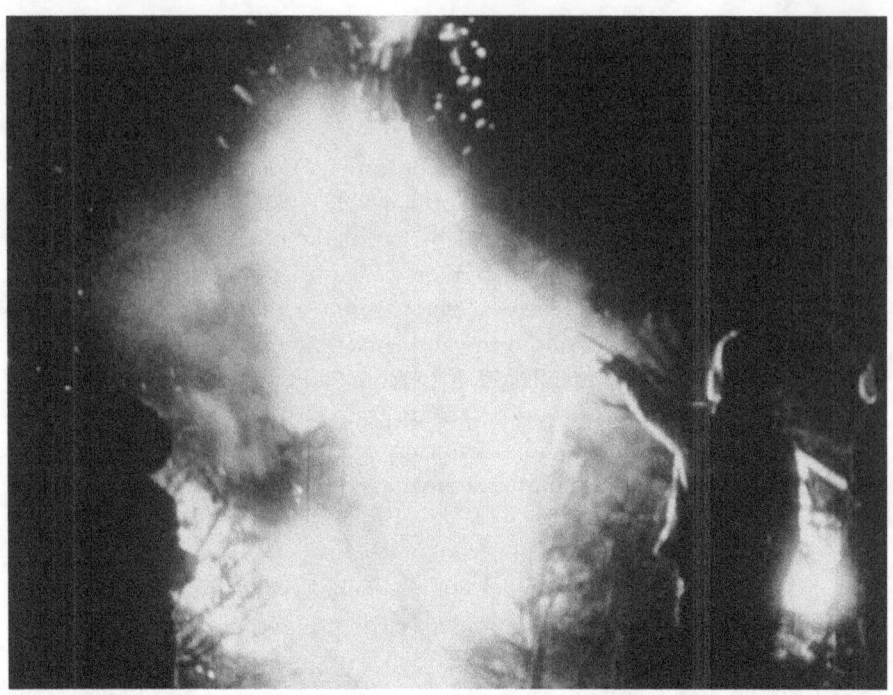

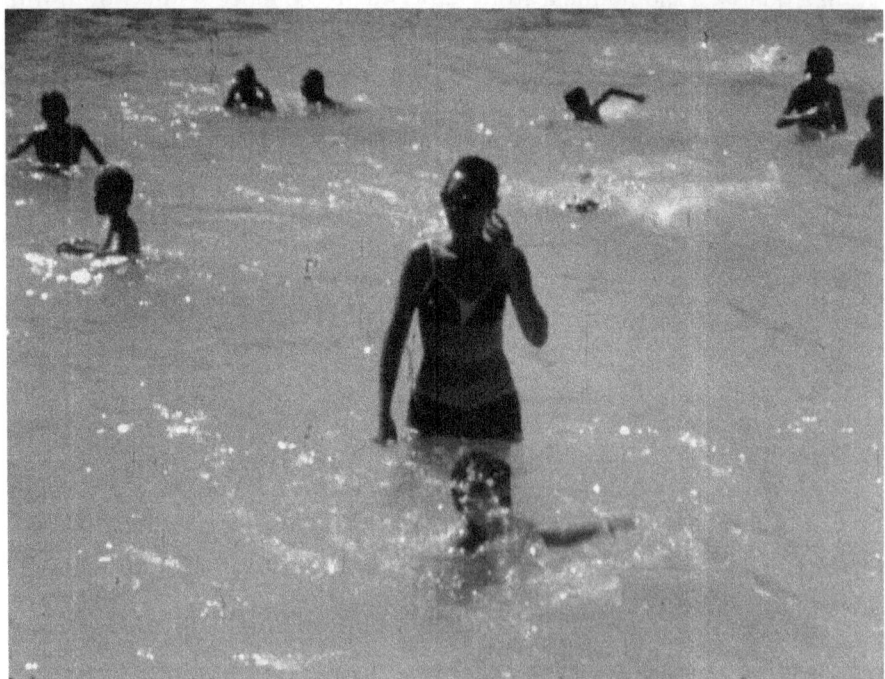

The Hart of London *[Film Stills]*, 1968-70
16mm film, 79 minutes, colour and black and white, sound
Courtesy of CFMDC

menace as the camera pans down the head of a slaughtered lamb.

The associative editing between the child, the animal and drip-ping water transitions into an editorial binary that joins scenes of lambs being slaughtered to a difficult birth. The lambs' throats are cut and the resulting death throes filmed in full, prolonged in discomfort and indig-nity. The birth is in a pale blue, the result of printing black and white negative to colour print stock, while the lamb is in vivid colour, its bright red blood coating a surface that is ambiguously a wooden slaughterhouse table and a stone altar. The birth footage shows forceps being used, skin cut, infant and afterbirth indiscernible. The intercutting of the birth with the abattoir suggests the implication of birth in death and vice versa, the closed loop of the circle becoming the symmetry of birth cries and death throes, recalling also the symmetrical maxims that frame T.S. Eliot's "East Coker": "In my beginning is my end," and, "In my end is my beginning."[23] On the soundtrack, the water has begun to play back in forward motion. The death throes of the lamb end in a light-struck tail of film that, for an instant, increases the exposure into pure red and yellow.[24] Images of the newborn are paired with those of an animal fetus, likely that of a lamb. The next substantial episode is bridged by footage taken by Chambers, of animal and human fetuses integrated with scenes of one of his children learning to swim at a public pool. In this footage, deer or sheep fetuses are shown in a slaughterhouse, their internal viscera moving; extreme close-ups of a fetus's eye and of a fetus in gel give way to shimmering, soft focus scenes of the sea; light reflects on water; a child breathes rapidly; and fi-nally, children play on a beach photographed in single-frame stop-motion. The sunlight causes rapid movements of light on the surface of the water.

This footage reinforces the elemental themes of the work, in par-ticular the relation of water to life, but the bulk of this reel soon comes to resemble the climactic sequence of *Circle*. Chambers has assumed further

---

[23] In his discussion of *The Hart of London*, Elder points to Chambers' use of contradictory or incompatible binaries, in particular, the interplay of innocence and brutality, ideas that have influenced this discussion and that resonate with these Eliot maxims. R. Bruce Elder, *Image and Identity: Reflections on Canadian Film and Culture* (Waterloo: Wilfred Laurier Press, 1989).

[24] The sacrificial lamb bears an obvious debt to Francisco de Zurbarán's *Agnus Dei* (1635-40), a still life of a lamb bound on a table, suspended in anticipation of the sacrificial ritual. Beyond the allegory shared by the painting and the film, Zurbarán was a primary influence on Chambers as a painter, for along with its relation to Veristic Surrealism, Chambers' painting activity has its technical roots in the exacting realism of Baroque Spanish paint-ing. In this sense, the staging of the lamb sequence and its overt allusion to *Agnus Dei* are other means by which the film has grown out of Chambers' painterly concerns, and, in a departure from the sanitized, bloodless, anticipatory rendering of Zurbarán's painting, the slaughter of this lamb extends the brutality of the sacrifice, a direct confrontation not only with the suffering of the lamb but with the human ordeals that the lamb embodies.

footage from London television, a mix of local stories and international news that assemble as a reverie, a rendering of the dream-life of the city.[25] Children sit on snowbanks watching a barn fire as firefighters work to put it out with dirt, wood and water. An infant in a baby carriage watches the blaze as its father stands vigilant. Fire, water and smoke rise up in plumes. Londoners watch the spectacle while stacking wood on the pyre to feed the flames. This fire is not such a threat, and the Londoners appear content to let it burn, gathering around the spectacle and then dispersing. As Chambers continues his integration of newsreels, the scenes and figures recall the grotesque nature of his Spanish representational paintings, the comic punctuation of an ordinary, ugly reality.

The next episode begins with London's Thames River icing over in a winter scene. Men undress on its banks. A policeman observes and retrieves a man after he has swam from one side to the other. Police lead the group of men to a paddy wagon and detain them. In short order, images change to the familiar binary of the military and the horticultural: a plane crosses the sky and parachuting soldiers jump from it, falling into a landscape that resembles a London winter; a man in a bomber jacket surveys plants in a greenhouse; at a veteran's fair, men barrel box in front of a crowd; and finally, an aged horticulturalist leads women through fields covered in umbrellas, under which he has been growing large dahlias. An elderly woman with a dog gathers a corsage from a garden; this transitions into a procession of children kissing an elderly couple as others look on with pleasure. A party of aged Londoners sifts through early twentieth century photographs that cover a dining room table, mementos of a bygone era, the children's kisses and the sifted photographs combining to bless the past.

In the coming series of found materials, the relation between man and animal is further developed and further taken into the territory of the nightmare as a group of hunters bring the carcass of a wolf to a woman. They hoist it up and pose it, showing its teeth. One appears giddy and bashful as he stands over it. A young girl pets a bird in a pen of caged birds. Birdcages are prepared for a delivery with what looks like a class photo placed in a sleeve at the bottom of the cage. At Christmas, a police officer and a man in formal attire collect and deliver a caged bird to a child with severe physical deformities. The boy's head is raised and steadied by his father's hand. He smiles apprehensively at the camera and looks puzzled by and fearful of the bird. The parents look at the boy, anticipating

---

[25] Like the found footage sequences of *Circle*, the sequences here that are borrowed from London television are discernible by an intermittent circle punched in the upper right corner of the frame.

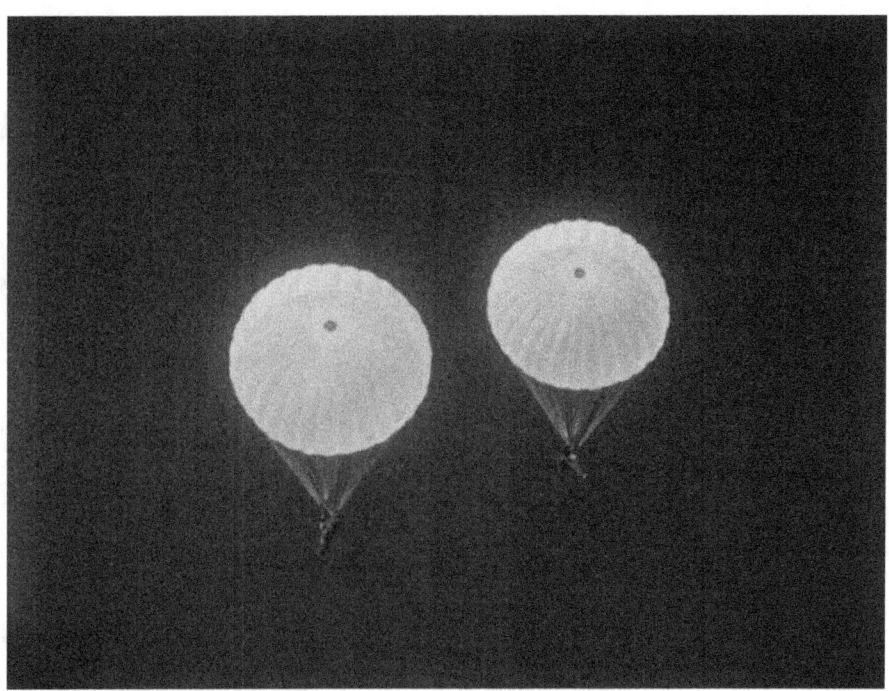

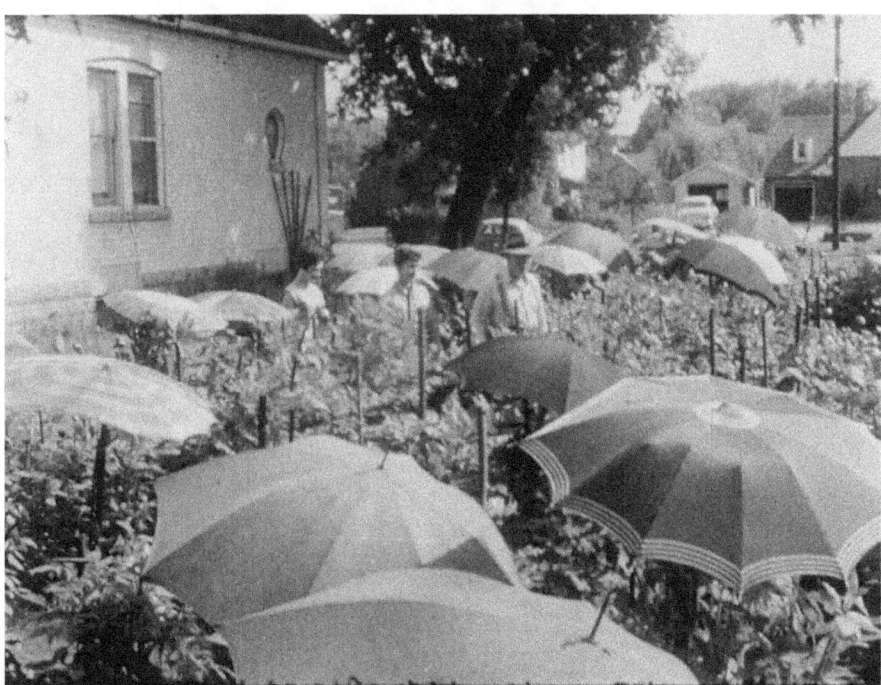

The Hart of London *[Film Stills]*, 1968-70
16mm film, 79 minutes, colour and black and white, sound
Courtesy of CFMDC

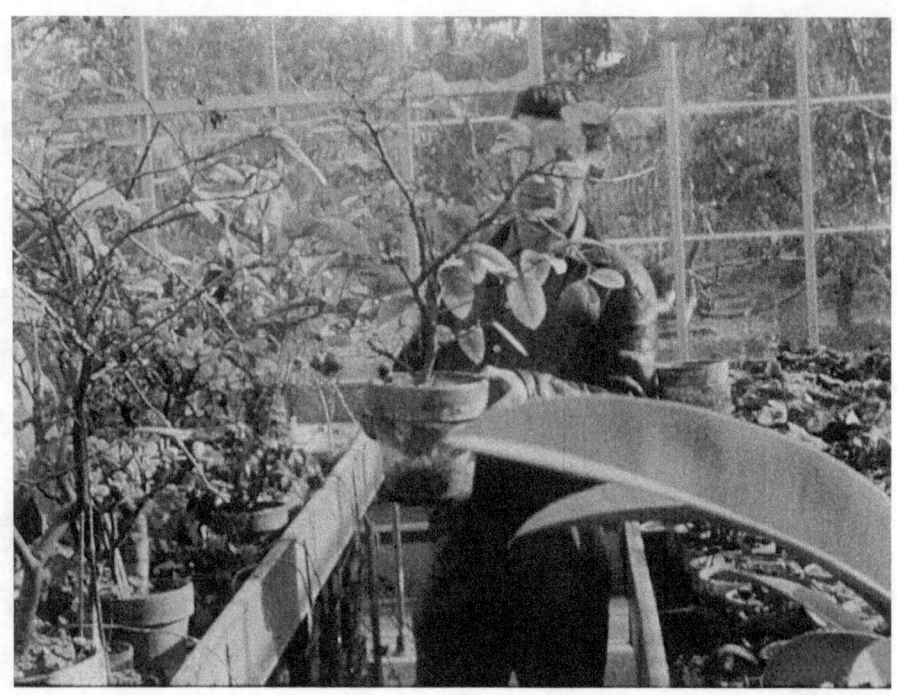

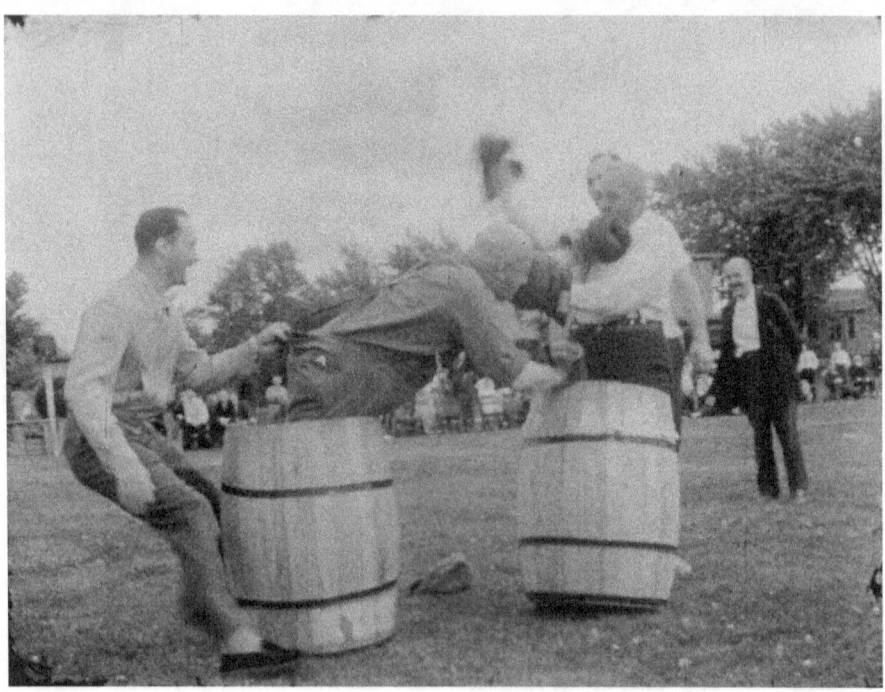

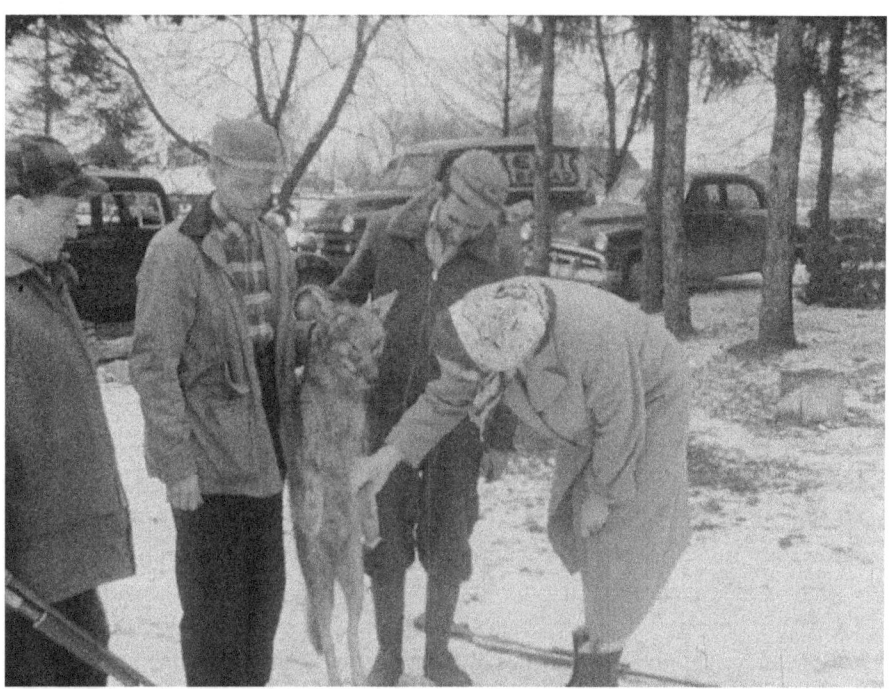

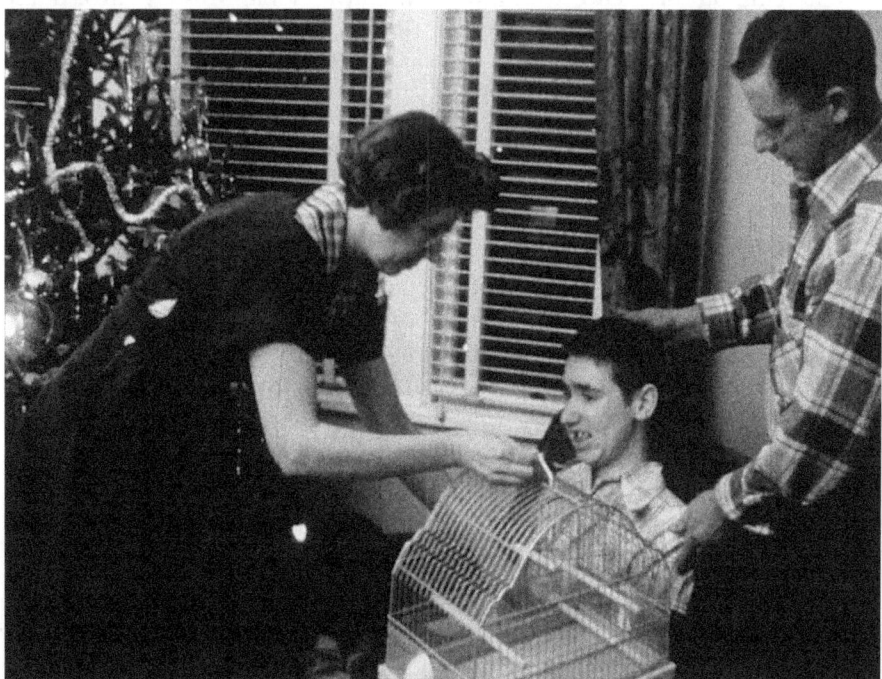

The Hart of London *[Film Stills]*, 1968-70
16mm film, 79 minutes, colour and black and white, sound
Courtesy of CFMDC

his reaction as one of delight. The boy's own face shows apprehension. Chambers, in conveying the suffering of beasts and of nature writ large, illustrates the fearful world of man, his isolation in a perceptual-spiritual mystery, above all, his relation to the animal as essential other, the beast a conscious being capable of fear, suffering and anger, made by these virtues into a metaphor for human experience, and yet, not human, inalienably different. The boy smiles at the cameras but looks to the songbird with trepidation.

These found scenes, the dream-life of London, are muddled by more elusive glimpses from other borrowed footage: Chambers has inserted images that are de-contextualized, that elude clear meaning in the sequence, for example, images of sailboats and of a woman's feet walking over a bridge. Trains billow steam up into the sky. Silos are tipped off of the roofs of commercial buildings and cleared from railroad grounds. Scenes from an unidentified Middle Eastern nation are integrated: men emerge from a hole in the ground, whether a collapsed tunnel or an ongoing construction project, and are greeted and embraced by men dressed in the garb of devout Muslims; bodies, either in sleep or death, lay in blankets along sand dunes and a primitive road; and finally, at the very end of the sequence, there is a brief glimpse of a man in formal Western clothes emerging out of a cave with a man in conventional Muslim garb. If the other parts of this sequence suggest the dream-life of London, these foreign scenes become a reverie for an exotic elsewhere, one that nevertheless resonates with the activities of London, the merging of disparate parts (East and West, positive and negative, forward and backward). Even as these dreams combine, they are also divided by the heterodoxy of their structure, by lack of transition, the episode as much an act of 'unmaking' vision as the silver chorus had been, unified in their ability to develop tensions between interlocking sequences.

As the episode nears its climax, an almost black, illegible image appears, then cuts to a man putting sunglasses on and shielding his eyes. Again, the black image appears, slightly more visible, and in it, a limp flag is set in photo negative. It becomes a macabre joke, the man putting on sunglasses to better see something that is already almost black. This marks a change in the soundtrack, from rushing water to the squawks of a bird, punctuated by a wooden clacking. The final dreams bring the viewer back into the film's present: a construction crew assembles around a monument to the Londoners killed in the Great War. The men are removing the crown of the monument, leaving it without a helm, for repairs or for gradual disassembly. This monument appears as an entrance pillar to London, Ontario. The disassembled monument, a simultaneous denigration of and memorial to human life, ends this reverie, returning to contemporary footage, of Jack Chambers mowing the lawn, maintaining the home, performing a fatherly chore. This begins the final sequence of the film, an exploration of Chambers' responsibilities as a father.

In the Heart of the Hart of London

The source of the running water on the soundtrack is finally revealed as London, Ontario's own Thames River, one of the city's most direct debts to its English namesake, photographed at sunset, its waters running along a dark bank speckled with distant houses. Diego and John Jr. approach a deer, in a patch of clear grass on the edge of woods. On the soundtrack, Olga's voice warns that they must "be very careful" as they feed it, not to move suddenly, not to startle it and thereby provoke it into a violent reaction of wild instinct. Jack and Olga give the children food for the deer to eat out of their hands. Olga's fretting about the children's safety is punctuated by her instructions to Chambers to film and other worried remarks to the children. The hart eats, and it moves toward the children to get more food, nudging them. They hold out their hands to show that they're empty. The sound begins looping, Chambers saying, "Here, Diego, I'll get you some more," "Don't get too near," and Olga whispering, "He's going, he's going," and "You have to be very careful."

Through the course of *The Hart of London*, the film moves from a portrait of fear to an urgent declaration of it. Fear, first seen in the terrified and disoriented gallops of the deer, becomes the immutable core of the film, as the disjoined presences of haunted London emerge as the silver chorus, as the sheep bleats its prolonged death throes in the abattoir, and as the exchanges between animal and man (the deer, the sheep, the wolf, the bird) increasingly reveal the estrangement of the two.[26] Throughout the film, visual and editorial tactics and scrutinized allusions had kept the work fixed in the modern, and rather than offer a narrow lesson, the film instead develops this relation between seeing and feeling fear. The anxiety of this final sequence refers back to the opening sequence: fear in the wild has moved from vision and allegory to a present, full-body perception of

---

[26] *The Hart of London* has enjoyed many parallels to the work of Stan Brakhage, and has received praise from Brakhage directly. While Chambers' film parallels Brakhage's birth films, *Window Water Baby Moving* (1955) and *Thigh Line Lyre Triangular* (1961), or the conscious mythmaking of *Dog Star Man* (1961-64), its strongest resemblance to any one work of Brakhage's might be to *Anticipation of the Night* (1958), a poetic assembly of Brakhage's anxieties that climaxes in a suicide attempt, with Brakhage filming the shadow of his own head in a noose. Brakhage and Chambers are working through similar anxieties, but they are also elaborating personal vision with thematic structures and motifs.

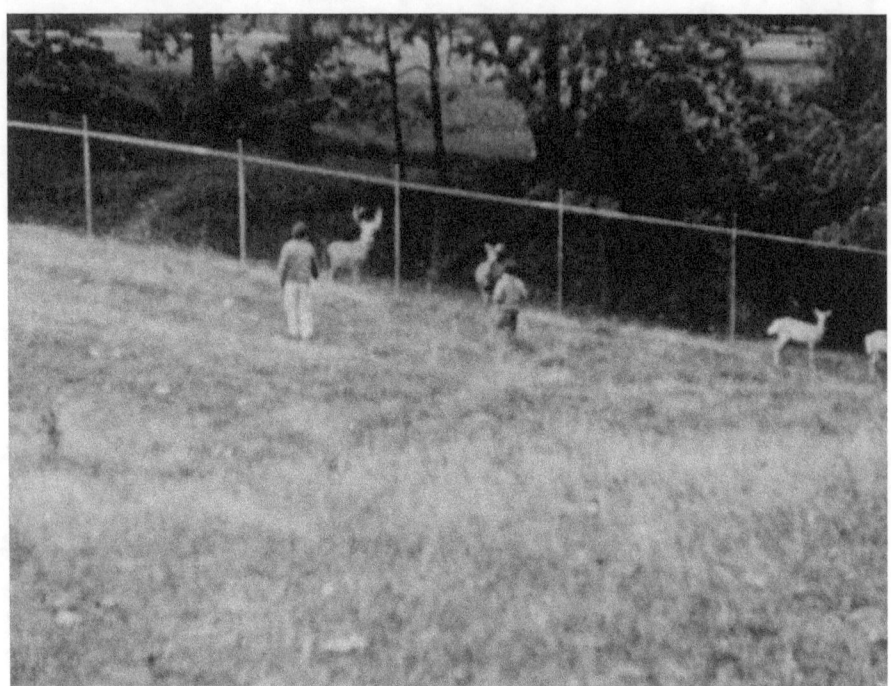

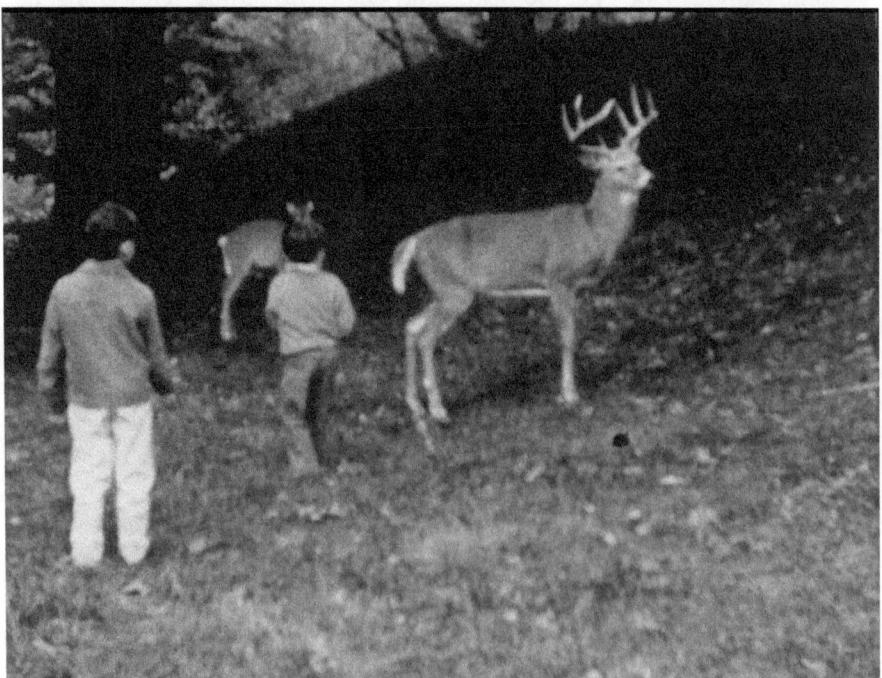

The Hart of London *[Film Stills]*, 1968-70
16mm film, 79 minutes, colour and black and white, sound
Courtesy of CFMDC

the menacing exchange between man and beast.

In medieval superstition, the bone in the heart of the hart would prevent it from dying of fear. This imagined hart could endure extremities of fear unknown to man, whose weak and unprotected heart was prone to rapid beats in moments of terror. The children's confrontation with the hart shows a final estrangement of beast from man; the children approach the hart at their parents' behest so that they can see and interact with the beast, but that interaction is fraught with the parents' fear that the beast, territorial, sensitive to the sudden movements of predatory man, could be startled into biting or kicking the children, or to goring them with its ant-lers. The film's first sacrifice was this beast, host to potential ferocity, and its presence extends through the interim scenes of the carcasses of hunted wolves, the silent bleating of the dying lamb, and the pet bird, eyed appre-hensively by its new owner, all sequences of man's essential otherness from beast. Beasts are predators, pets and meat, and man accepts them into a higher symbolic order as allegories of myth and faith. They commune with man by their consciousness, their fear, in which is seen a reflection of human suffering, and they are also his prey. By this, *The Hart of London* recalls the visionary poet William Blake's twinned *Songs of Innocence and of Experience*, "The Lamb" and "The Tyger." Man is entwined with beast in that they reflect the forms and machinations of a higher being. They become a mirror to Christ. Out of the same force that builds that symbolic communion comes a destructive and primal ferocity. The film ends with the scene of the children and the hart, beneath it the cautious pleas of Olga, an illustration of the blank question that Blake puts to his Tyger: "Did he who made the Lamb make thee?" Like Blake, Chambers builds a relation between the disparate symbolism of the beast, inhuman other and spiritual icon. *The Hart of London* fearfully poses an unknown and un-knowable future against a compromised present, a pall cast over it by the ferocious potential of nature, driven by instinct and hunger.

Difficult Aesthetics and The Hart of London

In pitching *The Hart of London* between formalism and folklore, Chambers established the modal difficulty of the work. This was the essential binary of the film, to at once offer something as communal and unifying as a founding myth, but to do so within a form of indirection, incomprehen-sion, and ambiguity. These ambitions continued from the branch of mod-ernism that explored and posed blank questions about being and meaning through works that assembled, in experimental syntax, flow, and juxtaposi-tion, histories of the world, assuming myths and parables from the ancients into the new language of the modern. *The Hart of London* was a film of totalizing ambition, enclosing the author's self-portrait within a menacing vision of his hometown, echoing his memories of childhood and casting them over the lives of his own children, and conveying his moral stance on nature and mastery, in the relation between man and animal. His folktale would not yield to explication, nor would his formalism yield to the perspectival and semantic conventions of classical art. Even when the film's folkloric aspects appear to clarify its relation to innocence or to brutality, or when its formal aspects give clear sight to something of definitive meaning, that relation or meaning only becomes enriched, only takes on further psychic associations that push the film's themes to greater ambiguity. When at the end its anxieties are stated, in Olga's commands to the children, those fears have become so all-consuming that there is no foreseeable resolution between the film's folklore and formalism.

The visual aspect of *The Hart of London* had evolved from Chambers' earlier films, in part, but like them, it also developed from his silver paintings of the mid-1960s. Where his earlier films had mirrored his painting activity in their fracturing of time and composition, *The Hart of London* assumed a density of colour and texture directly from the silver paintings, seen in the silver chorus sequence. In superimposing positive and negative renderings of the same image, he had created a largely new form of visual difficulty in both cinema and painting.[27] The dense and rapid passage of the images allows the work to open in different ways with each viewing, to survey a particular history (that of London) in glimpses, but also to survey a more universal conflict, of man and nature, man and memory, of the photographic memento in general, as faces, actions and places take on symbolic significance through discontinuity and disassociation. This energy field is rich with allusions, not only in the faces of historical Londoners, now anonymous, but also to iconic buildings and businesses of London that, through knowledge of the city's history, enrich the historical particularity of Chambers' sources. When Chambers begins to use found materials in the second reel, the city's military history emerges as another presence in the dream-life of London, in the parachuting soldiers and the veteran's picnic.

Chambers' own footage, which is most present through the second

---

[27] To say that this is new outright is to neglect work that had used negative images to the end of confusing or obscuring vision, or to thematic effect. Such activity lies at the root of avant-garde film practice. However, what is new about Chambers' use of this technique is, in part, his overprinting, and the way in which the negative inversion of the image assumed an overarching thematic consonance with the rest of the work, at once a representation of the 'energy field' of history and an illustration of the binary impressions of experience that haunt the film, positive and negative, backwards and forwards.

reel, includes black and white film printed in colour (taking on a vague blue cast), rich colour images from home movies of the Chambers family (in particular, scenes from the poolside and the final confrontation with the hart), and scenes from the slaughterhouse of a Spanish monastery. One of Chambers' central ideas in his painting activity was the use of colours "as spring-boards and magnets," to render tensions of spatial experience.[28] In other words, he believed in the conscious use of colour as a means to guide the eye through image space. In *The Hart of London*, attention wanes and focuses by colour, allowing the viewer to slip between a state of awareness and focus, and a state more open to the psychic activity of image association. These states align with Chambers' use of colour, which comes at moments that demand concentration (the parallels between animal and human fetuses, the wet back of the child by the poolside, the slaughter of the lamb), and his use of black and white, or in the case of the second reel, blue, which demand dispersed attention, best demonstrated by the free associative state of the silver chorus but resonating in the first parallels of child and beast in the second reel. The montage of childbirth and abattoir mixes both, in a sequence that demands both forms of attention to invoke what is simultaneously particular and universal. It places the viewer in a state of allegorical imagining, allowing these particular events to assume a greater allegory in the viewer's mind as the bright red of the lamb's blood tints their perception of the child's blue birth.

The soundtrack is composed almost entirely of the sound of the local Thames River. Through the first reel, this sound is run backwards, fading in and out in a loop. The sound is an elemental component of the film, water as life essence, water as an allegory for time, water as a force that permeates many aspects of being, the life-giving force that sustains man, animal and plant. And yet, through the silver chorus and after, the soundtrack has been conditioned by technology to come in distorted bursts, running backwards, shaped by the frequencies and effects of tape, obfuscated in such a way that the sound's source resists ready identification. As an abstract sound, it becomes a subliminal mirror to the accompanying images. It is the rifle blast that puts down the deer and the singing of a train track. It becomes sounds of hunting, industry and progress, the sound forming an association with receding memory. However, when it is run forward, bubbling familiarly, the water provokes a biological recognition of the relation between water and life, incompatible with the significances that it assumed throughout the first reel. The form of the soundtrack is not in itself menacing, but it takes on a menacing aspect,

---

[28] Ross Woodman, *Chambers: John Chambers interviewed by Ross G. Woodman* (Toronto: Coach House Books, 1967), 7.

not in chance associations with brutality and mastery, but in the uneasy exchange between water (in birth, in recreation, in the river itself) and instrument (the rifle, the garden shears, the train, the drill). Throughout the second reel, the water runs forward. As a child is born, the lamb bleeds out in the abattoir sequence, and the soundtrack becomes a sign of the water underlying all life and present in the blood, viscera and afterbirth of new life, as well as a substitute for the sound of blood rushing out of the lamb's neck and for the beast's unheard bleats.

The soundtrack's form, its shift between forward and reverse, is consonant with the negative-positive transit of the silver chorus. It is one of the symmetries and binary impressions that haunt the film—negative and positive, forward and reverse—all calculated acts of inversion by which *The Hart of London* reconciles discordant parts. This assembly of discordant parts also speaks to the film's sequential incongruities, an aspect of Chambers' films announced in *Circle*, with its dispersal of vision over its three parts. The two films have form that is free enough to defy the 'structural' label that would soon become dominant in avant-garde film discourse, for while Chambers' films were structured consciously, they also bore a more improvisatory mirror to personal vision, akin to the lyric films of Stan Brakhage.[29] Chambers' earlier films had complex structural conceits, or at least, resisted the improvisatory appearance that would come to mark much of lyric cinema. All of his films involved the reconciliation of two or more parts, as in the three ages of *Mosaic*, the binary of *Hybrid*, the integration of multiple documental forms in *R34* and the tripartite 'haiku' structure of *Circle*. *The Hart of London* is nearest in its construction to *Circle*, a series of parts linked thematically, but suggesting thematic redirection.[30] His earlier films had been difficult in their editorial sequencing, their use of fragmentary composition and their multiplicity of meaning.

Like the Perceptual Realist paintings, *The Hart of London* gestures to redemption. Where the paintings had aimed to redeem perception itself,

---

[29] When Brakhage would later champion Chambers' work, in particular *The Hart of London* and *R34*, he wrote of the apprehension with which he had approached *Circle*, and his avoidance of it because of his feelings toward the idea of structuralism as a movement, as this work appeared to embody those gestures. His admission suggests that, although these distinctions would later form the ground of common discourse through the work of P. Adams Sitney, the aversions and distinctions between these forms were palpable in the community of avant-garde film in the 1960s, making the modal turns in Chambers' work an impressive demonstration of an artist unhindered by the rigidity of the prevailing discourse.

[30] Among Chambers' film notebooks, preparatory notes on *Circle* give its title as *The Heart of London: Circle 4*. The relation between the two works is therefore one of prelude and body. It seems just as likely, by Chambers' own descriptions of his unfinished spatial study *CCCI* (1970), that it might also have held some direct relation to the suite of films Chambers had imagined comprising *The Heart*, or *Hart, of London*.

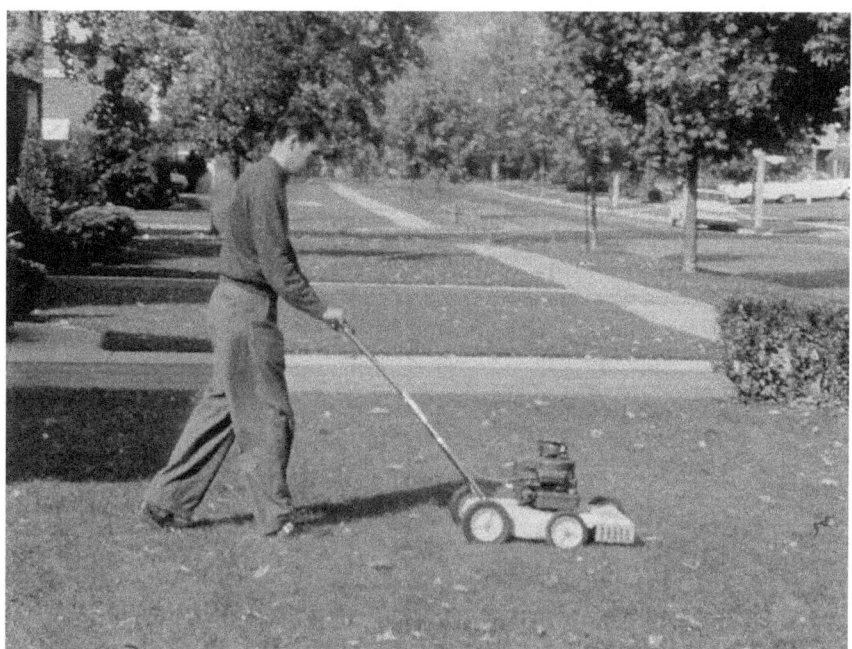

The Hart of London *[Film Still]*, 1968-70
16mm film, 79 minutes, colour and black and white, sound
Courtesy of CFMDC

Chambers uses the fractures of modern perception to address the redemption of man, a redemption implicit in the conceits and themes of his recombination. He aims to redeem man by the final cautionary utterance of the film, to his children, to be careful. They must be careful for their own being, careful in their exchange with nature and with the external world, careful in their dealings with beast and man. Man himself, in the symbolic continuity of the children, must be careful to recognize the brutal charm of a nature in which he is implicated, for knowing the fatal competition of earthly things becomes a path to the redemption of a whole-body spiritual perception. It is by this joining of romantic themes and modern aesthetic strategies that *The Hart of London* achieves an essential difficulty, with these fragments he has shored against his ruins.

The Hart of London as Final Testament

Jack Chambers had always imagined *The Hart of London* as a municipal team effort, and so despite its perceptual challenges, he had made the film with the intention of sharing it with his fellow Londoners whose pasts and ancestors had provided the raw materials for much of the film. *The Hart of London* received its hometown premiere through the London Public Library on November 27, 1970, alongside Greg Curnoe's film *Connexions*.[31] It was poorly received by the local press: Lenore Crawford, *London Free Press* art critic and longtime supporter of Chambers, was confounded by the film and dismissed it as an amateurish bore.[32] It is unlikely that its first audience, save for Chambers' friends and collaborators, would know how to approach the film, as by that time a general interest in Chambers was framed by the success of his Perceptual Realist paintings. By contrast to the ready pleasures of those paintings, as romantic landscapes executed with extraordinary skill, *The Hart of London* was dense, murky and determinedly against ready comprehension. Its folkloric and symbolic elements included disturbing and shocking violence and coexisted with a radical form so fortified against understanding, so against the conventions of mainstream cinema, that it invites intellectual and visual strain and frustration. Even those who had appreciated the relative didacticism of *Hybrid* and *Mosaic*, or the local colour of *R34* and *Circle*, would not be prepared by those works to see a film so devout in its obscurity. Chambers had planned other films and completed preliminary versions of two, *CCCI* (or, *centre, curve, circumference, insert,* 1970) and *Life Still* (1970).[33] However, during his prolonged illness, he would devote his time toward the more profitable efforts of his Perceptual Realist paintings, building equity for his family in the event of his imminent death. His reasons for abandoning filmmaking can only be speculated on, but he had always declared it an unprofitable pursuit, taken for pleasure and for freedom. In the prison of his illness, and in the aftermath of *The Hart of London*'s hostile public reception, pleasure and freedom may have proven insufficient.

Rebirth is a central concept in Chambers' cosmology, a natural mystical extension of the artist's preoccupation with birth and death. The bookends of corporeal existence are paired in *The Hart of London*, as in the tragic exchange of *Hybrid*, the ready substitution of life for death. When

---

[31] In *Connexions*, Greg Curnoe travels London speaking about the connections between his life and this place. It is a more direct work of autobiography than *The Hart of London*, but deals in the same ambition to link the artist's life and hometown, an exploration of the relationship between memory and environment.

[32] Lenore Crawford. "London artists' films show sharp contrast." *London Free Press*, 28 November 1970, 27.

[33] Although the date of *Life Still* is given as 1970, it has also been listed as finished or drafted circa 1972. Other planned films of Chambers, around which he had many considerable notes and treatments, include *Torero* and *Dogman*, the former a Spanish medieval picaresque fantasy in which a caped man woos a woman, dies and is buried (in the vein of magic realism, its treatment bearing references to Pluto cartoons); the latter a macabre story of a man eating with a dog, which is wrapped in plastic, force-fed and stabbed.

Chambers spoke of his series of births, he did not speak with the distance of a fully developed artist, but as an artist still in the midst of his spiritual preparation. For Chambers, reincarnation was a portal to higher levels of consciousness, the purification of a being's spirit. Chambers' work, in the arc of his own dark transit through the silver paintings and the affirmation of Perceptual Realism, takes on the dimensions of a spiritual quest, a journey deeper into the essential gesture that is reconciliation between being and nature. In this cosmology, the soul moves toward states of perfection beyond corporeal existence with each new birth. Chambers suggested this in his unfinished manuscript *Red and Green*, with a quotation, a second-hand reading of Plato pilfered from a 1967 Causeway paperback on reincarnation: "the soul ... may be capable of existing without the body, though it be imprisoned in it as in a tomb."[34] With each birth, Chambers attained a greater mastery. Out of the grief and fear of *The Hart of London*, he arrived at his ultimate birth in Perceptual Realism.

Jack Chambers passed away in 1978, almost a decade after his initial diagnosis with leukemia, defying expectations of a short life and contesting the illness through alternative medicine and spiritual therapies. The Chambers films remain as a record and expression of intimate perception, elevating his vision of his city, seeing its history from the fleeting present, his garden, his children and his wife. He recognized the mystery of these things and attempted, in building symmetries and harmonies in his portraits of them, to draw mysteries out of nature and into the very stones of London's houses. In Chambers' work, the life of London is raised to the mystical status of myth, then razed as ruins, the fading intimacies of the dead. *The Hart of London* becomes the founding myth of the city, its history an assembly of many lives gesturing in the invisible, the scale of which is magnified and enriched by Chambers' project, but never clarified.

---

[34] Qtd. in Tom Smart, *Jack Chambers' Red and Green: an artist's inquiry into the nature of meaning* (Erin, Ont.: Porcupine's Quill, 2013), 88.

Reason Over Passion *[Film Still]*, 1969
16mm film, 84 minutes, colour and black and white, sound
Courtesy of CFMDC

CHAPTER FIVE

Glowing Hearts:
Joyce Wieland's *La raison avant la passion /
Reason Over Passion* (1969)

Through the final years of the 1960s, Joyce Wieland longed to make a permanent return to Canada. Her mature work had gradually developed in
Neo-Dada and Pop idioms but was also more personal than those modes
might suggest; by 1967, Wieland had settled on Canada as her central
subject.[1] Her activities in painting, quilting and sculpture had gained the
attention of the Canadian art establishment, but that work remained obscure in New York. Whatever attention she gained stateside, she gained
through her films. In the mid-1960s her work had engaged with the repurposing of mass culture as an overtly personal expression, without a
strong sense of national affiliation, in paintings and sculptures that called
up the film frame, but which were also rooted in the design principles of
advertising. Wieland's work would become more explicitly Canadian in
content through the course of the nation's 1967 centennial, as her paintings and quilts began to consistently allude to Canada, for example, with
the collage sculptures *Puerco de Navidad* and *Confedspread* (both 1967). From
Wieland's adoption of mixed media in the early 1960s, through to her
shift away from the flat plane and toward her sculptural 'stuffed movies',
her work had moved toward the aesthetic philosophy she would form in
the wake of the centennial: a coexistence of de-familiarization, ambiguous
political comment and ironic comedy, under the umbrella of a militant
sentimentality. In the vastness of the Canadian terrain Wieland recognized
a "true north, strong and free," strong in its discipline, its espousing of bilingualism, in its codes and customs gained from a collision of British and

---

[1] In an unpublished interview with Barbara Stevenson (1986), Wieland said this of her
experience of the late 1960s: "I was sick of all these little groups, like little priesthoods of
understanding, groups that believed in one theory or another, and I found things drying up
(...) I also had been reading what the nationalist writers had been writing and I had been
reading my own history again and had been very much involved with American history and
various demonstrations (...) I realized that the statistics looked terrible in terms of Canada
surviving as a nation."

French colonial powers, its curious position of absorbing and in threat of being absorbed by American culture; free as a land nearing the centenary of its independence, where the government advanced a vision of Canada where intellect ruled, where reasoned calculation could better ensure the most sensible directions for government and a utopian protection of individual freedoms. It was free, also, in the possibilities posed by the sweeping canvas of the Prairies and of regions left uncharted or unpaved, free as a site where the New World's natural beauty was unobstructed and, by that lack of civilizing, preserved.

The ecological panic that Wieland had conveyed in *Rat Life and Diet in North America* focused on disparities between American and Canadian values. Her increasing attention to the Canadian political climate, and her fascination with the character of popular Justice Minister Pierre Trudeau who was then running for the office of Prime Minister, had extended from her past engagement with labour, social unrest and political iconography, even as Trudeau's iconographic value found a natural consonance with her semi-ironic ideas of marketplace sentimentality.[2] Her fascination with Trudeau, which steadily turned from adoration to a more critical regard, sprang from the same impulse that had drawn her interest to Napoleon Bonaparte and John F. Kennedy.[3] Trudeau, as a coldly reasoning man who stirred the nation's passion, was the essential embodiment of Wieland's ongoing project of pitching her work between sentimentality and irony, a paradoxical man who could simultaneously inspire patriotism in the hearts of Canadian liberals while proselytizing the advantage of a neutral, detached intellect. It was in the guise of the latter that Trudeau offered his motto, on the occasion of his nomination at the 1968 Liberal leadership convention, as the triumph of reason over passion. Wieland would develop a suite of works in response to Trudeau, composed of two quilts, one etching and a film, all titled *La raison avant la passion / Reason Over Passion*.[4]

[2] Political iconography in Wieland's work is never posed as direct political comment, so as to preserve, on the one hand, the personal dimension of her engagement with these figures, and on the other, the ironic detachment of the propagandizing mentality that she adopted in dealing with such figures. This treatment is supported by the cultural pervasiveness of their iconography, as men of the people, as messiahs of liberal reform, as late princes to no monarchy, as politicians who had captured the popular imagination so as to assume the apolitical stature of mythic heroes.

[3] These icons had both played roles in *Larry's Recent Behavior* (1963) and Wieland had written on Napoleon (in the 1960s Canadian little magazine *evidence*). Her interest in Napoleon re-emerged when, in 1971, on the occasion of her *True Patriot Love* solo exhibition at the National Gallery of Canada, Wieland included "the last letters of General Wolfe and the Marquis de Montcalm embroidered in crimson silk on linen." Hugo McPherson, "Wieland: An Epiphany of North," *Artscanada* 158-159 (August-September 1971), 19.

[4] This event is described in detail in Peter C. Newman, *The Distemper of Our Times: Canadian Politics in Transition, 1963–1968* (Toronto: McClelland & Stewart, 1968), 466.

This suite posed an indirect challenge to the motto. The works appeared to assume a mission even as they critiqued that mission, her use of the slogan steeped in formal discontinuity between statement and meaning, the inherent passion of forms undermining the preaching of reason, much as the necessary passion of the preacher undermines reason. By her challenge, Wieland served as both a critical respondent to Trudeau and as his willfully compromised propagandist. *Reason Over Passion* would be her most ambitious film to date, by its length, the complexity of its structure and the opaqueness of its component's relations.

In January 1968, Wieland travelled to the Vancouver Art Gallery which was staging a survey of her works of the preceding decade, including quilts, stuffed movies, drawings and paintings. She took the transcontinental train from Toronto to Vancouver, known as The Canadian, which cuts through a vast and sparely populated stretch of the prairies. The journey took one week, and led past the Lake of the Woods, through the Prairies, to British Columbia. She brought her Bolex camera and a tape recorder and began to film out of the windows of the train. The following June, Wieland would film the eastern part of Canada by car, passing along the Trans-Canada Highway from Toronto to Nova Scotia.[5] In the interim, in April 1968, she had filmed Trudeau at the Ottawa Civic Centre, on the occasion of the Liberal leadership convention at which he assumed party leadership. Sitting in the press section below Trudeau, Wieland had a medium-shot view of Trudeau taking his seat and staring out at the press corps. The footage was not ideal in its distance from the subject or in its wide capture of his surroundings. She would later re-photograph her footage, slowing it down and cropping it to form a more intimate portrait in which Trudeau's expressions became obscure, between menace and benevolence.[6] She put

---

[5] Wieland had travelling companions on these trips: en route to Vancouver, she was joined by Rose Richardson and critic Wendy Michener. Sequences from this journey appear in Wieland's unfinished film *Wendy and Joyce* (circa 1968), restored by the Cinematheque Quebecois in 2014. The film is dedicated to the memory of Michener, who died of an aneurysm in late 1968. For the eastern leg of the journey, taken by car along the Trans-Canada Highway, Wieland travelled with Richardson. In spite of its lonesome, isolated vision of the vast span of the nation, the making of *Reason Over Passion*, like the group dynamic of Wieland's quilting, served as a social occasion.

[6] Such binary countenances run through Wieland's work, in the mix of ecstasy and irritation or pain on the face of Sylvia in *Larry's Recent Behavior* (1963), and in the similarly ecstatic and suffering expressions of the woman golem that rises out of the dirt in *Barbara's Blindness* (1965). These expressions resonate in the comic ambiguity of Wieland's militant sentimentality, that is, the ability to join opposites within a single gesture or declaration, as in her relation to the phrase "Reason over Passion." She filmed Trudeau in a manner that led her to elicit these responses from friends: "I showed some of the footage to different people and I got different reactions. Some people said, 'That man is insane' and other people, 'That man is fascinating.'" (Joyce Wieland and Hollis Frampton, "I Don't Even Know about the

this footage away, along with her travel footage, unsure of what to do with it. Later she would show it to Snow and to Hollis Frampton, eventually deciding she would "make a sandwich," using the train and car trips as bread, with Trudeau in the centre, from which vantage point he would provide the reasoned counterpart to Wieland's passion.

In making *Reason Over Passion*, Wieland would reverse the trajectory of her journey, beginning with the June 1968 car trip, ending with the January 1968 train trip, bridged in the middle by a lengthy, re-photographed portrait of Trudeau, in which Wieland elasticizes and recomposes her convention footage. Her earlier films had gradually developed an individual sense of temporal and spatial relations, maturing rapidly through 1967. They would serve as a prelude to the more substantial project of *Reason Over Passion*. Wieland had described the film by its relation to Trudeau's theme: "I decided to unite the leader to the land and cement it with his words ... not so much cement as spread them across a continent ... REASON OVER PASSION!!! OVERWHELMED ... METAMOPHORSED INTO PASSION THROUGH USE."[7] As she made the film, Wieland imagined herself as Leni Riefenstahl. She became a propagandist whose work embodied an earnest declaration, but that by virtue of its intimate, passionate, irrational aesthetic, undermined its message.[8] The film was an act of subterfuge, a compromise of the rational by an omnipresence of passionate intensity, and by anagrams and chronological ruptures. Wieland would characterize the work as "a dialogue between Trudeau and myself ... but speaking to (and working for) Canada," a

---

Second Stanza," in *The Films of Joyce Wieland*, ed. Kathryn Elder [Toronto: Cinematheque Ontario, 1999], 178). Trudeau's motto ultimately becomes insane, inane, irrelevant to the ecstatic forms and the great white emptiness of Wieland's vision of the north. Years later, in an interview with Barbara Stevenson (1986), Wieland would clarify her own position in accounting the same story: "It really shouldn't be reason and passion in a person. But this man is only reason over passion, and ultimately he's a psychopath. (...) That is a psychopathic type. Not that I say 'reason over passion' is psychopathic, no. This man has a terrible imbalance. Though he believes himself to be so oriental and very balanced, he isn't. And what happens when people want the kind of power that he achieved in this country. It's psychopathic."

[7] Qtd. in Hugo McPherson, "Wieland: An Epiphany of North," *Artscanada* 158-159 (August-September 1971), 27.

[8] Wieland used this parallel—between Riefenstahl's *Triumph of the Will* (1935) and *Reason Over Passion*—in conversation with Hollis Frampton, published as "I Don't Even Know about the Second Stanza," 178. She also speaks, in the same breath, of the film as a land-travelling survey of Canada, oppositional to the aerial studies that came in the same era. She is specifically alluding to the National Film Board's *Helicopter Canada* (1966), a topographic survey of the land, directed by Eugene Boyko, a work of landscape tourism made on the eve of the centennial. The centennial's utopian ambitions, of the possibilities of Canadian civilization and wilderness, are pervasive throughout the National Film Board's mid-to-late 1960s output and its contributions to Expo '67.

definition that extends to the rest of this suite of works, including the quilts and etching.[9] But the film, in particular, takes on a staggering scale relative to her earlier film work, as an epic illustration of the relation of the land to the psychology and intent of its government and its people, an illustration of a Canada strong and free, and yet, menaced by Trudeau's proud imbalance, in which reason bests passion for the good of Canada, menaced also by the country's own ephemeral, increasingly abstracted sense of itself. Much as modern artists had vanished into their canvases, so too did the post-Dada subject vanish into itself.[10] With *Reason Over Passion*, Wieland not only builds a dialectic between logic and spirit. She cuts a path through the country by which it might reveal its own uncertain, indirect self-portrait.

Far and Wide

In order to form that national self-portrait in doubt, Wieland would, in her role as propagandist, reveal the nation through the title expression, the supremacy of reason and passion wherein the former might yield the latter by a forced translation, by transit into the irrational. In the film's first reel, reason comes under scrutiny almost immediately, as rational codes of cinematic space, time and communication are broken by voids, staggered, often muddied into opaque, abstract forms. Passion manifests in such fracturing expressions, but also in clearer presences, in the patriotic emotion demanded by the flag and by glimpses of familiar landscapes. Reason and realism have a particular relation, unified in their logical systems, and the film subverts both, not necessarily to lord passion over reason but to strike a balance between the two, to realize Canada as a land of passion *and* reason.[11] *Reason Over Passion* begins in discontinuity, the image shifting between several sequences of predetermined structure, rapid edits, the re-photography that will come to define large sections of the film, and finally, a direct act of self-portraiture that explicitly places Wieland herself, propagandist, as a central subject of (or voice within) the work.[12] Wieland's

---

[9] Joyce Wieland and Hollis Frampton, "I Don't Even Know about the Second Stanza," in *The Films of Joyce Wieland*, ed. Kathryn Elder (Toronto: Cinematheque Ontario, 1999), 178.

[10] George Lellis declares *Reason Over Passion* 'post-Dada', and his discussion of this is an influence on my subsequent discussion of the film's difficulty. A claim for this term might arise from the film's formal roughness that maintains ties to Wieland's Dada influences while departing from them into the post-modern project of conceptualism. George Lellis, "*La Raison avant la passion*," in *Form and Structure in Recent Film*, ed. Dennis Wheeler (Vancouver: Vancouver Art Gallery and Talon Books, 1972).

[11] Wieland viewed Trudeau's motto as an imbalance, and while she would state that the film was an attempt at reconciling reason and passion, it is evident that her own allegiance is to passion, and to seeing reason submit to passion.

[12] Wieland would later state that this is not a self-portrait of her, but of her Bolex camera,

ironic sensibilities are here a formal declaration that scrutinized reason will submit to passion. In practice, her scrutiny of reason does not transform it into passion, but has it pale next to passion.

The film has a running motif of Canadian flags placed at particular stations. These flags signal shifts in colour and serve to compartmentalize sequences, apparently at random.[13] Wieland described this structure as such: "the film is sewn together with flags 10 different kinds (different colours different shootings) meant to complement colour wise the clear and fogged leader (fogged in different tints) which they tie together." The flags appear, by her description, to elaborate the material fact of film as revealed by light-struck ends of varying tints. In practice, however, the flags appear to signal colour shifts in the film itself formed by colour filters, affected in printing, as they also tint text added in post-production. "Flag sew fogged ends together," she writes. "IMAGE ... TO ... FOGGED END ... TO ... FLAG LUMPS / RIBBONS AND KNOTS."[14] With this, Wieland gives the film an overarching structural conceit, one that echoes her process in quilting and sewn assemblages, and yet this also gives the film false or unreliable instructions. Her deviation from these notes makes the flag less an algorithmic marker than a motif. Her purposing of such a symbol, and its role in process, as sewn interstitials, serves a sign of the lingering resonance of Neo-Dada in Wieland's process. It is not clear whether the placement of the flags, in their adoption of tints, corresponds to a logical theory of colour relations, or whether, as in her text, they actually conform to the colours of fogged film.[15] The flags do not serve as stationary markers, but rather flash, interrupting the opening shots of their respective sections.

As *Reason Over Passion* begins, a looping voice repeats "from sea to shining sea," apparently a reading of "America the Beautiful" (evident by the word "shining") that also summons up Canada's national motto,

---

negating herself and giving agency (of 'self portraiture') to the camera eye, a parallel to the anthropomorphosis of the land itself in a film that is largely without human presence.

[13] I say 'at random' because they do not compartmentalize metrically or by divisions of subject. The flags are one of several aesthetic motifs that serve to irrationalize the film.

[14] Joyce Wieland, "Note on *Reason Over Passion*," printed as "Joyce Wieland: Interview and Notes on *Reason Over Passion* and *Pierre Vallières*," ed. Kristy A. Holmes-Moss, in *Canadian Journal of Film Studies* 15.2 (2006), 122.

[15] This play on the flag's colours recalls an earlier manifestation of the same idea in one of Wieland's 'stuffed movie' works. In *Confedspread*, the flag is subject to re-colouring and inversion, subverting the patriotic symbol and yet not subverting the patriotic ideal, rather reinforcing it by broadcasting the endurance of forms through variations. In this sense, both *Confedspread* and the flag insertions in *Reason Over Passion* recall Jasper Johns' flag paintings such as *Flag (Moratorium)* (1969), such objects that inspired Donald Kuspit's idea of Pop as a recapitulation of mass culture that is divorced from and even hostile to social reading.

A Mari Usque Ad Mare, From Sea to Sea.[16] The film's binary imagination has already begun: this fragment of "American the Beautiful" subliminally poses Canada as other to America, and to the poetic conceits of American patriotism embodied in that song, its lyric, like that of the national motto, uniting Atlantic to Pacific, much as the subsequent film enacts that journey across Canada. The camera aims through a windshield at a bend in the road; the image flickers; a maple leaf flag interrupts it. This sequence runs backward and forward. All of this is being re-photographed from the screen of an editing console, which gives Wieland the temporal control of an analytic projector. The frame falls out of alignment, but when legible, it shows the Canadian flag, lakes, mountains and farmland. Canada's pastoral vistas are transitioning in and out of the eclipse of the shutter, slowly coming into vision. Wind blows on the soundtrack. The landscape passes to the left, filmed from a car window. Through this fog of dismantled time, Canada will emerge as a nation of divisions, binaries, competing ideologies and plains.[17]

The Canadian flag appears with an electronic tone sounding under it. It fades out, comes again louder, cuts in, fades out, the tone shifting in pitch as it slowly sounds out the notes of the Canadian national anthem, "O Canada" (Weir/Lavallee, 1880). Waves strike a beach, dividing the frame into even bands, the image made gradually unfamiliar by the precise line of these bands. A patriotic march, possibly an arrangement of Canada's unofficial anthem "The Maple Leaf Forever" (Muir, 1867), sounds under it, joining the whir of the waves. The text of "O Canada" appears, music having preceded text, the 'reason' of language giving cohesion to the various anthems and patriotic songs that have come before it. As the prelude draws to a close, Wieland films herself in a mirror, mouthing "O Canada."[18] A title sequence, in French and then English, is followed

---

[16] The phrase was adopted by minister and writer George Munro Grant, tailoring it from the Latin Vulgate translation of Psalm 72:8—"Et dominabitur a mari usque ad mare, et a flumine usque ad terminus terrae," or, as in the *King James Bible*, "He shall have dominion also from sea to sea, and from the river unto the ends of the earth." Michael Ignatieff, descendent of Grant, has written that the minister used the phrase as a direct result of the progress represented by the construction of the Canadian Pacific Railway, a rail network that serviced Western Canada, one of John A. MacDonald's efforts at nation-building in the early years of the confederation. The new country's title, the Dominion of Canada, was also accommodated in the source quotation.

[17] Wieland wrote in a statement accompanying the film that this echo of her film through a re-photographed viewer is a "very beautiful idea of a doomed country," that as an act of preconceiving her journey, or foresight, the journey becomes an erasure to the landscape it passes.

[18] This sequence would also resonate in Wieland's lithograph *O Canada* (1969), a series of lipstick traces mouthing the national anthem, again engendering Canada but, more importantly, joining celebrations of nation, as in an anthem, to the ecstatic ohs of orgasm,

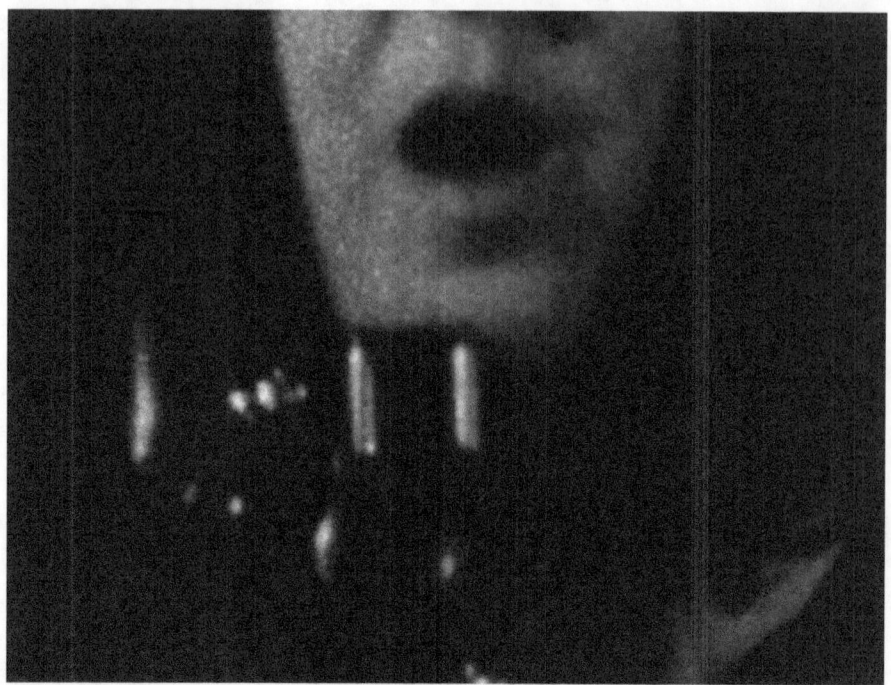

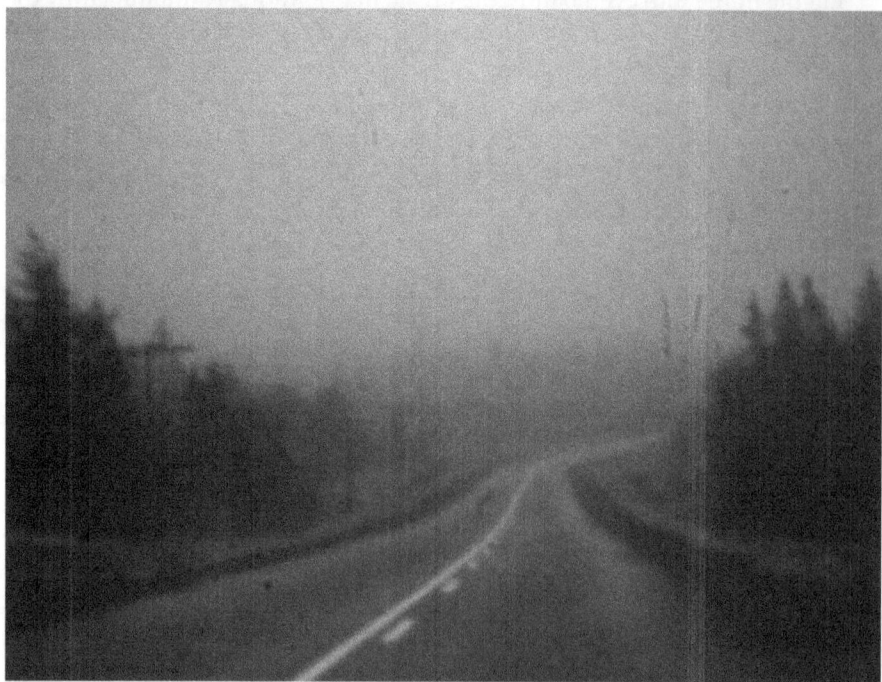

Reason Over Passion *[Film Stills]*, 1969
16mm film, 84 minutes, colour and black and white, sound
Courtesy of CFMDC

by Trudeau's quotation, "About Reason Over Passion ... that's the theme of all my writings ...", likewise given in French and then English.[19] This establishes the parcelled dialectics of the film, with languages in agreement with one another (in the sense that they share in meaning) announcing a division between reason and passion, mind and body, intellect and spirit.

The prelude gives way to scenes of even greater discontinuity, where particular logics—chronology, compositional and sequential ortho-doxy and the linear revelation of the journey itself—come under scrutiny. The image settles inside a moving car, its windshield streaked with rain, looking toward a vanishing point in the distance. Over the course of the next several minutes, the landscape changes from farmland and fence-lined highway, to other, less populated regions, to mountains and rivers. Hills lined with trees are reflected in lakes, and the sky becomes a pale, overcast wash against the rich scenery in the foreground. The nervous and uncertain energy of the handheld camera mirrors the shifting movement of the operator's body. Scenery repeats, countering any illusion that the journey is strictly chronological. When the Canadian maple leaf flag flash-es, at fluctuating scales and varying exposures, it is subliminal but for the richness of its red and white colour cast. Wieland enlisted Hollis Frampton to assist with algorithmic permutations of the words 'reason over passion' which are superimposed on top the image, the letters rearranged into non-sense, always divided into the same sets of six, three and seven.[20] That the resulting nonsense is a malformation of the title is evident to an attentive eye; a more casual eye to the text, one that strays instead to the scenery, might see the text on their periphery not as disfigured language, but as a non-English language, a reflection on the perception of French on the part of many English-speaking Canadians. The permutations make the text foreign, depriving the words of their comprehensible meaning much as the durational extension and slogan placement of *Sailboat*'s text had drained the word and the sailboat of their semantic consonance. On the

suggested by Wieland's plainly sexual lipstick smears. In another act of earnest declaration and irony, Wieland writes on her soundless singing of O Canada that it's "dutiful but I mean it too." This would repeat again with *O Canada Animation* (1970), in which stylized lips perform the same gesture.

[19] According to Wieland's notes, Trudeau's quotation was to be accompanied by applause on the soundtrack, which would serve as another layer of irony, Trudeau's remark met with immediate congratulation in a film that will make a case against it. She writes, "Irony came wandering in ... in the form of applause." On the two prints that I consulted, the sound was silent. Joyce Wieland, "Note on *Reason Over Passion*," printed as "Joyce Wieland: Interview and Notes on *Reason Over Passion* and *Pierre Vallières*," ed. Kristy A. Holmes-Moss, in *Canadian Journal of Film Studies* 15.2 (2006), 122.

[20] While Frampton is widely credited for the permutations, the permutations themselves are credited to Bell Labs employees William A. Burnette and Peter Neumann.

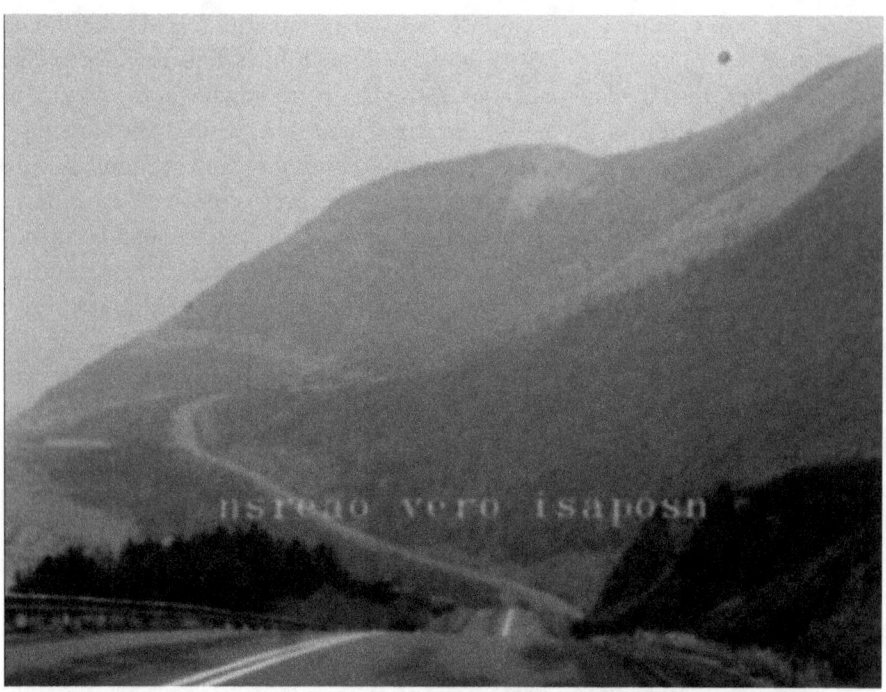

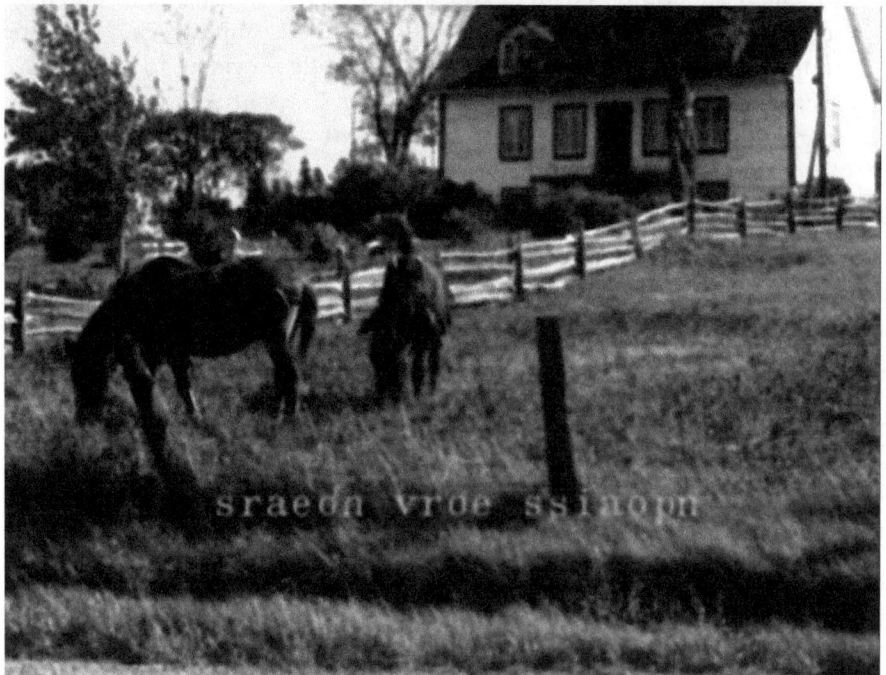

Reason Over Passion *[Film Stills]*, 1969
16mm film, 84 minutes, colour and black and white, sound
Courtesy of CFMDC

soundtrack, patriotic marches and a windstorm give way to an evenly measured electronic tone, a metronomic beep that synchronizes rhythmically with neither image nor text. In a statement on the film, Wieland wrote of this sound as being "like a space language or Russian [...] maybe the beep originated from this ... a space radio ... a country observed by another intelligence?"[21] This beep will sound continuously, barring some fissures and gaps, throughout the first reel, the three coexistent rhythms (image, text, sound) forming an overarching polyrhythmic whole.

The journey itself is filled with ruptures and breaks, moving west from Fredericton, New Brunswick, to Rivière-du-Loup, Québec and Québec City. Wieland's photography gives a partial view of the route from the Atlantic to the Pacific. Many critics, as well as Wieland herself, have posed the journey as an all-encompassing trek, as if it were an encyclopedia of the land, but Wieland is more precise in her arrangement of the journey than such descriptions suggest.[22] The elliptical path reinforces discontinuities that are elsewhere present in the film, and places Wieland's strategy in opposition to the reasoned chronology of the conventional travelogue. The spontaneity of her photography and editing mirrors this broken path, as scenes of the land, waterways and farms appear, sometimes in travelling shots, sometimes static, reassembled as a whole under the symbolic motif of the Canadian flag. The film is a late modern translation of the rousing, nineteenth-century structures of the New World's anthems, mottos and patriotic songs. The elliptical path takes Wieland through a landscape that, in its variance, becomes allusive, details emerging as familiar only to those with experience of the differing cultures and landforms of the provinces. The landscape appears rigid by its scale and pliable by its interaction with civilization, as if the supreme reason of the engineer has placed these roads as a fault line running through the center of miraculous, passionate, irrational nature. The Trans-Canada Highway has been placed by logic of planning to disengage the experience of the land, from ecstatic, spiritual communion into the commercial exchange of agricultural production,

---

[21] Joyce Wieland, "Note on *Reason Over Passion*," printed as "Joyce Wieland: Interview and Notes on *Reason Over Passion* and *Pierre Vallières*," ed. Kristy A. Holmes-Moss, in *Canadian Journal of Film Studies* 15.2 (2006), 122.

[22] Wieland's casual descriptions of the film, quoted in her biographies and in essays in Kathryn Elder's *The Films of Joyce Wieland*, appear to describe the work as such. P. Adams Sitney explicitly refers to it as "a moving excursion across Canada from east to west." P. Adams Sitney, "There is Only One Joyce," *Artscanada* 142-143 (April 1970), 44. It does account for the structure in a general sense, but I argue that the discontinuity of the journey is integral to Wieland's teasing of reason, as it demonstrates a more playful and loose sense of chronology than this description suggests. The film's improvisatory relation to the codes of structural film is in keeping with Chambers' *Circle*, in that neither artist is beholden to the conceits of their own structural predetermination.

tourism and human migration. The road is always the same, and the civilization growing around it is rendered consistently in the towns that Wieland travels through, their government buildings uniform in design with limp, mast-hung flags.

The photography is always in motion, but not always by vehicle along the highway. Wieland makes many stops on her journey and her handheld camera settles on wildflowers, fields, hydro dams and animals such as cows, ducks, horses and pigs. As her aperture closes, the land becomes a hulking darkness, split off by trees against the sky. In scenes from the Atlantic Provinces, the sea, lakes and rivers lead to misted vanishing points. When the camera occasionally turns to the road ahead, its horizon is stunted by buildings and curves, markers of civilization. In night shots, through the car windshield, the lights of oncoming trucks become almost abstract. In the daytime, cars rapidly pass to the left of the camera, in elliptical edits. Wieland films a war memorial and boats on water, the boats another resonance of the nautical theme common to many of her paintings, the war memorial a reflection of patriotic sacrifice and mourning, calling up the sinking ships and diving planes of Wieland's sequential paintings. With the appearance of another Canadian flag, the film takes on a distinct orange cast, tinting scenes from Fredericton in sepia. There Wieland films a Robert Burns monument, a fountain, a park, the steps of a house and a fire hydrant, scanning leaves, the whole sequence in autumnal colours.

Wieland's handheld camera is independent from the fixed counter-rhythms of text and sound. She allows her vision to occasionally settle on the ordinary activities of the land and its people, but the image is never entirely static, giving slight movements, like breaths, invariably turning back to handheld pans over the land, and tracking out the window of the car along passing scenery.[23] The more barren landscape of eastern Quebec is seen mostly from the car, in travelling shots of even and dim exposure. What few scenes are shot outside of the car involve leaves and plants twisting in the wind, woodchopping and the facades of churches and farmhouses. The image is conditioned by light leaks and sudden changes in exposure, the camera bounding along the tops of trees and over a lake, eventually settling on a boat. The image is abstracted by movement, and obstructed by tree branches and guardrails. The sky, lake and guardrails are photographed, the lens zoomed in and tracking so rapidly (with the speed of the car) that the lens gives sharp, abstract lines. As the car passes

---

[23] P. Adams Sitney writes of Wieland's similarity to Marie Menken. With Wieland's rapid photography out of car and train windows, *Reason Over Passion* might bear a resemblance to Menken's *Go! Go! Go!* (1962), a pixilation study of New York City. Where this superficial similarity would engender a sense of influence or shared sensibility, Wieland's techniques, much like Jonas Mekas's use of start-stop motion, are more suggestive of loss than levity.

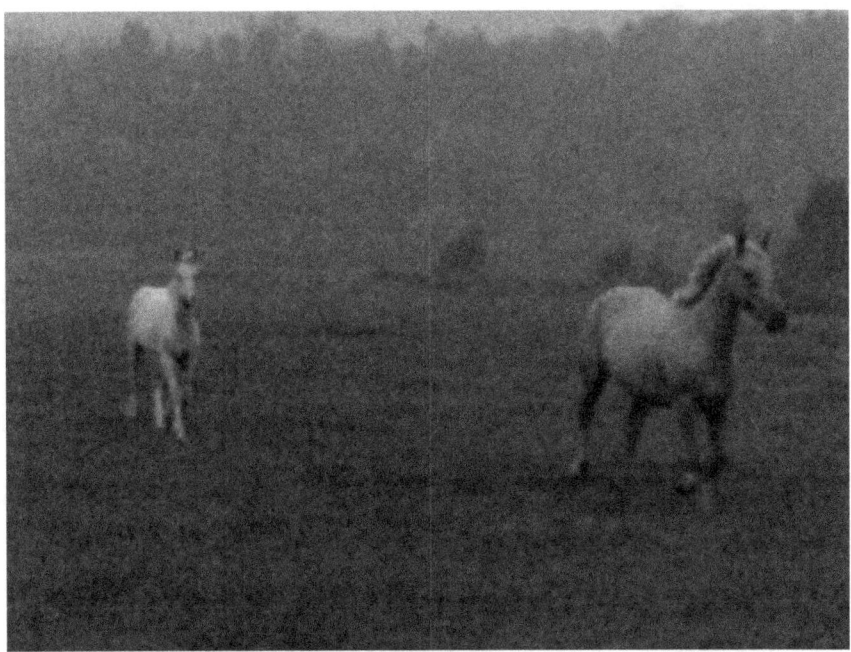

Reason Over Passion *[Film Still]*, 1969
16mm film, 84 minutes, colour and black and white, sound
Courtesy of CFMDC

a man on a horse, the film's montage editorial structure becomes increasingly evident: while the photography is structured by days, with gradual transitions between night and day, past compositions briefly repeat, another resistance to the realist logic of the chronological path.[24] This editorial montage forms another unity, recombining the fragments of her path into a new whole, alongside the enduring, overarching structures of the flags, the text and the beep that together give the film continuity.

When Frampton and Wieland discussed the film, Frampton expressed awe at the vastness and variance of the land, that a stretch of earth so great should naturally produce a wide variety of settlement and topography.[25] Wieland was decidedly partial to the outlying regions, where, under the vast scale of the wilderness, she was at her most isolated. As the

[24] This observation supports Wieland's claims of her intense editorial process, twelve hours per day for three months, and that the film is not, despite the presence of light-struck ends, a mere joining and elliptical cutting of camera rolls, but a careful and thoughtful integration of scenery, motifs and structured elements (as in the prelude and the portrait of Trudeau) to support the country's uncertain self-image.

[25] Joyce Wieland and Hollis Frampton, "I Don't Even Know about the Second Stanza," in *The Films of Joyce Wieland*, ed. Kathryn Elder (Toronto: Cinematheque Ontario, 1999), 178.

first reel ends, the film gives its first and only glimpses of urban Canada.[26] Villages become dense, highway signs more frequent, and the vantage point shifts from a ceaseless view of highway to the pastry window of the Maison Kerhulu in Quebec City. Quebec City is not seen in a fuller view, nor will the image ever explicitly cite Montreal; Ottawa, the capital; or Wieland's hometown of Toronto. Her passion for visions of rural Canada is affirmed in the final sequences of the first reel, as she turns again to her beloved critters: pigs eat flowers through a chain-link fence, the fence another civilizing act of man, separating himself from animal. Horses approach in the distance across a misted field. Dim exposures of tree-dense hills cause Wieland to turn the camera upward to the sky, where sunlight streaks across the lens. Clouds form thin wisps across the sky, above the farmlands, achieving a painterly stylization, but this is neither the flattened image of late modern painting nor the romantic evocation of the realist landscape, nor is it the consumable beauty of the picture postcard. These scenes pose the depth and force of experience, of reality, against the romance of painting, against the consumption of landscape.

Language Lessons

Joyce Wieland had used text in her earlier films as a means of disassociating components of semantic systems. In her visual art, words had rarely appeared. That would temporarily change with the textile work that she began in the late 1960s, when words began to play a role in her quilting and embroidery, not to the end of disrupting semantics, not as a lettered set like the permutations of text running through *Reason Over Passion*, but for the declarative power of words, as slogan and statement.[27] Wieland would depart from this in her later paintings, as her work began to take on more conventional landscapes and figuration in the service of Surreal and symbolic content.[28] Wieland understood the construction and

---

[26] George Lellis argues that the film appears to be assembled against figuration, that it has damned figuration out of the image. Of course, figures do appear—farmers, townspeople, Wieland herself—but this argument is sound in indicating the emphasis in the work on the land itself as the primary subject, and with that, a disavowal of the body. In this journey, the operator's body vanishes in the shadow of the sublime landscape, even when the image moves by the breathing of the operator or the vibrations of the car.

[27] This was not only true of the *Reason Over Passion* quilts, but also of *O Canada* (1970), *Canada* (1972), *Laura Secord* (1973-74) and *Lens* (1978-79).

[28] This return to figuration, and in particular, to the figuration that Wieland had practiced in the 1950s, would show in the early 1980s within paintings such as *Chopin with Other Polish Patriots at Lake Skootamata* and *Flying into Egypt (after Tiepolo)* (both 1981), and continued in such works as *Artist on Fire* (1983) and *The Paint Phantom* (1984). Iconography would remain, as in *Part 1, The Death of Wolfe* (1987), but her technique had become romantic. This

signification of language as an act of reason. The meaning of words can be challenged by placement or duration; declarations can be compromised by irony. In *Reason Over Passion*, keeping with the work's disaffiliation from reason, Trudeau's title declaration is disrupted by Hollis Frampton's textual permutations. This text runs throughout the majority of the film, but the experience of language in Wieland's Canada is explored beginning with the head of the second reel, as a French lesson begins to play on the soundtrack. A voice identifies itself as Pierre: "Bonjour, je m'appelle Pierre." The permutations stop. The colours of the Canadian maple leaf flag fill the frame, alternating between red saturation and white saturation. The maple leaf itself flashes occasionally. The language lesson continues under this in a series of statements and questions. Pierre states his name and asks yours; Pierre states his age ("huit ans") and asks yours; as it continues, he begins to count.

As the lesson ends, the alternating red and white frames cease as well. The Pierre of the language lesson is suggested to be Pierre Trudeau, as a cut introduces Trudeau, champion of reason, passing through the crowd of the Liberal leadership convention. Orchestral music is interrupted by a ringing telephone. The pairing of this sequence with the language lesson arises from Trudeau's response to the issue of separatism – that is, the notion of Quebec separating from English Canada as a nation in its own right. His sense was that the French-speaking Canadian must be made to feel "at home ... in Vancouver and Toronto as well as Montreal."[29] He believed in doing so through a program of immersive bilingualism and biculturalism, for example, legislating that public signs and government services be given in both English and French. Trudeau's bicultural platform was a position with which Wieland agreed, and the sequence responds to Trudeau's position toward and between languages. As a double to the speaker of the language lesson, he has a rudimentary grasp on the power of language, regarding it by its function and not for passion or poetry. The speaker could give his age, state his name, ask questions of the listener and count. Wieland describes her materials and the parallel: "I found the teaching record in a stack of our old records, luckily the man on the disk pretending to be a school child's name is Pierre. And he is supposedly only eight years old ... young like our eternally young Prime Minister."[30] The

represents not only a return to the figuration of the *Lovers* series (c. 1956), but also a return to material engagement more distant from the conceptualism that had overtaken her work through the late 1960s.

[29] Qtd. in Marc Levine, *The Reconquest of Montreal: Language Policy and Social Change in a Bilingual City* (Philadelphia: Temple University Press, 1991), 91.

[30] Joyce Wieland, "Note on *Reason Over Passion*," printed as "Joyce Wieland: Interview and Notes on *Reason Over Passion* and *Pierre Vallières*," ed. Kristy A. Holmes-Moss, in *Canadian*

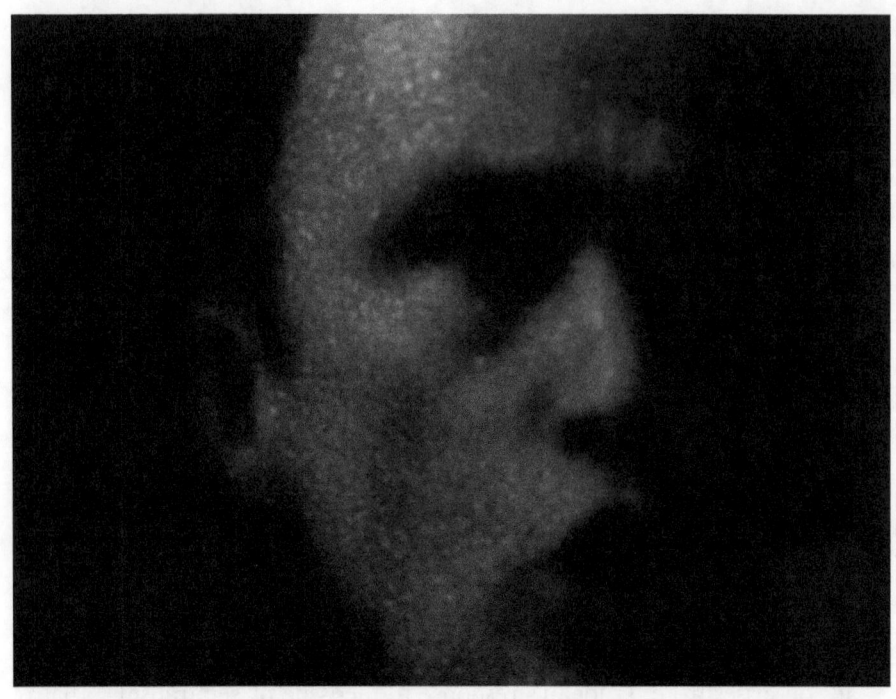

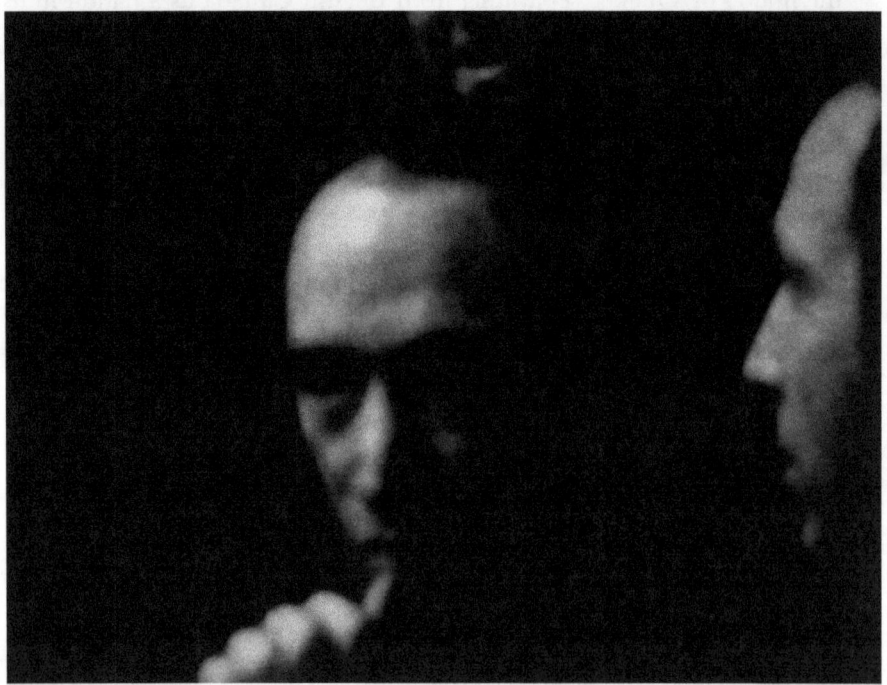

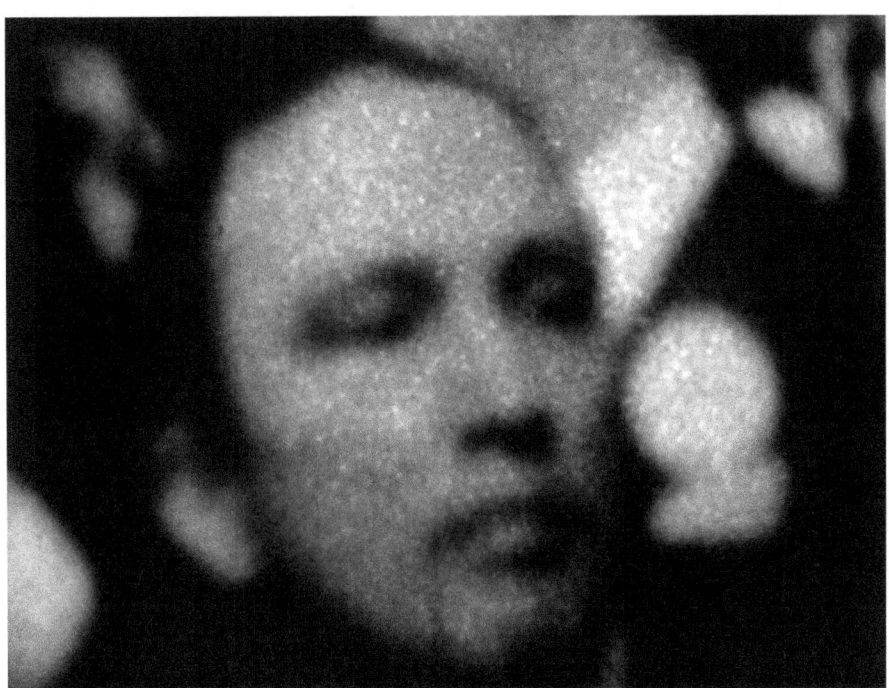

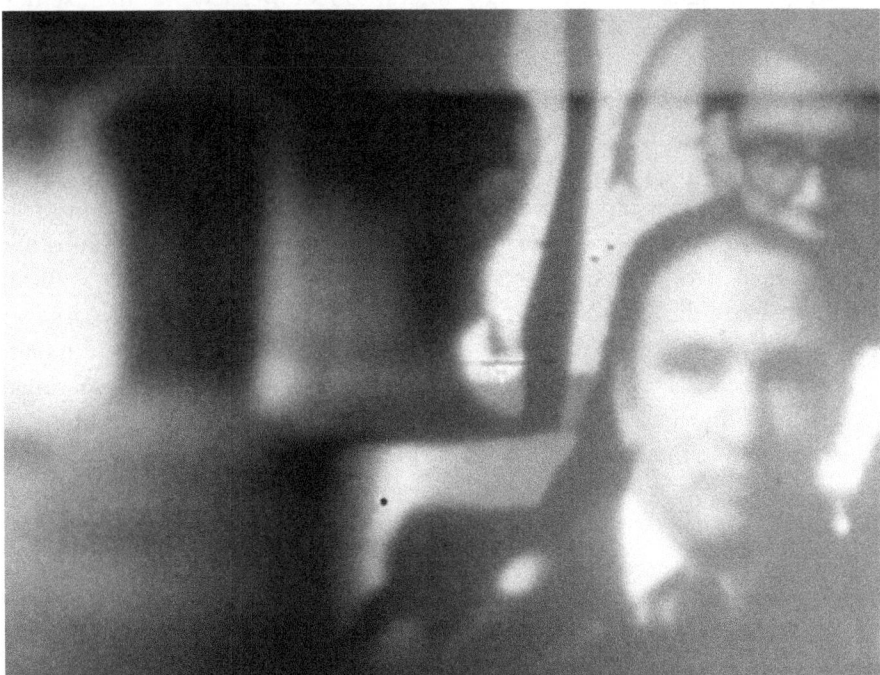

Reason Over Passion *[Film Stills]*, 1969
16mm film, 84 minutes, colour and black and white, sound
Courtesy of CFMDC

language lesson serves to alienate Trudeau from his image as a mature, articulate statesman, to strip the passion of language away from him and render him a mere ambassador of French-language fundamentals. This is achieved through de-familiarization, de-contextualization of materials and combining fragments in ironic juxtapositions.

Trudeau is first seen through a hole in a travelling matte, a flexing circle that follows him in a crowd. As he settles in his seat, the image becomes subject to looping and changes of frame rate. It is made elastic and stretched, a projection first cast in colour onto a coursing soft surface, likely a bedsheet, and then in black and white onto a textured surface. Trudeau smiles, talks and moves his head thoughtfully. On the soundtrack, a whistling noise is occasionally broken by what sounds like distant applause or waves. Trudeau's face is distorted in an angled projection, cast onto rough, cracked textures, his face becoming stone-like by those textures. His stare narrows its direction, in spite of movement and conversation around him, straight into the eye of the camera. In the distorted projection, his head swells up, is dissected by obstructions in the beam of the projector, and then reconstituted with passing frames. His head bends toward the camera, distorting, the sweat glistening on his forehead; the elastic interval is stretched so that the emotional tenor of his shifting expressions passes through a full range. His stare holds, past the camera, to its lower left and then settles. Trudeau smiles at the camera, his smile made menacing by an infernal red cast. Trudeau's head and face give a series of movements, turning left to attend to conversation, lolling slightly to the right, his every gesture magnified by temporal and visual distension. The Canadian flag begins to flash as if signaling another change of colour or scenery. Trudeau gives what may be a surprised look, but under Wieland's scrutiny, his every registration of emotion or perception becomes ambiguous. In a coda to this sequence, two projections are filmed off a wall: on the right, the Trudeau portrait; on the left, scenes from the Trans-Canada Highway. The images intrude on each other, and passion, in the form of the stuttering, emanating landscape, is literally cast over reason, in the form of the well-reasoned leader. This dual-projection sequence is the film's most explicit juxtaposition between passion and reason, and as it draws to a close, Wieland and her Bolex are seen in the interior of a train car, in the reflection of a window.

The language lesson, the elastic manipulation of Trudeau's image, and the dual-projection juxtaposition comprise the midpoint of the journey and of the film. The icon, Trudeau, is mocked by the ironic language lesson; his image is manipulated to evoke both rubber and stone; that

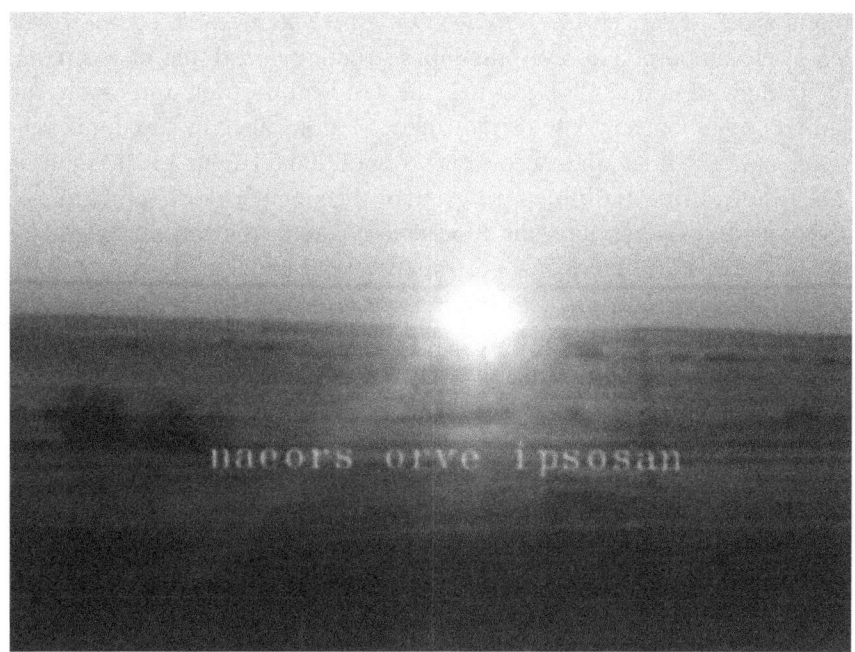

Reason Over Passion *[Film Still]*, 1969
16mm film, 84 minutes, colour and black and white, sound
Courtesy of CFMDC

image is dissected by elastic time so that his gestures are magnified to total ambiguity; and finally, his destabilized portrait is posed in contrast to the landscape, his infernal red glow pitched against the heavenly blue glow of the lingering wilds along the Trans-Canada Highway. If reason had been suggested earlier by signs of civilization, or by obscure patterns of text and sound, it is here given form in Trudeau himself, handsome, convivial, the seducer seduced by his own charms. It is reminiscent of Francisco Goya's ambiguous title to his etching *The Sleep of Reason Produces Monsters* (1797). Is it the lapse of reason, cradled to sleep, that draws out the nocturnal tormentors, the owls and the bats? Or could it be that reason itself, as in the triumphant reason of Trudeau, is a kind of sleep that produces monsters? *Reason Over Passion* cannot answer these questions, but by searching Trudeau in its dynamic, elastic time, it casts him stone-faced, a statue of a conqueror, imbalanced, corrupted by reason.

From Sea to Sea

According to Wieland's description of her use of the flag as a structuring motif, she had conceived of *Reason Over Passion* as a whole composed of ten or eleven parts. However, the film's structure is also that of a quartet: the prelude, the June 1968 journey, the Trudeau portrait, and finally, the January 1968 journey. The two journeys are equivalent in length but represent opposite sides, and, accordingly, oppositional visions, of the country. The beauty of the maritime spring and of the green fields of rural Quebec gives way to barren plains and mountain passes under an imposing blanket of snow. With Trudeau's portrait, Wieland allowed the leader, from within an ironic construct, to symbolize reason by his presence, even as she engaged in a formal critique of his championing of reason and its bearing on his biculturalism. In the wake of that portrait, the Canadian winter becomes an apocalypse. Even in its sublime beauty, the snowbound landscape serves as opposite to the earlier journey. The eastern provinces had been teeming with life, but the western provinces have become pale and vacant, save for CNR employees and homesteaders. At first, the train's carriage is not apparent, and so this journey starts as if seen by a bird, the handheld camera gliding past a mountain range and aimed down at snow-covered trees in a deep valley. Much of this journey will be filmed out of the windows of the train from Toronto to Vancouver, elevated and looking down or out to the passing scenery. When the train is stopped, Wieland continues her handheld filming on the ground, as in an early scene at a CNR depot where Wieland composes a shot of the depot so that the depot appears to have been overtaken by snow. The landscape has become almost monochromatic; ghostly traces of movement correspond to the mist of the winter air and to snow kicked up by the train. When the flag appears, it registers faintly against white. The trees take on a purple tint, as dense as the blues and browns of the maritime farmlands or the orange of Fredericton. The landscape bears few marks of civilization, only railway and telephone poles and the rare farm.

On the soundtrack, a modern electronic composition sounds as celestial feedback, the insistent beep sounding within it, a broadcast of Wieland's 'space radio'. This soon ends and the lone beep resumes. The textual permutations, which had ceased through the Trudeau portrait, resume at the same steady pace that they had before, still out of sync with the beep. Occasionally, the interior of Wieland's train cabin faintly registers in the window and bodies pass in that reflection when the image grows dark. For the most part, the window is revealed by plays of sunlight and melted ice upon it. Days pass and, as in the maritime footage, Wieland's photography becomes diaristic. Changes of colour, signalled by the flag, come more dramatically and frequently than they had in the first reel, owing to the dominance of white on the plains. For a long stretch, Wieland

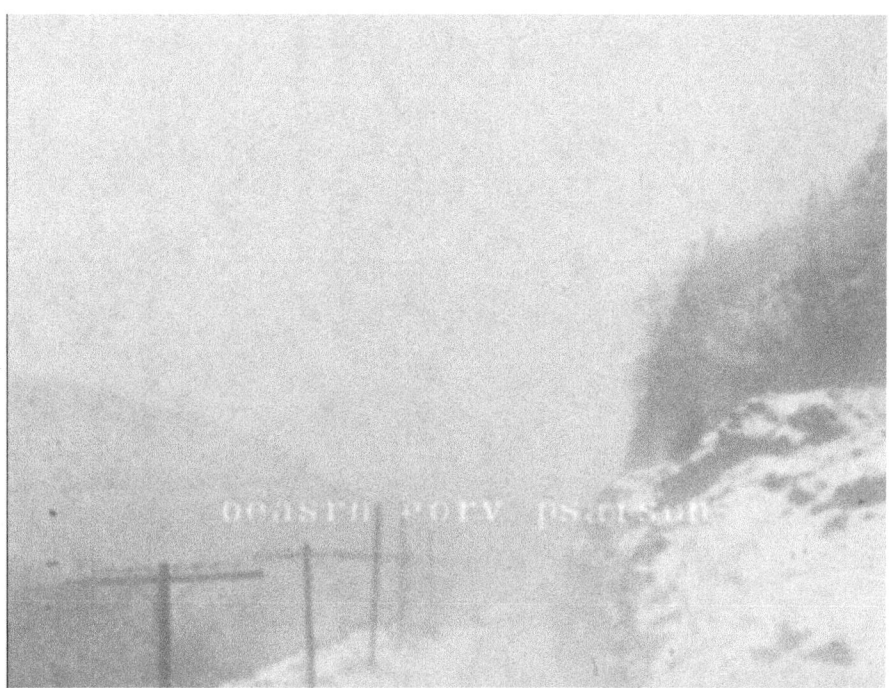

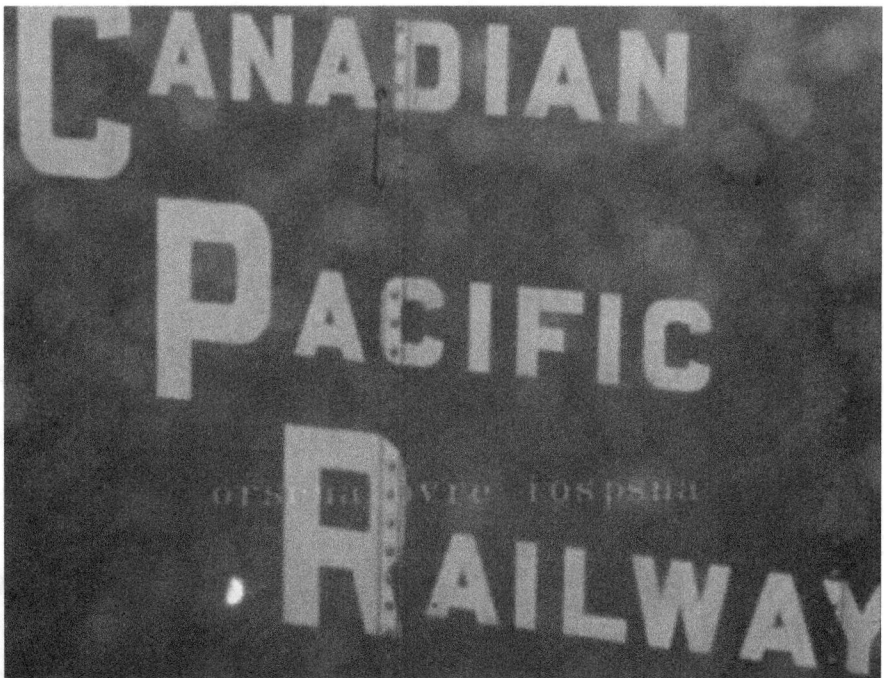

Reason Over Passion *[Film Stills]*, 1969
16mm film, 84 minutes, colour and black and white, sound
Courtesy of CFMDC

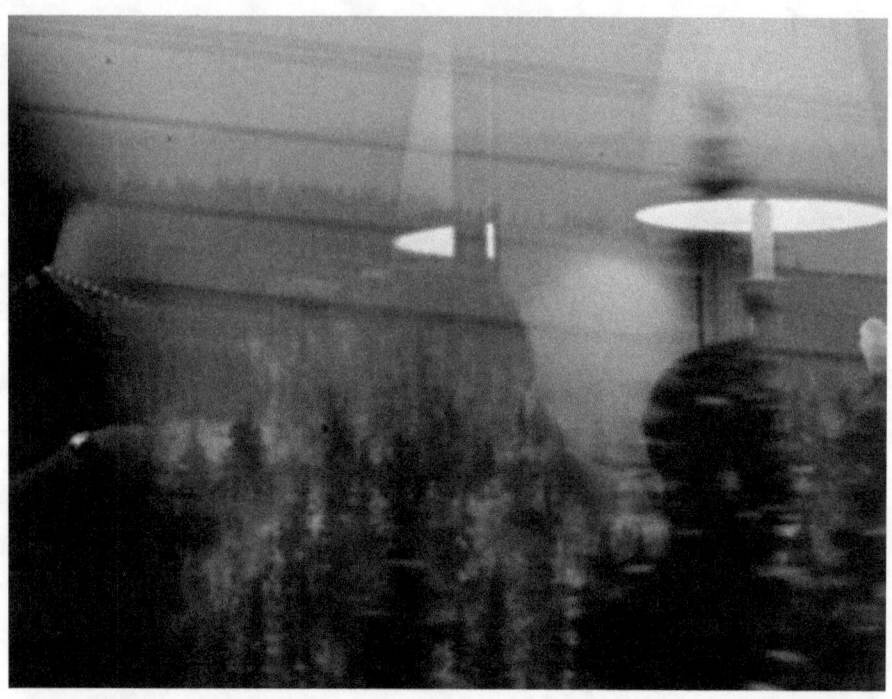

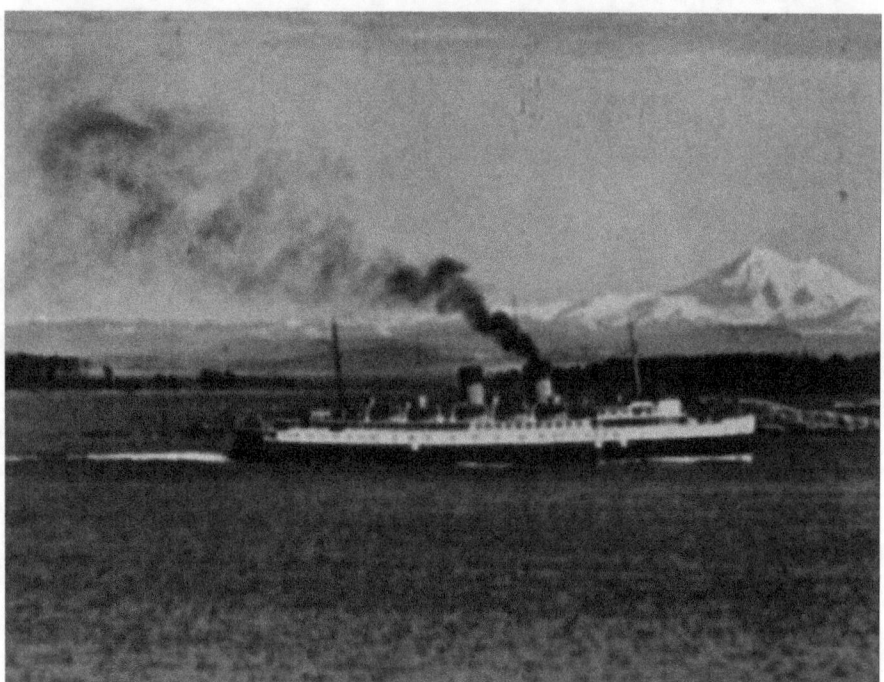

Reason Over Passion *[Film Stills]*, 1969
16mm film, 84 minutes, colour and black and white, sound
Courtesy of CFMDC

lingers on a sunset which backlights the mid-ground of rail and phone lines. It sets into darkness. The image resumes the next morning and the film begins to take on superimpositions, some caused by the window of the train car serving as a beam splitter, others performed in-camera or through optical printing.

Wieland oscillates between stationary photography (rough and handheld, as it was in the Atlantic journey), and photography taken from the window of the moving train. In both instances, Wieland's bodily vibrations, in the stutter of her hands on the camera, never allow the image to fully stabilize. The plains speed to the right in pixilation, her camerawork creating staggered rhythms. The camera passes farmhouses, and with the interruption of another flag, a pink tint is cast over the scene. When Wieland is on board the train, her camera is not always stationed at the side window. It strays so that the frames of windows and portholes are seen. The receding horizon is viewed from the back of the train. On this phantom ride, lines of snowbound trees flank the train to the left and right, ceaselessly marching toward a distant horizon. Canadian Pacific trains are glimpsed in rail yards. The flag signals again, first upside down and then upright. The days are marked by oppressive sunlight, the evenings by distant electric lights.

In this final sequence, which runs for the majority of the second reel, little changes. But it is never uninteresting. Activity is constant, though dense and repetitious. The camera is more nervous in its movements, an extension of the body trapped on the moving train, freed by capturing scenery from a bird's eye; her photography is nearer to nature in its movement, even as that nature has lost its vibrancy in winter. This activity, taken as a whole, does not engage in the same formal heterodoxy as had the earlier journey, even as a greater frequency of flags signal colour changes and give the film a unifying structure. Wieland fixes on her own isolated situation, isolation forming a clinical relation between camera eye and horizon. What fills the divide is much the same all through the long course of the ride. Isolation is uniform, even across such a vast landscape. Even so, Wieland finds ways to make the familiar landscape an unfamiliar presence. For example, while she films from the observation car, the train crosses a bridge overlooking a lake; Wieland turns the camera on its side so that the eye is guided up a vertical strip of land and sea. Her handheld rhythms become disorienting as more houses come into view, as the train reaches a more crowded west, and the camera, triggered in sudden jolts, produces the familiar sights of trees, mountains and water. These landforms interact through editorial disruptions, an open field suddenly cutting to a mountain, the rocky terrain of the mountain suddenly cutting to treetops.

Scenes shot from the observation car give the illusion that Wieland is on top of the train, that she is assuming the perspective of the train, a human consciousness cutting a forward path through nature, or viewing its own work in the retrospect of the receding horizon. Near the end of her journey, Wieland engages a split screen effect: the two sides of the image travel in opposite directions, a half moon skipping underneath scenes of twilit mountain ranges. Those mountain ranges dim to black, a light-struck end leads to a flag, and then to a picture postcard of a steamship. The smoke from the ship spells out the word "Sea," a command to see, a unity from sea to sea and a point of departure.

The train sequence does not insist on an indigenously Canadian identity. It represents the summit of Wieland's ecological panic, scenes of the harsh Canadian winter serving less as an affirmation of beauty than as a romantic, symbolic apocalypse. George Lellis has observed that, in its emphasis on landscape, *Reason Over Passion* is posed against figuration.[31] The human figure is largely absent, and when present, save for the Trudeau portrait, it serves only as an interference with the land. This was not only true of the human figure, but of the resonances of human presence in infrastructure, in the debris and depots of the highway and railway. But in the Atlantic journey, from the sea, even with a muted presence of humanity, that landscape showed signs of animal and plant life, and while lakes and rivers had served as sites of human activity, they also reflected a healthy ecosystem. With the second journey to the sea, the majestic Canadian winter buries these features of the land. The Canadian winter presents a sublime vision, by its great scale; its mystery; its white and blue emanations; and in its equal parts beauty and fearfulness. The whole of Canada, its Eastern paradise, its chilling, empty West, is united in this sublime vision, boundless and passionate, from sea to sea.

Difficult Aesthetics and Reason Over Passion

When *Reason Over Passion* premiered at the Museum of Modern Art in 1969, its program notes read: "HERE'S ANOTHER ONE OF YOUR LONG FILMS THAT HURTS AGAIN MY ASS."[32] At 82 minutes, Wieland's

---

[31] George Lellis, "*La Raison avant la passion*," in *Form and Structure in Recent Film*, ed. Dennis Wheeler (Vancouver: Vancouver Art Gallery and Talon Books, 1972).

[32] Program notes quoted in Douglas Pringle, "Review: *La Raison avant la passion*." *Artscanada* 134-135 (August 1969), 45-46. George Lellis includes this quote in his discussion of the work's difficult relation to its audience, and adds: "The fact that the film is difficult to take [...] suggests that Wieland, either intuitively or intentionally, is working toward finding a totally new approach [...] to producing nationalist feelings in her audience." George Lellis, "*La Raison avant la passion*," in *Form and Structure in Recent Film*, ed. Dennis Wheeler

film was ripe for such comic ribbing, but it was not a work of durational extension in the style of Andy Warhol. It held an agenda beyond its duration,
its ironies and obscurities marked by patriotic sentiment. For its length,
it became an underground epic, but its length also gave its audiences an
experience of duration that supported Wieland's message. It claimed an
ecstatic conversion to reason, and by that irony, offered an ecstatic conversion to passion. The work was difficult in its length, its codification and
its obscurity, but it was also patriotic in the manner of patriotic songs and
poems, songs that enrich citizenship, songs conceived to bind their listeners
and singers in the patriotic ideals that their lyrics described. *Reason Over
Passion* acquires a great complexity in its patriotism, a vehicle for Wieland's
irony. The film's modern roots, strategic disfiguration and abstract beauty
transcend its patriotic gesture, advancing its reverence for the land.

Reason Over Passion begins with a prelude of anthems, the film's
first demonstration of passion, not only for the power of music, but for
the poetic abstraction of anthemic lyrics that such music suggests. These
patriotic declarations evoke particularities of a nation's character through
poetic language, as in the claim of "America the Beautiful" that America's
"alabaster cities gleam / undimmed by human tears," as in the claim in
"O Canada" to a True North of divine providence under the patriots'
vigilance.[33] This affiliation with poetry is evident in the oblique reference
to Canada's motto, which shapes the trajectory of the work from sea to
sea, or rather to sea, to sea. Wieland's references to anthems, patriotic
songs and mottos form an underlying network of allusions that *Reason Over
Passion* operates within. These allusions do not arrive with instructions or
explanation. In the case of Wieland's silent performance of "O Canada,"
her performance demands that the viewer follow the implied relations of
music and text preceding the sequence. Much like Wieland's earlier films,
Reason Over Passion is not allusion-dense, or at least, it is not obscure in its
allusions, but it does follow a programme of implied knowledge, placing
an expectation on the viewer to recognize Canada's geography through
the course of the journey and, with slightly greater difficulty, to comprehend the references to Canadian politics, then taking considerable shape
in the popular imagination beyond the nation's borders.[34] The film is not

(Vancouver: Vancouver Art Gallery and Talon Books, 1972).

[33] The notion of a 'true north' is rooted in Alfred, Lord Tennyson's "To the Queen" (*The
Works of Alfred Lord Tennyson, Poet Laureate*, London: Kegan Paul, 1878), and in that text,
'true' refers to loyalty to the crown, an idea that had faded considerably in the intervening
90 years.

[34] In their dialogue, Wieland observes to Frampton that Americans are more aware of
Canada than Canadians are, although she would later complain that the ironies of her film
were lost on American audiences.

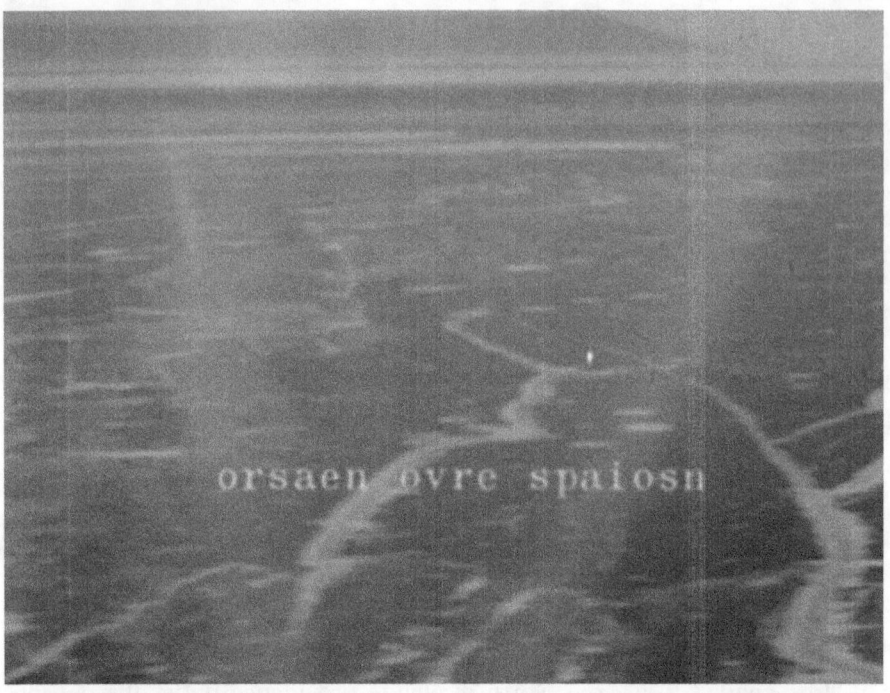

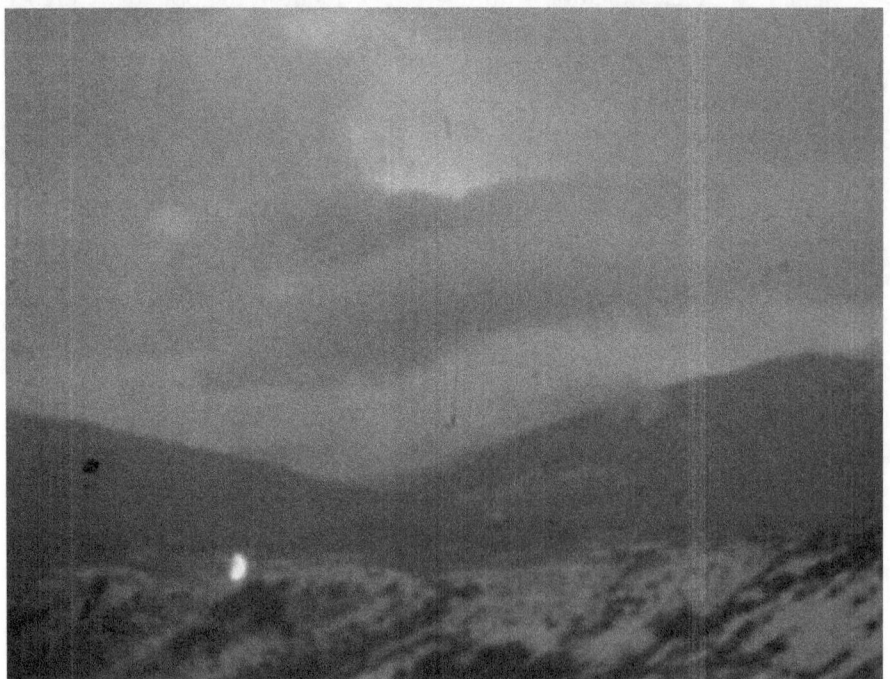

Reason Over Passion *[Film Stills]*, 1969
16mm film, 84 minutes, colour and black and white, sound
Courtesy of CFMDC

concerned with Canadiana, but with giving an overarching unity to the varied landscape, further codified by the red and white of the maple leaf flags, which, aside from their function in signaling slight colour shifts, serve as a frequent reminder of the Dominion cast over and bridging the land.

Wieland's ironic adoption of Trudeau's motto forms a semantic misdirection, one readily conquered by recognizing the passion of Wieland's aesthetic sensibility and the irony of her project. This early semantic misdirection set a precedent for the film, one that is further enriched and extended by the false instructions that run through it. Diaristic photography and structural conceits dominate, yet the viewer is lulled by the beauty of the land to receive a less autobiographical, less plotted understanding of landscape. False instruction also comes in parts that cannot be reconciled, such as the chance appearances of the flag, the exact nature of what it triggers in the image and the elusive implication of the rhythmic counterpoint between text, sound and image. As a work of studied poetic and political rhetoric, *Reason Over Passion* refuses to be anchored in any singular meaning. Wieland's implicit disaffiliation from Trudeau's motto is an act of irony, not cynicism, and her fragmentation and reassembly of the land reflect a search for passion, pursued through false instructions and polysemy, to the end of a new, immaterial Canadian constitution, founded on passion.

Yet another disconnection between meaning and form lies in the relation within the film between conceptualism and Neo-Dada aesthetics. This bears on its status as an art object, as a component part of Wieland's larger artistic activity and as an experiential work insistent on durational participation. Its programmatic conceits would classify *Reason Over Passion* as a work of conceptual art that probes a particular dialectic, and so the intellectual challenge of its semantic misdirection becomes its most immediately comprehensible gesture. It is a film about Canada and Canadian nationhood as ephemeral values, and so Wieland's journeying gives physical form to the immaterial, intellectual challenge of her concept. But against this, the film is anchored in materiality, in a Neo-Dada mode where its primary aesthetic gesture is that of 'sewing', a raw and rough editorial conceit that Wieland uses to describe the service of the flags, but which might be extended to the way in which her fragmentary photography reassembles into a structure. Wieland's structural conceits reveal the film's material base in her integration of text and sound, her elasticization of time and her self-conscious re-photography of images from a viewing console. These conceptual and material aspects are not easily reconciled as each one is a carriage for the other, a chicken and an egg. But by espousing reason over passion, turned by irony to passion over reason, Wieland uneasily bridges the conceptual and material dimensions, refusing both the notion that passion should be the province of detached conceptualism, or that the passionate material gesture be isolated from the concept of nationhood.

The primary difficulty of *Reason Over Passion* is that of its modal incongruity, as a work determinedly about the scale and glory of the landscape that yet endorses vision and experience on an intimate scale. By approaching the Canadian landscape with this sense of intimacy, Wieland dismisses any presumption that the scale of the landscape should make it any less personal, and that it reveals by its scale the same sentiments of passion and pride that are triggered by those patriotic songs. The land becomes anthemic, but form and content remain asynchronous, the landscape terminally dynamic, breathing, abstracted, brought into aesthetic territory that challenges our understanding of the subject by disconnecting from conventional representation. This modal incongruity serves the purpose of communicating, even converting an audience to, patriotic ideals, by turning away from picture postcard visions of the Canadian landscape, turning instead toward a representational mode that de-familiarizes, that forces the viewer into a direct perceptual relation not only to the shapes of mountains and lakes but to the experience of passing to sea and to sea. In hand with this, Wieland's tactical difficulties encoded *Reason Over Passion* with patriotic sentiment, enhancing her propagandistic intent. *Reason Over Passion* reflects Wieland's first steps toward what she wanted out of Canada as a subject, what she wanted also to give it: to comprehend its environmental and political needs, to construct a modern myth, to bring it into a state of unity. This desire to assemble a whole out of fragments is apparent in its insistence on a quartet structure, its use of motifs to form an underlying structure, its consciousness of film's materiality not only in the appearance of light-struck ends but in Wieland's tinting of entire sections of the film to the colours of those fogged ends. This not only acknowledges the material base but makes that base an essential part of its newfound unity.

After Reason Over Passion

Joyce Wieland's desire to return to Canada, in the wake of finishing *Reason Over Passion*, was exacerbated by one of the major controversies of the New American Cinema. In 1969, when Anthology Film Archives was founded in New York City, a committee formed to decide what works to include in the archive and what works to exclude. Many living women filmmakers were notably excluded, among them Storm De Hirsch, Shirley Clarke and Joyce Wieland. Despite the presence on that committee of two of her primary critical supporters, P. Adams Sitney and Jonas Mekas, Wieland's films were judged not sufficiently important to enter the collection. She would later say that she felt her work was downgraded for its feminine aesthetic, that the actions of the committee were merely chauvinistic.[35] She would describe New York in the retrospect of this experience: "In New York in the 1960s real art was never about feelings. It had a very patriarchal look. Not only do few women ever get into that world; their aesthetic is ignored. Men's dialogue, on the other hand, is always printed. Articles are written about it; big catalogues are compiled and their aesthetic becomes law, or the criterion that defines what the game is all about. In short, their theory becomes art history."[36] Her heartbreak over this event would be reflected in a steady departure from the comic stance in her work, a shift toward a more earnest, even bitter, longing for an idealized existence. This would be reflected in her work by way of a gradual dispersal of perceptual difficulties.

In 1971, curator Pierre Théberge arranged a massive retrospective for Wieland at the National Gallery of Canada, under the title *True Patriot Love*, a landmark show as the first retrospective given by the National Gallery to a living Canadian woman. With this exhibition, Wieland would exhibit her work across media, with quilts, paintings, soft sculptures, bronze sculptures, environmental installations, desserts and even a perfume. She would engage in mythmaking, illustrating a founding myth of her own invention, wherein the Spirit of Canada (a woman) has sex with a bear and conceives the French and English Beavers. This myth was illustrated in bronze sculptures. The exhibition included a large quilt, *109 Views*, containing 109 images that represented the journey of *Reason Over Passion*. These images did not appear in the conventional grid form of a traditional quilt, but were pieced in an arrangement of squares, fluctuating in size

---

[35] While this is likely true, and has been indicated as such by Wieland's supporters such as Ken and Flo Jacobs, the board's purported chauvinism deserves further contextualization. In Wieland's films, the superficial resemblance to the anthropomorphic fables of Beatrix Potter in *Rat Life and Diet in North America*, or the domestic setting and subject in *Water Sark* and *Cat Food*, may have led the disengaged viewer to dismiss the work as hobby art. Wieland's subjects might conceal the formal aspects that bring her work closer in spirit to both the contemporary vanguard of intellectual East Coast structuralism (her peers) and the wild, spirited picaresques of the West Coast that emerged out of the San Francisco Renaissance and the Beats (ironically, such filmmaking was the province of Anthology Film Archives committee member James Broughton). Wieland's work did much to enclose these disparate styles, and so its exclusion may have much to do with a superficial dismissal for its domestic values and its surface 'cuteness'. As much as this exclusion might be rightly blamed on gender inequity, the difficulty of Wieland's work started from her sophisticated concealment of irony within sentimentality, the very strategy for which it should have been readily assumed into the pantheon of avant-garde cinema.

[36] Qtd. in Iris Nowell, *Joyce Wieland: A Life in Art* (Toronto: ECW Press, 2001), 295.

to form an irregular diamond.[37] Although Wieland would continue her activities as an artist following the *True Patriot Love* show, and would receive major accolades in the years following, for example, a 1987 retrospective at the Art Gallery of Ontario in her hometown of Toronto, she nevertheless became increasingly disillusioned, retreating into the less difficult pleasures of earnest sentimentality and earnest propaganda, away from the paradoxical character that had given her work gravity and charm. Robert Fulford once referred to Wieland as "the visual poet of 1970s Canadian nationalism," and though her prolific output in the *True Patriot Love* exhibition cemented this title, little followed to reinforce it.[38]

Wieland's filmmaking activities following *Reason Over Passion* were less elusive in their politics and were strongly influenced by her friendship with Judy Steed. Together the two would make a series of films: *Pierre Vallières* (1972), *Solidarity* (1973) and Wieland's only fiction feature film, *The Far Shore* (1976). The difficult strategies of Wieland's filmmaking, primarily her sense of compositional intimacy, dislocation of image and sound and her use of text, were intact through *Pierre Vallières* and *Solidarity*.[39] *Pierre Vallières* was an interview with the Quebecois revolutionary Vallières, filmed in close-up on his lips. This narrow view maintained Wieland's interest in lips, in the intimacy of close-ups, in subverting the expectations of such a portrait, but the film also extended her ideas of semantic dislocation, reducing Vallières' statements to their vehicle, making him the mouth or voice of a revolutionary vanguard.[40] *Solidarity* was filmed on a picket line at Kitchener's Dare cookie plant, where the vast majority of striking workers were women. There she filmed the strikers' feet, and later superimposed the text 'solidarity', text that included the punning presence of the cookie company name (Dare) and that served a similar purpose of semantic disaffiliation between language and image as in her earlier films *Sailboat* and *1933*. While these strategies linked *Pierre Vallières* and *Solidarity* with Wieland's earlier work, her films would increasingly opt for direct political themes, resisting the creative ambiguities and subtle interrogations of meaning that distinguish *Reason Over Passion*.

The Far Shore had originated under the title *True Patriot Love*, planned

---

[37] This description is in part written from that which appears in Gunda Lambton, *Stealing the Show: Seven Women Artists in Canadian Public Art* (Montreal: McGill-Queen's Press, 1994), 88. Lambton does not appear to make the connection between *109 Views* and *Reason Over Passion*, regarding it instead as an impression of the Group of Seven.

[38] Robert Fulford, "Giving Us a Sense of Ourselves." *Toronto Star*, 10 July 1971, 55

[39] R. Bruce Elder discusses *Solidarity* and Wieland's difficult use of text in *Image and Identity: Reflections on Canadian Film and Culture* (Waterloo, Ont.: Wilfred Laurier Press, 1984), 258.

[40] Although Wieland would later express distaste for Vallières, she held his book *White Niggers of America*, about the exploitation dealt to the French Canadian working class, in high esteem.

in the spring of 1971. The film had no resonance with the difficult forms her art had assumed through the 1960s and instead resembled films made under the aegis of the Canadian Film Development Corporation.[41] The notion of a mythic Canada endured, as its narrative was an allegory for the life of Tom Thomson, the Group of Seven affiliate who predeceased the formation of the group when he vanished while canoeing on Canoe Lake in Algonquin Park in 1917. But *The Far Shore* represented the final disintegration of Wieland's stance, from an ironic militant sentimentality, toward sincere sentimentality. In the years after *The Far Shore* was released, Wieland and Snow divorced, and she would move away from filmmaking altogether, turning instead to figurative painting and drawing, now in a highly romantic style.

In the mid-1980s, Wieland began to show advanced symptoms of Alzheimer's disease. The condition ravaged her attention. In 1986, she would enlist Snow's niece Su Rynard in completing a series of films that had incubated since the 1960s and early 70s: *Peggy's Blue Skylight* (1964), *Patriotism 2* (1965), *A & B in Ontario* (1967) and *Birds at Sunrise* (1972). These films would not bear the same critical irony as those completed in the 1960s. Most were overtly sentimental portraits of her life in the 1960s as she would wish to remember it, *Peggy's Blue Skylight* an assembly of Wieland's New York family, *Patriotism 2* a eulogy for Dave Shackman, and *A & B in Ontario* a eulogy for Frampton. *Birds at Sunrise* recapitulated some themes from *Rat Life and Diet in North America* but lacked its formal difficulties, serving rather as an expression of solidarity with Israel, a sentimental allegory without her trademark irony.[42] Since her death in 1998,

---

[41] *The Far Shore* was largely funded independently, through fundraising by Wieland and Steed, but its crew included cinematographer Richard Leiterman, primary architect of the visual aspect of the Canadian feature film through his frequent work on films funded by the Canadian Film Development Corporation (including Allan King's *A Married Couple*, 1969, and Donald Shebib's *Goin' Down the Road*, 1970). The raw qualities of Wieland's avant-garde filmmaking were exchanged for a romantic formalism, the film drawing critical comparisons to Bo Widerberg's sentimental *Elvira Madigan* (1967). For a comprehensive study of the film, see Johanne Sloan, *The Far Shore* (Toronto: University of Toronto Press, 2010).

[42] With the eulogy films, Wieland turns her attention to her own past, and yet the act of remembering, steadily fractured by her illness, touched her most uncritical, sentimental tendencies. *Patriotism 2* is an extended portrait of Dave Shackman with the American flag wrapped around his shoulders, and it feels less a sequel than a didactic climax to *Patriotism*, the hot-dog-encumbered victim/victor now attired in the fashion of jingoism. It ends with a literal eulogy, a text of Wieland's memories of Shackman, declaring that she misses him. *A & B in Ontario*, finished in the wake of Frampton's death, features Frampton and Wieland filming each other, aiming and running off their cameras, re-loading to fire again, engaging in a kind of comic parody of war or of a gunfight. Much like *Peggy's Blue Skylight*, it is more fascinating as a social record than as an artwork. Of these films, *Birds at Sunrise* is nearest to the formal obscurities of the earlier films, for its visual composition (it is shot through a

Wieland's films have been the subject of an anthology of critical essays (*The Films of Joyce Wieland,* edited by Kathryn Elder) and of a touring retrospective of her work in conjunction with a home video release of her films by the Canadian Filmmakers Distribution Centre. In 2014, two more of her films, the film component of her expanded cinema performance *Bill's Hat* (1967) and the unfinished *Wendy and Joyce* (1968) were made available online by the Cinémathèque québécoise.

Reason Over Passion was not merely a suite of works that marked the maturation of Joyce Wieland's nationalism. It was the summit of her nationalism, a grand gesture resulting from years abroad and a longing for home. It marked home as her primary concern as the dwindling apocalyptic days of the 1960s, and with them fear of a weakening Canadian sovereignty, had left her wondering if there would even be a country to which to return home. She revealed that home in its vastness, in a premature mourning of the land. Her patriotism would extend further with the *True Patriot Love* exhibition, her founding myth of Canada a response to the centennial and its longing for definition, a nation founded again in the ironic and comic, genuine reasons for hope. *Reason Over Passion* became a dirge for a nation that, despite all competing definitions, was most accurately defined by its precarious position, on the verge of extinction or absorption into something else, back into the French and English colonial interests from which it had formed, or into the selfish individualism and ecological despair of America. The difficulties of the film, the indirect relationships and structures that Wieland assembles from symbols, texts and stuttering vistas, reflect difficulties of comprehension in the culture itself, where divides of language become excuses for the willful deafness, blindness and sensual disavowal that comprise a menacing indifference. Joyce Wieland discovers that reason cannot be "metamorphosed into passion through use," but that passion seeps out of Canada's green pastures and paved roads, out of the frosted air, into whatever eternal might remain glorious and free. It is a country founded and saved in the covert machinations of a difficult art.

---

cardboard tube) and for its use of allusions to Talmudic prayer. An ecstatic experience in Jerusalem had inspired her to finish *Birds at Sunrise* in 1984, and by virtue of this it is closer in spirit to her earlier work, anchored in passion.

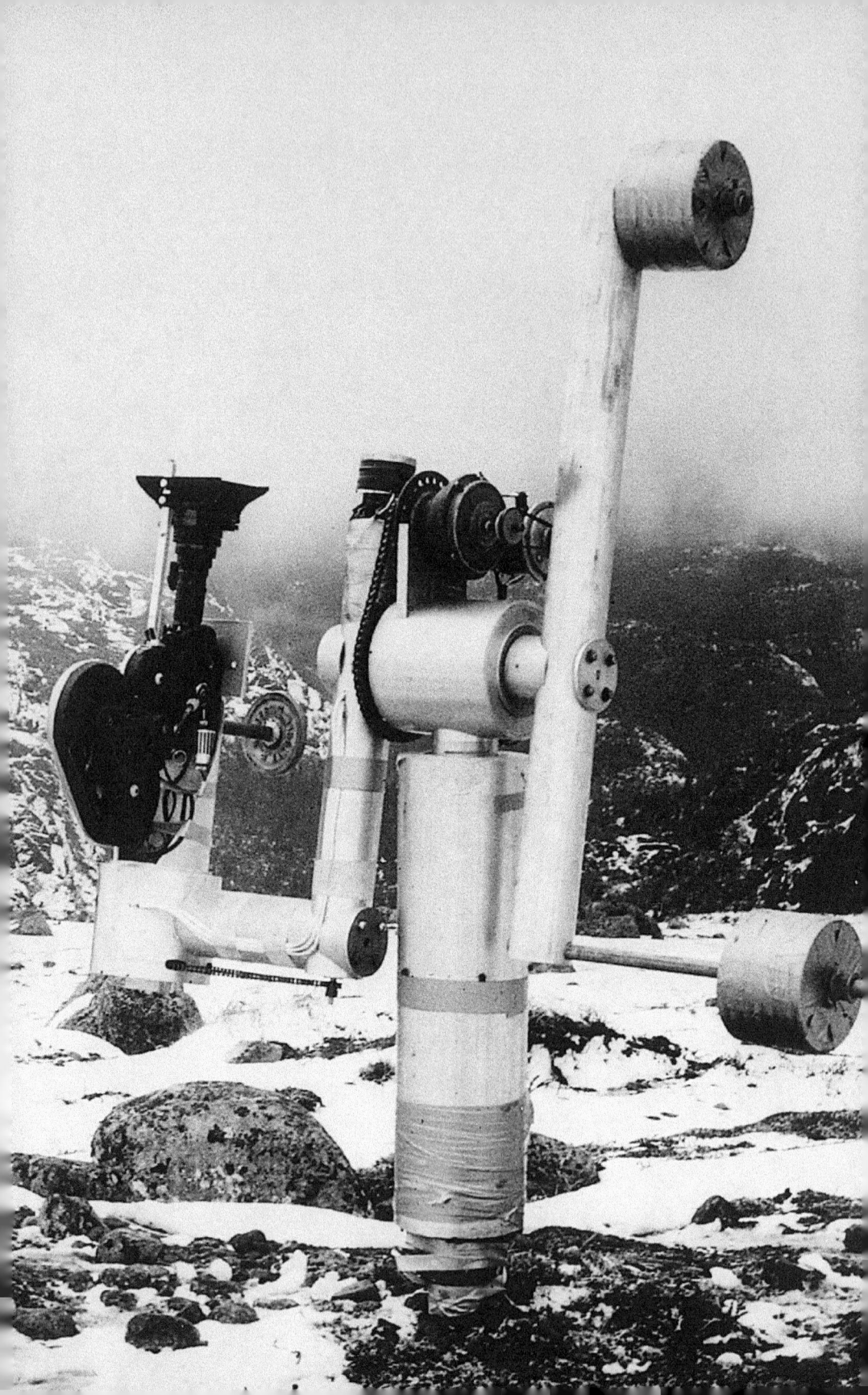

CHAPTER SIX

The Untethered Eye:
Michael Snow's *La Région Centrale* /
The Central Region (1971)

In 1971, Michael Snow and Joyce Wieland made their permanent return to Canada. Snow's film practice had steadily overtaken his work in other media in the years since leaving Canada in 1962. By the time that Snow made *Wavelength*, he had begun to think of his work as bearing a particular relation to the properties of the medium, to film's ability to engage the senses, and his pursuit of these aesthetic concerns would unify his activities across media. He had composed the Walking Woman as a theme on which to improvise. In cinema, he would likewise develop insistent continuities around which to improvise, as in the zoom of *Wavelength*, the mechanical pans and tilts of *Standard Time* and *Back and Forth* and the measured edits of *One Second in Montreal*. His cinema was already a dominant, individual force in the avant-garde film movement, recognized internationally, but at home in Canada he remained best known for his iconic Walking Woman works that had ceased with his exhibit at Expo '67. By the end of the 1960s, Snow's films were beginning to reflect an aggressive, ironic stance toward film time and attention, as in *One Second in Montreal* and *Side Seat Paintings Slides Sound Film*. With these works, revelations came in a winking strain on attention, and the films represented his most mature and difficult treatment of time in cinema.[1]

His return to Canada was marked by the realization of a project he had developed over the course of two years, one that would literalize the remoteness of the structural film and that would also serve as the supreme gesture of Snow's conception of the lens as a tool for visual construction. *La Région Centrale* (1971) fulfilled Snow's informal suite of axial composition films, following *Standard Time* and *Back and Forth*. Its vision of Canada was

---

[1] Snow's earlier works had attended to temporal experience through camera movements, whereas these works trapped the viewer into fixed attention, to slowly shifting compositions that changed in obscure ways. This not only strained the attention of the viewer but placed other (compositional, editorial, decoding) demands on their comprehension.

caught in an all-seeing, impossible eye, one that could at once encompass allusion to landscape art, modal incongruities, and a morphology in which shapes were stretched by lens and movement, coalescing in a harnessing of spirit, the mechanical eye a programmed ascent from the constricted, failing vision of man.

Snow first proposed *La Région Centrale* to the Canadian Film Development Corporation in March 1969.[2] He was then finishing *Back and Forth*, a film that, for its variable tempo and lens abstraction, had "opened up incredible possibilities" for Snow, even in its limited movements, described by one character within it as "back and forth, to and fro, hither and thither, hither and yon." He proposed an extension of these ideas, an orchestration of "all the possibilities of camera movement and the various relationships between it and what is being photographed."[3] Snow wanted to create a total record of the possibilities of camera movement and camera-subject interaction, and for his primary subject, he settled on a landscape. The recording of this landscape would be ultimate in its design and scope, "a kind of absolute record of a piece of wilderness ... a record of the last wilderness on earth, a film to be taken into outer space as a souvenir of what nature once was."[4] Snow's work in the visual aspect of cinema always had a correspondence to his painting activity, happenings and photography, and his exploration of the temporal aspect had assumed an increasingly specific effect. *La Région Centrale* would last three hours in length, a running time that would heighten the ordeal of its duration for some and prolong the experience of its ecstasy for others.

In order to survey all imaginable movements of a camera, Snow would have to conceive of a means by which to allow camera movement to probe space with 360-degree flexibility. To achieve this, he would need a machine that could not only allow the camera to move in 360 degrees, but that could vary in speed and motion and that could be operated by remote control, as a final means of removing the presence of the artist, erasing

---

[2] Snow originally wished to title the film *!?432101234?!*, by which he meant "that as you move down in dimensions you approach zero," aligning this film with the zero of an absolute centre. Charlotte Townsend, "Converging on *La Région Centrale*: Michael Snow in Conversation with Charlotte Townsend." *Artscanada* 152-153 (February-March 1971), 46.

[3] Michael Snow, "*La Région Centrale*," in *The Collected Writings of Michael Snow*, ed. Louise Dompierre (Waterloo, Ont.: Wilfred Laurier Press, 1994), 53. Snow's ambition to create this total record of the camera's ability corresponds in some obvious respects to the totalizing ambition of modern art; and it also reflects a mission that he would extend in his next and arguably most difficult work, *Rameau's Nephew (by Diderot) Thanx to Dennis Young by Wilma Schoen* (1974), in which Snow undertakes a similar total exploration of the possibilities and relations of technology and content—with sound recording and playback—a total record of hearing to *La Région Centrale*'s total record of sight.

[4] Ibid, 56.

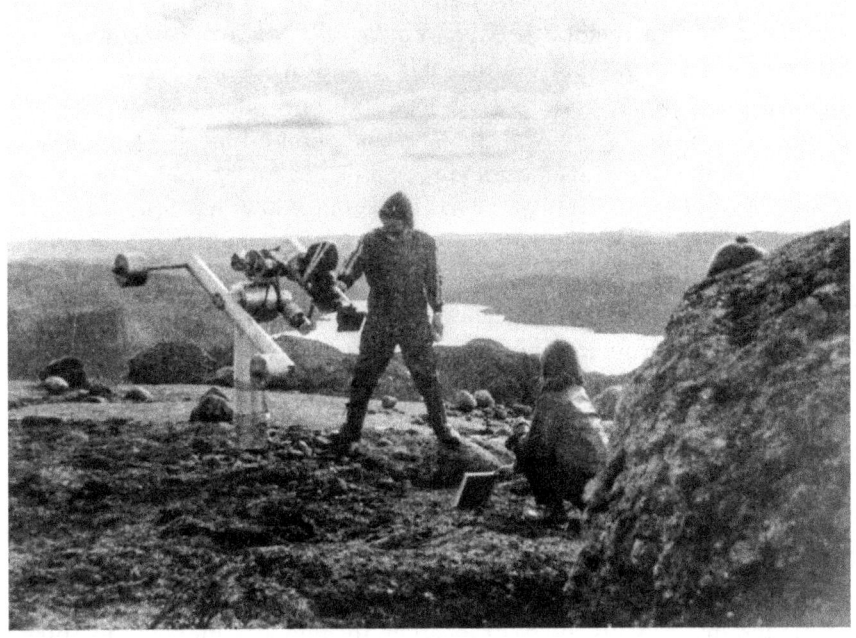

La Région Centrale *[Production Still]*
1970
Photograph: Joyce Wieland

human presence from the composition. To create such an apparatus, Snow followed the advice of Graeme Ferguson and approached engineer Pierre Abeloos, a technician working for the National Film Board in Montreal. The device that Abeloos conceived would guide the camera along the path of a sphere, making the camera capable of passing in lines across all of its surface area. The camera was to stare outward, never moving inside of the sphere by radius or diameter. Abeloos's device would also allow the camera itself to rotate in position. Snow would determine the camera movements by using signals on tape, operated remotely, so that apart from the shadow of the apparatus, there would be no sign of a human role behind this activity.

Such an apparent surrender of control to the apparatus was also a negation of human vision. In this, *La Région Centrale* would serve as the apogee of that strain in structural cinema that resists the mimetic relation between eye and camera so dominant in the films that came before it, in particular, those of Stan Brakhage.[5] In 1971, Snow, writing under the

---

[5] This discorporate vision does not set the film as against or indifferent to consciousness, as in, for instance, Warhol's durational films. R. Bruce Elder writes of *La Région Centrale* as

pseudonym Max Knowles, gave a summary of his film activity to date that concluded with a relation between *La Région Centrale* and the statement given by Edgar Degas on Cézanne: "He is only an eye ... but what an eye!"[6] In *La Région Centrale*, Snow is both less and more than an eye. The film achieves a spiritual unity with the land, its vision an inevitable disavowal of the human eye that its movements so little resemble, producing sight as a result rather than a process of composition. Snow has erased himself, vanishing into the remote station beyond the rocks where his triggers, dials and switches direct the camera to assemble a new geography.

To find his "last wilderness on earth," Snow would probe areas of familial significance to him, choosing between "the country north of Chicoutimi (my mother's birthplace) in Quebec," and an area where "in 1912 and 1914 my father was in surveying parties which mapped what are now partly the chief mining districts in Northern Ontario (Kapuskasing, Timmins)."[7] The work would ultimately be shot in a wilderness 100 kilometres north of Sept-Iles, Quebec, an area reachable only by helicopter, which Snow would describe as "a mountaintop strewn with extraordinary boulders, it had some of the kinds of slopes I wanted and a long deep vista of mountains."[8] By his choice of location, the film was attendant to Snow's ancestry, and it attended not only a generation back into the landscapes of his parents' youth, but to an undeveloped Canada, as it might have been seen by the first settlers of New France, as it might have been before the conquest of the new world.[9] Out of this encounter, not between man and wilderness but between machine and wilderness, the machine allows us, by

---

"a metaphor for consciousness," an ascent to ecstatic consciousness, that its de-anthropomorphosis of the camera, its disavowal of the relation between the camera eye and human eye and its placement in an unpeopled wilderness, allow us "to see camera movements for what they are in themselves," not beholden to object or character. R. Bruce Elder, *Image and Identity: Reflections on Canadian Film and Culture* (Waterloo, Ont.: Wilfred Laurier Press, 1989), 392.

[6] Max Knowles, "Michael Snow: A Filmography," reprinted in *The Collected Writings of Michael Snow* (Waterloo: Wilfred Laurier Press, 1994), 64.

[7] Michael Snow, *"La Région Centrale,"* in *The Collected Writings of Michael Snow* (Waterloo: Wilfred Laurier Press, 1994), 56.

[8] Charlotte Townsend, "Converging on *La Région Centrale*: Michael Snow in Conversation with Charlotte Townsend." *Artscanada* 152-153 (February-March 1971), 46.

[9] This idea comes from Bart Testa's writing on the film. Testa pronounced it "the first Canadian film," a transcendent encounter "between human sensibility and the terrible natural silence of the landscape," and a mythic film, mythic in its tracing to an origin experience, to "the first moment of the Canadian artistic sensibility." The film's aspiration to myth is another way in which the three major works of this study are unified—and unified against many of the other works emerging at the same time out of the Canadian underground—a distinction in the scale of their ambitions. Bart Testa, *Spirit in the Landscape* (Toronto: Art Gallery of Ontario, 1989), 61.

its mediation, to "see as a planet does," to look out at that landscape from the varying curves of its spherical path.[10]

The Allusive Eye

Michael Snow had conceived of *La Région Centrale* as a reckoning of the landscape genre in art. It was not indebted to the material tradition of that genre, as an inherently filmic expression, but it would be for film what "the great landscape paintings of Cézanne, Poussin, Corot, Monet, Matisse and in Canada the Group of Seven" were for painting.[11] The idea of landscape has always been a part of art, present in any expression of representational space, in acts of mapping to remember terrain, in antique panel paintings that predate the Common Era, as in the panels of architect Marcus Vitruvius Pollio, who would decorate chambers with "topia," evocations of places. In tapestries, murals and illuminations, through to its emergence as a recognized genre, the landscape commanded a role in representational art beyond its relegation as background in sacred paintings.[12] But its treatment as a genre evolved from the mid-sixteenth century onward, coming into common usage in ascription to a genre in 1604 when Karel van Mander devoted a chapter to the subject in a lesson book for young painters. Through the influence of Dutch Golden Age painting and later the Romantic Movement, landscape became the dominant preoccupation of prestigious western painters. Landscape remained a dominant genre through the mystical painting activity that emerged out of Romanticism, as in the work of Caspar David Friedrich and the formal experimentation of the Impressionists and Post-Impressionists, a body of work that developed in response to industrialization. Distorted landscapes would dominate the paintings of Veristic Surrealists, but through the twentieth century, the avant-garde would steadily eliminate representational subjects and realist perspective, dispensing with the landscape as anything more than a suggestion. The mainstream cultural imagination conceived its ideal painting, and in the twentieth century, that ideal would be enacted mechanically, culled out of the work of English Romantic J.M.W. Turner, French Post-Impressionist Paul Cézanne and Canada's Group of Seven, imitated or reproduced to be hung over hotel beds and sold as postcards.

---

[10] Charlotte Townsend, "Converging on *La Région Centrale*: Michael Snow in Conversation with Charlotte Townsend." *Artscanada* 152-153 (February-March 1971), 47.

[11] Michael Snow, "*La Région Centrale*," in *The Collected Writings of Michael Snow* (Waterloo: Wilfred Laurier Press, 1994), 53.

[12] For a more substantial survey on the evolution of the landscape, see Nils Büttner, *Landscape Painting: A History* (New York: Abbeville, 2006) or Malcolm Andrews, *Landscape and Western Art* (Oxford: Oxford University Press, 1999).

Snow's work arrives long after the emergence of landscape as a genre and toward the end of an epoch in which traditions of both value and perspective were being discarded or expanded. The most daring works of early modernist painting within the landscape genre would be celebrated in popular imagination for their resemblance to real things, and not necessarily for the power of their form. The dreamt landscape was taken out of the realm of academic fantasy and expanded by the Surrealist vanguard. Later, the ideal landscape was damned by the conscious flatness and raw action of Abstract Expressionism, annihilated entirely in post-painterly abstraction. One has the sense from Snow's list of Baroque and early Modern painters that it was not only a matter of craft mastery that had brought landscape to his consideration, but the transcendent aspect of these works, as in Claude Monet's *Water Lilies* series, works that, like *La Région Centrale*, served to not only represent the world beyond the canvas, but to enclose that world and the experience of vision itself within the canvas. To this end, the transcendent scale of Snow's work was not only influenced by the landscape genre in painting, but by the great religious choral works, like Johann Sebastian Bach's "St. Matthew Passion, B Minor Mass, St. John Passion, Ascension oratorio," for in "philosophies and religions there (had) often been the suggestion, sometimes the dogma, that transcendence would be a fusion of opposites."[13] The aim of transcendence was one of the primary goals behind Stephane Mallarmé's books to end all books, and in its own way, although it did not contain explicit allusion, *La Région Centrale* was a totalizing gesture of the same order, not a recitation of all history but an encapsulation of all manners of looking at this wilderness, through a survey of all imaginable camera movements.[14] Snow's fused opposites might include the horizon and sky, left and right, up and down, the metaphysical and the corporeal, the closed visual field of X and the open field of O, the Cartesian coordinates of X and Y. Why? All of these opposites undergo a rapid exchange and become fused throughout the course of the film.

La Région Centrale begins with an X that will become a recurring symbol and structuring device through the course of its three-hour running length. X is the only trace of language in the film. Its function is not set in language, nor in the various meanings that X has assumed: X marks the spot; the sign of multiplication; it is an algebraic variable, an unknown value, following on Descartes; in Cartesian coordinates, it refers to the horizontal axis; it serves as a sign of negation; and on topographic maps, the

---

[13] Charlotte Townsend, "Converging on *La Région Centrale*: Michael Snow in Conversation with Charlotte Townsend." *Artscanada* 152-153 (February-March 1971),

[14] Encyclopedism, in its broadest definition, would include the cataloguing of minutiae and the cataloguing and attenuation of gestures.

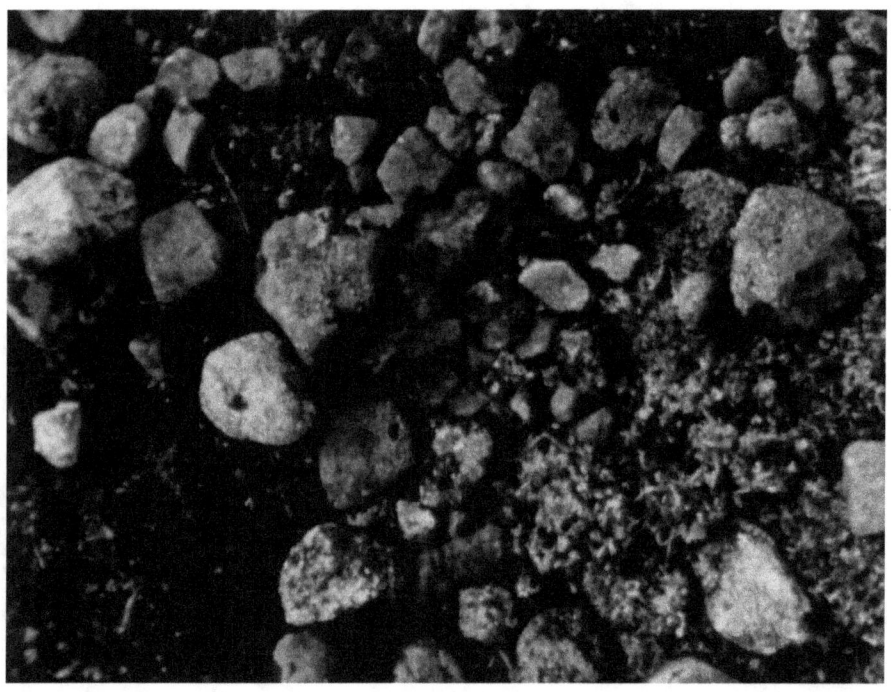

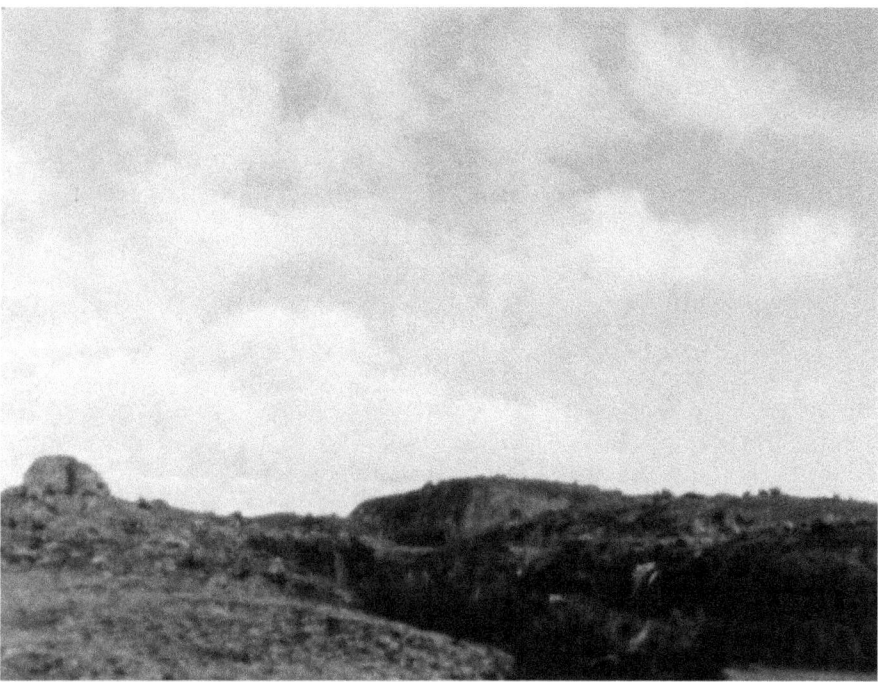

La Région Centrale *[Film Stills]*, 1971
16mm film, 180 minutes, colour, sound
Courtesy of CFMDC

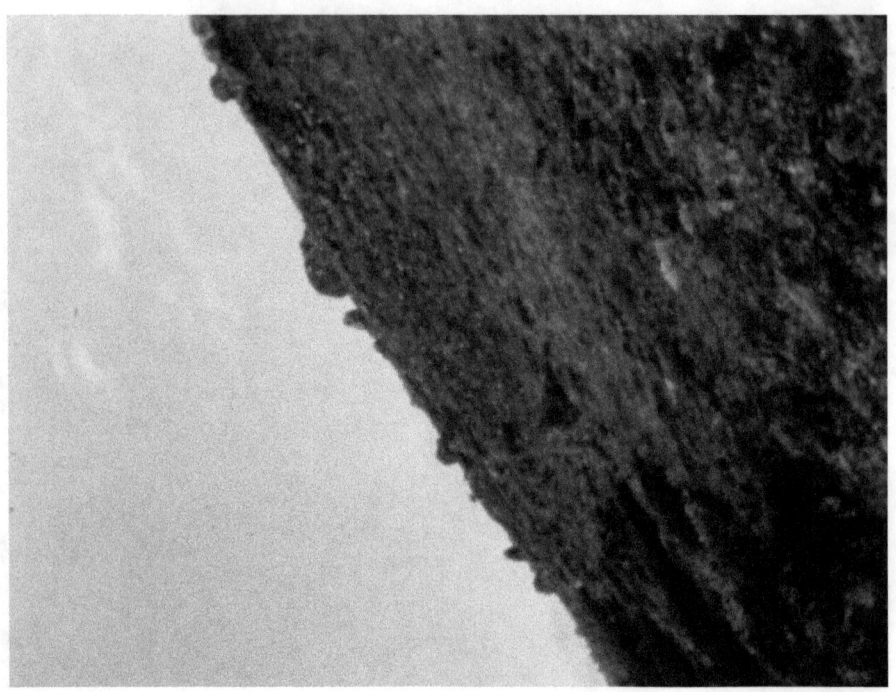

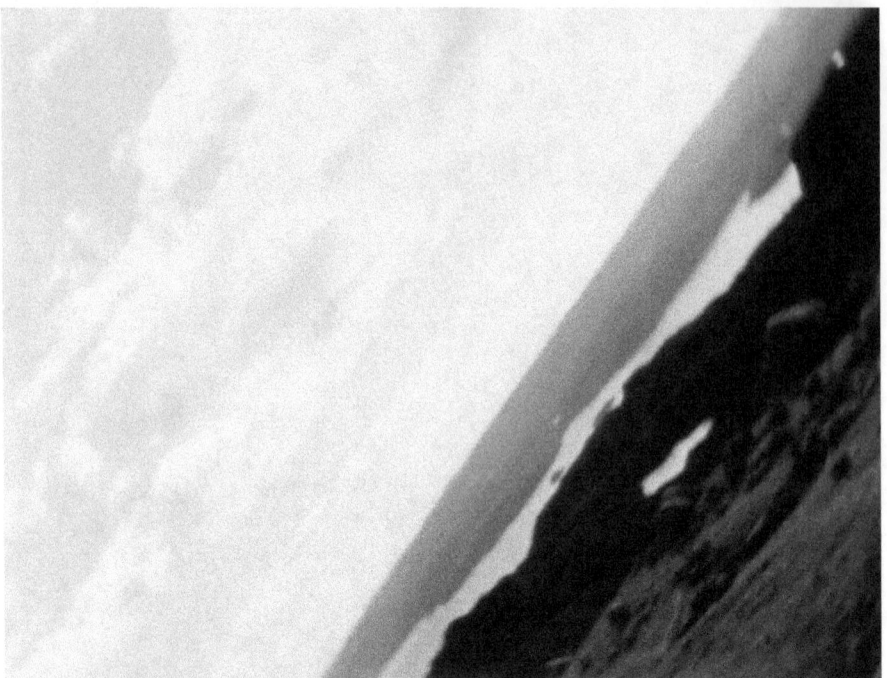

La Région Centrale *[Film Stills]*, 1971
16mm film, 180 minutes, colour, sound
Courtesy of CFMDC

X represents an elevation. In *La Région Centrale*, X is graphic form, a saltire, a St. Andrew's Cross; it becomes a structuring principle that, like the flags in *Reason Over Passion*, bridges movements. In this case, it bridges seventeen sections comprised of camera movements occurring along a 360-degree rotation (in all directions) in the Quebec wilderness. Throughout, that X recurs at each bridge to draw focus to the vanishing point at its juncture.[15]

The camera moves on a curve over stones and earth. They distort at the edges of the lens, by their proximity to the wide angle of its focal length. The camera turns along this curve slowly. With a sound, it speeds up. As the sound stops, it returns to its slow scan. The relative quiet of this frequency causes the camera to survey on its curve slowly. Breaks in unseen clouds cause the sun to reflect on the stones. The shadow of the apparatus comes into view. The tones that Snow has used to trigger and correspond to changes of movement are sounding, beginning with a synthesized tone that, as it begins to sound more frequently, aligns with minor upward adjustments of the lens. The stones are now more fully revealed by the sunlight, and faint activity, in weeds blown by wind, disrupts what is otherwise a movement so smoothly mechanical and inhuman that it suggests the re-photography of stills in an optical printer. The sound now comes at even intervals. The shadow of the apparatus appears again, an impression of the artist's strange instrument. That shadow resembles an oil well, a sign of the film's underlying ecological concern, or a satellite, a symbolic reinforcement of Snow's cosmic theme.

With a cut, the quality of light changes. The film will change frequently as its magazines are reloaded, but the qualities of light will remain variable as the camera movements pass over a landscape under cloud cover. The camera has reached a horizon, a vast horizon that crosses several fields, nearby stones, and in the distance, a graduated landscape that becomes blue in atmospheric haze. In the distance is a lake so stylized by the haze that it could be a Lawren Harris painting of the Canadian north. The clouds and horizon would take on the look of landscape painting, except that the movement of the camera remains insistent, still stuttering in little bounds upward with each sounding of the synthesized tone. It circumnavigates and is carried back to the lake, crossing a boulder. Sounds have now begun to conflict on the soundtrack, playing in different rhythms, one an almost continuous, distant metallic sound. Another sound is guiding the lens so that each time it passes over the same scene, it is at a higher elevation. The landscape gathers at the bottom of the frame until

---

[15] Bart Testa has argued this, writing "its brightness leaves an afterimage on the eye, suggesting another centre, the beam of the viewer's gaze." Bart Testa, "An Axiomatic Cinema," in *Presence and Absence: The Films of Michael Snow, 1956-1991*, ed. Jim Shedden (Toronto: Art Gallery of Ontario, 1995), 61.

it disappears, the clouds overtake the composition and the camera looks skyward.

The apparatus is mechanized against the random assembly and carriage of human vision. It does not illustrate or linger in caesura. It gives movements, and those movements in the continuity of the curve pass over the real things of nature. These natural things, in comparison to the plotted path of the apparatus, are arranged by chance: a wilderness of clouds, rock forms and earth. The film is anchored in this reality even as the surveying, mechanical vision will strain these natural forms and speed them into abstraction and other forms of illusionism, paradoxes, fused opposites. Reality vanishes into the transcendent illusion, but reality never really vanishes. It is only made to morph by the apparatus. A synthesized bass tone begins to sound, giving no apparent effect to the image. The tones begin to sound at different intervals, a round of sounds that would perhaps align with discernible movements if the image were not turned up to the clear, vacant blue sky. When the last cloud forms disappear, and the blue sky remains with these movement-guiding tones sounding under it, the film's durational aspects become pronounced. The blue sky, emptied of clouds, is part of a system of compositional elements that Snow is containing in the film, and as the part of the wilderness that most clearly signifies absence and nothingness, this sky becomes one of the film's first transcendent visions. But this sequence also shows that the presence of things in the world does not align in any significant way with the mission of the machine, that the machine, which shapes and surveys things of visual interest, is disinterested in anything but the continuity of its own movement.

An X appears, and then the camera pans from a clouded blue sky upward, and finds the horizon there, at the top of the composition, as if gravity has been annihilated and the eye is falling upward to earth. The machine is now moving faster, and the competing tones on the soundtrack have become denser. The camera moves over stones until the horizon is again at the bottom of the screen and the camera resumes its horizontal pan. The landscape is dimmer, assuming a pure, undetailed form under the detailed sky. The camera begins to rotate, spinning and tilting so that the horizon travels along all sides of it, a continuous, mechanical movement and a revelation of the growing distances between the lens, its carriage and the human eye. The lens has achieved a movement that is entirely against the anthropomorphized movements of a cinema that would align the camera lens with the human eye. As the sounds become louder, more aggressive and insistent, this movement speeds, spinning the vista in the continuous motion of a 45 RPM record, even as the camera moves further along its curved trajectory, further across the hypothetical sphere

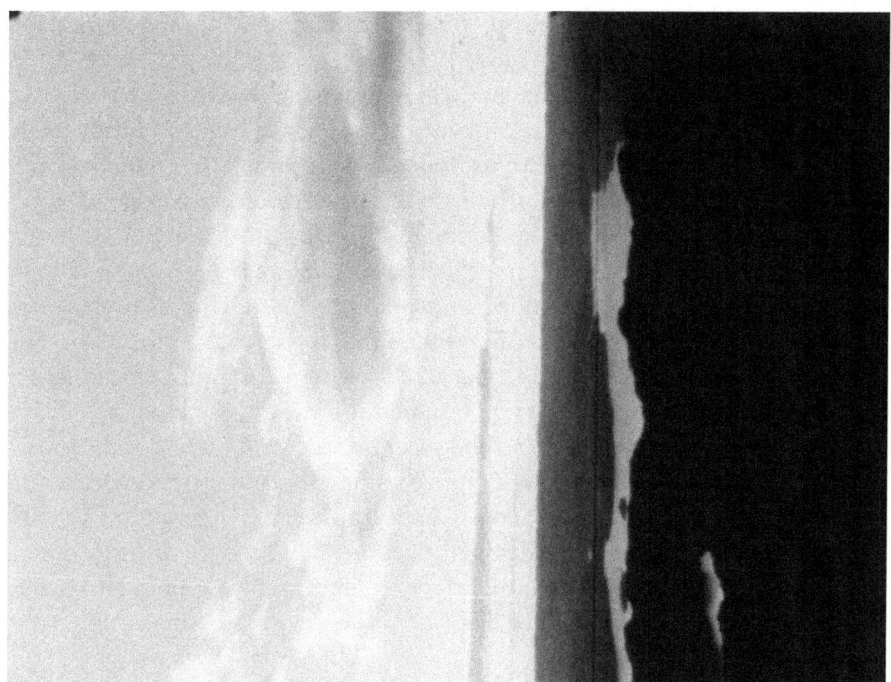

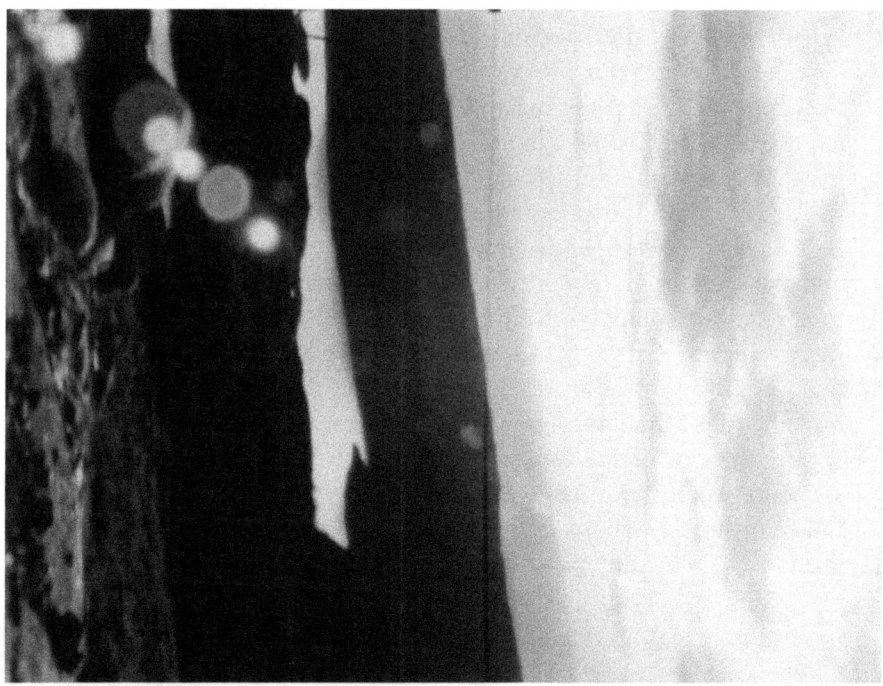

La Région Centrale *[Film Stills]*, 1971
16mm film, 180 minutes, colour, sound
Courtesy of CFMDC

that guides it along the horizon. That horizon, now wrapping around the image, no longer serves as a guide.

With this new movement, any sense of pathway that the film had established is disrupted. The landscape is now at the whim of mechanism, and that mechanism is able to transform it into something so unlike landscape painting that it cannot be reconciled with our knowledge of earth and vision. To experience this continuity, and the distortion that it causes, an eye might be deceived into seeing the distant vanishing point of clouds and sky as a centre surrounded on all sides by earth. But that illusion is being created by means that are mechanistic. It enchants and enriches the subject of its vision even as the machine itself remains indifferent. Another X appears, and when the image resumes, it is moving on a curve, quickly passing over the landforms and sky, reconnecting with the sky at the top of its composition. The shadow of the apparatus appears several times in this movement, and the camera tilts on angles, always in the service of its panning movements. Image and sound slow down. The camera turns downwards to its initial survey of the rocks around it, moving on a curve over dense earth. The first reel, for all of its variation, ends in this symmetry.

The Incongruous Eye

When Michael Snow settled on the formal construction of *La Région Centrale*, he removed a prologue that would show himself, Abeloos, and their crew setting up the machine and leaving it there. He described the sequence: "The first 30 minutes shows us the four people who have set the camera and machine in motion doing various things, talking, looking, but after that we are gone and the remaining [time] is entirely made by the machinery (you?) There are no other people but you (the machinery?) and the extraordinary wilderness."[16] Such a prologue might have made the process of composition explicit, or might have made the camera's activity more mysterious for the actions of its makers, who with such a sequence less resemble artists than land surveyors. It might also have cast over the film a human presence that is otherwise absent but for the surrogate presence of the viewer. But whatever end it may have served, the sequence would have made the carriage of vision explicit, assuming the didactic, representational style of the National Film Board films that foreground or follow any process with its explanation.[17] Snow removed this

---

[16] Charlotte Townsend, "Converging on *La Région Centrale*: Michael Snow in Conversation with Charlotte Townsend." *Artscanada* 152-153 (February-March 1971), 46.

[17] In the same article, Snow says that Wieland had wanted to make a film about the making of *La Région Centrale*, entitled *A Humane Use of Technology*, punning on the inhuman vision of the film, the apparatus taking the place of the operator, the humane use being the removal

sequence, perhaps deciding that revelation of the process of composition would impact on the work's transcendence. The documental approach to reality would remain in the work, to Snow's end of creating an "absolute record of a piece of wilderness." It records that wilderness in continuous gestures, and by its duration, the subject becomes familiar and is rendered secondary to the gestures, camera movement itself coming to the forefront of the viewing experience as the most immediate and knowable reality in the image. With the removal of this prologue, the film has lost its internal explanation of its mechanized vision. Its constitution challenges viewers to surrender their broad expectations of engagement, as well as their specific expectations of mimetic vision, in order to enter the work.

As the film emphasizes camera movement, it suspends the viewers' expectations of subject content and forces the eye to search the landscape to confirm a mode of representation, to pin it into a familiar discourse by which to enter it. But that familiar discourse is not forthcoming. The work is fortified against this, in particular, in its disconnection from the landscape, historically and presently. The film departs from the fixed vantage point of landscape painting, assembling a new geography in fragments. In doing so, it becomes the ultimate manifestation of landscape in its relation to reality, but for its mechanization, it is always apart from the landscape, situated at its centre and yet floating above and through it. In its relation to landscape and to reality, *La Région Centrale* manifested a spiritual-ecological anxiety that corresponded to that of *Reason Over Passion*, less concerned with the specific weight of rhetoric and more with the vanishing wilderness. Snow would admit that "like a lot of other humans I feel horror at the thought of humanizing the entire planet," and so the film, as a final sight of the isolated landscape, was a "visit of some of our minds and bodies and machinery to a wild place but I didn't colonize it, enslave it." By Snow's estimation, he "hardly even borrowed it."[18] This mode cannot be understood through our expectations of the landscape, or our expectations of mimetic vision, but only by its discorporate isolation of rhythm, in gestural continuity and in repeating figures. Those rhythms become attenuated through the course of the experience and are exhausted in gestures of abstraction, of falling upwards, of an ultimate fusing of opposites. Snow achieves this through continuities, among them, the static X that signals a new sequence.

As the second reel resumes from the X motif, the apparatus begins a new series of movements. It enacts a continuous pan along the landscape

---

of humans. But this also shows their self-consciousness of the machined vision, which becomes difficult to reconcile in the film itself, where vision becomes total and totalizing, even as its carriage remains largely invisible but for its shadow.

[18] Charlotte Townsend, "Converging on *La Région Centrale*: Michael Snow in Conversation with Charlotte Townsend." *Artscanada* 152-153 (February-March 1971), 46.

that stops and returns, a repetition of the continuous, stunted, returning pans of *Standard Time*, or a 360-degree elongation of the back and forth motions of *Back and Forth*. The motion is not aligned with the synthesized noise in any particular way.[19] A tone sounds that had previously signalled slight raises in the camera's relation to the horizon. Now, that relation appears to be adjusting more dramatically; the land and rock forms, densely packed near the apparatus, give way in the pan to an open sky and clouds. The return of the motion is always marked by a shift that is undeniably mechanical.[20] The landscape is not in any way a traditional landscape. If traditional landscapes encompass a swath of painterly activity from the commerce of pretty pictures to the grand, transcendent gestures of Cézanne and Monet, that tradition develops around the composition of vistas. Film allows Snow to assemble his landscape out of fragments stamped out at twenty-four frames per second. Its restless compositions are also acts of fragmentation, of a landscape that can be recombined in sequence, that can be explored in continuities of gesture, but which cannot be encompassed within any individual frame of the film.

In a new section, the pan now crosses a darkened, upside-down landscape. The zoom adjusts while in motion, a perfect mechanical execution. It speeds and slows, and rather than bound back and forth, it continues in full 360-degree turns, eventually at such a speed that it begins to abstract the contents of the image. It aims at the sky, zoomed in so that distant clouds become continuous streaks interrupted by the hulking shadow of the landscape. It slows as the zoom draws back, movement slowing and quickening with the change of focal length and not of the apparatus itself. The landscape is surveyed, as are all the same forms—boulder, lake, hills— now slowly crossed, the horizon passing along at an angle that, after several minutes, changes into another continuous rotation, the camera simultaneously panning at 360-degrees so that the panning mirrors the action of the rotating camera. The camera stops and passes back to the landscape, panning over it in dimmer light, a long stretch of black that gives way to cloud forms, a pan that continues back from the sky to the darkened earth. This occurs on a 90-degree angle so that, when it settles, the horizon has

---

[19] Here, at the beginning of the second reel, is where the film begins to show signs of internal distress, the tones that so clearly indicate certain forms of movement slightly out of alignment with the image. Regardless of whether these misalignments are intentional, they give the two central and interdependent mechanical operations a frightening agency, as vision is no longer obeying sound.

[20] Snow's project is much like that of Jack Chambers' *Circle* in the sense that, while the camera mechanism is performing its programmed duty—in Chambers' case, a human-operated exposure of 4 seconds each morning, in Snow's case, a programmed machine performing movements by audio signal—qualities of light and of real things become conditioned to the presence and activity of the mechanism.

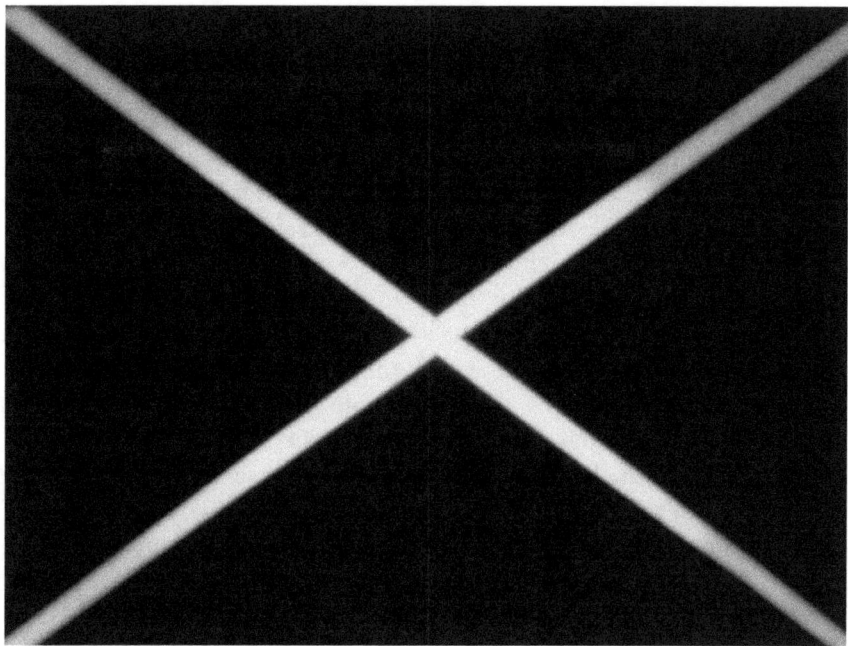

La Région Centrale *[Film Still]*, 1971
16mm film, 180 minutes, colour, sound
Courtesy of CFMDC

become vertical. The image appears to be divided down its centre, the horizon on its the right, the sky to its left. It then begins to move leftward along the horizon, which in the composition becomes a downward vertical motion. The landscape, no matter how it is angled or distorted, eventually gathers itself. This vertical landscape cuts to an X.

The image resumes on clouds, the camera moving on a curve, readjusting upward by synthesized tones. The same action plays out over the stones at the base of the mechanism. The camera moves up to the clouds and eventually finds the horizon again, entering over the top of the composition, this Y-axis movement repeating. The camera rotates, its rotations mirroring the 360-degree activities of the axial movements. That activity is focused on the dimming landscape, and details slowly emerge therefrom, sunlight streaking in and clouds parting to illuminate the earth until it assumes a warm brown tint. The image settles vertically, on a 90-degree angle, the horizon occupying the left, the sky on the right. Again it moves downward, the silhouette of the landscape becoming a shifting perforation between heaven and earth. Eventually, the camera shifts to the right and the sky overtakes this image. With another X, the image resumes on its 90-degree angle, the horizon to the left, the sky to the right. As it passes, sunlight falling on the lens refracts, casting the shutter onto the image. The components of the composition are real things—a horizon, a sky—and yet by the angle of taking and the ceaseless downward pan, the mechanism abstracts forms.[21] When this becomes too clearly the mission of the activity, it changes again, shifting to another of its continuous movements, that of the rotating camera, finally settling on an upside-down horizon, panning to the left, surveying it. Through a shifting Y-axis, the earth once again overtakes the frame, and soon after, once again, accedes it to the sky. Snow's camera enhances the glory of the landscape, but such reverence is of no interest to the camera. Its lens is not, as the film taken in abstract terms supposes, an all-seeing godly eye, but a tool for visual construction that surveys, stamps out, pieces together and recombines the component parts of this landscape, seen in ceaselessly stable pans, into its new transcendent whole.

The sound has become faint, staccato, sounding out a variation in four tones. The continuities of the various camera movements are mirrored in this sound, regardless of its precise correlation to the motion. The camera pans across an upside-down horizon repeatedly, and this repetition combines with the repetition of the sound to become transfixing, to remind, in its constant activity and lack of variation, of the durational, minimalist achievement of this vision. An X leads into the next sequence, and when the image resumes, still upside down, the vantage point has changed, the lake now in view. The sound has changed slightly, and soon the image begins to move again on a curve, over the rock forms that surround the apparatus, eventually departing from the horizon, toward the sky, which in turn tenders the other side of the horizon, entering upside down. The camera returns to its 360-degree rotations, over the ground, up into the sky, ground reappearing at the end of this same continuous motion. With a slowing of the frequency, the motion slows as well. The final moments of the second reel achieve a compositional precision in the way the camera departs from and delivers the land, a gesture and sight so continuous in its delivery across the vast sky as to be completely inhuman. This is how the film's modal incongruity shows itself, by the glory and indifference of its instruments.

---

[21] One might argue that it comes to resemble the colour field manifestations of landscape in Richard Diebenkorn paintings, where sightline and topography become ambiguous and the artist builds around shape and line rather in a manner that subverts orientation.

The Impossible Eye

Michael Snow believed that the visual constructions tendered by the apparatus were "cosmic-planetary as well as atomic," that in addition to the general implications of the camera's spherical movements, and of the remote landscape, the film was also casting its vision on a molecular level.[22] Snow would pun that the film was a "cosmic strip," for its fracture and recombination of the landscape, and for the isolated wilderness and its relation to the planet and cosmos. Snow's work was richly conceptualized, but it was also dependent upon the divining and executing of his programmed movements. Snow's project is premised on the apparatus and its techniques. As the landscape becomes elastic and abstract, the camera movements become visible. But Snow's programmed actions are as much about restrictions of motion and vision as they are about possibilities. What the apparatus aspires toward, as it produces its impossible visions, is a totality of vision that will never be achieved. The camera will never be able to overtake its periphery. As the film goes on, this manifests in a number of techniques including zigzags, figure eights, Möbius strips.[23] It does not only survey movements; in its acceleration through a series of attenuated gestures, it pursues an ultimate gesture. When it achieves this, in the final sequence, it gives the appearance of falling upwards. Snow's tactical difficulty is strategized not around bringing the camera into sympathy with man's breaking vision, but around the generation of continuous gestures. These continuities are attenuated, as in his earlier films, to exhaustion. On the course to exhaustion, they bear the fluctuation of variables and frustrate by the insistence of their repetition.

La Région Centrale is therefore formed in a union of concept and process. The movements are conceived, charted, programmed and executed by mechanistic means, and encompass the overarching continuities of the film. The camera movements were achieved through patterns given to the moving parts of the apparatus by way of sound tapes. Directions would correspond to frequencies of sine waves. Snow explains: "it makes up a layer of tones divided into five sections starting very high, about 10,000 cycles per second, down to about 70 cycles."[24] Beats or pulses would guide

---

[22] Charlotte Townsend, "Converging on *La Région Centrale*: Michael Snow in Conversation with Charlotte Townsend." *Artscanada* 152-153 (February-March 1971), 46.

[23] Regina Cornwell expands the list: "rolls, spins, circles within circles and cycles within cycles, figure eights, arcs, scallops, sweeps, zigzags, horizontal shifts, mobius strips, etc." Regina Cornwell, *Snow Seen: The Films and Photographs of Michael Snow* (Toronto: PMA Books, 1980), 111.

[24] Charlotte Townsend, "Converging on *La Région Centrale*: Michael Snow in Conversation with Charlotte Townsend." *Artscanada* 152-153 (February-March 1971), 47.

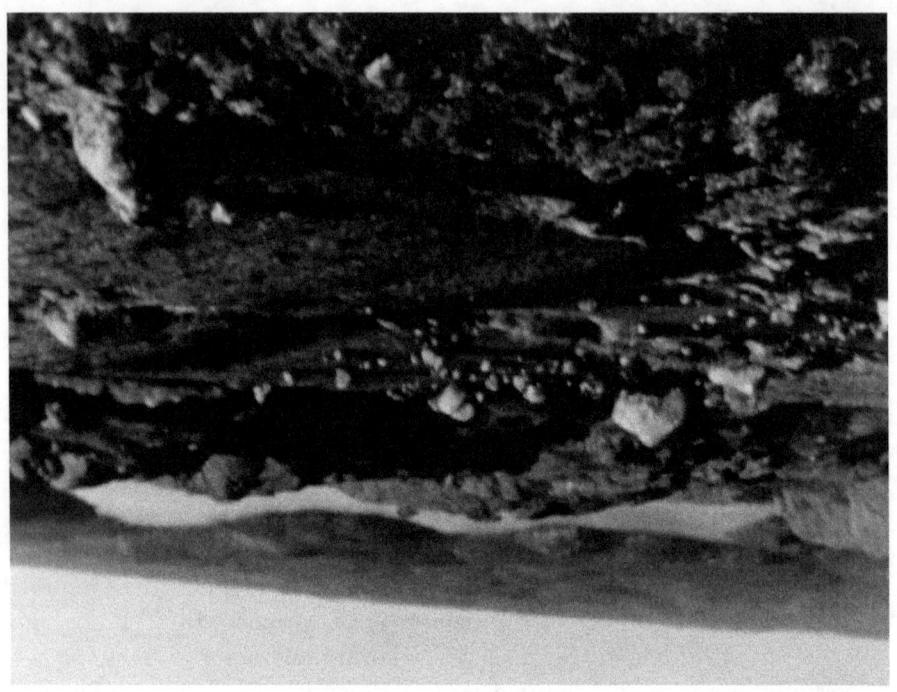

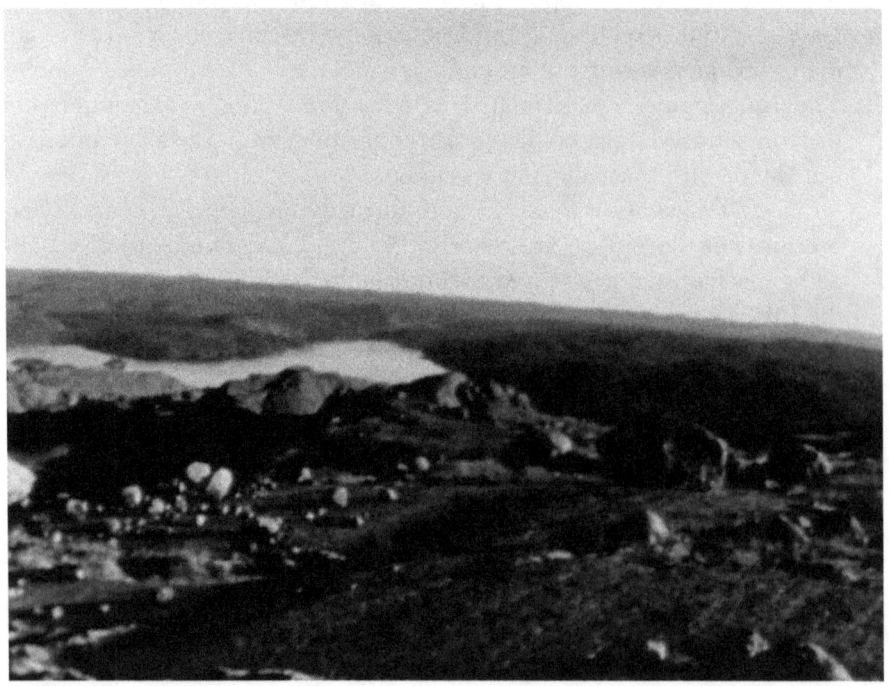

La Région Centrale *[Film Stills]*, 1971
16mm film, 180 minutes, colour, sound
Courtesy of CFMDC

the arms along horizontal divisions. Snow would later further clarify the guidance of the image as being controlled by "a series of dials and switches ... dials for the Horizontal, Vertical, Rotation (centered on the lens) and Zoom."[25] This would draw sound and image into an unconventional dialogue, in Snow's words, "a whole world of conversation in itself."[26] This system also creates effects that Snow could not anticipate, as the lens, regardless of careful surveying or deliberation of motion effects, becomes subject to natural variation, as in the vagaries of light and the passing cloud cover, and to the unpredictable textures of motion blurs. The work is finally assembled in a structure that is pointedly uneven, a series of rhythmic exercises that fluctuate in time from three minutes to thirty minutes.

If the first reel deceived the spectator into anticipating symmetries to run through it, the subsequent reels would subvert that expectation. The reels become increasingly unpredictable in their structure until, late in the film, movements begin restarting, anchored at the same station, as in the controlled stagger of *Standard Time*. As Regina Cornwell reports, the film's structure mirrors the structure of roughly a day: "the film begins about noon, proceeds to mid-afternoon, continues from sunset to night to sunrise, and ends about noon."[27] Throughout, these rhythm studies are truncated by unpredictable edits, most but not all sequences running for the course of a 400' camera magazine, and arranged in such a way as the structural fragmentation becomes unpredictable, with Snow marrying planned rhythm studies to studies that are more experimental in their conception, and inserting long sequences that wander through a series of disconnected movements. Snow's strategy is present across the planning, execution, and final construction of the work: he conceives of a system that will survey in fragments; activates the system to transform and abstract the subject; and finally, fuses opposites—design and improvisation—through his disjointed X-marked sequencing.

As the third reel begins, the lens resumes panning along the boulders. It begins to reverse, and then moves downward. It enacts a tilting movement, which continues into the night. The tilt occurs even as the image pans slowly right along the landscape, forming a zigzagging action. The horizon becomes an all-consuming darkness against the faint light of the night sky. The zigzag motion is accompanied by, or determined by, a

---

[25] Introductory note to "Converging on *La Région Centrale*: Michael Snow in Conversation with Charlotte Townsend," in *The Collected Writings of Michael Snow*, ed. Louise Dompierre (Waterloo, Ont.: Wilfred Laurier Press, 1994), 57.

[26] Charlotte Townsend, "Converging on *La Région Centrale*: Michael Snow in Conversation with Charlotte Townsend." *Artscanada* 152-153 (February-March 1971), 46.

[27] Regina Cornwell, *Snow Seen: The Films and Photographs of Michael Snow* (Toronto: PMA Books, 1980), 111.

sounding of two tones against each other, operating in a round, releasing at steady intervals. The boundaries of the movement become dramatically pronounced and then, with a recession of both sounds stripping down to a steady intermittent frequency, the camera begins again to pan to the right continuously. The subject of that pan is now too dark to identify, but moonlight occasionally breaks across a cloud, which indicates the direction of movement. After an X, the image resumes on the moon. The camera's motion has animated the moon in a curving motion, as it spins in and out of the upper right of the composition. The synthesized tones now sound loudly, and their frequency, combined with the spinning moon, suggests that the camera is moving very fast. The moon appears less a moon than a controlled spotlight, assigned agency by the mechanism that animates it.[28] The moon becomes the focus of attention as the sole light source on the plain. With an X, the image turns black, with no discernible movement but with wildly fluctuating sounds. Without light, without anything of visual interest to photograph, the mechanism continues operating. This is signalled by the faintest impression of the forms over which it is passing, but more concretely, by the interplay of frequencies and tones that imply rapid, dynamic movement of the apparatus. The camera breaks away from the darkness, departing from the land and into the early stages of sunrise. It soon returns to darkness, presumably the darkness of the still dim earth surrounding the apparatus.

The sun rises. The camera rises from the ground to move skyward. The cloudless sky mirrors the flat darkness of the preceding night, again attenuating focus, awaiting the camera's return to earth and to familiar, representational content. The relation of sky to earth has assumed the same binary of light and dark, black and white values that had been central to *New York Eye and Ear Control* and certain Walking Woman variations. After a sustained sequence of sky, the camera returns to the earth, now still soft in focus by the faint light. The camera turns back up to the sky. This exchange repeats. The landscape returns to the relative stability of the day before, and the pans continue downwards, from sky to land and through to sky, neither sky nor earth fixed in relation to one another, one giving way to the other in a continuous 360-degree movement, giving the effect of falling upwards. Long episodes of darkness, presumably with the lens aimed at the feet of the apparatus, are broken up by cloudless sky. After

---

[28] This observation has its roots in R. Bruce Elder's remark that the movements of the camera confuse us into seeing agency in the contents of this landscape: "we know that it is actually the camera that is moving, but, try as we might to see it this way, we still seem to stubbornly take the movement as the movement of the moon through the sky." R. Bruce Elder, *Image and Identity: Reflections on Canadian Film and Culture* (Waterloo, Ont.: Wilfred Laurier Press, 1989), 397.

another X division, the relation between earth, which is now dimmed to a hulking, darkened mass, and sky, which is cloudless, becomes one of dramatic, dynamic transition, the camera settling into one, either in light or darkness, and breaking away from it by the silhouette of the land entering or receding from unpredictable corners of the frame. Details have been shorn away by calculated exposure or by light itself. Expectations of light have been annihilated as it becomes ambiguous as to whether the horizon is experiencing sunrise or another sunset. If the earlier sequences of the film had been demonstrations and announcements of continuities, of aesthetic themes, this section emphasizes duration and through that, the apparatus's visual disinterest.

Another X comes and when the image resumes, the detail in land and sky have returned to their original state, the earth a warm brown, the sky a gradating scale of blue. The camera begins to move in its 360-degree upwards gesture again, but it now absorbs more detail, making the transit less unpredictable. It follows the sky and earth on a curve, a constant circuit of arrivals and departures. Even as the film has become insistent in the continuity of its gesture, and is beginning to realize this 360-degree tilt as the dominant, conquering gesture of the work, it is also giving less variation. With a new sequence, the image is now shifting on a curve, still passing through earth to sky and from sky to earth in one continuous motion, moving in one vertical direction. Changes in sound signal the camera to move on a bend, turning and coming around to earth, passing over the earth in a slow swoop, down and then up. The camera is again rotating while moving on its axes, giving a motion wherein the landscape comes into vision but is then subject to this distorting survey before the camera turns to the sky. The effect of this motion is to disorient by undermining the logical orientation of the horizon. Eventually the image reorients itself along a straight linear axis, again moving from land to sky and through to land again. This gesture begins to reverse itself, assuming a tilt that moves through the land to sky, and then bounds back, returning down to land again, the earth rendered a narrow strait through the surrounding sky. The zigzagging motion repeats, the camera simultaneously moving up and down and undergoing faint horizontal shifts. Eventually, this evens out to a steady leftward pan.

The Eye Freed

Even if Michael Snow were unconcerned with infusing a human presence into the wilderness, the actions of the camera would deliver the beholder an ecstatic experience. The movements of the camera carried the beholder through a system of visual experience that assigned no value to the experience that it created. But the ecstatic and sublime vision that resulted from that system was shaped for the beholder by the metaphor of remoteness itself, by an integration of technology and wilderness that removed man as witness, and that by his devices created the impossible camera vision. What made it impossible was not that this untethered eye could move elastically at such speeds, but the mechanical executions of its repeating rhythmic figures. Snow had spoken of this as a record of earth to pass beyond the last gasp of earth as we know it, a time capsule for an unknown future. The camera eye could chart this experience mechanically, but as it was interrogated after the fact by an intelligence that might resemble the human eye, it would form a statement of man's relation to earth, sensed in metaphor out of the isolation of machine and wilderness: a statement of man's impulse to be emancipated from gravity. The core of the film's ecstatic experience lay in an emancipation from gravity, as in man's aspirations toward space conquest, as in the launching of the Sputnik satellite, but also as in the unknowable yet universal experience of being freed from the mortal coil of corporal being. The ultimate difficulty of *La Région Centrale* lay in this ecstasy of falling upwards and its complex metaphors that extend the scope and power of the apparatus into unknown territory. In this it probes the limits of perceptual and perspectival enigmas.

As its final reel begins, *La Région Centrale* continues the motions with which the prior reel had ended. The image pans steadily to the right, from the same station where the last movement had ended. The image soon begins to zoom into the mountains, panning right along stones at a telephoto focal length, giving the illusion of rapid speed, and then zooms out to a wider view. This brief sequence announces a movement that will be repeated after an X, as the camera restarts from the same position, panning steadily and continuously to the right; again it zooms into the mountains, farther this time, surveying the distant mountains until its sightline is overtaken by nearer stones seen in detail. The camera again zooms out, continuing its slow pan. The speed of the pan is being dictated by the illusion of proximity given by a shifting focal length. The camera suddenly begins rotating again as the pan continues. The rotation becomes increasingly aggressive. Eventually this rotating pan not only begins to speed but becomes concentrated around unpredictable movements, circling over the ground in circular motions, rising up to the sky in wider motions, performing an uneven figure eight. As the film begins its final sequence, the camera is performing a circular movement, indiscernible in pattern, that allows the landscape to enter the frame at right and then push away to the left, immediately followed by its mirror gesture, the landscape entering the frame at left and pushing away to the right. As the tones fluctuate and intensify on the soundtrack, the image continues what appears to be a consistent pace of moving across the landscape, signifying a final disconnection of interplay between sound and vision. With a cut, the image changes, now speeding violently so that the land simply becomes a green-brown blur punctuated by the blue of the sky. The sounds sustain; that, or its pulses are coming in such speed that they are forming into a singular tone. The camera spins 360-degrees so that it crosses from sky to land to sky, but even this begins to slow into a more legible reality, even as the alien effect of returning to earth by upward passage remains disorienting. The landscape becomes familiar again, but in a final departure, the camera crosses slowly over a white, formless sky. A final X shows clear through to a landscape, followed by a faint O. The film has arrived at what Snow called the "nirvanic zero, being the ecstatic centre of a complete sphere," marked by these final hieroglyphs.[29]

By freeing the lens and eye relation, and by his modal disconnection of the landscape from its traditional representation, Snow was able to subvert the contract of intelligibility between the work and its beholder in a way that was not easily reconciled. This combined with the interaction of wilderness and mechanism, and the erasure of man from that equation, to create an ecstatic and unfamiliar experience. *La Région Centrale* arrives at an obscure truth of the relation between art and landscape, great in scale if ambiguous in meaning, that of art's ability to make the land simultaneously flexible and rigid. Solid ground, stones and mountains are recast as something collapsible and flexible, but also transcendent of physical matter. Snow showed himself to be an omniscient and supreme listener, one who could relegate his own role to that of conceptualizing and programming the work. The machine's total knowledge was one of mystic necessity and simple computation, translating sound cues into actions. Through Snow's commands, its surveying and scanning opened onto a spiritual action that drew the work further from intelligibility. In the third and fourth reels of *La Région Centrale*, the viewer witnesses a liberation from gravity. Liberation from gravity meant, in the eye's final movement toward sky, a liberation from the limits of periphery and from the perspectival conventions shaped by human vision on the earth. The impossible eye, at last freed from gravity, was one that could float and fly. But it could also heal the fractures of human consciousness so that in its vision, at last, the wilderness might be perceived as it is, or as it was, or as it might have been.

---

[29] Charlotte Townsend, "Converging on La Région Centrale: Michael Snow in Conversation with Charlotte Townsend." Artscanada, 152-153 (February-March 1971), 46.

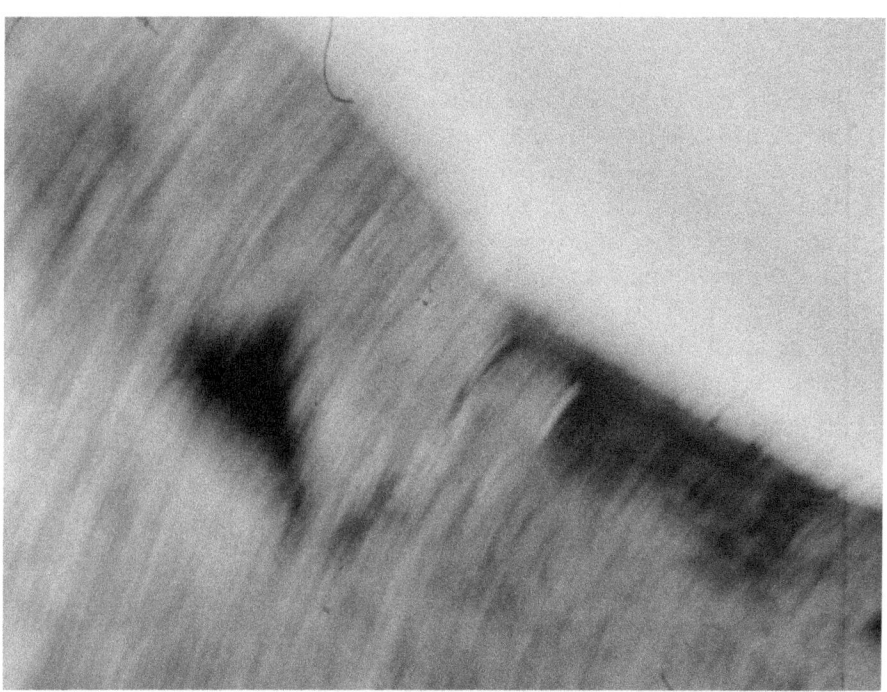

La Région Centrale *[Film Stills]*, 1971
16mm film, 180 minutes, colour, sound
Courtesy of CFMDC

Goodbye to Earth

From the zoom of *Wavelength* to the pans and tilts of *Standard Time* and *Back and Forth* to the variations explored in *La Région Centrale*, Snow had set himself to the task of cataloguing camera movement and its effects. With *La Région Centrale*, the mechanistic nature of his greater project clarified its stance as to where the eye was, and what it was. It was not a human eye in any conventional sense, although his work conflated his viewer and his contraption; it was not guided in its movement by human hands, as a metaphor for vision or a substitute sight; instead, the lens was a tool for visual construction. Though the project has behind it Michael Snow's conscious mediation of these elements, its authorship was not merely conceptual. From concept and programming to structure and exhibition, it arose from the difficult heritage of Snow's aesthetics. In Snow's earliest work, difficulty was present in the mediation of a subject, as in *Lac Clair* (1960), to reveal and insist upon the material construction of the image, a Neo-Dadaist disavowal of presence and symbol. In the Walking Woman variations, symbol reigned over the work and allowed Snow to brand himself in the art world, but through it he had also discovered a new way in which to concentrate his activities, in idioms translated from the mechanistic boogie-woogie vamps of his pianist mentor Jimmy Yancey, what would mature in short order from variations on a theme into the continuity and attenuation of gestures. Snow would establish continuities of gesture and pursue them until they exhausted and modulated into something new. This paradox, of variational continuity, or continuity producing and subject to variation, becomes one of the dominant markers of difficulty in Snow's work, a modal and tactical difficulty that, by the time it manifests in his mature films, resists the label of difficulty by its minimalist simplicity. Attenuations of gesture, and the durational effect on an audience, reveal its difficulty. Repeating rhythmic figures, translated to camera movement, are not freeing. They entrap the spectator in restrictions of movement, like those inherent in any system of rhythm. Here lies the essential difficulty of *La Région Centrale*, in its aspiration to see as a planet does, and the impossibility of that vision. The nearest it comes is in the wild 360-degree fluctuations that come to see the landscape as a thin cosmic strip, repeating, divided by sky.

Although Snow had taken great lengths to conceal the machine in the final film, eliminating his prologue and in doing so allowing the machine to become an omniscient presence, he was not interested in abandoning or obscuring the machine altogether. Through the course of filming, he had decided that Abeloos's machine was itself a beautiful object, and wanted to integrate it into his body of work in a more explicit way.

Within the year, Snow had created *De La* (1971), a video and sculpture in-stallation built around the machine. In the process the machine was trans-formed from a 16mm film camera mount into a closed circuit television system. In its installation, the machine is equipped with a video camera that broadcasts images in real time to four monitors that are stationed around the machine, the audience passing between the machine and the monitors. Eventually, the monitors show all space, including the spectator and monitors. It was a declaration of the draftsmanship that had formed *La Région Centrale*, a re-enactment of the gesture, but one in which the force that formed the sphere and the playback itself were made visible, active components of the work.

In the films that Snow would make over the following decades, he would continue a program of difficulty. However, the durational difficulty, cataloguing and formal self-consciousness to which his work had aspired through the late 1960s would reach its apotheosis in *Rameau's Nephew by Diderot (Thanx to Dennis Young) by Wilma Schoen* (1974), one of the most en-duringly difficult Canadian avant-garde films for its obvious contingencies but more importantly, for its survey-investigation of all manifestations of sound in film (its mission twinned to that of *La Région Centrale*, an aural complement to the earlier film's totality of vision). Snow would continue thereafter to expand his filmmaking in new directions, always returning to his basic interest in the variations and modulations created through the continuity and attenuation of gestures. Through the 1980s and 90s, Snow made a series of long films no less challenging in their aesthetic conceits but less concerned with totality. This strain would re-emerge in Snow's feature-length video work, **Corpus Callosum* (2002), in which a series of tracking shots through an office space reveal increasingly elastic and comic forms, culminating in a return to Snow's origins in animation, collaps-ing half a century of distance into a new container. Likewise, attenuation of action would re-emerge almost two decades after *La Région Centrale*, in a work more decidedly fixed to earth, *Seated Figures* (1988), in which the camera, mounted looking downward on the rear of a truck, speeds over various terrains, making a literal road movie, a topographic landscape.

When Michael Snow first proposed *La Région Centrale*, he described it as an "absolute aloneness, a kind of Goodbye to Earth which I believe we are living through."[30] Even as it served as a culmination of the difficult aesthetics of his work, it was also a mythic declaration of cultural and ecological anxiety, an apocalyptic reckoning of Canada and of the new world itself. From its station in the isolated landscape of northern Quebec,

---

[30] Michael Snow, "*La Région Centrale*," in *The Collected Writings of Michael Snow*, ed. Louise Dompierre (Waterloo, Ont.: Wilfred Laurier Press, 1994), 56.

it returns the viewer to the origins of that first encounter with the vacancy of the Canadian wilderness, like that of a planet waiting to be born or set reeling. By removing man from that encounter, Snow posed a good-bye to earth that took a subject common to artist, surveyor and explorer, and in parting, he set the machine to collapse earth and sky. But what the machine reveals is not necessarily an apocalyptic climax, but landscape's endurance, as in the final sequence, when the stones and distant hills are scanned in a parting gesture before the camera spins up to the sky.

POST-SCRIPT

Difficulty and After

At the time of Canada's 1967 centenary, the focal point of the era in which these works emerged, Northrop Frye delivered three lectures, published as *The Modern Century*, which conclude with a somber reflection on Canadian identity. Frye's terms began from his reading of Blake, of the tiger and the lamb, of brutality and innocence. He concluded that we live in the world of the tiger, a world that "was never created or seen to be good."[1] Canada reflected, to itself, by its own long-studied preoccupation with self-definition, an uncreated identity, an unachievable Utopia. Its underlying myths were not merely drawn out of its true symbols, "a flag perfunctorily designed by a committee, a national anthem with its patent pending, an imported Queen," but a straddling of physical reality, a "tearing apart [of] the physical world to see what lies beyond or through it."[2] Some would wrestle from it the spiritual rewards where thistle, shamrock, rose entwine, a song swelling loud and long till rocks and forest quiver. Canadian artists would discover more mysteries, more blank questions, not posed by their art but explored by the relations within it. The real Canada, Frye proposes, is an ideal with nobody in it. It is no place, populated by nobody but the tragic and triumphant figures dreamt out of its myths. Frye did not argue this as an obstacle but as a fact of Canadian nationhood, its uncreated identity giving the same myth as that which other nations faced struggling into being, as in "Blake's new Jerusalem [...] built in England's green and pleasant lands."[3] For a brief time, between 1969 and 1971, the Canadian avant-garde film assembled its vision of the country: regional, national, spiritual, fractured and recombined, of semantic enclosures and distentions and visual constructions.

The Canadian avant-garde film movement, at its outset, consisted of a small group of artists working within a framework of common values, their work sharing a purposeful difficulty. For Jack Chambers, that

---

[1] Northrop Frye, *The Modern Century: The Whidden Lectures, 1967* (Toronto: Oxford University Press, 1969), 121.

[2] Ibid, 122.

[3] Ibid, 123.

difficulty lay in the interstices between lyricism and outrage, and the rare, transformative experiences of heightened perception. For Joyce Wieland, purposeful difficulty came in a collision of earnestness and wit that composed a deeply ironic militant sentimentality. And for Michael Snow, difficulty came in another paradox, that of variational continuity, an aesthetic theme that unified his work through a decade and a half of near-constant evolution. These three were able to assemble their own aesthetics, as did their peers in the broader Canadian underground film community, by freeing themselves of the impediment of a search for a national aesthetic, or even of a sense that their art must reflect their origins, a condition to which it inevitably aspired. But unlike that underground, which became increasingly dispersed and influenced by American culture, Chambers, Wieland and Snow each focused his or her energies on creating major works that were not only cumulative achievements of purposeful difficulty, and by that represented profound perceptual challenges, but which were also distinctively about Canada the ephemeral, about Canada as it was understood, or not understood, within its own culture, a fog in which it is terminally obscured. Haunted by its uncreated identity, the nation slowly formed as concept, contour and country.

For their parts, Chambers and Wieland formed myths, his regional, hers national, both situated in personal vision, his to redeem perception, hers to reconcile a philosophical imbalance. Snow's mythic gesture was to bring the landscape itself into an ultimate state, where it came to enclose, extend and surpass all representations of landscape that came before it, a gesture that has not been surpassed since. Chambers and Wieland would abandon film not long after their major works were completed. In neither case was this matter one of willful abandonment, and in both instances their departure from filmmaking arose in circumstances that suggest heartbreak, and in a more concrete sense, out of the interminable condition of making art without cash value. Their illnesses further influenced this, Chambers' diagnosis coming as he was completing his last film, Wieland's illness becoming apparent even as she was beginning to complete her old, abandoned films. Snow carried on, and while he continues to produce music, painting, sculpture and photography, filmmaking maintains a central focus, and his perception of himself as a 'time-light-sound' poet endures in his work across media.

The subjects and forms of the Canadian avant-garde film were carried on in the work of the artists who would emerge in the 1970s and 1980s. The template for this cinema had been laid down by 1971, in its distinct response to the landscape, the diary, the frame. In *The Hart of London*, Chambers had built a collective diary of London akin to William Carlos

Williams' *Paterson*; he offered a galvanizing Canadian vision of place and history equal to Charles Olson's Gloucester or Henry David Thoreau's Walden Pond. With *Reason Over Passion*, Wieland declared an extremely personalized view of Canadian identity, placing her identity in a national dialogue. By the time he made *La Région Centrale*, Snow assumed the role of a proto-ecologist, finding a way to make a non-human film of the world. The challenge of these works was unique in its collision of formal radicalism, political awareness and social power, and its themes and methods would inspire work that followed its lead, forming through regional movements, production cooperatives and non-commercial distributors.

To make a film of indigenously Canadian vision, the artists who followed would work with the landscape and the diary form, insisting as their forebears had on the presence of the frame and a disavowal of the relation between eye and lens. The best of this work emerged organically, as had that of the first wave. It did not always engage formal difficulty, often instead embracing a didacticism inherited from the National Film Board of Canada. However, difficult pleasures would maintain a primary role in the aesthetics of Canadian experimental cinema, sustained by our need for experiences that defy resolution.

The difficult aesthetics of the foundational, major works of the Canadian avant-garde film have been an implicit theme in the critical discourse surrounding them. Such essential difficulties have marked vanguard forms of filmmaking from cinema's inception. Humanity's appetite for meaning, that force that created philosophy and faith and conceived the systems of mathematics and the sciences, created also, by modern aesthetic inquiry, the modes of purposeful difficulty in art. Purposeful difficulty shall never be wholly resolved, acclimated to or accepted, but it opens onto an edifying experience, extending the experience of art into the dislocated discourse of the new, bringing with it new feelings and new knowledge. Difficulty remains, in its endless variation, the last redemption of art.

BIBLIOGRAPHY

Andrews, Malcolm. *Landscape and Western Art.* Oxford: Oxford University Press, 1999.

Argüelles, José A. *Charles Henry and the Formation of a Psychophysical Aesthetic.* Chicago: University of Chicago Press, 1972.

Armatage, Kay. "Kay Armatage Interviews Joyce Wieland." *Take One* 3:2 (November-December 1970), 23.

Battcock, Gregory (ed.). *The New American Cinema.* New York: E.P. Dutton, 1967.

Bowie, Malcolm. *Mallarmé and the Art of Being Difficult.* Cambridge: Cambridge University Press, 1978.

Büttner, Nils. *Landscape Painting: A History.* New York: Abbeville, 2006.

Chambers, Jack. "Assemblages, the Found Object and Art." *Region* 4 (1962), unpaginated.

– "Letter to Daryl Duke, January 29, 1964." Reprinted in *The Capilano Review* 33 (1984), 20-21.

– "Perceptual Realism." *Artscanada* 136-137 (October 1969), 7-13.

– "Perceptualism, painting and cinema." *Art and Artists* 7:9 (September 1972), 28-33.

– *Jack Chambers.* London: Nancy Poole, 1978.

Cheetham, Mark. *Jack Chambers.* Toronto: Art Canada Institute, 2013.

Cornwell, Regina. *Snow Seen: The Films and Photographs of Michael Snow.* Toronto: PMA Books, 1980.

Crawford, Lenore. "London artists' films show sharp contrast." *London Free Press,* 28 November 1970, 27.

Cullinan, John. "Interview with Anthony Burgess." *The Paris Review* 56 (Spring 1973), 118-163.

Dalí, Salvador. *The Secret Life of Salvador Dalí.* New York: Dial Press, 1942.

Diepeveen, Leonard. *The Difficulties of Modernism.* New York: Routledge, 2002.

Diepeveen, Leonard and Timothy van Laar. *Art with a Difference: Looking at Difficult and Unfamiliar Art.* Oxford: Mayfield, 2001.

Dompierre, Louise (ed.) *The Collected Writings of Michael Snow.* Waterloo, Ont.: Wilfred Laurier Press, 1994.

Duval, Paul. *The Tangled Garden: The Art of J.E.H. MacDonald.* Scarborough, Ont.: Cerebrus, 1978.

Elder, Kathryn (ed.). *The Films of Jack Chambers.* Toronto: Cinematheque Ontario, 2002.

– *The Films of Joyce Wieland.* Toronto: Cinematheque Ontario, 1999.

Elder, R. Bruce. *The Films of Stan Brakhage in the American Tradition of Ezra Pound, Gertrude Stein and Charles Olson.* Waterloo, Ont.: Wilfred Laurier Press, 1999.

– *Image and Identity: Reflections on Canadian Film and Culture.* Waterloo, Ont.: Wilfred Laurier Press, 1989.

Ellenwood, Ray (ed. and trans.). *Total Refusal (Refus Global): the manifesto of the Montréal Automatists.* Holstein, Ont: Exile Editions, 2009.

Farber, Manny. "The Arts: Farewell to a Lady." *Time* (Canadian Edition), 24 January 1969, 17.

Foucault, Michel. *The Order of Things: An Archeology of Human Sciences.* New York: Vintage Books, 1970.

Frye, Northrop. *The Modern Century: The Whidden Lectures, 1967.* Toronto: Oxford University Press, 1969.

Fulford, Robert. "Wieland." *Toronto Star*, 2 February 1962, 30.

– "Giving Us a Sense of Ourselves." *Toronto Star*, 10 July 1971, 55

Hall, Michael D. and Eugene W. Metcalf Jr. *The Artist Outsider: Creativity and the Boundaries of Culture.* Washington and London: Smithsonian Institution Press, 1994.

Holmes-Moss, Kristy A. (ed.). "Joyce Wieland: Interviews and Notes on *Reason Over Passion* and *Pierre Vallières*." *Canadian Journal of Film Studies* 15.2 (2006), 122

James, David E. *Allegories of Cinema: American Film in the Sixties.* Princeton: Princeton University Press, 1989).

Jenkins, Bruce (ed.). *On the Camera Arts and Consecutive Matters: The Writings of Hollis Frampton.* Boston: MIT Press, 2009.

Karl, Frederick R. *Modern and Modernism: The Sovereignty of the Artist 1885-1925.* New York: Antheneum, 1985.

Kilbourn, Elizabeth. "Art and Artists." *Toronto Star*, 23 November 1963, 36.

Kilgour, David. *A Strange Elation: Hart House, the First Eighty Years.* Toronto: University of Toronto Press, 1999.

Kritzwiser, Kay. "What's So Special About New York? Ask an Artist." *Globe and Mail*, 15 April 1967, 13.

– "Artist Michael Snow Wins Prize for Movie." *Globe and Mail*, 3 January 1968, 10.

Kuspit, Donald. "Pop Art: A Reactionary Realism." *Art Journal* 36:1 (Fall 1976), 31-38.

Lambton, Gunda. *Stealing the Show: Seven Women Artists in Canadian Public Art.* Montreal: McGill-Queen's Press, 1994.

Leclerc, Denise and Pierre Dessureault. *The 60s in Canada.* Ottawa: National Gallery of Canada, 2005.

Levine, Marc. *The Reconquest of Montreal: Language Policy and Social Change in a Bilingual City.* Philadelphia: Temple University Press, 1991.

Lind, Jane. *Joyce Wieland: Artist on Fire*. Toronto: Lorimer, 2001.

– *Joyce Wieland: Writings and Drawings 1952-1971*. Erin, Ont.: Porcupine's Quill, 2009).

Lipton, Lawrence. *The Holy Barbarians*. New York: Julian Massner, 1959.

MacDonald, Scott. *A Critical Cinema 2: Interviews with Independent Filmmakers*. Berkeley and Los Angeles: University of California Press, 1992.

McPherson, Hugo. "Wieland: An Epiphany of North." *Artscanada* 158-159 (August- September 1971), 17-27.

Medjuck, Joe. "The Life & Times of Michael Snow," *Take One* 3:3 (January-February 1971, published April 1972), 6-12.

Merleau-Ponty, Maurice. *The World of Perception*. New York: Routledge, 2004.

Michener, Wendy. "Underground Movies Begin to See the Light." *Globe and Mail*, 6 January 1968, 21.

Nasgaard, Roald. *Abstract Painting in Canada*. Toronto: Douglas & McIntyre, 2008.

Newman, Peter C. *The Distemper of Our Times: Canadian Politics in Transition, 1963-1968*. Toronto: McClelland & Stewart, 1968.

Nowell, Iris. *Joyce Wieland: A Life in Art*. Erin, Ont.: Porcupine's Quill, 2001.

O'Brian, John. *The Flat Side of the Landscape: The Emma Lake Artists' Workshops*. Saskatoon: Mendel Art Gallery, 1989.

Pearson, Roger. *Mallarmé and Circumstance: The Translation of Silence*. New York: Oxford University Press, 2004.

Perelman, Bob. *The Trouble with Genius: Reading Pound, Joyce, Stein and Zukofsky*. Berkeley: University of California Press, 1994.

Porter, John. "Maya Deren and Hans Richter in Toronto." *The Funnel Newsletter* (November-December 1983).

Pringle, Douglas. "Review: *La Raison avant la passion*." *Artscanada* 134-135 (August 1969), 45-46.

Purves, James (ed.). *The Idea of Difficulty in Literature*. Buffalo: SUNY Press, 1991.

Renan, Sheldon. *An Introduction to the American Underground Film*. New York: E.P. Dutton, 1967.

Rockman, Arnold. "Same Woman, But In All Shapes and Sizes." *Toronto Star*, 6 July 1963, 26.

Rooney, Anne. *Hunting in Middle English Literature*. Woodbridge, Suffolk: Boydell & Brewer, 1993.

Rosenblum, Robert. "The Castelli Group." *Arts Magazine* 31:8 (May 1957), 53.

Sanouillet, Michel. "The Sign of Dada." *Canadian Art* 78 (March/April 1962), 111.

Sax, Boria. *The Mythical Zoo: An Encyclopedia of Animals in Myth, Legend, and Literature*. New York: Overlook, 2013.

Seaver, Richard and Helen R. Lane (eds.). *Manifestoes of Surrealism*. Ann Arbor: University of Michigan Press, 1969.

Shedden, Jim (ed.). *Presence and Absence: The Films of Michael Snow, 1956-1991*. Toronto: Art Gallery of Ontario, 1995.

Shetley, Vernon. *After the Death of Poetry: Poet and Audience in Contemporary America*. Durham, Duke University Press, 1993.

Sitney, P. Adams. "There is Only One Joyce." *Artscanada* 142-143 (April 1970), 43-45.

– *Visionary Film: The American Avant-Garde.* New York: Oxford University Press, 1974.

Smart, Tom. *Jack Chambers' Red and Green: an artist's inquiry into the nature of meaning.* Erin, Ont.: Porcupine's Quill, 2013.

Stein, Gertrude. *Tender Buttons: Objects, Food, Rooms.* New York: Claire Marie, 1914.

Steinberg, Leo. *Other Criteria: Confrontations with Twentieth-Century Art.* London: Oxford University Press, 1972.

Steiner, George. "On Difficulty." *The Journal of Aesthetics and Art Criticism* 36:3 (Spring 1978), 263-276.

Tennyson, Alfred Lord. *The Works of Alfred Lord Tennyson, Poet Laureate.* London: Kegan Paul, 1878.

Testa, Bart. *Spirit in the Landscape.* Waterloo, Ont.: Wilfred Laurier Press, 1989.

Thomas, Ralph. "300 flee from far-out film." *Toronto Star*, 5 April 1965, 22.

Townsend, Charlotte. "Converging on *La Région Centrale*: Michael Snow in Conversation with Charlotte Townsend." *Artscanada* 152-153 (February-March 1971), 46-47.

Tyler, Parker. *Experimental Film.* New York: Grove Press, 1969.

Webster, Bill. "On Entertainment: Underground Film on London Planned." *London Free Press*, 20 January 1968, 43.

– "On Entertainment: Back to *Heart of London*." London Free Press, 22 January 1968, 27.

Wheeler, Dennis (ed.). *Form and Structure in Recent Film.* Vancouver: Vancouver Art Gallery and Talon Books, 1972.

Wherry, Matthew. "The Silence of Jack Chambers" *20 Cents Magazine* 1:9 (May 1967), unpaginated.

Wigmore, Donnalu. *Isaacs Seen.* Toronto: University of Toronto Hart House, 2005.

Wilhelm, James. *Il Miglior Fabbro: The Cult of the Difficult in Daniel, Dante, and Pound.* Oronto: National Poetry Foundation, 1982.

Woodman, Ross. "London: Regional Liberation Front." *Globe and Mail*, 13 December 1969, 27.

– *Chambers: John Chambers interviewed by Ross G. Woodman.* Toronto: Coach House Books, 1967.

Wordsworth, William and Samuel Taylor Coleridge. *Lyrical Ballads, with a Few Other Poems.* London: J. & A. Arch, 1798.

INDEX

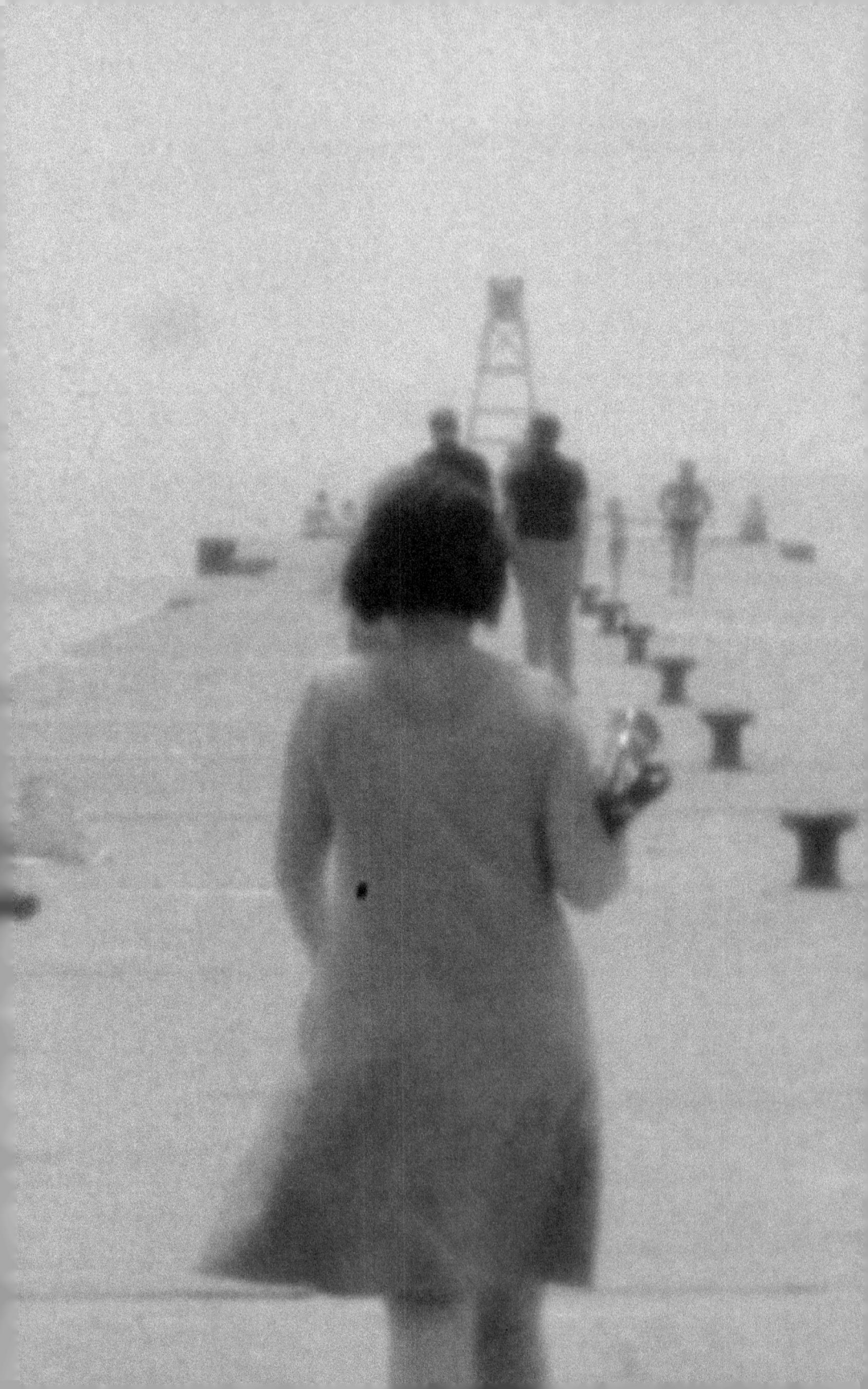

www.ingramcontent.com/pod-product-compliance
Lightning Source LLC
Chambersburg PA
CBHW072131170526
45158CB00004BA/1328